PSYCHOLOGY
THE STUDY OF
MAN'S MIND

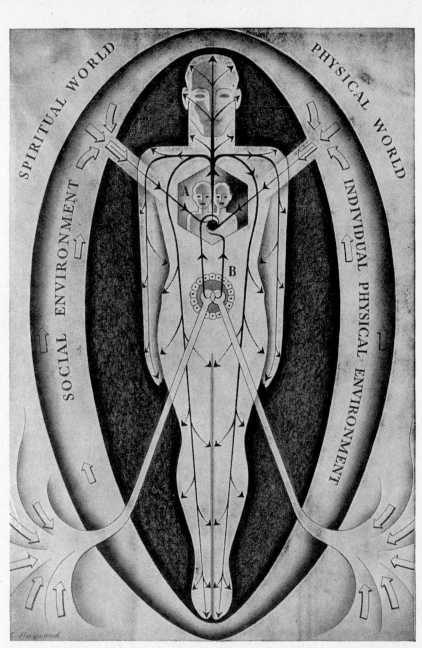

Human personality is formed by the interaction between the individual and his total environment. The twin nature of that personality (A) is explained by Fig. 86. Those physical, mental and emotional tendencies which are normally regarded as a legacy from our ancestors are symbolized by (B). Equally our own individual environment and our social environment act and interact on our personality and help to condition our psychological make-up.

PSYCHOLOGY

THE STUDY OF MAN'S MIND

AN INTRODUCTION TO THE
STUDY OF THE NATURE, STRUCTURE AND FUNCTION OF
THE MIND, AND OF THE INFLUENCES OF ENVIRONMENT
ON BEHAVIOUR, TOGETHER WITH A BRIEF SURVEY OF
THE APPLICATIONS OF PSYCHOLOGY TO THE PROBLEMS
OF EARLY DEVELOPMENT, OF EDUCATION, CHOICE OF
CAREER, INDUSTRIAL EFFICIENCY AND MENTAL DISORDER

CONTRIBUTORS:

Agatha H. Bowley, Ph.D.   Mary Collins, Ph.D.
Professor James Drever, D.Phil., B.Sc., F.R.S.E., F.B.Ps.S.
R. G. Gordon, M.D., D.Sc., F.R.C.P.E.
E. Patricia Hunt, M.A.   H. G. Maule, M.A. (Cantab.)
Arthur Pinsent, M.A., B.Sc.
Percival Smith, M.A.

ODHAMS PRESS LTD · LONG ACRE · LONDON

CONTENTS

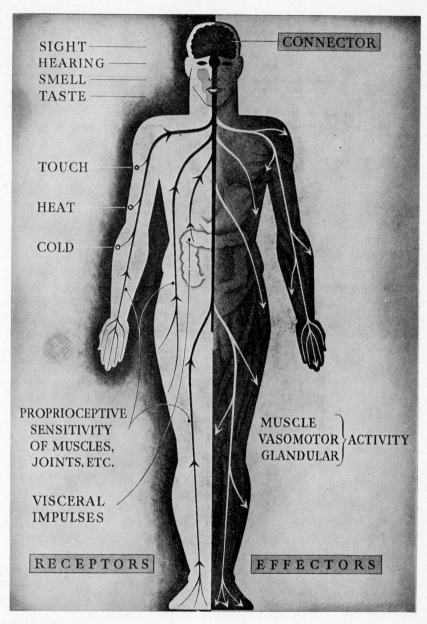

SIGHT
HEARING
SMELL
TASTE

CONNECTOR

TOUCH

HEAT

COLD

PROPRIOCEPTIVE
SENSITIVITY
OF MUSCLES,
JOINTS, ETC.

MUSCLE
VASOMOTOR ⎬ACTIVITY
GLANDULAR

VISCERAL
IMPULSES

RECEPTORS

EFFECTORS

FIG. 1. *The psycho-organic system comprises three main groups of organs and nerve-cells—receptors, effectors, connectors. The "receptors" receive stimuli; such are the sense organs, touch and temperature corpuscles, and the "proprioceptive" or self-tensing tissues. The "effectors"—muscles, glands and vessels—respond to stimuli; while "connector" cells—the brain and nervous system—convey messages between the two former groups.*

6

CHAPTER I

WHAT IS PSYCHOLOGY?

WHAT is psychology? Popularly it might be described as "the study of human—and animal—nature". That is at least the sense in which one would understand the word as used in ordinary conversation, or in the daily Press. No one, however, would regard that as a scientific definition of psychology. As a systematic study in University or College, how would it be described?

Two centuries ago the answer to this question would have been very different from the answer today. Then the answer might have been something like this: "Psychology is that part of philosophy which studies the mind and mental processes; together with Logic and Ethics it makes up that division of knowledge generally spoken of as Mental Philosophy." However much they might vary with respect to details, the great majority of those who attempted to answer such a question today would reply in some such way as this: "Psychology is a positive science, belonging to the biological group of what are called the Natural Sciences." Beyond that, some differences of opinion might be expressed according to individual points of view.

The fact is that something like a revolution has taken place with regard to this subject during the past hundred years or less. A hundred years ago the word "psychology" had barely established itself as a word in the English language. In Germany the word appears to have been used a century earlier, but in Great Britain as late as the time of Dugald Stewart (1753–1828) the rival terms "phrenology", "pneumatology" and even "pneumatics" were still being put forward for recognition as the accepted terms for the science. Many writers on what we now call psychology preferred to speak of the "philosophy, or physiology, of the human mind".

Not only had the name not yet established itself, but people were far from understanding clearly where this new science should begin and end. Fierce controversies raged round every attempt to lay down the fundamental principles of the subject, and the methods of investigation relied upon were, as a rule, crude in the extreme and to a high degree subject to individual bias. Today the boundaries of the science are perhaps not quite so clearly defined as they might be, but an enormous advance has been made towards agreement

7

on what they should be. Controversies inherited from the philosophical past are unfortunately still with us, but no psychologist now regards them as involving fundamental principles or allows them to interfere seriously with the essential nature and aims of the science, or with the progress of investigation. Moreover, today's methods of investigation are those of other recognized sciences, physical and natural, so far as these methods are applicable.

A description of the science of psychology which would be acceptable to most psychologists of the present day would be: "the positive science which studies the behaviour of men and animals, so far as that behaviour is regarded as an expression of that inner life of thought and feeling which we call the mental life". By calling it a positive science we mean that it is concerned primarily with the investigation of facts, with what *is*, not with what might be or ought to be. The immediately observable facts which it investigates are those of the behaviour of men and animals. We cannot, however, really understand the behaviour of either man or animal without reference to that inner life, which has always been regarded and spoken of as the life of the mind, of which the behaviour is the outward expression. Moreover, the behaviour is the only indication of human or animal nature. Hence, the modern description of the science really joins hands with the older view, and also with the view of the man-in-the-street—that psychology does study the mind and mental processes. The only difference is that from the modern point of view the mind and mental processes are studied in order to understand the behaviour of men and animals, not to support this or that philosophical theory, or this or that political doctrine or ethical teaching.

WHAT IS BEHAVIOUR?

The practical value of this understanding of the behaviour of ourselves and other people is undoubtedly very great, certainly not less than the value of the understanding of the phenomena of the physical universe in which we live. From that point of view, also, psychology claims a place alongside the other positive sciences. It also has numerous and valuable practical applications, to be worked out by the various branches of Applied Psychology. As a pure science its aim, like that of the other pure sciences, is a knowledge and understanding of the facts with which it has to deal, such knowledge and understanding being sought without bias, for the ascertainment of the truth, and for that alone.

What, then, do we mean by the behaviour of men or of animals? Briefly, behaviour is the total response which man or animal makes to the situations in life with which either is confronted. Such a definition, however, demands some expansion. To make clear its significance let us consider the activities of any living organism, which are continually going on so long as the organism remains living. A living organism is built up of living cells, in which and by which the various activities are carried on. In the higher and more complex types of life, like human life, the cells are organized into the great organs and structures of the body.

The activities of an organism may be said broadly to fall into two groups or classes. On the one hand there are those activities which are concerned directly in maintaining the life of the organism, or in performing what might be called vital functions. On the other hand there are the activities involved in responding to the various influences and changes in the environment, in such a way as to secure the best conditions for the performing of the vital functions. These other activities might be regarded as the performance of adaptive functions. The adaptive functions, taken as a whole, might be said to represent the behaviour of the organism. It must be borne in mind, of course, that there is all the time the most complex interaction between the vital and the adaptive functions, and to this extent even the vital functions may play a part in the behaviour.

In the higher animals and in man the vital functions are usually performed by great organs with large systems of interrelated structures, as, for example, the heart and the circulatory system of the blood, the stomach and the digestive system, and so on. In the same organisms, the cells concerned in the adaptive functions also form a great system of interrelated structures, which may be called the "psycho-organic system". This system comprises three parts, each part consisting of cells specialized to play a definite role in

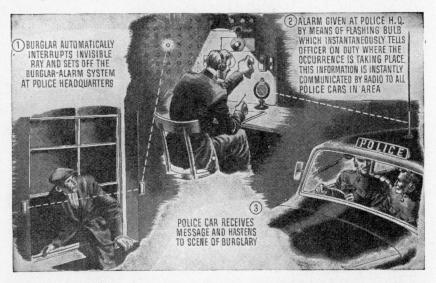

FIG. 2. *The interrelation of the three components of the psycho-organic system* (FIG. 1) *may be illustrated by comparison with a modern automatic burglar-alarm system. The invisible ray represents the receptor, and the policeman in the patrol-car the effector, while the connector is represented by the wiring, the duty officer at police headquarters and the radio, which, when taken together, form the connecting link.*

the behaviour as a whole. One part, usually called the "receptor" part, is composed of cells specially adapted to receive stimulations of various kinds from the external surroundings or from within the body. These stimulations are signals that some change has taken place in external or internal conditions, and are, as it were, a call for adaptive action.

A second part, called the "effector" part, consists of cells specialized to make, by their activity, the necessary responses to the stimulations received, representing the answer to the call for action. The third part, the "connector" part, very complex in the case of the human being, is composed of cells specialized to make connexion between the receptors and the effectors, so that the responses may be relevant to the signals received. The first part is represented by the various sense organs, the second by the muscles and glands, and the third by the nervous system.

With the activity of the cells in the nervous system, or at least a section of them, is associated, in some way we do not at present understand, what we know as the life of the mind, or the inner world of thought and feeling. It is the business of the physiologist to investigate the nature of all the different types of cell in the body, inclusive of those which compose the psycho-organic system. He can tell us less about the activities of the cells in the nervous system, and especially of the processes underlying thoughts and feelings, than about what takes place in the receptor cells or the effector cells, that is, in the sense organs or in the muscles and glands. We can say, therefore, that it is particularly at this point that psychology comes to join physiology and investigates these processes from the side of the mind.

PART OF THE EVENT

What, then, of this other side? That is a longer and somewhat more intricate story. The most fundamental and characteristic feature of the mental life is what we know as "consciousness". This is an entirely new feature, which need not enter into the physiological story at all. It is impossible to define a term like "consciousness". It is unique. Nevertheless, some sort of description may be attempted. Consciousness is not a place, though we frequently speak of things "being in consciousness". Nor is consciousness a thing or entity, though we are exceedingly prone to think of it as if it were. It is merely a character, at least as far as psychology is concerned, that belongs to certain events or processes, such as perceiving, or remembering, or imagining—events as real as any other events that take place in this universe of ours, as real as the rising and the setting of the sun, and as familiar to every human being. Probably this character may be best described by saying that it is a seeing of the event as it were from the inside, or an inside view of the event. We are, as it were, inside what is happening, and have, therefore, a corresponding view of it. All other events in the universe we can only view from the outside; in this case alone, the individual who perceives or imagines

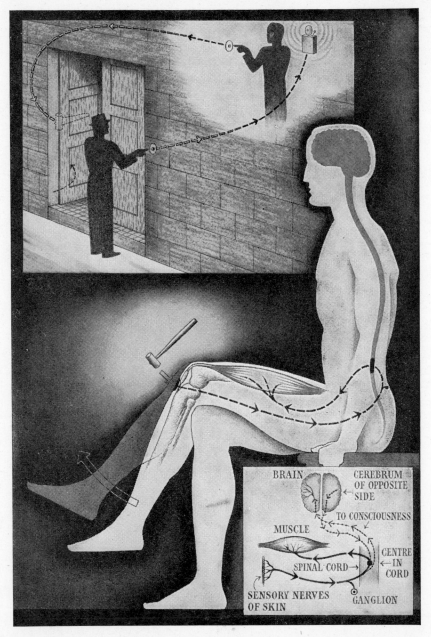

FIG. 3. *When we consciously move a limb (see* FIG. 4), *the nerve current is initiated in the brain, and travels to the muscles through the spinal cord. But a reflex path functions like an automatic door-opener. The message from an external stimulus is transmitted to a nerve centre in the spine; this centre sends out a nerve current that causes the muscle to contract.*

11

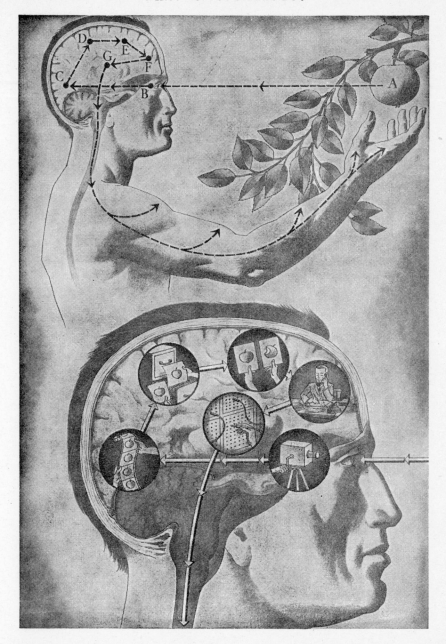

FIG. 4. *In a conscious reaction in which an external object (A) is concerned, the nerve currents pursue paths involving the following mental processes: sensation (B); perception (C); cognition (D), reached through association; affective emotion or desire (E), through further association; will (F). Finally, motor impulses (G) stimulate the muscles to attain the desired end.*

—but no other individual—can view it from the inside, because he is in a peculiar and unique way inside it.

There is another fundamental characteristic of the mental life, which is inseparable from consciousness, but nevertheless distinguishable from it. That is what we call "intelligence". Again, there is difficulty in defining the word, since it also is a term designating something which is unique. For ordinary purposes it would be taken as meaning, in the concrete, "putting two and two together" or, more abstractly, "the ability to apprehend the relations between things". Neither is a very scientific definition, but both would be recognized as near enough to the truth to serve ordinary purposes. Such attempts at definition do not help us much when we seek to understand the precise nature of intelligence in what may be called its lowest terms, so that we may be able to distinguish clearly between what is essentially intelligent and what is essentially unintelligent behaviour in man or animal.

AN EXPERIMENT

Some illustrative examples may assist us here. In one of a classical series of experiments with chimpanzees described by Köhler in his book *The Mentality of Apes*, he brought the chimpanzee into a room arranged as in Fig. 5, with a window looking out on the courtyard, and a door at the far side of the room opening into a passage which also led into the courtyard. He opened the window, threw out a banana, and closed the window. The chimpanzee immediately made for the door, although this meant going in a direction away from the banana, passed out through the passage, and seized the banana. The whole behaviour was a unified action. It was intelligent behaviour, because at every point it was obviously consciously relevant to the animal's objective, the getting of the banana. The chimpanzee knew what he was doing and why he was doing it.

The same experiment in principle was carried out with hens, a wire-netting enclosure taking the place of the room. Food was placed outside the enclosure, to be reached by a passage as before, but a much shorter passage. The hens made straight for the food, came up against the wire-netting, and fluttered aimlessly backwards and forwards in a flustered state, every now and again agitatedly making straight for the food and coming up against the netting once more. At length, apparently by chance, one hen after another, on coming near the door, took the path by the passage and got to the food.

How are we to describe the behaviour this time? Obviously, when a hen was moving directly towards the food, it was aware, however dimly, of what it was doing and why it was doing it; its behaviour, therefore, was consciously relevant to its objective, and so far was intelligent, though unsuccessful. While it was fluttering aimlessly backwards and forwards, we may regard its behaviour as approaching the limit of being quite unintelligent. Here, then, we have an illustration of what intelligence may be in its lowest terms. By comparing the behaviour of the hens with that of the chimpanzee we can also obtain a clear view of what is involved in different degrees of intelligence. Thus apparently, and as a limiting case, we may have consciousness without intelligence, or with varying degrees of intelligence, but we cannot have intelligence without consciousness.

Closer examination of the mental life reveals phenomena of two distinct orders. Consider the following phenomena, which are familiar in our everyday intercourse and conversation: perceiving, remembering, imagining, fearing, believing, deciding. In all these cases the words plainly refer to

FIG. 5. *The arrangement of Professor Köhler's experiment, described on page* 13.

processes or events in the mental life; the processes quite analogous to, and the events quite as real as, those occurring in the physical world which is around us.

Now consider these: prejudice, sentiment, ideal, complex. It is clear that these words do not refer to processes or events, but to something of an entirely different order, something more or less analogous to the things or entities of the physical world around us. They describe what might be called parts of the make-up or structure of an individual's personality, or at least what you would enumerate if you were giving a description of an individual's personality.

It is clear that the first group of phenomena—perceiving, remembering, etc.—are all what we call conscious processes. Our second group—prejudices, sentiments, etc.—are not conscious processes at all, or even processes. An individual may be conscious that he has a prejudice or a sentiment, just as he

14

may be conscious that he has a scar on his face, but that is an entirely different matter. In that case the prejudice or the sentiment is exactly analogous to any other object perceived or remembered or imagined. A prejudice or a sentiment may affect conscious processes such as perceiving, remembering, or imagining—is, in fact, constantly doing so in all sorts of ways—but is itself no more a process than the pupil of the eye is a process in seeing.

There is really good reason for thus stressing the distinction between conscious processes, making up an individual's experience, and the constituent elements in an individual's character or personality. Once we have really grasped that distinction, the whole psychology of "the unconscious" becomes clear. The basal sense of "the unconscious" in the psychology of Freud, Jung, and their followers is the totality of those elements in an individual's make-up which are neither conscious processes, nor, as such, capable of becoming conscious processes. Unfortunately, many of the psychologists who have discussed the unconscious are not themselves clear about this distinction, and, as a result, the unconscious becomes for them and their readers a veritable night-cap country, "a tumbling-ground of whimsies", as the American psychologist, William James, once called it.

UNCONSCIOUS PROCESSES

These elements in the make-up of the personality are dynamic. It has just been pointed out that prejudices, sentiments and the like may influence perceiving, remembering or imagining. There are thus processes or events in, and of, the unconscious, not merely in this influencing of conscious processes, but also in interaction among the elements themselves, inhibiting, reinforcing, conflicting with one another. Such processes are not conscious processes. They are of a different order altogether. They are processes in the unconscious.

This was to be expected, since these are all parts of a living organism. In consequence of this activity, impulses may spring up in our minds, apparently coming from nowhere; or impulses which never become conscious impulses may affect our behaviour, often to the bewilderment of ourselves and our friends. These and other similar phenomena are specially emphasized by Freud and the analytical psychologists, and it would be well to mark them off from conscious processes by a term employed by Freud in his theory of dreams—the term "endopsychic". This is all the more necessary, because, if we speak of them simply as unconscious processes, there is danger of confusion with the processes which have been called "subconscious". This confusion has, in fact, already shown itself too frequently, and has contributed considerably to that obscurity so often present in psycho-analytical literature.

Subconscious processes are really processes of the same order as conscious processes. Before the psychology of the unconscious, as represented by

Freud and Jung, came upon the scene, the term "subconscious" had become popular, largely under the influence of the French psychopathologists. It was employed for phenomena differing from the phenomena for which the term "unconscious" was used by Freud and Jung. When, however, the latter became popular, the new word came to be used indiscriminately of both groups of phenomena, the word "subconscious" tending to disappear altogether.

This word, however, can be usefully employed in the sense originally given to it. There are certain phenomena—some of them quite normal, others less usual but not abnormal, still others definitely abnormal—in which an individual exhibits behaviour of which he himself may be quite unaware, but which nevertheless presents the appearance of being intelligently directed. Such phenomena range from comparatively common absent-minded acts, talking in one's sleep, and sleep-walking or somnambulism, to the rarer automatic writing, and alternating or multiple personality.

AUTOMATIC WRITING

Perhaps the clearest illustration of these phenomena is given by automatic writing. In this case the individual, while sitting reading apparently with concentrated attention (though that is somewhat doubtful) may be seen to make writing movements with one of his hands, which is resting on the table; and if a sheet of paper be placed under his hand and a pencil between his fingers, he may write continuous sensible material, without knowing what he has written. He may even answer in writing questions put to him, without being aware of the questions asked or of the answers he has written. The material thus written is as much evidence of conscious process and intelligence as we normally regard a letter written by another person at a distance to be, and yet the writer is quite unaware of the writing until he reads afterwards what he has written.

Obviously we have here something which is scarcely distinguishable from conscious processes, except that the individual is unaware of its occurrence, and something which is clearly of a different type altogether from what we have called endopsychic processes. The term "subconscious" seems, therefore, quite appropriate.

Summing up, then, we find that in his study of behaviour the psychologist is concerned on the mental side with four groups of phenomena requiring to be investigated. These fall into two categories, the conscious and the unconscious, and may be tabulated thus:

Conscious	*Unconscious*
(*a*) conscious process;	(*c*) structural elements;
(*b*) subconscious process;	(*d*) endopsychic process.

The bodily activities which enter into and form the pattern of behaviour also fall into four groups, since the types of effectors are four—two types of

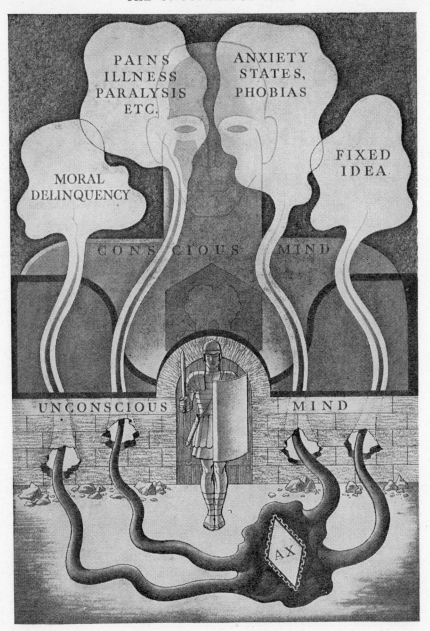

FIG. 6. *A neurosis (or complex) may be caused by an idea (AX) which is associated with a painful emotion and which has become buried in the unconscious mind. Since this idea is forgotten and cannot come into consciousness in the normal way, it breaks through in disguise and may cause symptoms of mental or physical disease.*

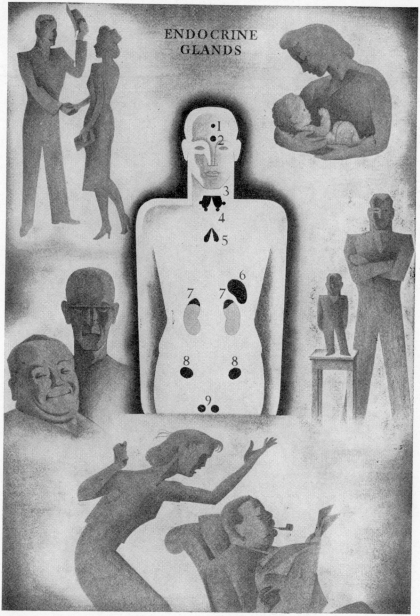

FIG. 7. *There is undoubtedly a close connexion between mental and especially emotional life and the activity of certain of the endocrine glands. These glands are:* (1) *pineal,* (2) *pituitary,* (5) *thymus (bodily growth and development);* (3) *thyroid (temperament—excitability, sluggishness, etc.—and physical constitution);* (4) *parathyroid;* (6) *spleen;* (7) *suprarenal;* (8 and 9) *ovaries and testes respectively* (*sex activity, procreation*).

18

muscle and two types of gland. We have, therefore, a similar tabulation of activities:

Motor	*Glandular*
(a) activity of the voluntary, or striped, muscles;	(c) activity of the duct glands;
(b) activity of the involuntary, or smooth, muscles;	(d) activity of the ductless, or endocrine, glands.

The detailed investigation of these activities, and of the organs, with their associated structures, in which they take place, is, as we have already pointed out, the more particular concern of the physiologist. The anatomist concerns himself only with the structural aspects of the organs. Though the psychologist gratefully avails himself of the results of the investigations of both anatomist and physiologist, his point of view is different from that of either. His main concern is with behaviour as a pattern of adaptive activity in response to a definite situation.

There is, naturally, considerable overlapping of the investigations of the psychologist with those of the physiologist. An early development of experimental psychology was named, and rightly named, "physiological psychology". In particular, there may be considerable overlapping with the work of the neurologist, that is, the physiologist who specializes in the functioning of the nervous system. It could hardly be otherwise, considering the part which the mental aspects of this functioning must play in the psychologist's interpretation of behaviour. Each science has its own special task according to how it views its aims and purposes. Physiology and neurology will nevertheless often throw light on the problems of the psychologist, and, similarly, psychology will often throw light on the problems of the physiologist or the neurologist.

It must be added that a considerable number of psychologists—some of them the most important names in the history of the science—prefer to confine their investigations to the mental field. The modern tendency in psychology is different, but it must be realized that valuable work in psychology may be done without trespassing on the work of the physiologist at all. The field of psychology is wide, and there is plenty of room for all.

SCIENTIFIC METHODS

The methods of study and investigation employed by the psychologist are today similar in principle to those employed in other natural sciences. As in all positive sciences, the primary aim is the ascertainment of facts and of their mutual relationships. This involves careful and patient observation and experiment. These are not in reality two different methods, since experiment is merely observation under carefully arranged, and, as far as possible, controlled, conditions. Merely casual observation, no matter how accurate it may be, is not observation as the scientist understands it. Similarly with experiment. Scientific experiment is not the trying out of any sort of combination of conditions to see what will happen. In order to be of scientific value, observation and experiment must be directed towards a definite objective—usually the solving of some problem, or the answering of some question which presents itself to the investigator as demanding a solution or an answer before his investigation can proceed.

To put the point in another way, if observation is to be fruitful the observer must have a definite idea of what he is looking for. As often as not this will arise out of some tentative theory or hypothesis which he has formed. The forming of hypotheses is legitimate in psychology as in other sciences. At the same time, a hypothesis, however tempting it may appear, must not be regarded as an established fact in the science until it has been verified by observation or experiment. A hypothesis is merely a possible connexion or relationship, imagined by the investigator, from which certain inferences with respect to possible facts may be drawn. Its usefulness consists in its being a guide to the direction investigation must take in order to ascertain if these possible facts are actual; and, until this investigation has been carried to a conclusion, the hypothesis remains in the realm of fancy, not of scientific knowledge. It should be stressed here that in no science is it more important to bear this in mind than in the science of psychology.

DIFFICULTIES OF SELF-INVESTIGATION

In the older psychology observation was directed mainly, if not exclusively, to the workings of the mind itself. This type of observation is usually spoken of as "introspection". To some of the early writers on the subject, such as John Locke, this kind of observation seemed simple enough and more or less a matter of course—as it does, indeed, on the surface. As we have seen, consciousness is a view of events from the inside. We are aware of our hunger, or our anger, or our sorrow, and have no difficulty in making the statement that we are hungry, angry, or sorry. Such introspection is an everyday affair. But as a method of scientific observation it is subject to marked limitations and grave defects.

In the first place, the direct observation of what goes on in the mind can only be carried out by one person, even under the most favourable circumstances. That difficulty, however, is more apparent than real, since, if a number of people, each observing what passes in his own mind, agree in the results of their observation, that would appear to be all the confirmation required. Unfortunately, even then the influence of an individual's idea of what he ought to find, or his knowledge of what other people say they find, may bias his observation to an extent that makes it quite unreliable. In the second place, a difficulty of a still more serious character arises out of the fact that the attentive observation of what is going on in the mind may change the whole mental situation, so that what we wished to observe eludes us entirely. Introspection, it is said of such cases, tends to destroy its own object. In emotional states like anger, for example, it is easy to see how, by paying more attention to what we are experiencing ourselves than to the object of our anger, the anger itself would tend to change and even to disappear rapidly.

Not only may the attempt to observe attentively some mental states which we hope to investigate alter them profoundly, but in certain cases it may be quite impossible to fix our attention on the state we wish to observe. As William James has so aptly put it, "it is like trying to turn round quickly so as to catch our own eyes looking". Under these circumstances it is not surprising that the older pyschology should have been such a raging sea of controversy regarding what actually took place in the mental life. Yet, in spite of these disadvantages, a trained observer can attain considerable success with this method; and, of course, it must be remembered that information obtained in this way can be obtained in no other way.

STUDYING THE MIND IN ACTION

The point of view and the objective of the newer psychology tend, however, to diminish the relative importance of the method of introspection. The main interest of the psychologist is not now the nature of the mind and mental life, but the external results produced by this mental life in behaviour and other expressions of mental process, and in the various permanent products which arise or have arisen from mental process. In all such cases, observation in psychology is not different in principle from observation in any of the other sciences. Accordingly, it tends to become more accurate and more reliable, and it is largely this change in the direction of interest that accounts for the remarkable progress that has been made in psychology in recent years. This change also accounts for the important and diverse applications of the science in our own times, resulting in Educational Psychology, Vocational Psychology, Industrial Psychology, Clinical Psychology, and so on.

In some cases self-observation may still be necessary, but such self-observation is usually of the everyday sort, not that systematic, subtle, analytical self-observation which was deemed to be necessary by the older psychology in its search for the nature of mind itself. Consequently, the older controversies now seem to the psychologist to have been about matters which are really of minor importance to psychology, and which may well be left to the philosopher to worry over.

It is now realized that psychology is a science which touches every one of us, and not merely the philosopher, far more intimately than does any other science, physical or biological. Confining our attention to the human animal, and leaving aside the practical issues involved in the development of the various branches of applied psychology, we find a wide range of interesting and important problems opening out in all directions, problems which hardly presented themselves to the older psychologists and which, even if they had presented themselves, could not have been studied in any scientific way from the older point of view.

Consider, for example, problems of development. We have equated behaviour to adaptive responses. In the case of the human being this is a very schematic description of behaviour, since the adaptive activities of the human being are multifarious and highly complex, even in the childhood of the individual or of the race, to say nothing of the highly civilized adult of the present day. In all cases, however, we begin with the relatively simple adaptive activities of the human infant at birth. From the beginning, and throughout the whole course of development to adulthood, these adaptive activities show two distinct phases. These have sometimes been spoken of as "active" and "passive" respectively.

These terms are not entirely satisfactory, especially the latter, which suggests the occurrence of a passive activity—an apparent contradiction of terms. All behaviour is essentially active, even in its very beginnings. It is not easy to suggest a more satisfactory word for "passive", unless we employ a word expressing simply the negation of the other phase. We should then have the phases characterized as "constructive" and "non-constructive" respectively. The essential difference between these two phases is that in the one case—the "non-constructive"—the conditions in which adaptation or adjustment takes place are, so to speak, accepted, and the form of the activity alone is altered to meet different conditions; whereas in the other case—the "constructive"—the conditions themselves are altered by the individual, either with or without alteration of the form of the activity. As the child increases in years, the constructive phase becomes more and more prominent in the total behaviour, and the higher his development the less is he found to be, so to speak, the slave of his environment.

INDIVIDUAL AND RACE DEVELOPMENT

The development of the human race from early prehistoric man to the civilized man of today shows very similar phenomena on a vastly larger scale. On that larger scale the details of the process are much more clearly exhibited. The bringing of these two fields of psychological investigation into juxtaposition also brings into relief the distance to be traversed by the infant of today in becoming the civilized adult of tomorrow. He starts where the prehistoric infant started. As the race has passed through the nomadic, the pastoral and the agricultural phases of civilization to the industrial phase, so has the behaviour of the individual become progressively more complex, and his adaptation more and more constructive.

The conditions of the environment have also become progressively more complex, particularly with the development in complexity of the social and economic environments. Psychological problems of great interest and importance face us here on every side. The conception of what has been called the "social heritage" gives us the key which makes intelligible the manner in which the human infant is enabled to reach the stage reached by the civilized adult of today. The term is applied to the accumulated results of what has been achieved by preceding generations through toil of mind and body, to be utilized as a basis for further advance by each succeeding generation. Such achievements as the production and use of fire, the making of tools, the smelting of metals, the invention of language, oral and written, the creation of government, with laws and institutions, the acquiring of all kinds of knowledge and skill and short cuts, by the systematic assimilation of which the child of today can acquire in a few years what has initially cost thousands of years of human effort.

Here again we have a vast field, presenting at one and the same time data and problems for the psychologist—the field of the products of mental process in the past. To these products adaptation must be made constructively and non-constructively. The psychological results are not all on the credit side. As Graham Wallas has pointed out, the human being becomes more or less dependent on his social heritage, and the uncivilized man may learn to do things which the civilized man does not need to learn to do, but which under certain conditions might become absolutely essential for survival.

FIG. 8. *The modern psychological laboratory is equipped with ingenious apparatus for determining the mental processes of men and animals. Here a psychologist (Right) is measuring a subject's reaction time, that is, the time taken to respond to a stimulus, such as a signal.*

23

Relevant to these points is the Culture Epoch theory in its application to the education of the child. This theory is an application, or rather extension, of the biogenic law that "ontogeny recapitulates phylogeny". This means that the individual in his development passes through the stages passed through in the development of the race. With certain qualifications, it is in a measure true of the physical development of the embryo. But the extension of the law, in the shape of the Culture Epoch theory, to the post-natal development of the child has to be qualified to such an extent as to make it of relatively little practical importance, particularly if taken as a guide in the education of the child. It is true that the child in his play may, and does, reproduce more primitive types of attitude and behaviour. Even here, however, any close parallelism is very difficult, if not impossible, to trace, though it is true that we do find activities occurring which are suggestive of forms of behaviour characteristic of remote epochs of racial history.

To make this theory a guide in the education of the child is an entirely different matter. The aim in education is to bring the child into adjustment with an existing social and cultural environment. The method by which this must be done is the wise utilization and wise guidance of the child's interests as they develop. If the course of development of these interests were closely analogous or parallel to the successive cultural and social phases of development in racial history, a study of these would without doubt be of considerable assistance. Even so, we dare not forget the primary aim of adjustment to the cultural and social conditions at present existing; and the most serious dangers lurk in any educational practice which permits this primary aim to be displaced by entirely secondary considerations. Nothing can take the place of clear consciousness of the final aim of education, on the one hand, and direct knowledge of the developing interests of the child, on the other.

Test Yourself

1. What are the two main groups into which the activities of an organism can be classified?

2. What are the two chief methods used in the science of psychology?

3. What constitutes the social heritage of the child?

Answers will be found at the end of the book.

CHAPTER II

THE WORLD OF OUR SENSES

W<small>E TAKE</small> very largely for granted the knowledge that we have of ourselves and of the environment around us. And it is not until we begin to ponder over things that we realize that our knowledge arises from experience primarily based on the information we receive from the different senses with which we are endowed. Through them we see, hear, touch, taste and smell, and gradually from the knowledge so gained we become aware of the world around us.

Almost from the beginning of life our sensations become modified. For example, if we see before us an orange, we know from previous experience how it will taste, how it will feel, its approximate weight and so on. In other words, all our previous experience of an orange will modify the sensation we are experiencing at the moment. Further, we identify the object, name it, and so place it in its own category. Similarly, when we look at a piece of velvet it looks smooth to us. The effect of smoothness has been obtained from touching the velvet on some previous occasion, and it has become linked up with the visual appearance. In the same way, we find that white snow *looks* cold to us, whereas white sugar *looks* sweet.

Perception, which is the name given to this more complex process, belongs to the cognitive aspect of our experience, and is cognition at its most fundamental level. Examples of perception are: seeing a friend or animal, hearing the sound of a whistle or of a violin, tasting chocolate, smelling the fragrance of a rose, touching an object, experiencing a pain, etc. In each of these examples some stimulus is present which affects one or other of the sense organs, such as the eye or the ear, the tongue, the nostrils, the skin, or some of the internal organs of the body.

At a higher level, at what is called the level of "ideation" or "ideal representation", cognition involves imagery, memory and imagination. We can see the animal or the flower in our mind's eye without its actually being before us. In other words, we can have the experience again, but this time in the form of an image. This type of experience indicates a greater degree of freedom in our mental life, for we are independent of the presence of the stimulus. In this way, we can remember things or events from the past, or we can combine images in new ways and imagine them as different. As we shall see later, images are not confined to vision, but are characteristic of all our senses.

At a still higher level, the level of "conception" or "intellection", we are able to abstract a quality from an object and compare it with a quality from another object. We may then conclude that the colour of one object is lighter or darker than that of another, that of two notes one is higher or lower in pitch, or that a pain is more acute than its predecessor. The two objects we are comparing need not necessarily be before us, for we can compare them mentally by means of the images we have of them in our minds. This is the level of comparison, abstraction, generalization, and all the higher levels of mental activity, including thinking.

These three levels are interdependent. We are constantly returning to our percepts to clarify our images and our concepts. If the picture in our mind of a kangaroo or of an emu is vague and uncertain, we may visit the Zoo in order to perceive the animal once again, or we may look at a picture of the animal in an authoritative work. If our memory of a Beethoven sonata is faulty at one part, we may turn to the printed music or a gramophone record to refresh our memory. In very much the same way, our concepts are constantly developing and being enlarged, and this process in turn leads to our thinking becoming stimulated and broadened in scope.

CONSTANCY OF PERCEPTION

It is a curious, yet common, experience that, although objects are seen from different angles or in different illuminations, they still look pretty much the same to us. A person at a distance does not look unduly small. Our perceiving, in other words, is relatively constant, although the stimulus itself is actually different in different situations. If this constancy did not exist great confusion would result, as we should not be able in many cases to recognize familiar objects around us if their appearance were always changing.

Interesting research has been carried out in brightness and colour constancy. Objects exhibit the same brightness although they may be reflecting more or less light according to circumstances. For example, the strength of illumination at noon is about one hundred times that in the early morning or late afternoon. Yet, in spite of this great change of illumination, the colours of objects do not change at all, or at least change to an almost imperceptible degree. The white paper of this book does not appear black in the afternoon, although it is actually reflecting less light than the black letters do at noon. A sheet of white paper at the back of a room is actually darker than a sheet of black paper near a window. Yet the white paper appears white to us, and the black paper appears black. The phenomenal appearance (that is, what the paper looks like to us) is not the same as the actual sensation. We are not perceiving what is actually there. The physical appearance of these papers

26

can be tested by using a reduction screen, a piece of grey paper or cardboard with two small holes in it. If it is so arranged that through one hole one sees the far-away white paper, and through the other hole the nearer black paper, the black paper will appear to be the lighter of the two.

The same brightness constancy is found to exist in the case of animals. Köhler carried out experiments on chimpanzees and domestic fowls. The fowls were trained to take grains of corn from the brighter of two papers. When the darker paper was placed in bright sunlight, so that it reflected more light than the brighter paper, which remained in average illumination, the hens chose the paper which reflected less light, that is the paper which was actually brighter and which they had been trained to choose. This they would

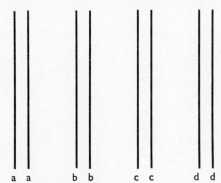

a a   b b   c c   d d

FIG. 9. *Perception is largely an active process; the mind makes its own contribution to the image upon the retina. Thus, the lines in this figure are not seen merely as independent lines, but are grouped mentally into a pattern of bars.*

not have done if the brightness constancy had not existed in their case. A similar result from a differently arranged experiment was obtained with the chimpanzees.

The shape and size of objects also remain constant. Distant objects do not look unduly small. If we move a pencil away from us, the retinal image is smaller, but we see the pencil in its normal size. A round plate is generally seen as round, although from the various angles at which we regard it its appearance is actually that of an ellipse.

One of the earliest experiments which drew attention to the difference between what is perceived and the actual image on the retina was carried out by Wertheimer in 1912, and is known as the phi-phenomenon. If two lights at a certain distance apart are switched off and on independently one after the other in quick succession, the observer actually sees movement, as if one light moved backwards and forwards from one position to another. The stimuli recorded on the retinas of the two eyes are those of two separate lights, but the experience is actually that of movement. This is the same kind of phenomenon as that which occurs in the cinema. A film strip consists of separate, stationary pictures, each one very slightly different from its predecessor. When they are shown in succession at a certain speed, the onlooker sees movement. If the rate of exposure is too slow, only static pictures will be seen.

This is also the basis of the changing electric signs used in advertising. In such signs there is no actual movement of the signs, although we perceive them as moving. The movement arises from the switching off and on of the lights at regulated intervals and in a pre-arranged sequence.

Perception must not be regarded as a passive process, for it does considerably more than merely mirror the objective world around us. For example, in Figure 9 are eight parallel lines: a a, b b, c c, d d; the spaces between a and b, b and c, etc. are greater than the spaces between a and a, b and b, etc. But we tend to group these elements into a pattern, so that what we actually perceive is a figure made up of four vertical bars; we are not primarily conscious that this pattern is composed of eight unconnected lines and the spaces between them.

If we now look at Figure 10 we have an example of an ambiguous figure. It is seen either as a vase or as two silhouettes. In such a case we have a reversal of figure and background taking place. When the vase is dominant, the black surface becomes the background. When the silhouettes are dominant, the vase drops into the background. The same thing happens in puzzle pictures. When we suddenly see the hidden picture, the rest of the drawing, which was up to that point the figure, now becomes the background. As the physical object has remained exactly the same, the difference between

FIG. 10. *A vase or two human heads? This figure makes a totally different impression according to whether we concentrate upon the white or the black portion.*

the two ways of seeing the picture must be attributed to the mind, to some subjective factor modifying the original data.

The subjective factor entering into our perceiving is clearly shown in geometrical optical illusions. These can be divided for convenience into the following three groups.

(1) *Illusions of Reversible Perspective.* The drawing in Figure 11 shows no perspective, that is, it has no figure and ground and can be seen in either of two ways. At one time the central line appears to be in front of the whole drawing, at another time behind it, so that we see an open book with its back either projecting outwards or inwards. Once these two aspects can be seen, the reversal from one to the other takes place very rapidly. The more complex

figures are even more striking; examples of these are the figures known as Scripture's Blocks (Fig. 13), Schröder's Stair (Fig. 14), and Scripture's Changing Rings (Fig. 15).

(2) *Illusions of Extent or Distance.* If two lines are drawn of equal length, but one horizontal and the other vertical, the vertical lines will appear longer than the other. This is known as the vertical-horizontal illusion. When a perfect square is drawn, with the four sides mathematically equal, it always looks higher than its breadth. In Fig. 16 is shown the Müller-Lyer illusion. The two parts of the horizontal line are actually equal, but the part bounded by the obtuse angles looks much longer than the part

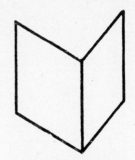

FIG. 11. *The central line can be made to appear behind or in front of the rest of this drawing at will.*

bounded by the acute angles. Many explanations of this illusion have been offered. The one most generally accepted is that the angles of the short end lines affect the apparent sizes of the two portions, the obtuse angles making one portion appear longer, while the acute angles make the other portion appear smaller.

Another type of illusion which fits into this category is that in which two spaces look different in size owing to one being filled. For example, if we mark off two equal distances with dots (Fig. 12) and fill up the space between two of the dots, then that distance immediately looks greater.

FIG. 12. *The unfilled space at* (*b*) *appears to be, and is, the same size as that at* (*a*). *But the filled space* (*B*) *appears larger than the unfilled space* (*A*), *although in actual fact, measurement shows that both spaces are of the same size.*

This illusion is said to be due to the greater number of eye movements required for the eye to pass along the line from one dot to another.

(3) *Illusions of Direction.* A number of illusions may be included in this group. We find here straight lines appearing bent or curved or broken. In Fig. 17 the two thick lines appear to be bent. In Fig. 18 the diagonal line does not appear to be continuous. The lower half of the line seems to be parallel with the upper half rather than continuous with it.

Many explanations have been suggested to explain illusions. As we have already indicated, eye movements are said to be the cause in many cases. It requires greater effort to move the eyes vertically than horizontally, hence a vertical line seems longer. In the reversible perspective type of illusion, it is suggested that when we look at one part of the figure it stands out in one aspect, and when we change our point of fixation the other aspect of the illusion appears. Eye movements, however, cannot be the whole explanation, for illusions can still be experienced when eye movements are ruled out. Again, some authorities say that illusions arise owing to the angles of the lines, or that they are due to the curvature of the retina. One interesting explanation of the Müller-Lyer illusion is that it results from "empathy". The end lines seem to possess energy, pushing in one portion of the horizontal line, thereby causing it to contract, and stretching out the other portion to its fullest limit. In most cases, such illusions still persist even when we are familiar with them.

In addition to the geometrical optical illusions, other illusions abound in everyday life. We mistake one object for another, such as a shadow in the dark for an animal. The stimulus is there, but we are not perceiving it correctly. The illusions produced by the conjurer represent another category.

HOW WE SEE COLOURS

Let us now turn to the senses themselves and discuss some of the interesting facts which have been discovered about them.

Colour Vision. Our sense of seeing is more wonderful than many of us imagine. Its complexity is taken as a matter of course, and we seldom pause to ask how such a delicate organ as the eye can yield us so many different sensations. The eye gives us all our colours and shapes and enables us to enjoy the beauties of the world around us.

Colours are caused by rays of light originating in the vibrations of the ether which surrounds us. These strike the inner coating of the eyeball, which is known as the retina, and the nervous impulses initiated there are carried by the optic nerve to the brain. The sizes of the ether waves vary considerably; of all colours, the colour red has the longest wave-length, and the colour violet the shortest. All the other colours fall intermediately between these two. Ether waves which are longer than the waves giving us the experience of red are not seen, but we feel some of them—the infra-red waves—as heat. Among the ether waves shorter than the violet waves are the ultra-violet rays and the X-rays, both of which, again, are invisible.

Ordinary sunlight is composed of ether waves of different wave-lengths. The intermediate or visible rays we see as white light, which is composed of the colours we know as red, orange, yellow, green, blue and violet. These are the colours of the rainbow or of the spectrum. If we hold a prism in the path of a sunbeam, the prism will separate out the white light of the sun into these six colours.

Our visual sensations divide themselves into two distinct groups—brightnesses and colours. In the brightness group, we have the light experiences ranging from dazzling white through all the shades of grey to a deep black.

These form the "achromatic" series. In the other series, the "chromatic" series, are all our colours—reds, greens, yellows, blues, etc. Generally, in everyday life, these two series combine to give us the different shades and tints with which we are so familiar, and of which the number is said to be about thirty thousand.

The Blind Spot. How many people are aware that there is one part of the eye with which we see nothing? In the eye there is a blind spot, at the point where the optic nerve enters the retina. This can be demonstrated very easily. Hold up the book (open at page 38) in front of you; close the right eye and look steadily at the black cross in Fig. 19. Move the page slowly towards and away from the eye, and at one point the rectangle with the black triangle will completely disappear. This is because it has been focused upon the blind spot. The other eye can be tested in the same way, if the book is reversed. The reason that we are normally unaware of these blind spots in our eyes is that both eyes function together and that we subjectively fill in the "blind" portions from the surrounding areas.

Seeing in Twilight. During the war years, we became gradually accustomed to darkened streets. Most of us realized through experience that when leaving a brightly-lit room to go into the dark outside, it was better to wait in the dark for a little until the eyes became accustomed to the change of light, before venturing forth. The eyes require time to become "dark-adapted", for dark-adaptation is a relatively slow process. Moreover, people differ in their ability to become dark-adapted and also in their rate of dark-adaptation, which explains why some people see better in the dark than others. A very slow change takes place during the first ten minutes, followed by a rapid increase of adaptation during the next half-hour. This is the reason why often a householder, on walking round his premises straight from a brightly-lit room, saw no light showing from his windows during the black-out, whereas a warden who had been in the darkened streets for some time could see a light showing. The householder's eyes were not yet sufficiently dark-adapted.

When passing from the dark into light, as in leaving a cinema, time is also

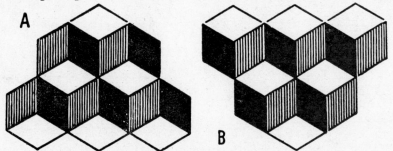

FIG. 13. *The illusion known as Scripture's Blocks. At (A) there are three cubes, and at (B) five cubes: these persist if the book is turned round slowly. But if the book is reversed rapidly, five cubes appear at (A) and three at (B).*

31

required for the eye to become accustomed to the light, or to become "light-adapted". The adaptation this time is much more rapid, but sometimes, before the eye becomes accustomed to light again, we have the unpleasant experience of glare.

The sensitive light-cells in the retina of the eye are known as "rods" and "cones" on account of their shape. According to one theory, the "cones", which are concerned with colour sensations, function in daylight, whereas the "rods" function in twilight vision, and are concerned with the production of sensations not involving colour. In the fovea (that part of the retina associated with the most acute vision) only cones are found, so that in the dark the fovea is no longer the most sensitive part. The periphery of the eye, which contains rods, is better adapted for night vision. One fact which supports this theory (although it is still debated) is that the retina of nocturnal birds, such as owls, contains only rods or at least has very few cones.

The Field of Vision. When we look at an object directly, it is focused upon the fovea of the eye. Images of other objects in the immediate neighbourhood fall on other parts of the retina outside the fovea. Colours may look different as they fall on different parts of the retina. The extreme periphery cannot see colours at all, only blacks, whites and greys. If we mark a point on a wall on a level with our eyes and close one eye, this can easily be demonstrated. Imagine a horizontal line to be drawn through this point. Fasten a little square of coloured paper (say, red) on the end of a wire, and gradually move it along this horizontal line. If the right eye is open, move the coloured paper from the right; if the left eye is open, move it from the left, keeping the gaze of the open eye steadily fixed on the little square. At first, the paper may

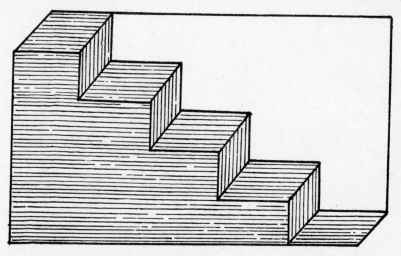

FIG. 14. *According to how our eyes focus, this may be seen either with the large shaded surface as the front wall or the white surface as the front wall.*

be too far out for the observer to see anything at all. Then, as the paper is moved nearer to the centre, it may be seen as grey; and as it is moved still farther in, the red may appear as yellow, but it is not until it is very near the mark or centre that we can see the true colour.

We shall find, if we test the eye with different colours in this way, that we shall be able to divide the horizontal line into three parts: the outermost part where we can only see greys, the middle part where we can see blues and yellows, and the inner zone where all the colours are seen, including reds and greens. The same type of result appears when the vertical field of vision is investigated, although this field is more restricted.

That the outer zone is best for seeing greys or brightnesses is easily verified on a starry night. If we look at the constellation of the Pleiades we can count a certain number of stars; but if we turn our head a little aside so that we are looking at the stars with the periphery of the eye, we shall be amazed to find that we can see stars which were quite invisible to us before.

BEAUTIFUL EFFECTS

Successive Contrast. Some very beautiful colour effects can be obtained very simply through contrast. If we look at a piece of yellow paper for about twenty seconds, try to focus the centre of it without moving the eyes, and then transfer the gaze to a sheet of grey paper, a blue patch of the same shape will appear on the grey paper. If we fixate a piece of green paper in the same way, a red patch will be seen. These colours—yellow and blue in the one case, red and green in the other—are called complementary colours. No matter what colour we focus, its complementary colour will always appear. White and black behave in the same way as colours. White gives, when fixated, an after-image of black or of dark grey, whereas black gives an after-image of white or of light grey. Try this with Fig. 20.

The complementary colour which appears occupies the same shape and is of the same brightness as the original colour. In some cases the successive contrast colour, or the "negative after-image" as it is called, lingers for some time, and may appear and disappear at intervals. It is possible to project these after-images at different distances. Instead of looking at a sheet of white paper, try fixating the after-image on the ceiling or on a wall. The farther away from the eye it is projected, the larger will it appear.

The existence of these negative after-images may explain why a certain shade of material bought in a shop after the purchaser has looked at many colours may prove so disappointing next day when looked at by itself. Contrast effects have been at work, enriching the colour of the material, or at least affecting it in some way.

Positive after-images may also be obtained by looking at a colour in bright sunlight for three or four seconds, and then looking at a piece of white or grey paper. The positive after-image is of the same colour as the original.

If a piece of red paper is looked at in good illumination for three or four seconds, and then a piece of grey paper is fixated, red will appear and will take the same shape as the red stimulus paper. The blowing out of a candle often produces positive after-images, the flame appearing wherever the gaze is projected. Also, on looking at the sun and then away, positive after-images of the sun are readily experienced.

Simultaneous Contrast. Simultaneous contrast effects can be obtained by placing a small piece of grey paper on differently coloured backgrounds in turn, and covering them with a sheet of tissue paper. The grey paper looks yellow on a blue background; on a yellow background it appears blue, on a red background green, on a green background red, on a white background dark grey, on a black background light grey. The role of the tissue paper is to soften the edges of the grey paper and so facilitate the contrast effect. With practice, the tissue paper can be dispensed with.

COLOURED SHADOWS

Beautiful effects are obtained with coloured shadows. If a red light is arranged so as to shine on a sheet of white paper which is already illuminated by an ordinary electric lamp, a pencil held between the source of the red light and the white paper throws a shadow on the paper which is green. If a green light is substituted, the shadow of the pencil this time will be red. A blue light will give a yellow shadow, and a yellow light a blue shadow. These coloured shadows exist all around us, but we rarely notice them. If an artist paints coloured shadows, we are apt to think they exist in his imagination, and we find it difficult to see the colours which he has faithfully reproduced on canvas.

Colour-blindness. Three varieties of colour-blindness seem to exist, but they are not all of equal importance. Total colour-blindness is, fortunately, not very common; only about eighty cases in all having been reported. To a totally colour-blind person no colours are visible, but generally the brightness series is unaffected. For instance, red may appear black, orange a dark grey, blue a light grey and so on. The second variety of colour-blindness is blue-yellow colour-blindness, in which blue and yellow are the difficult colours. This type of colour-blindness is very rare and generally is associated with some pathological change in the eye. In one case which has been recorded, blue was seen as a dazzling white.

The third form of colour-blindness, red-green blindness, is the most important because of its frequent occurrence and because of the colours involved. When it is recalled that red and green are the colours used in signalling on the railway, at sea, in the air, and for traffic control on the roads, it is evident that this defect is one which cannot be overlooked. It becomes increasingly important when it is realized that the existence of this defect in the male population is estimated at about seven per cent. In the case of

FIG. 15. *We can see these as solid rings either with their front edges towards the centre, or facing outwards to the corner of the page.*

women, only about one in five hundred suffers from this disability. Unfortunately, this defect is inherited and incurable.

Colour-blindness must not be confused with "colour-ignorance", which, of course, can be put right, for this is only a case of learning the names of the colours and associating them properly. Colour-blindness is an inability to see certain colours, although visual acuity of the eye may be normal.

TONE AND NOISE

Our world of sound is as interesting as our world of vision, and as rich in experience. In our daily life we are constantly hearing sounds of all kinds and descriptions and of different intensities—the rumble of a cart in the street, the noise of a motor-car passing by, the sound of a bicycle bell, the conversation around us, the sound of a friend's voice, the music of the radio or a concert.

It is customary to think of sounds as being separated into musical tones and noises. The division is an arbitrary one and is not clear-cut. In practising a violin the beginner produces noise more often than anything else, but as he becomes more accomplished tones are heard more frequently. An orchestra, when tuning up, produces noise, and yet this noise is brought into being by a combination of musical instruments, all of which are producing tones.

If we accidentally strike a tumbler, we hear a ringing sound, and often we can see the tumbler vibrating. If we touch the tumbler, so causing the vibrations to cease, the sound stops also. Before we can listen to the note of a tuning-fork, we must set the prongs vibrating. If they are not set in motion, no sound is heard. Sound is caused by the vibrations of the air around us. When air vibrations strike the drum of the ear at regular intervals, we hear tones. When the intervals are irregular, noises are heard. Middle *C* on the piano has

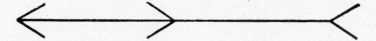

FIG. 16. *The Müller-Lyer illusion. Which portion of this line is the longer?*

a vibration rate of 256 vibrations per second; the octave *C* above has a vibration twice as fast—that is, 512 vibrations per second. The higher the vibration rate, the higher is the tone; the lower the vibration rate, the lower is the tone.

The air-waves in vibration strike the drum of the ear, which in turn vibrates at the same rate. Its movement is communicated to one delicate structure after another in the middle ear, until the cells in the inner ear are reached. When these are stimulated, nervous impulses are initiated, and are conducted by means of the auditory nerve to the auditory centre in the brain.

The ability to hear high notes decreases with age, and it has been said that no one over forty hears the squeak of a bat. Some people suffer from what is called "high-frequency deafness", that is, they are unable to hear any sound which has a high frequency, but can hear sounds of middle or low frequencies. This affects very considerably their hearing of speech and conversation and constitutes a very serious handicap. This defect is not characteristic of old age, but is found to exist at any age. Some children accused of inattention at school may be unwitting sufferers from this defect. Fortunately it is found that this particular type of deafness does not occur very frequently.

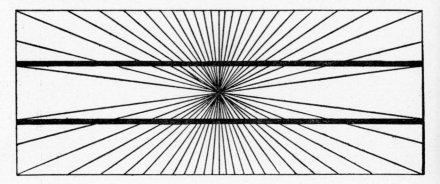

FIG. 17. *An illusion of direction: the two thick lines are really quite straight and parallel.*

The other special senses include those of taste, smell, touch and other sensations derived from the skin.

The Sense of Taste. The organs of taste are situated on the upper surface of the tongue, but sensations of taste may also be experienced in the soft palate and its neighbourhood. Only four simple qualities of taste can be distinguished: sweet, bitter, sour or acid, and salt. These correspond to the tastes of sugar, quinine, lemon juice and common salt respectively. Certain papillæ yield only one kind of gustatory sensation, others yield two, three, or even four kinds. The tip of the tongue is most sensitive to sweet and salt sensations, while the back of the tongue gives the sensation of bitter ones; the sides of the tongue yield the sensation of sourness or acidity. Saccharine tastes sweet over most of the tongue's surface, but at the back of the tongue it tastes bitter.

The sense of taste consists really of four senses in one, and most tastes are either combinations of some of these four simple tastes, caused by simultaneous stimulation of different papillæ, or they are not pure tastes at all, but are

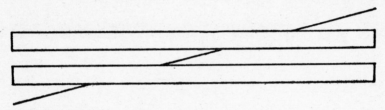

FIG. 18. *The diagonal lines, although parts of one continuous line, seem to be "staggered."*

linked up with sensations of smell and of temperature and with contact and organic sensations. What is our experience when we taste lemonade? It is quite complex, and consists of a sweet taste, a sour taste, a scent, sensations of temperature and a pricking skin or touch sensation. Taste and smell are closely bound up together; that is why a cold in the head destroys the sense of taste—it really takes away our sense of smell. Touch and temperature sensations are also obtained from the tongue. As the tongue is a muscular organ, it also assists taste by causing movement of the fluid.

The Sense of Smell. In the case of the sense of smell, the end organs are situated in the inner and upper part of the nostrils. The stimulus for smelling consists of very minute particles, emanating from the odoriferous substance, which pass into the nostrils in breathing and stimulate the olfactory cells.

It is not easy to analyse the sense of smell into its elementary qualities. Some authorities suggest that there are six qualities, while others say that there are nine.

The six elementary smells have been described as fruity, resinous, flowery, spicy, burning and putrid.

In the nostrils a second set of nerve fibres exists which gives us the tickling or irritating sensation accompanying some of the so-called smells, such as that of ammonia.

Both in taste and in smell, great individual differences exist. Some people have an acute sense of taste and smell, others a poor sense of taste and smell, while others, again, may suffer from an actual defect in either or both of these senses. In the case of smell, the defect may extend to certain smells only. One person reported was unable to smell vanilla, while another was unable to smell mignonette.

Skin Sensations. Our cutaneous sensations are more complex than we normally imagine them to be. If we move a rod or a pencil lightly over the skin, say over the back of the hand, we experience a touch or tactual sensation. If the rod has been immersed in ice before being drawn over the hand, then we shall experience here and there distinct "flashes" of cold, due to the stimulation of the so-called "cold spots" in the skin. If the rod is warmed to a temperature of between 45 deg. and 50 deg. F., heat spots will be felt here

FIG. 19. *The eye contains a "blind spot", with which we can see nothing! Its presence can be demonstrated with the aid of this figure and the explanation on page 31.*

and there when it is moved slowly over the skin. If we substitute a needle or a pin for the rod, we shall experience sensations of pain when the "pain spots" are stimulated. Pain may also arise when any stimulus is too intense, such as a very loud noise, or when actual damage to the skin takes place.

Each of the sensitive spots, whether of pressure or touch, cold, heat or pain, yields only its own sensation. A cold spot gives only the sensation of cold, a heat spot only the sensation of heat, and similarly with the spots responding to pressure and to pain. We do not notice these different spots as individual points in the skin, because, generally, larger areas are stimulated. These different spots are distributed all over the body, but clusters of one kind may be grouped together at different parts. Touch spots, for example, are very numerous on the tips of the fingers, as one would expect.

Other sensations arise from the muscles and tendons which give us feelings of strain and tension, while sensations from the joints are important in determining for us the position of our limbs. When we move a limb or a finger we experience a sensation of movement or what is called a "kinæsthetic sensation".

The common sensation of dizziness or "swimming in the head" arises from disturbance of the three little semicircular canals inside the ear. If by any chance these canals are damaged, it is difficult to maintain one's balance.

There are also organic or visceral sensations, which include all those sensations which come to us from any internal part of the body, except from the muscles, tendons or joints. These give us our feeling of wellbeing or otherwise, and are largely bound up with the vegetative and nutritive life of the organism. These organic sensations play a very important part in all our emotions, particularly in all strong emotions, such as intense fear and anger.

STRANGE ABNORMALITY

Synæsthesia. It may be novel and surprising to some readers to learn that colour and sound often combine, and that some people "see" sounds coloured. Coloured hearing, or "synæsthesia", is more frequent than is generally supposed. In addition to an auditory stimulus giving its own auditory response in the form of a sound, it seems to call forth also a visual response in the form of a visual image which is associated with it. This often occurs in the field of music. In the minds of some people the hearing of music is closely associated with colour. Different notes call forth different colours, and different musical instruments are associated with their own characteristic colours.

Some composers have even suggested the showing of colours during musical recitals. Those in whom synæsthesia is strongly developed may have a coloured background which is constantly changing as they listen to the orchestra, or to a pianoforte solo, or even to a song.

With some people, the coloured hearing may be even more extensive. Days of the week, months of the year, letters of the alphabet may all be coloured. Even vowels may have colours attached to them which vary according to their sounds. Galton has an interesting section on coloured hearing, with illustrations, in his *Inquiries into Human Faculty*. He records that wallpaper was translated into words and sounds by one of the individuals studied, and sounds into different colours of wallpaper!

Those who have coloured hearing are unaware that there is anything unusual in it, and do not know that they differ from others until they chance to read about it. It seems to be inherited, and members of a family all seem to be

FIG. 20. *Fix the gaze for about two minutes upon the white cross, and then quickly place a sheet of white or grey paper over the illustration. A negative after-image will appear.* (*See page 33.*)

39

"coloured thinkers", although they do not have necessarily the same associations between sounds and colours. In one case studied the individual was always conscious of a coloured background. The colour did not remain constant, but varied according to the person spoken to, the conversation listened to, or the music that was heard. In listening to a lecture, the topic of the lecture evoked a colour which remained constant as long as the hearer devoted her attention to the lecture. If her attention were diverted to the lecturer, the lecturer's colour predominated. Chemistry was visualized as green, anatomy as red, psychology as white.

In this girl's mind books and authors were also associated with colour. Scott was grey, Masefield's poems were blue, and Shaw was red. Music, too, had its appropriate colours: MacDowell's music was red, the music of Bach and Beethoven brown, and Grieg's music green. If this girl listened to music without seeing colour, she did not enjoy it, which meant that the music was too intricate for her to follow. When music was enjoyed, the colour pervaded the concert hall, and natural colours in the environment were repressed.

In this girl's case, tastes and smells were also coloured, as, indeed, were most of her other senses. Toothache, for example, was green. In the case of vision she possessed a complete colour alphabet. *A* was straw-coloured, *B* blue, *C* blue, *D* black, *E* white, *F* pink, *G* green, *H* auburn, etc. The colours of the vowels varied according to their sound. Days of the week and months of the year were also associated with colours.

This girl, who only discovered through hearing a lecture on synæsthesia that it was not common to all people, was amazed, and found it difficult to imagine the content of other individuals' minds. Her remark was to the effect that their minds must be very empty!

Test Yourself

1. What do we understand by a *percept* and how does it differ from an image?

2. What is understood by the constancy phenomenon in perception?

3. What do you understand by a *concept*? How far is it dependent upon the senses?

Answers will be found at the end of the book.

CHAPTER III

IMAGERY AND IMAGINATION

MOST of us are familiar with Wordsworth's lines in which he expresses his joy when "a host of golden daffodils", whose appearance has given him so much pleasure, later flash upon the inward eye. When we recall a scene such as this, we often do so in the form of a visual image. That is, we do not require the daffodils to be actually before us, but we can see them represented ideally in our minds. It is possible to image objects perceived not only yesterday, or the day before yesterday, but indeed after any lapse of time.

We can picture in our minds fairly easily an animal or a flower, a person or a landscape, which we have seen on only one occasion. But most of our images are not based on one percept, but on a number of percepts experienced at various times. We see our pet spaniel over and over again, and when we picture it the image we have is a composite one derived from its appearance on different occasions. Or we look at trees in winter, then in summer, and again our image of them is a composite one. An image such as this tends to be sketchy, since only the parts common to all trees are retained in the image; the other parts fade away, or are blurred and indistinct. It has been suggested that an image of this kind cannot exist, for when we try to call up an image of trees or dogs in general, it does not seem possible to do so, and the image either becomes very sketchy or resolves itself into an image of a particular tree or a particular dog.

COMPOSITE PORTRAIT

The general image is analogous to the composite photograph devised by Sir Francis Galton. Galton was interested in heredity, and one ingenious line of research carried out by him was to photograph on the same plate all the members of a family, either all full face or all in profile, and so obtain the "family face". The parts of the features common to all members of the family appeared clear and distinct in the photograph, whereas individual idiosyncrasies were blurred and indistinct.

In a way, the formation of a general image is much the same, in that the common elements are retained and individual peculiarities drop out or are vague. So sketchy does this type of image become that some people declare that they have no images at all when they think of an object. Their thinking is not accompanied by concrete images, but only by verbal or word images. For example, when they hear a word, say, "house", they mentally speak the word, or they may see it as printed before them, but they have no picture of the object "house" itself. Whether thinking can take place without any imagery at all is a nice point in psychology, and one that has caused no little controversy.

How can we distinguish an image from a percept? To the uninitiated this question may seem rather absurd. Surely, it will be argued, we know when we are looking at a dog in front of us, and can distinguish that experience from imagining we see one. Surely we know when we actually hear a bell ringing and when the sound is only an auditory image? But are we quite so sure? Is it so easy to distinguish between what really exists in the physical world and what it is that has its existence in our mental world?

PERCEPT AND IMAGE

There are certain characteristics which enable us to draw the distinction between a percept and an image. An image, for example, has not the same vitality that a sensation has. It has been said that the strongest image is still inferior to the dullest sensation. Trying to experience the heat of the sun in the form of an image is not the same as actually feeling the heat of the sun. Smelling a rose is more potent than trying to bring back its fragrance in the form of an image.

Again, a percept is not under our control, as an image is. We can choose, to a certain extent, what we wish to see or what we wish to hear or taste, smell or touch. We have in this way a measure of control. But an image is completely under our control and is, moreover, independent of space and time. We can perceive the Sahara Desert only if we are in its vicinity, but we can have a picture of it in our mind's eye no matter in what part of the world we may be. We can, in other words, carry our images about with us.

Further, because we have control of our images, we can picture things in a different way from that in which they actually exist. We may perceive a rose as red, but have an image of it as yellow, and these two experiences—percept and image—can exist simultaneously.

Another difference between a percept and an image is that a percept is the property of all. A landscape can be seen by anyone, as can a play in a theatre or a picture in an art gallery. An image, on the other hand, is our own private property. We alone can know what images pass through our minds. Other people can know about them only if we choose to tell them.

Still another difference is that a percept has a context or a setting into which it fits. A book lies on the table, or the sun shines in the sky, or the fragrance is distilled from the rose. It is not only that we actually see or hear or smell at the moment of the perception, but the percept fits into the surroundings and it is the whole situation that we are aware of. An image, on the other hand, does not do this. It is quite detached from any perception we may be experiencing, and it may not fit into the total situation, although occasionally

42

there may be an exception. For example, if we are thinking of a polar bear, an image of a polar bear may flash into our mind. This image, quite definitely, does not belong to our present perceptual experience!

It is because of these and other characteristics that we are aware of the difference between a percept and an image. Sometimes, as it happens, one or other of these criteria fails. When they all fail we mistake an image in our own minds for a real object, and so we experience a hallucination. Probably the most frequent sources of hallucinations are to be found in the visual and auditory fields, where we mistake a visual or an auditory image for the real things.

Many abnormal people experience auditory hallucinations, when they imagine they hear voices. These are generally persecutory in character.

In an interesting experiment the subjects taking part were led to mistake a sensation for an image. They were asked to image a banana and to project their image on a screen before them. As they were concentrating on doing this, one of the assistant investigators in an adjoining room threw a very faint picture of a banana on the screen, and gradually increased its intensity. The edges of the banana were blurred, and it was made to vibrate gently. All the 27 students, men and women alike, mistook this picture for their own efforts.

Different Kinds of Images. Most of our recollections are obtained by means of visual images. When we recall a concert which we have attended on the previous evening we generally recall the scene inside the hall and the singers and the audience as visual pictures. Or, if we are recalling a meeting with a friend, we have usually a visual image of that friend. The majority of us are visual-minded, but this does not rule out the use of images from other sense departments from time to time. Instead of recalling a meeting with a friend in terms of vision, we may have an auditory image of his voice and of the conversation, or both visual and auditory images may be present. It is possible, also, to have taste and smell images as well as those of touch, and many people recall movement in the form of kinæsthetic images. (The sensation we experience on moving a limb, which tells us to which position the part in question has been moved, is known as a kinæsthetic sensation).

TYPES OF IMAGERY

At one time it was thought that people could be divided into groups according to their dominant type of imagery. Most people belong to the visual group, and these were called "visiles". Others, a smaller number, could be placed in the auditory group, the so-called "audiles". Still others use chiefly motor imagery, and they were described as "motiles", and so on with the other sense departments, the groups being mutually exclusive. It is now realized that individuals cannot be placed in categories in this way, for the majority, although employing visual imagery more than any other type, may on occasion have auditory, touch, smell, taste or movement images. In other words, most people do not belong to any one type, but are mixed in type so far as imagery is concerned.

People vary very considerably in the strength of their images. In the case of visual images, some people may have such vivid imagery that it is almost as clear as the original sensation. Others, again, have medium or very faint images, and some declare they have no concrete visual imagery at all.

One of the earliest, and at the same time one of the most interesting, investigations into imagery was reported by Galton. He devised a questionnaire on imagery which he sent to a number of people. They were asked, for instance, to imagine a definite object, such as the breakfast table as it had been seen that morning, and to reply to the questions with the image of the breakfast table in their minds. Below is a sample of the questions asked:—

(1) *Illumination*. Is the image dim or fairly clear? Is the brightness comparable to that of the actual scene?

(2) *Definition*. Are all the objects pretty well defined at the same time, or is the place of sharpest definition at any one moment more contracted than it is in a real scene?

(3) *Colouring*. Are the colours of the china, of the toast, bread-crust, mustard, meat, parsley, or whatever may have been on the table, quite distinct and natural?

Other questions in his questionnaire were attempts to determine individual differences in imagery, such as "Can you, at will, cause your mental image of any person to sit, stand or turn slowly round? Can you deliberately seat the image of a well-known person in a chair and see it with enough distinctness to enable you to sketch it leisurely?"

If the reader tries out these questions on his friends, he will be surprised, as Galton was, at the differences revealed by their responses.

With reference to visual imagery, Galton quotes the Bushmen of South Africa, who used to draw accurate pictures of men and animals on the walls of their caves. The method apparently employed was to place on the medium isolated dots which seemed to have no connexion with any outline of any object. Once the artist was satisfied that there were enough dots, a bold line was drawn from one to another, and gradually the figure of an animal appeared. Galton argues that this method would not have been successful unless a clear picture of the object to be drawn existed already in the artist's mind.

An image is not necessarily an accurate reproduction. Very few images are exact replicas of the original sensation. We tend to omit a detail here or to add a detail there. There is, in fact, a certain amount of creative activity at work. Very often the image is altered according to our interests. We recall in the image what we perceived in the original, and often only the parts that are of interest to us stand out. Those with good visual imagery often take advantage of this in memorizing. They are able to recall the page on which the facts they wish to remember are written or printed. Many a student at an examination visualizes the page of his notebook when answering a question, and knows that he has missed out something which fills a certain area of the page. It is reported of one orator that his strong visual imagery proved somewhat of a handicap. He not only saw the page with his speech written on it, but also any corrections he had made. This caused a slowing down of his oratory and a certain amount of confusion.

A woman known to the writer improves her game of golf when she is unable to sleep, instead of counting sheep. She visualizes the golf course and plays a round of golf, using the different clubs and seeing the different lies of the ball. She is aware of playing well or badly. Sometimes the round is played in good weather conditions, sometimes in bad, such as in a strong wind. Strong visual and kinæsthetic imagery seem to be present here.

How can we determine the type of imagery possessed by any person? Probably the most satisfactory method is still that of the questionnaire, in which the person who is being tested has to answer a number of questions specifically relating to the strength and vividness of his imagery.

Another method is that of asking the subject to write down a list of objects that are characterized by their colours, such as "grass", "pillar-box"; secondly, a list of objects characterized by their sounds, such as "whistle", "piano"; thirdly, a list of objects characterized by their smells, such as "rose", "gas", and so on. The subject should be allowed the same time for the writing of each list, usually five minutes. The assumption is that the type of image which comes most easily to mind, and so produces the longest list, indicates the dominant type of image used by the individual.

TESTING IMAGERY

A method employed fairly frequently is the letter-square method. A card is prepared (Fig. 21), divided into nine, twelve, or sixteen squares, each of which contains a letter. The subject reads the letters from left to right. After a lapse of twenty seconds, during which he counts aloud from one to twenty in order to prevent recall during the interval, he is asked to reproduce the letters in columns, or from the bottom upwards. If he is a strong visualizer, this presents no difficulty to him. The auditory type or the motor type, however, would find this task practically impossible. Sometimes the learner may be told to utter a sound like "la" all the time he is reading the letters. This will interfere with the auditory type of person, but not with the visual type, and so on.

As we have already stated, most people belong to the "mixed" type so far as imagery is concerned. Although visual imagery plays an important part in the life of many, it is said that auditory and kinæsthetic images also occur with fair frequency in the case of adults.

In his book *The Distribution and Functions of Mental Imagery*, Betts describes an investigation into imagery by using the questionnaire method, much in the same way as Galton did. The subjects were asked to call up images from the different sense departments: visual (landscape, face), auditory (voice, tune), touch (velvet, sand), taste (sugar, salt), smell (roses, onions), kinæsthetic (running, kicking), organic (headache, hunger). Each image had to be ranked by the subjects on a scale ranging from 0 (no image) to 7 (perfectly clear image). Betts found that when a subject ranked himself high on one type of image, he also ranked himself high on all the other types; and if a subject ranked himself low on one type, he was low on all types. This result confirms the need for the recognition of mixed types. Visual and auditory images were only slightly higher in rating than the other senses.

Z	M	B	E
R	D	X	H
F	J	M	C
W	G	K	Q

FIG. 21. *The letter-square for determining the type and strength of imagery.*

Eidetic Imagery. Those people who are capable of what is known as "eidetic" imagery have not only very strong visual imagery, but are able to project their images on an external surface, such as on a piece of paper or on a screen. This type of imagery seems to diminish and disappear with age: it is not very common in the case of adults, but is possessed by many children. The child appears to see the picture on the screen so clearly that he moves his eyes to and fro as though looking at the details of a real picture before him. Some people can project a design to be embroidered on to the material so clearly and vividly that they do not require to have the design stamped on the material, but can sew it while following their image on the cloth.

To test for the presence of eidetic imagery, a picture very full of detail is shown for a brief time, say about thirty seconds, and then the children are asked to describe it. This was tried on 30 children by one investigator. Their reproduction of the picture was amazing in its detail, even to the extent of reproducing accurately a German word of 16 letters which appeared over a shop door, although none of the children knew German. Some of the children could spell the word as easily backwards as forwards.

It is important for all those engaged in education to realize that as many avenues of sense as possible should be utilized in learning. One person may learn better if he sees words written on the blackboard, another if he hears them spelled aloud, a third if he himself writes them down, so ensuring a kinæsthetic image in the future. Some people may require all three methods.

In his *Introduction to Experimental Psychology*, Valentine has described a very interesting experiment to illustrate how remembering is helped when accompanied by a visual image. He has devised two pieces of "imaginary" history, each consisting of three short paragraphs and each of fairly equal difficulty. In both cases dates and numbers are mentioned, as well as names of persons, towns and rivers. When one of the "histories" is read over, reference is made to a simple map illustrating the reading, and the names and dates are pointed to as they occur in the story. This is done by the experimenter, who reads the story aloud. The other section is read without illustration. Pre-arranged questions are asked about each abstract. Undoubtedly the section with the accompanying map is much easier to remember. This is due to the presence of the visual image of the map during recall. Students taking part in this experiment in the writer's evening classes all testified to the benefit derived from the map.

Betts, on the other hand, obtained a result which indicated that visual imagery is not essential for everyone. He asked his subjects to imagine a large cube, painted only on the outside and divided into 27 small cubes, then to answer the following question: how many cubes are painted on three sides, how many on two sides and how many on one side only? This is a problem in which one would expect visual imagery to be helpful. It proved to be so in some cases, but it is reported that 35 per cent of the subjects solved the problem without using imagery, and did so just as quickly as those did who possessed a strong visual imagery.

IMITATION AND CREATION

Imagination. The word imagination has a wider connotation in psychology than it has in everyday speech. It includes more than simply "imagining things" and "building castles in the air". We use our imagination, for example, when we are reading a book. When we come across a description of a scene or the delineation of a character, we picture to ourselves the scene or the character. These are new creations helped out by the author's description. This kind of imagination, in which we follow a given model, is called "imitative" or "receptive" imagination. The author or the poet, on the other hand, who writes the scene or describes the character is using not imitative but creative imagination. He has no model to follow, unless it be an inner one of his own.

Imitative and creative imagination are generally thought of as taking two directions, termed "pragmatic" and "æsthetic" respectively. The architect planning a new building, or the engineer who has been asked to design a bridge, require to make use of their pragmatic imagination. The engineer wishes to create a new model which will be of outstanding beauty, but at the same time it is essential that he take into account the conditions of the site on which the bridge is to be built, the kind of soil, the nature of the rocks, the depth of the water, and also whether it is for passenger or goods traffic, and so on.

Although the design of the bridge may be good, it will, nevertheless, be valueless if these external conditions are not considered. Thus imagination of the pragmatic type is ultimately determined by conditions in the real world to which it must be adjusted. Aesthetic imagination is not so determined or tied down. Our flights of fancy, our "castles in the air", can rise to any heights untrammelled by limits imposed by conditions in the real world. If there are limits, they are self-imposed, as in the case of the artist or the poet.

"CASTLES IN THE AIR"

Daydreaming. One of the forms of æsthetic imagination is daydreaming. When we daydream, our thoughts take wing. To the uninitiated, daydreaming may seem an aimless activity, but a study of daydreaming often gives us an insight into a person's mind.

Daydreaming, or autistic thinking, is well illustrated in Miss Rose Fyleman's verses when she writes:

> I wish I liked rice pudding,
> I wish I were a twin,
> I wish some day a real live fairy
> Would just come walking in.
>
> I wish when I'm at table
> My feet would touch the floor.
> I wish our pipes would burst next winter
> Just like they did next door.
>
> I wish that I could whistle
> Real proper grown-up tunes.
> I wish they'd let me sweep the chimney
> On rainy afternoons.
>
> I've got such heaps of wishes,
> I've only said a few.
> I wish that I could wake some morning
> And find they'd all come true.

Many adults declare that they do not daydream, but once their attention is directed to the matter they find that they daydream as much as others do. One characteristic of daydreaming is that it is soon forgotten, and so we are apt to think that it has not taken place at all. Whenever we become bored, as in listening to a lecture, hearing a dull play, or looking at a mediocre film in which we are not interested, our minds wander and we are apt to indulge in a pleasant daydream and build "castles in the air".

When we begin to investigate daydreams, we find they may be very revealing. Most of us find ourselves in an environment with one or other of our needs unsatisfied and some of our wishes unrealized. These deficiencies are often compensated for in our daydreams or in our imagination. This is the general principle underlying daydreaming of the simple type. Very few people exist in an environment where all their wishes come true. The only child, with no companions to play with, creates imaginary playmates. The boy living in a dull, uninteresting environment has daydreams full of adventures. In such cases the daydreams compensate for the deficiencies felt in the environment.

No matter what form a daydream may take, the individual himself is always the central figure. He is generally in some kind of situation in which he is fêted and fussed over, where his ego can find satisfaction. The more his ego is denied satisfaction in everyday life, the more will it tend to find satisfaction in daydreams. In the daydream, the dreamer may save a person from a burning building and win the approbation of the huge crowd gathered round. Or he may kick the goal which saves his side from defeat, again in the presence of thousands of applauding spectators! As individual needs differ, according to development and environment, daydreams also will vary. But underlying each daydream is this fundamental need to find gratification for the self.

This kind of daydream is a form of recreation, and helps us over many of the rough places of life. If a person daydreams to excess, however, it will be detrimental to development. He will always be waiting for things to happen as they do in his daydreams. One insidious and vague daydream which is very satisfying is the relegation of all effort to some distant future. The daydream takes the form of the comfortable self-persuasion that some day we shall achieve something worth while. This type of vague daydream stands out in clear contrast to the well-defined daydream of the little American boy who, seeing a long row of clerks on his arrival at the office to begin his first job, is said to have exclaimed: "Gee, is all dem guys ahead of me fer President?"

REVEALING DRAWINGS

Daydreaming is often expressed in the form of drawings. "A girl of six, who was very fond of food and who was poor, always drew dozens of eggs, oranges and apples. A boy of nine, who always went away with the family on his holidays, painted a large bus drawn up outside the front door of his home. He was indignant when some one mistook it for a car, and warmly assured her that he did not like going for his holidays in the car—he liked to go in a bus with 'lots of people'. A girl of eight, who had little chance of self-assertion, either at home or at school, very often drew a king sitting on his throne. His attributes of office were very clearly drawn: there was no mistaking his crown and sceptre. From her conversation it was obvious that the king was for her the personification of power. By her drawing, she indicated the attribute which she admired and envied." We have quoted these examples from Oldham's *Child Expression in Colour and Form*.

If daydreaming becomes excessive, it may prove harmful, because it gives rise to the development of wrong impressions of life. We all have to learn to face life as it is, and not as we picture it *might be* in our imagination. That way leads to mental shipwreck.

FLIGHT FROM REALITY

Daydreaming becomes dangerous also when it is used in order to dodge important issues or to avoid disagreeable situations which ought to be faced. In such cases it is regarded as constituting a "flight from reality". One little boy, referred to a Child Guidance Clinic for poor arithmetic, was seen by the writer. After one or two interviews it came to light that he had a fairly complete fantasy life, to which he retreated when conditions at school became too unpleasant. In this fantasy life he owned a castle in the Highlands of Scotland, and as he walked along the corridors the servants, all clad in white satin breeches, bowed before him. In other words, he was King of the Castle, admired and fêted, and the centre of attention. His castle was an escape from the prosaic and real world of school. Barrie's *Peter Pan* illustrates this phenomenon very clearly—the story of the little boy who did not want to grow up, who did not want to face life with all its responsibilities in the world of reality.

Test Yourself

1. Try to recall a recent meeting with a friend with whom you conversed. Do you recall the incident as a visual image or as an auditory one or both?

2. How does a study of a person's daydreams give us an insight into his mind?

3. In these lines of poetry, imagination is called to aid our understanding of the poet's meaning. Explain how this aid is given:

> "I warmed both hands before the fire of life,
> It sinks and I am ready to depart."

Answers will be found at the end of the book.

CHAPTER IV

LEARNING AND REMEMBERING

A N INDIVIDUAL begins to learn from his earliest days, and learning continues throughout his lifetime. We are aware of the helplessness at birth of the human infant, and how gradually he learns to adapt himself to his environment. This may be partly explained by the factor of maturation, but learning—the ability to profit by experience—plays a very important part. The ability to learn varies from one individual to another, and individual differences are very striking. Some people seem to learn easily and quickly, whereas others are slow and they find learning laborious. A slow learner requires far more time, and a considerably greater number of repetitions, than does the quick learner.

The ability to learn does not, however, remain constant, but varies with the years. Improvement in learning ability is said to take place up to the early twenties. After this period there seems to be a very gradual decline. The decline is not very marked, and it reveals itself in some kinds of learning to a greater extent than in others. If the new learning grows out of, or is established on, material or skills already learned, the older person is as efficient as the younger person. He can learn easily, for example, new knowledge relating to his business or profession. If, however, the new learning entails learning something which necessitates the acquiring of new skills or the forming of habits contrary to those already well-established, greater difficulty in learning is experienced.

ADULT AND CHILD LEARNERS

It has been said that children are better learners than adults, but this popular belief requires some modification. One reason for it may arise from the fact that the adult has a higher standard than a child and, in consequence, demands from himself a better performance. If a child makes mistakes when learning, he is not unduly worried or upset, whereas an adult is conscious of his shortcomings. Furthermore, an adult may not have the same motivation or incentive to acquire knowledge in different fields, as he can manage with the knowledge and skills he already possesses. He does not exert himself, therefore, to acquire new facts outside his immediate interests.

But no matter at what age learning is attempted, there are general principles which, if applied, can be of inestimable service to the learner, and which will make all the difference to ease of learning and permanency of remembering.

The Curve of Learning. In laboratory experiments in which learning is studied the process is, perhaps, seen more clearly than in everyday life. Very often learning to use a typewriter is made the subject of study. If the learner practises for half an hour every day and the number of letters correctly typed is counted for each period, the degree of progress made can be fairly accurately assessed. At first the typing is neither speedy nor accurate. As the learner perseveres, errors diminish and the correct letters are struck more frequently. In this way, improvement takes place, which is indicated by the increasing number of letters typed in the allotted time. Gradually the typing becomes more and more automatic and increasingly accurate.

If we set out this increase in skill in the form of a graph, it appears as in Fig. 22 (Left). This is the shape of a typical learning curve. Learning does not proceed so smoothly as the graph depicts, for sometimes there are setbacks and the number of letters typed may be fewer than on the previous

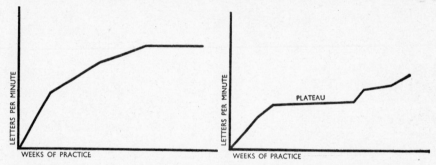

FIG. 22. *A typical learning graph (Left) showing progress from commencement of learning to complete proficiency. On the right is a "plateau of despond", which can, nevertheless, be overcome by encouragement and by persistent effort on the part of the learner.*

occasion. Such fluctuations in learning are due to various causes, such as fatigue, inattention or lack of interest. If the graph is smoothed out, however, the shape is as shown.

In all learning, whether muscular or mental, considerable progress occurs at the beginning, shown in the curve by the rapid rise. Then a slowing down of the learning takes place, and, although there is still improvement, it is not so swift. Finally a stage is reached when learning comes to a standstill, as if the maximum had been attained. In other words, the learner has arrived at a "plateau" [Fig. 22 (Right)]. Despite practice, no improvement is shown, and the level of attainment reached remains fairly constant. This period of constant attainment has been named by Kitson the "plateau of despond". Various explanations of the plateau have been proffered. It has been suggested that the plateau is a necessary stage in learning. It enables the learning so far achieved to become consolidated. In typing, the lower units of learning require time to be co-ordinated, and the learner needs to associate the letters with their positions on the keyboard until this becomes automatic.

If learning is unduly hurried, retrogression may set in, and the learning will actually deteriorate.

Other explanations of the plateau have been put forward. It has been suggested that the learner has become discouraged and requires a new motive to spur him on to greater achievement. Or the explanation may be that bad methods of work have been acquired, which are preventing progress. Other factors contributing towards a plateau may be poor physical condition, fatigue, a weak incentive, worry and so on.

If the learner perseveres and continues practising long enough, he will be rewarded one day by reaching unexpectedly a higher level of ability. Improvement will again continue until another plateau is reached. Learning over a period of time consists of a number of such steps and stairs—improvement and then a plateau, improvement and then a plateau. It is at each resting period that a teacher can spur on his pupil to better endeavour. A student without the influence of a teacher can spur himself on by trying to beat his own record. Self-competition is a good stimulus to better achievement.

LEVELS OF ABILITY

The American psychologist William James has suggested that the majority of us have not reached the heights of learning and skill we could aspire to, because we have not made the necessary effort to advance beyond the first, or it may be the second, plateau. As a consequence, we remain fairly mediocre in our achievements. James takes the analogy of a runner who becomes winded. If he makes an effort and continues running, he obtains his second wind. James conceives of a third wind, and a fourth wind etc., if effort continues long enough.

Although it is largely true that most of us are far from having reached a maximum performance, yet it stands to reason that it is impossible to rise to high levels in all achievements, and we must be content to remain poorly skilled in many things. What James undoubtedly meant was that even in the case of our one achievement, whatever it may be, we remain at a lower level than is desirable.

The highest level that can be reached is the physiological level, which is the limit beyond which no learner can advance any further, for this level is determined by his psycho-physical make-up. The cognitive limit is generally lower than the physiological limit. It is the highest level that an individual can reach because of faults in the method he is using, or some such reason. A change in method may be all that is necessary to effect improvement. A third level is the motivation level. This is the highest limit reached because of the limitations of the motive accompanying the learning. A new incentive may be sufficient to spur on to higher levels. The output of individuals performing the same work may vary in these three ways. Two typists, for example, may differ in output or skill. The reason may be that one has a superior method of work (cognitive limit), or a better incentive or zeal (motivation limit) or a different psycho-physical make-up (physiological limit).

One method of improvement tried successfully in recent years, both in education and in industry, has been referred to above, namely, that of self-competition.

The dull boy in class is not expected to surpass the top boy, an impossible task and a disheartening one, but is urged to beat his own record. The clever boy who finds competition with others too easy has also to surpass his own record, and so there exists for him a spur to further endeavour. When the same idea has been applied in factories, the workers have been furnished with an extra incentive to make progress in their skill.

Habit. When learning becomes established and the activity is frequently repeated, it becomes a habit. Many of our everyday actions are habitual ones, such as the way we hold our pen, or cross our "t"s. The act of dressing is largely habitual, and the act of putting on a coat, for example, is accomplished by most people in a regular and unvaried way.

FORMING NEW HABITS

Habit plays a significant part in our lives. In the first place, it makes for economy. An habitual action can be performed in less time than an action which is not habitual. A little child takes much longer to put on a shoe or coat than does the practised adult. Second, a habit makes for accuracy. Before a person has formed the habit of typing or of playing the piano, he strikes many wrong keys or notes. As the activities become more habitual, the erroneous movements diminish. Third, habitual actions can be performed without our having to think about them too much. The child beginning to play on an instrument has to concentrate on every note and every movement made. As he becomes more efficient, less attention is required. Knitting affords another good example of the saving of time and energy which habit brings about. The beginner has to concentrate on every stitch, whereas the practised knitter can knit at great speed, and some are so skilled that they can read a book and knit at the same time. Attention is only required when a stitch is dropped or when a difficult pattern is being followed.

The more that can be handed over to habit, the more time is there left for other things. Some individuals waste time because of the failure to do this. They are unable to decide at what hour they should rise in the morning or go to bed in the evening. They wonder if they should do this, or whether it would be better to do that. In fact, a great part of their lives is spent in a state of indecision.

In his book *The Principles of Psychology* James has formulated four laws for forming new habits.

1. Launch yourself with as strong an initiative as possible. Accumulate all the possible circumstances which will strengthen the right motive—make

engagements that are quite incompatible with the old habit. This is to ensure a good send-off, for failure at the beginning is a disaster.

2. Never suffer an exception to occur until the new habit is securely rooted. Each lapse he compares to the letting fall of a ball of string which one is carefully winding up—a single slip undoes more than a great many turns will wind up again.

3. Seize the first opportunity to act on every resolution you make. No matter how good the resolutions are, they must be put into action. Write the resolution down, or express it in some way.

4. Keep the faculty of effort alive by a little gratuitous exercise every day, or be heroic in little unnecessary points. As James puts it, do something every day for no other reason than that you would rather not do it.

Kinds of Learning. If we watch an animal in a puzzle-box or one placed in a maze trying to get out to reach food outside, we notice it begins by making many random movements, most of them unnecessary and valueless. If shut in a puzzle-box, it tries to squeeze through the slats of the box, or it stretches out a paw to reach the food, or it bangs against the sides, until by some lucky chance it pulls at the catch which opens the door. If this is repeated the following day, much the same kind of performance will be observed. In later repetitions, the number of unnecessary movements gradually diminishes and the time taken each day to reach the food becomes less and less, until one day the animal undoes the catch, opens the door and walks out. In other words, it has succeeded in learning the trick.

VALUE OF IMITATION

This "trial-and-error" learning, as it is called, is not confined to animals, but is also characteristic of human beings. In trying to solve a puzzle our efforts may be largely trial and error; and in learning a new skill or a new game the same method is adopted. Many erroneous movements are characteristic of this type of learning.

We may take a short cut, however, by watching another person engaged in the task, and then endeavouring to imitate him. Such a procedure gives us a short cut in learning, for it enables us to dispense with some of the useless, erroneous movements. The learning, in consequence, takes place more quickly, and a considerable saving of time is effected. It is essential, it need scarcely be said, to have a good model to imitate. This is a very important point, which has a practical significance in the home, school and factory.

In trial-and-error learning—learning in which insight is not always possible —improvement takes place gradually. This is partly because repetition plays an important part. "Practice makes perfect" is a true maxim, and we require to continue practising if we wish learning to be effective. The repetition must not, however, be carried out mechanically, or the results will be negligible. The learner must take part in the learning, and *actively* learn. Indolent learning or passive learning is of little avail. Repeating movements, nevertheless, cannot be the whole explanation of our improvement, for we repeat wrong movements, at the beginning of learning at least, as often as we repeat the right ones. The strengthening of the correct movements is said to be due to the "glow of satisfaction" experienced when the right movements take place. We feel pleased, and this pleasure helps to impress on us the right movements, for there is a tendency to repeat that which gives pleasure and satisfaction. On the contrary, when a false movement occurs dissatisfaction is experienced, so that the movement is not impressed and there is no urge for its repetition. The two factors, repetition and the feeling-tone, work together in learning of this kind.

Criticism has been made of the trial-and-error experiments undertaken with animals, to the effect that animals are unable to grasp the problem as a whole because of the lay-out of the experiment. It has been argued that if an arrangement could be set up whereby the animal could perceive the lay-out as a whole, results would be better. This has actually been tried, and undoubtedly the result has given a different angle of approach to animal learning. The so-called "Gestalt" psychologists are the chief critics of those animal pyschologists, such as Thorndike, who observe animals threading their way out

| M | F | R | O | S | A | Q | V | P | E | J |
| I | Y | C | U | Z | K | W | B | N | G | L |

FIG. 23. *A mental maze, for trial-and-error experiments with human subjects. In this example the "right way out" could be found by choosing the italic letter in each case.*

of mazes, note errors and record times. A human being, in the same circumstances, they declare, would act in much the same way as the animals do. Probably the nearest approach to such a situation in the case of the human being is the mental maze experiment.

In a maze, the animal has each time to explore two possibilities and discover which one leads farther on, and which one is blocked. In the mental maze (Fig. 23) the human subject is given a choice of two alternatives, represented by the two letters, M and *I*. He has to explore the possibilities, as it were, by selecting one of these. If he choses correctly, then he is given a choice from the next two letters. If he has made an erroneous choice and lands in a blind alley, he must start from the beginning again. The number of trials required to learn the maze is noted. The original method, devised by Peterson, allows retracing. With this technique, the individual may wander backwards and forwards, for he is not given any information as to his progress or lack of it. This type of situation is certainly analogous to that with which the animal has to cope, the learning of paths without any possibility of insight into the situation as a whole.

Köhler is one of the severest critics of Thorndike's puzzle-box experiments and maze-learning, and he devised experiments to give the animal a chance of "inspecting" the situation as a whole, in order to ascertain whether it can solve the problem in any other way than by trial and error. In one experiment a dog was placed in front of a wire fence, and food was placed on the other side of the obstacle. The dog immediately made a detour round the end of the fence to reach the food. The direct path to the food was blocked, but the animal overcame the obstacle by following a roundabout path. In other words, the dog had insight into the whole situation, and in this instance the blind trial-by-error method of learning was not employed.

AN APE SOLVES A PROBLEM

The same indirect or roundabout solution to problems was also observed in chimpanzees during an interesting series of observations carried out by Köhler which are described in his book, *The Mentality of Apes*. In order to seize some bananas suspended from the roof of the cage, normally well out of reach, these animals would individually pile up three or even four boxes, one upon another. Although the structure thus formed was not very stable, it was sufficient for the purpose.

The most intelligent of Köhler's chimpanzees, known as Sultan, arrived at another ingenious way of capturing a banana which had been placed outside his cage, too far to be reached with his paw. The two sticks in the cage were not long enough to reach the fruit. Köhler relates how Sultan solved the problem. "Sultan first of all squats indifferently on the box, which has been left standing a little back from the railings; then he gets up, picks up the two sticks, sits down again on the box, and plays carelessly with them. While doing this, it happens that he finds himself holding one rod in either hand in such a way that they lie in a straight line; he pushes the thinner one a little way into the opening of the thicker, jumps up and is already on the run towards the railings, to which he has up to now half turned his back, and begins to draw a banana towards him with the double stick." This is an illustration of genuine insight on the part of the animal.

Distribution of Learning. Learning takes place more rapidly when we distribute it over a period of time, instead of massing it all together in an endeavour to absorb the whole at one sitting. If we want to learn to play golf or any other game, it is better to play for a short time every day than to practise all day long. If we are studying for an examination, it is better to work for a set time every day over a period of time than to attempt to cram it all up the day before. In other words, cramming is not the most beneficial method of learning. Further, when our learning is spread out or distributed, retention is improved. Learning crammed into the evening before an examination is readily forgotten. If we have six hours available in which to learn, it is better to set aside one hour every day for six days, or one half-hour every day for twelve days, than to attempt to learn for six hours consecutively.

FIG. 24. *A chimpanzee makes use of boxes, piling one upon another, to reach some bananas. This example of animal insight shows a great advance upon trial-and-error efforts.*

Why is it that distributed learning is better than mass learning? There are various factors which cause the distributed learning to be the more beneficial. The chief of these is the pause which occurs between each of the learning periods. The pause allows the learning to become consolidated, and bad habits to be dropped.

In addition to this, the learner is much fresher after a pause, for fatigue is not allowed to accumulate. Further, during the pause between the learning periods the individual can practise recalling what is learned. In mass learning, when the learning is carried out all at one time, there is no opportunity for recall or for the learning to become consolidated. Jost has formulated a law to the effect that if two associations are of equal strength but of unlike age, repetition favours the older association. In distributed learning, the association will gradually become older with each re-learning; whereas, in massed learning even at the end of the learning period the association is still very young. The older association is also retained better.

That pauses favour learning is confirmed by the well-known fact that improvement often takes place after a pause. If we have not played a game of golf for some time, we play a better game than usual after the break. Learning seems to be continued during the rest period. This is the explanation of James's cryptic statement that we learn to swim in winter and skate in summer.

Further, short periods of learning mean better concentration. When we are learning for a long stretch of time we become restless and fidgety and our attention wanders. We are more likely to pay attention, even if we have to force ourselves to attend, when the period is not too long. We must be careful, of course, not to make periods of learning too short. Periods which are too short are wasteful, for then the learner does not get under way before it is time to stop.

Some people take longer than others to settle down before they are free from distraction and completely immersed in the task.

The optimum distribution of learning periods will vary slightly from one individual to another. Each person must determine for himself what yields the best results in his particular case. Children will, as a rule, require shorter learning periods than adults.

Importance of Recall. Recall in learning is beneficial, and the greater the amount of time spent in recalling what one is learning the more efficient is the learning.

In an experiment conducted by Gates, the learning of some nonsense syllables was compared with the learning of meaningful material consisting of short biographies, and the amount of time spent in recall was varied. The results were as follows:

TABLE A

Nonsense Syllables	Percentage remembered immediately	After four hours
(1) Continuous reading without recall	35	15
(2) 1/5 of time spent in recall	50	26
(3) 2/5 of time spent in recall	54	28
(4) 3/5 of time spent in recall	57	37
(5) 4/5 of time spent in recall	75	48

TABLE B

Meaningful Material	Percentage remembered immediately	After four hours
(1) Continuous reading without recall	35	16
(2) 1/5 of time spent in recall	37	19
(3) 2/5 of time spent in recall	41	25
(4) 3/5 of time spent in recall	42	26
(5) 4/5 of time spent in recall	42	26

The total time spent in learning nonsense syllables (Table A) for all five methods was exactly the same, but in each case the distribution of learning and recalling was varied as indicated in the first column. In the first method, the subjects read the material over and over again with no attempt at recall.

Table A shows a clear-cut and definite result in favour of recall. Continuous reading without recall produces the poorest return. Furthermore, when four-fifths of the learning time is spent in recalling, the greatest benefit accrues, both for immediate recall and even after an interval of four hours.

MEMORIZING

With the meaningful material (Table B) there is benefit from practising recall, but it is not so marked as in the case of the nonsense syllables. This is probably due to the fact that when one is reading meaningful material there is a certain measure of recall going on in one's mind all the time, for one is conscious of anticipating what is coming. The benefit due to recall is probably greater than is shown by the actual results.

The advantage of recall is partly that one is reproducing the material subvocally and so reinforcing the visual impression; partly that one is recalling the material as one wants to recall it finally and in the same form; and partly that by comparing what one recalls with the original, errors can be corrected and weak links can be strengthened. One writer, Aveling, expresses it thus: "Recitation furnishes an immediate goal to work for, and is more stimulating than continued reading of the lesson. It is somewhat like running a race against a competitor as contrasted with jogging along the track all alone."

Methods of Learning. It has been found more economical to learn by wholes than by parts. For instance, if we take as an illustration the learning of a poem, we can learn it in the usual way verse by verse or section by section, or we can employ the "whole" or "entire" method, which consists of reading the poem through from beginning to end over and over again. The "entire" method is superior to the sectional method. Fewer repetitions are required, and the material so learned is retained better.

A typical experiment is that reported by Aveling. A comparison was made of the two methods of learning 240 lines of poetry. One method involved the learning of thirty lines at a time every day, the other, reading the 240 lines over in their entirety three times a day. "When the two passages could be recited equally well by heart, it was found that twelve days (or 431 minutes) had been taken to learn by the first ('partial') method, while only ten days (348 minutes) had been necessary to learn by the second." In this case, saving of nearly a fifth of the time of learning was effected by the use of the "entire" method—an economy well worth securing.

There are several reasons why the sectional method is not the most favourable one. It has the disadvantage that, once the verses have been separately learned, it is difficult to recite the poem as a whole. When the learner reaches the end of the first verse he hesitates, for the word that comes to mind is not the beginning of the second verse, but the first word of the first verse! When he is prompted, by being given the correct word, off he goes again triumphantly to the end of the second verse, but only once more to come to a pause, for he is unable to remember the beginning of the next verse. This may continue throughout the whole of the poem, as many a teacher knows. As we have indicated, with this method wrong associations between the end and the beginning of the same verse are formed during the learning, and these require to be broken. This makes it all the more difficult to form the correct associations between the end of one verse and the beginning of the next. In the "entire" method, no wrong associations are formed, and in consequence there is not the same difficulty in repeating the poem as a whole. Associations between each verse and its successor have been formed while the learning is in progress. The only association which is unnecessary is that between the end of the poem and the beginning, an association which can be eliminated without difficulty.

The "entire" method is, however, not without its disadvantages. It is not easy to practise recall, and the learner is apt to feel discouraged at the apparent lack of progress. Further, the "glow of satisfaction" when a verse has been learned, which spurs the learner on to further effort, is absent. In practice, it is generally found that the two extremes of a poem are learned more easily than the middle parts; this necessitates extra repetitions before the whole poem is committed to memory.

The success of the "entire" method also varies with the age and intelligence of the learner. It seems to be a beneficial method for those with average and superior intelligence, but is not so helpful in the case of those with intelligence below normal. It is doubtful if the method can be recommended for children. To give children as big "wholes" as they can tackle seems, so far as our knowledge goes, to be the soundest solution.

PART-PROGRESSIVE LEARNING

Further difficulties arise when the material to be learned is not homogeneous in character. If some parts are more difficult than others, such as obscure meanings or unusual phrases, it may mean extra repetitions of the whole poem in order to commit the difficult part to memory. To overcome this difficulty, a modification of the "entire" method has been suggested, to the effect that the difficult words or phrases be mastered to begin with, and then the "entire" method employed. In the part-progressive method, the first section is learned, then the second section, then the two together. The third section is now mastered, and then the first three together, and so on. Another modification which has been suggested is to learn the first section, then begin at the beginning again and learn to the end of the second section, then return to the beginning again and learn to the end of the third section, and so on. These modifications of the "entire" method have all been found to be superior to the sectional method. The "entire" method has been tested to the extent of 240 lines of poetry.

These different methods have also been studied with reference to the acquisition of skills, but the results have been conflicting, and more research must be carried out before any definite conclusion is reached.

Transfer of Learning. When one skill is learned, it may help in the acquisition of another skill, particularly if there is a marked similarity between the two. Efficiency at tennis helps in learning to play badminton, largely because the same kind of technique is used. This is what is called "positive" transfer of training. Sometimes the opposite effect is obtained, and the acquisition of one skill may interfere with the learning of another skill. When this kind of result is found, it is referred to as "negative" transfer. An illustration of such is learning to type with one arrangement of the keyboard, and then switching over to a different arrangement. Skill with the second arrangement is slow in appearing because of the habit already formed.

At one time there were many disciples of the doctrine of "formal discipline". They held that certain subjects such as Latin, Greek or Mathematics were good disciplinary subjects for the strengthening of certain mental

FIG. 25. *Visual aids to learning are increasingly employed in schools, for it is found that objects apprehended through the eye—such as the picture of a giraffe above illustrating a Geography lesson—tend to be lastingly impressed upon the memory*

faculties such as reasoning, memory, attention and the like. As these "faculties" are necessary in different spheres of activity and achievement, their exercise would effect improvement in these spheres. In other words, a transfer effect could occur, so that in later life memorizing anatomical parts would be made easier for the medical student by the practice he had had already in memorizing Latin or Greek verbs.

One of the earliest attempts to explore this assertion was made by James and is recorded in his book, *The Principles of Psychology*. He learned 158 lines of a poem and recorded the time taken. He then practised committing poetry to memory over the period of a month, after which he learned a further 158 lines of the same poem. To his great surprise, he required a longer time to commit this second part to memory, and was forced to conclude that his month's practice had not improved his ability to learn poetry.

Although James's experiment was not ideally set up, for he was in a fatigued state at the end of the learning and, moreover, there was no guarantee that the two sections of the poem were of equal difficulty, it led to others investigating the problem with a more careful procedure. Generally, two groups of subjects are equated as regards learning ability. Both are tested in a certain skill; then one group is given practice in similar learning, whereas the control group receives no such training. At the end of the specified training, both groups are re-tested in the first type of skill: if the first group shows improvement, it can justifiably be attributed to the specific practice given.

This type of experiment is frequently used in mirror-drawing, in which the subject is required to trace a star-shaped figure following the movement of his hand in a mirror. Direct vision of his hand is cut off. Group 1 traces the figure with the left hand, and time taken and errors made are recorded. Then practice in tracing is done with the right hand, and finally a second trial with the left hand is made. The control group has no practice with the right hand. Such an experiment yields positive results, and the final tracing by the left hand shows definite improvement after practice with the right hand. This is an example of cross-education or bilateral transfer, in which learning responses by one side of the body facilitate learning by the other side.

The general conclusion seems to be that transfer only occurs when the activities are very similar in content, or where a technique can be carried over from one activity to another. A student who is accustomed to learning can utilize his methods to master a new activity. He can transfer his habits of study, his powers of attention and concentration, his thoroughness, etc. to the new material with satisfactory results.

Permanency of Learning. We have shown how recall helps in both learning and in remembering. The retaining of what is learned is most important, but even under the best conditions forgetting occurs. Sometimes forgetting is due simply to lapse of time, or oblivescence, as it is called. We find fragments of poems coming to mind which we learned as a child. If, for some reason or other, we want to relearn the poem, we find we can do so much more easily than learning an entirely new poem. The same occurs in the case of skills. In swimming, although we have not indulged in it for years, we readily return to our former level of ability. Likewise cycling, if learned when a child and not practised since, can easily be brought back to its previous state of perfection.

RETENTION OF LEARNING

The duration of retention has been studied in animals by means of the delayed-reaction experiment. An animal is trained to associate food with the showing of a light in a compartment. Generally there are three compartments in the set-up of the experiment, and the light appears irregularly in any one of these three compartments. When the light is shown, the animal is immediately released and seeks the food in the appropriate compartment. The food provides the motivation for the learning. If the animal goes into the wrong compartment, it experiences a slight electric shock. After the association between the food and the light has been firmly established, a delay is introduced into the experiment. The light appears, and then is switched off. The animal is not released immediately, but after an interval which is varied in duration. If the animal goes straight to the correct compartment after the interval of time, it can be assumed that it has remembered in which compartment the light appeared. It was found under these conditions that rats and dogs did not respond correctly unless they kept their heads steady and pointing in the right direction. The longest interval obtained by the psychologist W. S. Hunter, who conducted experiments upon these lines, was: for rats ten seconds, for dogs five minutes. If, however, the animals had moved during the intervals, so that they were facing in a different direction, mistakes occurred. Racoons, on the other hand, seemed to be able to select the correct entrance, even although they might have turned round during the delay.

Köhler, who suggests that building up an association between the food and the light is an unnecessary complication, tried simpler experiments with his chimpanzees, such as burying fruit in the ground in their presence. In one case the fruit was correctly located after an interval of sixteen-and-a-half hours, although the animal had been doing other things in the meantime. With further experiments the period of delay may even be longer.

These results indicate the great superiority of the human being over the animal. Even with young children the period of retention is much longer. The human being has the advantage that he can formulate the problem in verbal terms, which is undoubtedly a considerable asset.

With children and adults, recall is generally assessed by means of the memory span, which tests immediate or rote memory. The material consists of series of digits gradually increasing in length. Each series—if it be visual

64

memory span which is being tested—is shown only once, and then the subject attempts to reproduce them. The digits must not only be reproduced correctly, but they must also be reproduced in the correct order. The subject's visual memory span for digits is assessed by the longest series of digits which he can reproduce without error after seeing them once (Fig. 26). The auditory memory span is tested by the experimenter's repeating the digits aloud to the subject, one series at a time, the digits being spoken at the rate of one per second and the subject attempting to reproduce them after each series. Memory span for words, forms, or other material may also be determined.

Memory, or recall, may also be tested for continuous narrative. A story is read out and the subject is asked to reproduce all that he remembers of it. Generally the main theme is reproduced, but with omissions or alterations. If, without further perusal of the story, the subject is asked to reproduce it after an interval of time, more errors creep in and there may be a tendency to distortion of the theme. The distortion is in the direction of making the story more conventional and more in accord with the subject's own interests and experiences. Interesting records of this tendency have been made by F. C. Bartlett in his book, *Remembering*. When the story is passed on from one individual to another, great distortion often appears.

1.	9
2.	75
3.	416
4.	5297
5.	81527
6.	386105
7.	6140725
8.	29583741
9.	972684316
10.	1847352694

Fig. 26. *Digit series, for testing rote memory.*

Reproduction of forms shows the same tendency. An example of serial remembering is shown in Figure 27. The original, labelled "Portrait of a Man", was shown to a subject, who reproduced it from memory. His sketch, similarly labelled, was shown to a second person, who was required to reproduce it, and so on. It will be seen from the reproduction how the drawings gradually changed until a more conventional form appeared.

An allied, and an interesting, experiment has been recorded which again demonstrates that in remembering there is a tendency towards the conventional. A number of ambiguous line drawings appeared in a series, but before each drawing was exposed a remark was made by the experimenter to the effect that "The next figure resembles . . . ." In many cases the suggestion which he made influenced the recall. When two circles, joined together by a short horizontal line, were shown the suggestion was made of eyeglasses, and in the reproduction the two circles appeared as in the stimulus, but the short horizontal line between them curved upwards; the whole drawing definitely resembled eyeglasses. When it was suggested that the same stimulus represented dumbbells, two lines appeared in the middle, joining the circles.

It is often asked if speed of learning has any effect on remembering. It is popularly believed that the quick leaner rapidly forgets what he has learned, as is suggested in the phrase "Easy come, easy go". When this belief is tested under experimental conditions, there is found, however, to be no basis for the statement. The quick learner shows, on the contrary, superior retention and less forgetting.

Other factors which may produce forgetting are retroactive inhibition and interference. The first of these is caused by learning a second sample of the same material immediately after the first learning is finished. The learning of the second sample retroactively inhibits the first learning. The greater the

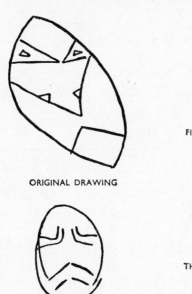

ORIGINAL DRAWING

FIRST REPRODUCTION

THIRD REPRODUCTION

SECOND REPRODUCTION

FOURTH REPRODUCTION

FIFTH REPRODUCTION

Fig. 27. *The original abstract drawing on the left was shown to the first subject, and it was suggested to him that it represented a portrait of a man. This subject's reproduction of the original from memory—already slightly more naturalistic than the original drawing—was shown to a second subject, the latter's version of this reproduction to a third subject, and so on. With each successive reproduction there is a progressively wider departure from the original. In the desire to make his reproduction as much as possible like the object that he has been told it represents, each subject in turn has altered or suppressed peculiarities that did not conform to the familiar image of the human face. The last reproduction shows a conventionalized human face which is almost entirely unlike the original drawing.*

resemblance between the two samples being learned, the greater will be the influence of this factor. It seems that the associations made in learning require a certain time to become stabilized or set; and if this interval is not forthcoming, because of the too quick onset of new associations, the first associations become considerably weakened. A pause after learning and before any new learning is tackled seems essential for good results.

The other factor, interference, is a common phenomenon. If we start to learn a new skill and have practised a wrong movement, the latter persists in interfering with later and more efficient movements. Hence the importance of a good beginning. A common experiment frequently used to test the influence of interference entails card-sorting. A box with a number of pigeon-holes is used, the holes being numbered non-consecutively. The subject is given a pack of cards which have been well mixed, each card of which bears a number, and he has to sort them one at a time into their respective pigeon-holes. This is done until the sorting becomes automatic. Then the box is turned over, and on the reverse side is a similar number of pigeon-holes with the numbers rearranged. This time the sorting of the cards takes longer, because the former associations of the numbers and the pigeon-holes persist in consciousness and interfere with the new learning.

In addition to these various conditions which influence learning and memory, there are two others which have been mentioned but perhaps not sufficiently emphasized. All learning must be accompanied by the "will to learn", and the learner must have adequate motivation. Indolent learning, reading over the task with no "will to learn", produces little or no result. One can sit for hours aimlessly reading the text, and there will be nothing to show at the end of the period, whereas the presence of the intention to learn will soon produce results. A good incentive or good motivation is also essential. This will vary from one individual to another. The effects of praise and blame on learning have been studied, as well as the goals to which the learning may be directed, and results have all pointed to the desirability of good motivation. The goal in view should not be too remote, nor should it be set so high as to be beyond the power of the learner. But a goal of some kind there should be, towards which the learner is aiming. Learning without any goal or purpose is aimless, lacks drive and is poor in achievement.

Test Yourself

1. Explain why there sometimes occurs a halt in the progress of learning. To what causes may this halt be due?

2. What is the value of habits?

3. Why do we encourage the learner to recall deliberately what he is trying to learn?

Answers will be found at the end of the book.

CHAPTER V

HEREDITY AND ENVIRONMENT

How far the adult human being is what he is, physically, intellectually and morally, through inheritance from his parents and ancestors, and how far because of the environmental influences he has encountered in the course of his own individual life, and his own reaction to these influences—this question has become, in our time, an important and highly controversial problem. The controversy has become acute because of the extreme positions taken up by the contending parties. On the one hand, there are those who would make heredity all-powerful, and contend that the only hope for the progress of humanity lies in selective breeding. On the other hand, we have those who, without denying the fact that children do resemble their parents, contend nevertheless that environment plays the predominant part in determining what a child shall become, intellectually and morally at least, as an adult. Both parties can cite evidence which, superficially regarded, appears very strong, but in the case of a highly complex organism like man, and in the present state of accurate scientific knowledge of the actual facts, it is difficult to assess the real value of the evidence adduced by either party in support of its contentions.

THE BEGINNING OF LIFE

In weighing the validity of such evidence there are certain principles which may serve as guides. The first and fundamental principle is to the effect that what will eventuate in the case of any developing organism, whether single living cell or complex of living cells, must inevitably be determined by two factors: the nature of the organism itself, and the nature of the conditions with which it interacts. Nothing can depend on heredity alone or on environment alone in the interchanges between an organism and its environment. We now know that the living organism, the human being, begins life as a single cell. The *chromosomes*, the bodies within the cell determining development and carrying inheritance, are contributed in equal numbers by both parents. They are arranged in pairs, one of each pair being derived from each parent. The actual carriers of the hereditary factors are the *genes* contained in the chromosomes. There are a great many of these genes, and they have been likened to little packages of chemical substances.

At one time it was held that there were certain "unit-characters" which were, so to speak, carried by certain genes—such characters, for example, as mental defect, partial colour-blindness and the like. That view must now be

68

given up. These "unit-characters", it is now known, do not depend on any single gene, but on a great number. The absence of one, out of fifty or more, may alter the whole situation. Further, they do not appear always to be brought about in the same way. Hence, to take a concrete illustration, if both parents are mentally defective, and if the same collocation of genes is associated with the condition in both, there is high probability—but no more—that children of their union will be mentally defective. Otherwise there is no such probability. The principle we have stated, therefore, holds at all stages in the development of the child from the initial single cell up to the time of birth and after. After birth, however, new types of environment, with new influences, are brought to bear, and here a second principle requires to be stated.

The second principle is that a stage in development of an organism is always reached when stable conditions are established, and further modification in any radical sense becomes impossible.

NEW INFLUENCES

The new environmental influences which begin to affect the child from its birth are of an entirely different kind from those which have been in operation up to that point. Also, the development which takes place—in one of its aspects, and that possibly the most important—is of an entirely different sort from ante-natal development. The new influences are those affecting the growing individual through experience; they are now influences of a definitely psychological and not of a physical character. The development is a development of knowledge, skill (in a wide sense) and inner organization.

Our first and second principles, then, still hold. The behaviour of the individual still depends on the nature of the individual at that time and on the circumstances in which he is placed, or the conditions to which he reacts. A certain stage is still reached where certain types of knowledge, or of skill, or of inner organization become stable, or relatively so, and in certain corresponding respects behaviour becomes stabilized. But in the nature of the individual at any time, and in his behaviour at that time, we must recognize a new factor, the influence of which may be unpredictable. That factor is the developing personality of the individual, dependent partly on past and present experience, but also dependent more and more as development proceeds on his aims, ends and purposes. Here we seem to have a third principle.

The stimulus for this inquiry into the relative importance in the development of the human being of heredity and environment came from the formulation in modern times of the theories of evolution. All evolution theory assumes the transmission of characteristics from parent to child. The essential difference between the two main forms of the theory, as they exist at the present time, lies in the kind of characteristics that are transmitted, or more specifically, in the possibility of the transmission of acquired characteristics, that is, characteristics acquired by the parent in his or her lifetime. It is generally agreed that this possibility is not consistent with all we know of the process by which a new organism is formed and developed before birth. No one, however, now thinks of denying that hereditary factors, however they originated, and environmental factors both determine, especially in their interaction, the course of human development. The only difference is in the emphasis placed on one side or the other. Coming into the world with a certain "nature", that is, with certain possibilities of development, the child can only develop in the way that its environment permits.

We may assume, then, that the individual child at birth is in possession of certain endowments, physical and mental, in a certain measure, very few of these endowments being very obvious at the outset. How far can they be measured from our knowledge of similar endowments in the parents, or in the ancestry of the parents? When we put the problem in this way its difficulty and complexity become at once apparent. Our knowledge of these endowments in the parents must usually be very imperfect; for, remember, we are thinking of natural endowments, and not attainments or achievements. How much more difficult, too, to try to assess the endowments of their ancestry! Under the most favourable circumstances the evidence obtainable must necessarily be subject to innumerable sources of error, and only the most rigorous sifting can give us even a modicum of reliable fact. Physical characteristics can be directly observed and measured, but for the rest we are mostly dependent on vague qualitative data derived from the life histories of the various individuals; and obviously this kind of information must be, as a rule, fragmentary and unreliable in the extreme.

PHYSICAL RESEMBLANCES

The physical resemblance to their parents and to one another of members of the same family is a matter of common observation. Even in the same family, however, there may be marked differences in stature, length of arm, head measurements, colour of hair, colour of eyes, and the like. Even in such physical characteristics each member of the family has his or her own individuality. When we are dealing with twins, it is true, the situation may be different, and more especially when the twins are "identical", that is, twins who are believed to arise from the same fertilized ovum. In the latter case, the resemblances are so great that even the parents may have difficulty in distinguishing one from the other. Galton records a case where one of the twins was courting a lady, and the other twin sometimes took his place, "and neither the lady nor her parents could distinguish between the two". Physical characteristics are, however, usually fixed before the influences of the external environment come into operation.

On the mental side, the position is very different in almost every respect. When we reduce to the lowest terms the various aspects of the mental endowment of the child, the original endowment is represented in the main by drives, aptitudes and capacities. But the outward and visible signs of these are disposition, temperament, tastes, interests, skills, achievements, attainments, and, ultimately, knowledge, efficiency and character. How are we to set about the estimation of the relative importance of the parts played by heredity and environment, respectively, in this complex field? Let us consider the different kinds of inquiry which are likely to afford us data.

FAMILY RECORD

The first line of inquiry we may call the "family-tree" type of investigation. This has been pursued with considerable success, so far at least as the accumulation of factual material is concerned. The detailed records of a number of families which have been closely investigated present an impressive and, at first sight, convincing mass of data in support of the view that heredity plays an overmastering part in determining the future and fate of the human being. The records of the Kallikak family are perhaps the most significant. Martin Kallikak, while serving as a soldier, met at a tavern a feeble-minded girl, by whom he became the father of a feeble-minded son. Of 480 known descendants from this son, 143 were known to be feeble-minded, and many others were probably of low mentality; 36 were illegitimate, 24 were confirmed alcoholics, and 33 were sexually abnormal. After leaving the army, Martin Kallikak married a girl of good family. Of direct descendants from this union, 496 have been traced. This group contained doctors, lawyers, judges, educators, merchants and landowners, no feeble-mindedness, no illegitimates, one man sexually abnormal and two alcoholics. Here, then, we have for comparison two groups, one with an easily traceable taint of feeble-mindedness, the other without any such taint, both starting from the same point. These data, however, are much more important to the investigation of the social significance of feeble-mindedness in a stock than they are to our present problem of the relative importance of heredity and environment in the development of the individual.

SOCIAL ASPECT AND ENVIRONMENT

Mass records of this kind can throw little light on the influence of environmental factors. These are essentially individual in their character and operation. At the same time it is necessary to note that the "Kallikak" data are not entirely without significance on the environmental side. In the case of the human being, the environment has a social aspect, which is effective from the very beginning of a child's post-natal life. Moreover, this is probably the most influential of all the aspects of the environment, as far as the development of behaviour and personality is concerned. It is a legitimate deduction from the facts as known that the social environment of the individuals in the first of the Kallikak groups must, from the very beginning, have been anything

71

but healthy. The sombre tones of the picture derive from more than one source.

At this point it is necessary to give some consideration to environmental factors, and to the way in which they exercise their influence on the development of the human being. At the start, the human child is quite helpless, and entirely dependent on others for the conditions that enable him to survive at all. Relative helplessness continues for a period of years, during which time influences in the environment are operating powerfully in producing a certain type of human adult. Some of these influences may be introduced deliberately, in the hope that certain desired results may follow; others are accidental, unintentional, and even unconscious. It would be expected that the earlier environmental conditions would exert a more profound influence than the later, and, generally speaking, this has been confirmed by observation; but exceptions to the general rule cannot be excluded. We know also that physical conditions have a less direct, and usually more superficial, effect on the character and personality than psychological and social conditions, though the indirect effects of physical conditions, such as lack of nutrition and similar factors, may be quite considerable.

HOME INFLUENCES

The earliest environmental conditions, physical, psychological, and social, are those of the home, or such substitute for the home as the human child encounters during these early years. Can one imagine, for example, the illegitimate son of the feeble-minded mother, even though he were himself free from any hereditary taint of feeble-mindedness, developing normally under the conditions in which he would be likely to find himself in his early childhood? On their face value, and in view of these factors, the "Kallikak" data would almost appear to prove too much if interpreted only from the side of heredity.

Regarded as part of the child's environment, psychological and social conditions can be effective in two ways; on the one hand they afford opportunities to the child for the normal development of those aspects of his mental life involved in feeling, thinking and "willing"; and on the other hand, they influence his development through the nature of his relations to his father and mother, to his brothers and sisters, and to others outside his immediate circle. "As the twig is bent, so is the tree inclined." There are many ways in which the twig may be bent, even within, and through the influences of, the family circle. It is usual to think of all the members of the same family as living in the same environment, and as being subjected to the same environmental influences. Surprise is often expressed that members of the same family turn out so very differently in afterlife. This view of the family situation is now recognized to be superficial, and in many respects erroneous. No two members of the same family, except possibly twins, share the same social environment.

The social environment varies with the child's place in the family. The oldest, the youngest, and the middle of three children in the same family are subject to quite different social influences, so far as their relations to each other are concerned, and these differences will be all the greater if there is a sex difference among them.

A second line of inquiry, taking into account to some extent facts of this kind, has been the study of twins. Early and important work by Galton has been supplemented by much work done since his time in the tracing of the developmental history of twins. In contrast with the mass studies of the "Kallikak" type, these studies must be essentially individual. Mass studies can only obscure the issues. Twins seem to offer conditions as favourable as they can ever be for the study of our problems. We can assume that, so long as the twins are brought up together, their environment, in its main features, remains the same for both. This last assumption, however, is sometimes apt to mislead us, since, although the main features in the environment are apparently the same, there may be slight differences, dependent, for example, on the relations of the twins to one another, the results of which may be far from slight. Twins, we have already seen, fall into two groups—the *identical* twins, who are always of the same sex and closely resemble one another in almost every respect, and the *fraternal* twins, who may be of the same sex or of different sexes, and whose resemblance to one another is not markedly closer than the usual resemblance between two members of the same family.

Galton's general conclusions may be summarized in the phrase "Nature is far stronger than Nurture"; in other words, the influences of heredity greatly outweigh those of the environment.

FORMATION OF COMPLEXES

Certain facts noted by Galton are interesting and significant. One of them is the fact that handwriting is generally markedly different in twins who resemble one another closely in almost every other respect. Another is the fact that dissimilarity may develop as the result of the influence of some deformity or defect, either natural or the consequence of accident at an early age. A third, on which Galton himself is disposed to lay considerable stress, is that dissimilarity may arise as a result of early illnesses of a serious nature. Though the significance of these tendencies is minimized by Galton, they are precisely of the type which would specially interest the psychologist. In the light of recent analytical work, particularly that of Adler and his school, deformity, defect, or special weakness, no matter how arising, are exactly the types of deviation from normality which are likely to lead, through interaction with the social environment, to well-marked phenomena of behaviour, character, and personality, by way of the formation of "complexes," and the various results following on that.

The tendency to attribute developments of an unexpected or abnormal

FIG. 28. *From his starting-point of heredity—pre-determined before his birth, for good or ill—man begins the long upward climb towards the attainment of his ideal personality. His footholds are the social heritage bequeathed by his forebears, education, experience; but he has to bear the unending drag of his own animal nature, to which he is eternally fettered*

74

character to some more or less serious illness in early childhood is a very familiar phenomenon to anyone who has had some experience in the clinical examination of children, when taking evidence from the mother. As in the case of the "family tree" inquiries of the "Kallikak" type, reading between the lines and discounting the obvious bias of the investigator, we can see in Galton's data evidence that environmental influences are not so wholly without significance as he would have us think.

Later investigations have aimed at supplying one serious deficiency in Galton's investigation, namely, the case where the members of a pair of twins are subjected to different environmental conditions, whether the differences are experimentally introduced or occur independently in the respective life histories. In the case of experimental procedure of this sort, psychologists speak of the "method of co-twin control".

EXPERIMENT WITH TWINS

The method of co-twin control has generally been used with reference to the phenomenon of what is called *maturation*, that is, the process of natural development of a function. One experiment may be cited, since its results bring out principles which are wider than its immediate purpose. The object of this experiment was to study the relation of maturation to learning. The experiment consisted in training a pair of twins to climb a short stair. To begin with, neither twin could climb it. One twin was given practice in climbing it for a fixed period every day for six weeks, while the other twin was doing something else. At the end of the six weeks the first twin was an expert climber. The second twin was again tried at this point, but could not climb even the first step. A week later, however, she climbed by herself to the top. She was now given two weeks' training on the same lines as those given to her sister. At the end of this period she was as expert a climber as the latter. This experiment is more fully described on pages 159–160.

How far was the apparent expertness in climbing the result of maturation rather than of learning? It was one of several experiments with the same twins, and the results of these experiments were held to show that maturation played an essential part in the success achieved by the subjects. The wider significance of the results of these experiments lies, however, in the evidence they give of a fourth principle, regulating with the others we have stated the relationship between heredity and environment. This further principle may be regarded as the converse of the second, and can be formulated thus: environmental influences are dependent for their effectiveness on the readiness of the individual to respond to them, and that readiness in turn is dependent on the stage of natural development attained by the individual.

In order to bring them together here, the four principles may now be re-stated. They are:

1. What will eventuate in the development of any living organism at any

stage in its development will necessarily be determined by the nature of the organism itself and by the environmental conditions with which it interacts.

2. A stage is always reached in the development of any living organism when stable conditions are established, and further radical modification becomes impossible.

3. With human beings a new factor is introduced in the interaction of organism with environment. This factor is the development of the personality, dependent partly on past experience, and expressing itself in aims and purposes.

4. Environmental influences depend partly for their effectiveness on the readiness of the individual to respond to them, and that in turn is dependent on the stage of development attained.

The first principle applies to all organisms and throughout life, from its earliest beginnings to its end. The second and the fourth principles are complementary to one another, and apply particularly to the processes of growth and development throughout their course. The third principle, as formulated here, applies more especially to the human being, and is the principle which has been most frequently forgotten in past discussions of heredity and environment.

PHYSICAL DEFECTS

It is now possible, in the light of these principles and of the data made available by observation, experiment, and every type of investigation, to give a general summary of what appear to be the main facts with respect to the human being.

I. As regards the physical structure, with the various organs and organic systems, it would seem that a stable condition is reached at a relatively early stage of ante-natal or post-natal development, and radical changes do not thereafter take place, except by way of impairment, due to disease or accident. Such impairment does, however, in many cases arise from influences in the external environment, and may bring about changes in mental functions, intellectual and emotional, in which the psychologist as such is interested. Defects also, affecting particularly the sensory systems, may be congenital, and nothing may be possible to remedy such defects through nurture. Particular examples are blindness and deafness, total or partial. All such defects will modify the possibilities of direct sensory experience, and may thus modify mental development so far as it is dependent on such experience.

Although congenital, these defects need not necessarily be inherited in the strict sense. A specially interesting case is that of colour-blindness, which is usually regarded as inherited, and, for practical purposes, rightly so regarded. In its commonest form it appears to be sex-linked, since it shows itself to an enormously greater extent in males than in females,

II. General mental endowment, or what is usually called "general intelligence", also seems to depend on factors which have reached a stable stage of development at birth, so that we may regard it as a congenital endowment. It varies through a wide range from individual to individual, but is found to be practically constant for each individual all through the course of development. Moreover, it is relatively little affected by considerable variations in environmental conditions, and even of physical health. Here we must again, however, distinguish between different possible origins of defect. In some cases defect may be due to accident, if one can so describe birth injuries and the like, or to disease. In others, and these presumably the majority, it represents simply an extreme deviation from the average—the average balancing, as it were, defect against extreme deviations in the opposite direction, which we call genius. If we can assume normal distribution of general intelligence, that is, a frequency of occurrence of different levels, corresponding to what might be expected according to the theory of probability (page 173; Fig. 52) as applied to chance distribution, we might be able to calculate the numbers to be expected at any level in a total population, and thus determine the number falling under this last head. Again, from a practical point of view, such cases may be reckoned as due to heredity.

III. As regards disposition and character and, generally, the phenomena associated with the mainsprings of action, we must assume certain basal factors as being congenital, and presumably inherited. In this case, however, the stage of stability is not attained at birth, except with respect to what may be called individual human needs and impulses. Radical modifications may, without doubt, take place during post-natal development, and some of them even at a relatively late stage in post-natal development, as in adolescence, or later still. With respect to inherited needs and impulses it must also be recognized that there may be innate differences in the relative strengths of different impulses in different individuals. Even with respect to such differences, radical modifications may take place as a result of the experiences of life. Moreover, the formation of interests, sentiments, and "complexes" is quite definitely the work of environment, and not of heredity, and in this whole field nurture may be taken to rule supreme, as far as the structures reared on original needs and impulses are concerned.

THE SOCIAL HERITAGE

IV. There is a still more important manner in which environmental, rather than hereditary, influences determine the development and the course of life of the human being. That is through what has been variously called "social heredity", "the social heritage", "social inheritance", "tradition", and the like. This consists of knowledge, expedients, habits, and so on, handed down from one generation to another, and acquired by each new generation through training and education, formal and informal. Man has

77

become in the course of his history on this planet so increasingly dependent on his "social heritage" that now the highly civilized white man has become in many fundamental respects even "parasitic" upon it, as Graham Wallas has put it. In his book *The Social Heritage*, Wallas has described in somewhat lurid language what would happen if some great catastrophe wiped out at a blow the whole of the "social heritage", leaving man with his individual powers unimpaired. "Nine-tenths", he says, "of the inhabitants of London or New York would be dead in a month, and 99 per cent of the remaining tenth would be dead in six months. They would have no language to express their thoughts, and no thoughts but vague reverie. They could not read notices, or drive motors or horses. They would wander about, led by the inarticulate cries of a few naturally dominant individuals, drowning themselves, as thirst came on, in hundreds at the riverside landing-places, looting those shops where the smell of decaying food attracted them, and perhaps at the end striking on the expedient of cannibalism." This is possibly rather exaggerated, and there is much more; but there can be no question of the importance of the "social heritage", and it is perhaps well that a counterblast of this kind should be made to those who lay all the stress upon biological heredity.

Test Yourself

1. State briefly what you understand by the controversy on "Nature versus Nurture".

2. Is the environment of children of the same family necessarily similar?

3. Character has been described as "the sum total of our habits grafted on our natural temperament". How may habit formation balance temperamental defects?

Answers will be found at the end of the book.

CHAPTER VI

PARENT AND CHILD

IT IS TRUE to say that nowadays people are beginning to realize that parenthood is a big responsibility. At the same time, they recognize it to be a responsibility that is very worth while. The Child psychologist, who has studied the development and the difficulties of children, has an important part to play here. He or she will be able to help parents to understand and accept those responsibilities, as well as to learn to understand their children.

It is often said that wise parents are born, not made. This, however, means that only those mothers and fathers are happy, serene and well-balanced people who had a happy childhood themselves; such are eager and able to create a good family life for their own children. They possess a natural sympathy for children; they are genuinely fond of children; they understand the needs and the rights of children. Marriage, to them, means not only a satisfying sexual life and mutual love and companionship, but also the joys and sorrows of healthy family life.

What, then, of the folk who were not so fortunate in their own childhood, who had many difficulties with which to contend, and who embark on marriage and parenthood with many misgivings? It is just these people whom the psychologist can help. Of course, the family doctor can help too, and there are many excellent little books on mothercraft and child welfare which will give a great deal of valuable information on hygiene, nutrition and baby care. But the contribution the psychologist has to make is of equal importance. Parents will learn from Child Psychology what to expect from their children, when to expect it, how to facilitate the child's natural development, and how to deal with the child's natural difficulties of development. Some parents will read books about it all; some will attend lectures; some will consult a psychologist when family problems are too difficult for them to solve alone.

But too much psychology is not good for parents. It is not wise to be too intellectual and scientific about family life, to become self-conscious or over-anxious about the upbringing of children, or to analyse one's motives and methods too earnestly or closely. On the other hand, it is surely a mistake to treat the important business of bringing up a family in a haphazard or careless way. Although it may not be possible to train to be a good mother as one would train to be a good cook or a good motorist, it is not impossible to learn something about mothercraft from the Infant Welfare Clinic, from the Child Guidance Clinic, or even from one's own mother. The County Colleges of the future may well run courses in babycraft, which will explain not only how to bath the baby, but also how to treat a tantrum!

LEARNING FROM PSYCHOLOGY

The chapters in this section will explain in detail the teachings of psychology as they apply to the growth and development of children from babyhood to adolescence. Here are a few general statements, based on the teaching of Child Psychology, which the reader may find useful as a help to his further reading:

1. Mothers and fathers should co-operate in the care of their children and try to share the responsibility equally with the enjoyment of parenthood.

2. The close relationship of the mother to the young child is of first importance, but the father can also play a valuable part in the upbringing of very young children.

3. It is a great mistake to look for unfortunate hereditary traits in offspring.

4. Never discuss a child's character or behaviour with other grown-ups in the child's presence. Even if the child does not understand all that is said, he or she frequently understands more than grown-ups imagine. Never say in the hearing of a girl child that you wanted a boy, or vice versa.

5. The first four years are probably the most important years of a child's life, and that they should be years of happiness and serenity will be the first concern of good parents.

6. No two children are alike in intelligence, physique and character (except, possibly, identical twins), and comparisons between brothers and sisters are odious and harmful.

7. The two most important needs of a young child are security and affection. Good and wise parents will ensure that their children experience both of these in full measure.

8. The gradual development of a child's mind and personality is a remarkable phenomenon. Often the role of the parent or the teacher must be a passive one. To know when to be an observant onlooker is just as necessary as to know when to offer advice, or when to be a companionable friend.

9. If married couples do not want children, their wisest course is obviously not to have any. Unwanted children so often become the neurotics and delinquents of society.

10. If a marriage relationship is fundamentally and chronically unsatisfactory, it is usually in the best interests of the children to sever the relationship sooner rather than later.

Newly-married people usually look forward to the prospect of a young family with mixed feelings. Babies can be, and often are, noisy, messy, exacting and expensive individuals, who wear their parents' tempers raw and their patience thin. Their needs are immediate and insistent, and during the first year or two their demands require attention before those of husband or wife. Husbands tend to feel a little neglected now and then. Wives tend to feel overburdened with household cares and find their leisure time greatly reduced.

Nevertheless the great majority of parents greet the arrival of the baby with undisguised pride and joy. Babies, however ugly or puny or disturbing they may be, readily win the appreciation and affection of their parents and of most grown-ups. Their helplessness claims adult sympathy; their vitality excites admiration; their very minuteness and the perfection of their form evoke wonderment, and their growth and development during the early years seem little short of a miracle.

Fig. 29. *At ten months, the normal infant enjoys the experience of crawling about on all-fours, to the great benefit of his bodily and mental development.*

Before the baby arrives, there is all the fun of preparing for it. The layette begins to take shape. Play-pen and perambu'ator are obtained. The wife consults the family doctor and learns to take a serious interest in her own health and well-being. The husband usually becomes over-anxious about his wife's welfare. The nursery and the infant's name are chosen, and probably even its school, university and successful career also, long before the baby appears on the scene. This is as it should be, for the keynote ought to be one of expectancy and happy anticipation.

Unfortunately, this is not always the case. Some babies are unplanned and unexpected. Some are quite definitely unwanted. Some are accepted grudgingly, and some—happily only a few—are abandoned or neglected. Naturally, all such babies have a bad start. Growing up is made unusually and unnecessarily difficult for them, and they will need expert care—in some cases State care—if their bodies and their personalities are not to be warped from the very beginning.

Babies need both mothers and fathers. The illegitimate child is always at a disadvantage compared with others. The loss of the father or mother later is probably less harmful to the child's future development than to have no knowledge or experience of a father's love and care during infancy. However, the loss of the mother, by death, desertion or divorce, for instance, is usually found to be more serious to the young child than the loss of the father. Substitute mothers or fathers in the guise of grandparents, aunts, uncles or foster-parents can heal the wound the child has suffered to some extent, but, naturally, they can be only second best.

In the happy family—and, fortunately, there are a great many of them— the baby labours under no such handicap. He is wanted, planned for, and eagerly awaited by both parents, and the beginnings of a well-adjusted personality are safely and truly laid in babyhood.

INFANCY

When the baby is born, he brings into the world a body and mind adequately prepared to meet some of the experiences of his new environment. He is as yet ill-prepared to face dire disturbances or shocks. Noise, sudden movements or sharp contrasts seriously disturb his equanimity.

He spends much time in sleeping, thereby conserving his energy and allowing nature to build up his body and mind. In his waking moments, his main interest is in the taking of nourishment.

The satisfaction of his hunger is his mother's prime concern. His first introduction to the breast should be made gently and tenderly. Although he will suck instinctively, for he is equipped with a sucking reflex whereby the touch and taste of the nipple will stimulate sucking movements of his lips automatically, it may take a little time and patience on the mother's or nurse's part before he will feed willingly or peacefully. It is of very great importance to establish a good breast-feeding contact, for obvious physiological reasons; the psychological reasons are less obvious. Good feeding means good physical health. It also means good mental health. The tie established between mother and child by this means is of immense value for future satisfactory emotional development. A well-nourished, contented baby regards his mother as a giver of all good things, a source of goodness and love, and it is no exaggeration to say that he will learn to pattern his life on his early experiences at his mother's breast. The world will, no doubt, appear bountiful to him. It will seem a safe, secure and kindly place when he is suckled by his own mother without flurry or disturbance, and when his craving for nourishment is adequately satisfied.

If he does not feel secure or satisfied, if neither his physical nor his psychological needs are adequately met in these early days, his attitude to the world is likely to be one of apprehension, distrust and discontent, and his personality development may well be distorted.

NEW-FOUND POWERS

There are many obvious and unavoidable difficulties in the way of good breast feeding. If the quality or quantity of the mother's milk is unsatisfactory, if illness or anxiety prevent breast feeding, after a proper trial it should be abandoned as the baby's only means of nourishment, and supplementary bottle feeding should be introduced. As the baby learns to take the bottle (at his mother's hands, if at all possible), breast feeding can gradually be given up altogether. In this way, he can gain adequate satisfaction and security.

Assuming, then, that the baby is taking nourishment properly, his body will begin to grow rapidly and his parents will have the delight of watching his discovery of new-found powers.

Certain bodily movements are "reflex" responses. That means that they are automatic, perfectly prepared activities which require no conscious attention. A baby will *blink* at too strong a light. He will *cough* when something irritates his throat. He will *grasp* reflexly if a pencil or a finger is pressed against his palm. This last is supposed to be a relic of our close relationship to the monkey, who will cling to a branch for support, even in infancy. In the human infant this reflex does not persist for long. He will also fan out his toes when the sole of his foot is touched by a finger (the "Babinski reflex"), but this movement does not persist either, being replaced by a curling movement of the toes, as if to protect them or remove the irritation. Other reflex responses are the actions of *sucking, swallowing, sneezing,* and *knee-jerking* when the lower part of the kneecap is tapped (the "patellar reflex").

These activities obviously help to preserve the organism. They are either positive, e.g. for obtaining nourishment, or negative, e.g. for defending the body from harm.

Certain vague, apparently purposeless, movements also begin to appear soon after birth. They seem to be random movements, probably in response to some internal stimuli—wriggling, stretching, bending movements which usually involve the whole body. They are very slight at first, but gradually, in a few months' time, they assume great importance, and by this means the baby begins to explore and investigate the world around him and his own body. He touches his bed-covers, his clothes, his mother's nipple and her breast. Later he finds the side of his cot and his pram, and usually later still he discovers, to his huge delight, the existence of his own fingers and toes.

By about the end of the first month, usually, he can lift his head now and again. This clearly increases his range of vision and widens his environment a little. At the age of three-and-a-half months he can often hold his head up quite steadily without support. At five months he can sit with slight support, as when propped by pillows. He should not be allowed to do this until he is ready; and most doctors do not recommend pram cushions, but advocate a soft, firm, flat mattress to encourage good muscular development and a straight, strong back. When he is six months old he can usually sit alone for a short time, but here again he should not be allowed to do this often, or for long at a time, for fear of straining his muscles. The baby himself is the best guide. If he is strong and eager enough, it will be difficult to prevent him from sitting up when he wants to. When he feels tired, he will slip back on his pillows of his own accord. At seven-and-a-half months he will probably be able to sit alone, steadily and securely.

At seven months many babies learn to roll over from their backs

FIG. 30. *By the end of the first year curiosity is strongly developed in the average baby, and he should be afforded plenty of opportunity for satisfying it by handling and playing with suitable toys. Playthings for the child of this age need not be elaborate: empty cotton-reels, a wooden spoon, small boxes—all provide interest for the baby's developing mind.*

FIG. 31. *At the age of ten months most babies can stand, clinging to their cot or play-pen. About their first year they usually learn to walk.*

on to their stomachs, or vice versa. From this it is a short step to crawling, and by nine months of age, lively, healthy children may be crawling into all kinds of mischief —from waste-paper basket to coal-scuttle explorations! But, of course, some children never bother to crawl at all, or more commonly adopt their own characteristic mode of locomotion. An infant known to the writer learned to "beetle" along the floor on his buttocks, using one hand and one leg to propel himself along at great speed. This contented him greatly because it got him where he wanted to go with the minimum of time and effort. The damage to his clothing was his mother's concern, not his! Shortly after this, he learned how to climb up stairs on all-fours, and he would chortle with delight at this new achievement. Most babies learn to stand by pulling themselves up against a cot or play-pen at about ten months and learn to walk at about thirteen to fourteen months.

Naturally, given no encouragement or appreciation, babies will not achieve these feats so quickly as those who are allowed to kick or splash in the bath or to roll on a blanket without any clothes on, or are held firmly while they explore a soft carpet with their bare feet. If they are weakly and their musculature is not well developed, or they are very large, heavy babies, they should not be over-encouraged; and indeed they will safeguard themselves to a considerable extent, because they will show no inclination to get on to their feet until they are sufficiently mature. Every child has his own maturation rate, and the "norms" that have just been quoted serve only as an approximate guide to normal "gross motor development". Girls usually develop locomotion more quickly than boys, probably because they are usually not so heavily built and have less weight to carry.

The precision of movement, or "fine motor co-ordination", is another indication of how the infant's body grows. When the strength of the early reflex grasp decreases, the baby's grasp of his rattle or similar object is loose and insecure. He may make fanning and curling movements of the fingers, but at first these seem purposeless and undirected. Gradually they

85

become more definite, and at about four months he can hold and handle objects with greater precision. At this time he seems to be busy exploring his surroundings with his hands, his feet and his mouth, as well as with his eyes and ears, but he does not appear to co-ordinate his impressions. It is not until the age of five months or so that he follows the action of his hands more closely with his eyes, and begins to convey his beads or his rattle directly to his mouth. In the first year he uses his mouth a good deal to discover the properties of objects—sometimes with unfortunate results, as, for instance, when a baby swallowed the clapper of a handbell, in his enthusiasm, no doubt, to find out how it worked!

THE DAWN OF INTELLIGENCE

From now on the baby's reaching and grasping activites become more accurate, but it is not until about the age of twelve months that he can oppose his thumb to his finger in picking up small objects. At about the same time he can learn to hold his cup to drink from and can build a tower of two bricks if he is given the opportunity. By two years of age his tower may be six bricks high, and he will delight to knock it down as well as build it up again.

By two years most children can fold and tear paper, and a little later learn to cut it (with round-ended scissors). All such activities give the two-year-old a great deal of pleasure. By the end of the second year the baby will be in, on, under and "up to" everything, and it is most necessary to see that he has enough to do and the right kind of toys with which to play. A full account of suitable playthings will be given later in this chapter.

There are, perhaps, two types of mother in particular who deserve mention: (1) those who insist that their babies understand everything, and (2) those who declare, "Baby is much too young to understand anything at all".

The Child psychologist holds that neither statement is true. In his waking moments, the normally intelligent baby is very alert indeed, even in the first month. He will stare at a moving object. He will watch a person's face if it is within his range of vision. He will keep hold of a bone ring when it is put into his hand. Recognition and signs of memory often occur first in regard to the feeding situation. Very soon indeed he seems to recognize the preliminaries of feeding and learns to adjust his body and limbs to facilitate the feeding process. At an early stage, too, he seems able to appreciate the signs of preparation for going out in his pram, or for having his bath.

At three months his eyes will follow a moving object and he will turn his head freely to look at something which attracts him—the source of an unusual sound, a bright light, or a sudden movement. He will finger one hand with another in play. He seems aware of strange places, though not of strange faces in any definite way. He is usually readily quietened by a familiar voice or by music.

By six months the normally healthy and intelligent baby, who can sit for a while with only slight support, will reach for an object when he sees it. He can pick up a cube brick, for instance, from the table; he can bang a spoon or pat the table in play; he can hold something in each hand simultaneously for a moment or two. He can distinguish between strangers and familiar people.

By twelve months evidence of intellectual activity—of perceiving, judging, comparing, imitating, recognizing, discovering, experimenting—is manifest to the careful observer. The baby can hold a crayon and imitate a scribble. He can put a small brick in a cup when asked. He can put a round block in its right hole. He can unwrap a small toy enclosed in paper. He can hold a cup to drink from.

With the mastery of walking, usually before eighteen months, a wider field of exploration is opened to the child. He is busy trying to discover the properties and the nature of his environment. His perceptions are wider and more organized. He is busy learning about the qualities and functions of things—that jam is sticky and sweet, that rain is wet, that gravel paths are hard to fall on, that flowerpots will break easily, that if a cat's tail is pulled she will scratch, and so on. The world must be a fascinating, surprising and puzzling place to the toddler, but the intelligent toddler learns quickly. He learns to connect certain properties with certain things. He learns to expect certain actions from certain objects. He is particularly interested in colours, shapes, sizes and sounds.

SUITABLE PLAYTHINGS

At first the baby needs few toys, but only sufficient opportunity to lie down, preferably out-of-doors, and look at and listen to whatever is going on around him. As he grows older, he needs sufficient stimulation and encouragement from his environment to allow him to use his maturing mind and his growing body. Bath-time is an important playtime. He will soon learn to slap the water and splash his feet about and enjoy handling rubber toys. Mother should not be too busy or too hurried to prevent him from enjoying a short play in his bath. A rattle with bells and a few cuddly toys will keep him happy for some time in his cot while his mother is preparing his feed or his bath. A bone ring will help him during teething time.

When he is able to sit up in his play-pen, indoors or out-of-doors, he will enjoy a more varied assortment of toys—a string of bright (but fast-coloured) beads, a large, soft ball, bricks of all sizes (though not small enough to be swallowed), empty cotton-reels, a kitchen spoon and a saucepan, an empty powder tin with rounded ends, boxes of different sizes, and similar objects which can be banged, thrown and pulled about or fitted into each other. He does not need expensive or elaborate toys, and can be relied upon to suck or tear or break anything that can be sucked or torn or broken. It is just his own way of finding out about things, and an important part of his education.

In baby's second year bricks are usually still very popular, and he will enjoy a truck or a barrow or a pull-along toy. A sand-pit and sand implements are greatly appreciated, for the joy of making and destroying "mud pies" in childhood is surely universal. Water play is a real need for little children, and the garden tap or the scullery sink will attract a child like a magnet. Some provision, such as a paddling-pool out-of-doors, should be made, if possible, for this form of play.

For indoor play, simple fitting toys such as peg-boards or nested boxes or a graduated cone will be much appreciated. Large wooden animals, wooden trains, teddy bears and rocking-horses gradually come into their own, but the keynote should be simplicity, durability and good æsthetic value. Very young children can appreciate beauty of colour and design in their surroundings. A two-year-old will pluck a dandelion head and gaze with wonder at its glowing colour, before tearing it to bits to see how it is made. A three-year-old can be seen to watch the clouds scudding by overhead with great absorption and genuine delight.

It is most important to make clear that the age at which a child can perform certain feats, such as sitting up or walking or putting his toe in his mouth, cannot be determined exactly, and parents should never become worried or anxious because their child does not behave just as the baby books say he should. Defective health, previous illnesses, unusual weight, a poor standard of nutrition, will tend to handicap a baby. Lack of opportunity, encouragement or interest will, of course, also delay development, as will serious home disturbances or frequent changes in environment, or of nurse or of guardian. All-round retardation in walking, talking and general alertness may indicate a low level of general intelligence and even mental deficiency, but this can only be determined with confidence by the doctor or psychologist, and usually not until the child is considerably older.

SPEECH DEVELOPMENT

Language development shows great variability and depends on a number of factors. General intelligence is one factor—the dull or defective child starts to talk late and his vocabulary is very limited. The cultural level of the environment is another factor. The child in a cultured home hears good, clear speech used to him and around him continually. Speech also depends on the companionship the child receives; he will learn to speak readily if his mother takes time and trouble to talk to him, and if he has children near his age around him as soon as he is old enough to appreciate their company— at the age of about twelve to eighteen months, perhaps.

It is best to use simple words and a clear, quiet tone when talking to a young child. Baby talk may be necessary at first, but should be given up as the child shows his ability to pronounce words correctly. Well-known, tuneful songs, nursery rhymes and jingles help speech development considerably.

During the first month the baby's only language is a cry—it may express hunger or pain, discomfort or loneliness. It is perfectly natural for him to cry when he needs something, for it is his only way of gaining satisfaction for his needs. From about the fifth month he vocalizes a great deal. This is sometimes known as the "play-stage" of language. He appears to be experimenting with sounds and enjoying the discovery and sensation of new sounds. He coos and crows, babbles and gurgles, and a careful listener can detect most of the recognizable vowel and consonant sounds and syllables. It is at this age, too, that he shows some recognition of familiar simple words and syllables, such as "No" and "Dada".

THE BABY'S VOCABULARY

At about ten months the first recognizable word may be spoken, and by twelve months his vocabulary may consist of two or three words. At eighteen months he may have about nine words at his command and often uses one word to convey the meaning of a whole sentence, e.g. "Gone," indicating that he has dropped his ball out of his pram and wants you to pick it up at once. The growth of language proceeds rapidly during the second half of the second year, and by two years of age the toddler's vocabulary may consist of some two hundred words and sentences, which are still very short, but increasing in number and complexity. Words usually appear in this order:

1. Exclamations
2. Nouns—a child shows great delight in naming things
3. Verbs—a child is interested in action
4. Adverbs
5. Adjectives
6. Prepositions, conjunctions and relational elements, which usually come last.

Until walking is well established, speech usually does not develop very fast. It is as if the child can only devote his energies to one important aspect of development at a time, and while he is concerned with learning to walk he cannot concentrate on learning to talk.

Speech is, however, closely associated with practical activity. The child vocalizes as he plays — he verbalizes his fantasies to some extent. He imitates sounds and voices he hears around him—the puffing of the train and the steam engine, the call of the coalman and the milkman, the miaow of the cat and the bark of the dog. He uses speech to gain further information from others or to bring past experiences to bear on to his immediate problems.

Girls tend to talk earlier and more readily than boys—and many people, of course, contend that women remain more loquacious than men well into adult life! It has been found that twins are frequently retarded in linguistic development because they understand each other so readily by gestures and expressions and do not need, to the same extent, to make each other understand by words. Children brought up in institutions are usually handicapped

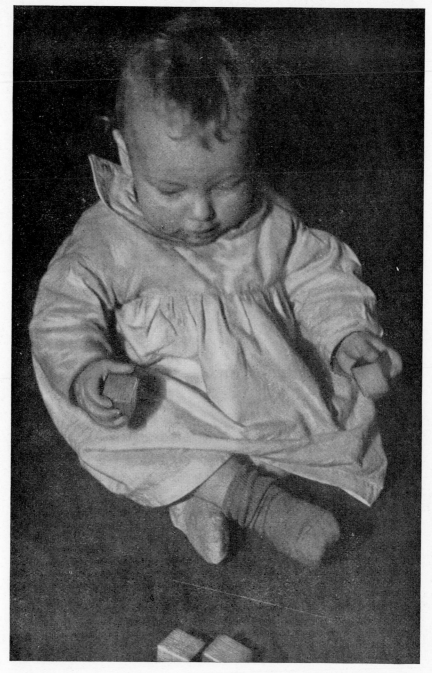

FIG. 32. *Infant play—first stage upon the long and difficult road of education.*

in speech development, because they do not receive sufficient encouragement and individual attention.

Some account has already been given of physical and intellectual growth during the first two years of the child's life. It would, however, be an incomplete picture if no reference was made to the emotional aspect of development during this period. Naturally, it is far more difficult to know or describe how the baby feels than to explain how his body grows, or how his intellectual activity manifests itself. But modern psychology lays great stress on the importance of understanding the emotional life of the child, and psycho-analytic studies of both children and adults have shown that in the first two years feelings are intense, though fluctuating and short-lived.

The bond between mother and child is very close. The child is helpless, defenceless and very dependent on his mother. Normally, the mother responds readily to the child's need, and maternal feelings of protection and affection are strong. There is evidence from psycho-analytic studies that the infant quickly feels deserted, insecure and deprived when his mother does not attend to him the moment he demands attention, or satisfy his hunger adequately, or comfort him when he is in distress. We have constant evidence from Child Guidance work that the children who cannot rely on maternal love, who never feel secure or safe in their early relationships with their parents, find great difficulty in building up good relations with other people and may feel insecure and inadequate all their lives.

ANGER AND TEARS

Anger is an emotion which is commonly expressed in babyhood. It can be observed when feeding is delayed, or when the baby is restrained against his will from free movement of his limbs. It is usually shown by screaming attacks or biting. It is perfectly normal and natural that the infant should feel hostile to the grown-ups around him at times, and parents must recognize the normality of this emotion. The baby is soon aware that such hostile conduct earns disapproval from his mother, and he soon learns to modify it.

Screaming, when due to feelings of anger and hostility, needs careful treatment. Although it is usually best to ignore a sudden outburst of angry tears, which serves as a relief of emotional tension to the child and from which the child should be given time to recover, it is most unwise to allow a child to scream himself out. He needs comfort and reassurance from a familiar and friendly adult. He needs the assurance that he is loved, despite his inner hostile feelings towards his parents.

Screaming, of course, may be due to pain of a physical nature—to indigestion, teething, ear-ache, skin irritation and other troubles. Naturally, such physical disturbances must be given correct physical remedies, but it is very probable that the infant, whose knowledge of reality is so meagre, may imagine such pain to be a hostile attack on himself by his parents. His need

91

of affectionate care from his mother is, therefore, very great at such times, and it is most unfortunate when infantile illnesses necessitate prolonged treatment in hospital. The hygienic atmosphere of the hospital and the expert care of a trained nurse cannot compensate for the temporary loss of the baby's mother.

The occasional temper tantrum of the toddler is a modified form of infantile screaming. It occurs when he is frustrated, when he cannot achieve or obtain what he wants immediately. A two-year-old appears to have a philosophy which may be termed a "here and now" and an "all or none" attitude to life. He has little understanding of time, and disappointment and postponement are hard indeed for him to bear. If something is taken away from him, he has little confidence in its return. He cannot be sure that grown-ups' promises or threats are always fulfilled, and, of course, in many cases grown-ups are not reliable in this respect. A tantrum at this stage is a very necessary part of emotional growing-up. It is a safety valve for hostile feelings. It is a child's means of self-assertion against his parents and against the external world. Intelligent parents will recognize and understand this phenomenon for what it is, and be tolerant and tactful in their handling of the angry child.

To give in to a child's temper is, of course, foolish and does not help the child. It will, indeed, be disturbing to him if he finds his hostility can control his own parents. This will ultimately terrify him and make him feel very insecure. He needs to make sure to himself that his parents are strong enough and wise enough to control his own aggressiveness—and some children need constant proof of this. A little wholesome neglect of the temper display, followed by friendliness and kindness to show the child that you want to help to heal the hurt that the child feels he has suffered, is the best psychological method.

THE NEED OF AFFECTION

Affection is certainly another feeling we may credit to the baby. An affectionate relationship to his mother or nurse is very quickly established. Recognition is clearly shown by the age of five months, but before this a baby will snuggle against his mother and will pat her breast or her cheek. His smile of welcome is his usual greeting in later babyhood, and as a toddler he will bring his most treasured possessions, as well as his damaged knees, for her inspection. Clearly, his affectionate response to his parents will be dependent on their mutual love and appreciation of him. It is quite possible to meet serious, sullen and surly two-year-olds who appear to greet the world with a scowl, just because their parents do likewise. The young child's need of affection is the most fundamental and important of his psychological needs. Its satisfaction is the keynote of satisfactory emotional development. Its frustration means unhappiness and often delinquency and neuroses.

Fear is the third important emotion of this period. It is shown when the baby is startled by a loud noise or by a sudden movement, or when support is taken from him. Probably it is experienced when anything happens to increase his feeling of helplessness and defencelessness. Sometimes he seems afraid of being alone, sometimes afraid of the dark.

The effect of fear is now known to be so damaging and so far-reaching that every care should be taken to prevent the very young child from experiencing this emotion, so far as is possible. A baby needs a stable, settled environment. He needs parents who are not anxious and apprehensive themselves. It is most essential that he shall feel able to rely on them in any and every emergency. Very young children have been observed to show hardly any fear at all during a heavy air-raid, provided their parents have remained calm and close at hand. Probably the fear of the loss of the parent and fear of the parents' hostility towards him are the most profound and the most severe of a young child's feelings, and he needs constant reassurance and protection against these feelings.

PANIC AND ITS TREATMENT

Screaming on account of fear is a kind of panic reaction to a terrifying experience. It is more likely to occur after than during babyhood. If the infant screams in this way—and such screams are easily distinguishable from cries of anger—he needs immediate comfort and consolation. Sucking at the breast or the bottle is probably the most effective remedy, unless the baby has been fully weaned. Doctors sometimes prescribe mild sedatives in such cases.

It is clear that the very young child has strong feelings and that during the first two years he is struggling to gain mastery over these feelings. As he gains some stability and has good experience of security in his environment, he will begin to make advances to, and seek responses from, the people in his environment. He is quite definitely aware of his mother, as distinct from any other grown-up, by about five months. By six months some babies have been observed to take notice of other babies and even show some jealousy of them. By eight or nine months he may attempt to communicate with others by rudimentary speech—the "babble" stage of speech development—and he may begin to welcome strangers and respond playfully to them. If the father takes an important role in upbringing and shares some of the routine work—even bathing, nursing or dressing the baby now and again—the child will build up a close and affectionate relationship to him and will recognize the value of his strength, support and assistance in helping him to tackle some of the manifold practical problems of babyhood.

During toddlerhood—up to three years at least—the child is very dependent on his parents, but it is quite possible to teach a young child to enjoy playing by himself for part of the day. He will learn to occupy himself in his play-pen with his toys for a considerable time, if he is sure that his mother is at hand and within call. A two-year-old can be left to amuse himself in a safe garden if he is allowed to visit his mother from time to time, but it is equally important that his parents shall find time and opportunity to play with him now and again. A lively romp with his father, a quiet story-time with his mother before bed, are greatly appreciated and probably enjoyed as much by the parents as by the child!

Young babies ought not to have too many grown-ups around them. The devoted grandmother, aunt and "in-laws" should not usurp the mother's role. As the baby gets older, occasional visits are stimulating to him. Before two years of age the company of other children is not greatly appreciated, but by the time the toddler is on his feet, however unsteadily, he will enjoy playing beside other children in the sand-pit or in a paddling pool, for instance. He will not usually play *with* other children (he may seem highly indifferent and aloof from them and intent on his own toys), but gradually he will come into contact with them, and though disagreements, tussles and tears will often ensue, he will have made his first attempt at social adjustment. Older children will be protective or bossy towards him: he will sometimes accept their protection and refuse their domination. Adult interference may be necessary sometimes to see that justice is done, or that the younger child is not exploited by the older, but, on the whole, children are best left to settle their own differences and learn to fight their own battles from the beginning, without undue intervention by adults.

Test Yourself

1. What are the normal steps in motor development during the first two years of a child's life?

2. Outline suitable play material and play occupations which will stimulate the growth and development of a child between two and three years of age.

3. Discuss the young child's need for affection.

Answers will be found at the end of the book.

CHAPTER VII

EARLY CHILDHOOD TO ADOLESCENCE

T HE PERIOD from two to five years, or from three to five years, of age is commonly known as the "pre-school period". This does not mean that the child learns nothing. On the contrary, he usually learns a very great deal, but he is not yet ready for book learning or formal work. At this stage of his development he is learning much about other people and much about himself and how to use his limbs and his lungs, for instance. He also learns a good deal about his parents and the people immediately around him. He discovers a certain amount about his immediate environment, but he has still a great deal to find out.

He can walk—usually well by eighteen months. In the next year or two he learns to run, climb, jump, balance, hop, skip and dance. Whenever he discovers a new feat, such as hopping or skipping, he keeps on doing it— just like Hoppity in the A. A. Milne poem; he delights in practising each new achievement again and again, and demands adult appreciation of his efforts. To insist that a three-year-old shall "sit still" when his whole body is tingling with restrained energy is to demand the impossible. At the same time, a young child needs a great deal of sleep and at least one rest period in the day. In the Nursery school this is insisted upon, and three-year-olds will often sleep quite happily for 1-1½ hours in the afternoon. A children's curfew—to prevent children playing in the streets after normal bed-time hours—has much to recommend it, but is unlikely ever to be enforced strictly in this country.

GROWING SKILL

The child also learns many new ways of using his finer muscles more precisely and more accurately. The two-year-old can build a tower of bricks. The three-year-old can copy a circle or draw a schematic "man"—usually a large round with two strokes for legs and two marks for eyes. The four-year-old can copy a square with right-angled corners. The five-year-old can draw a "man", with a body, eyes, arms, hands and a suggestion of a neck.

Children of these ages are keenly interested in colour, shape, size and volume. It was Madame Montessori who emphasized this aspect of perceptual development so clearly. The two-year-old will enjoy fitting bricks into a box, and putting pegs into holes. By three years of age most children enjoy matching colours and shapes. By four years a child can fit a simple three- or four-piece jig-saw puzzle together. The five-year-old can name the common colours, e.g. red, yellow, blue and green, and often can distinguish some numbers and letters; but many five-year-olds are not so advanced, nor so interested, and it is a great mistake to urge any kind of "formal work" upon them until they show readiness and keenness. The author knew one two-year-old who could count up to 100, and also a six-year-old who could not count out five bricks correctly.

Play Occupations for the Pre-school Child. It is most important that children of this age should have enough to do. A bored child frequently gets into mischief. The first essential is to have enough play space. Quarrels are far more frequent when children are cramped and continually bump into each other. For the country child there are lanes and fields, trees and brooks. Many a child of four or five years can be happy for hours with a bucket, a jam-jar or two, an assorted collection of hips and haws and leaves and pebbles, and a shallow, muddy brook. Most country children go out in all weathers; frost and snow offer a thousand new play possibilities.

But city children are not so lucky. Parks and public gardens and playgrounds are poor substitutes for the country, and are inaccessible to many. The backyard, the gutter and the busy street are unsuitable playgrounds. The Nursery school or Nursery class is the obvious answer. From three years of age a young child can gain much valuable experience in such a school or class. Sufficient indoor and outdoor play space is provided. Apparatus for active play, such as climbing-frames, chutes, see-saws, swings, planks and boxes, is part of the nursery equipment. Pull-along toys, wheelbarrows, kiddy-cars, tricycles, etc., are included. Materials for sand and water play are provided in modern schools of this type.

Then, too, indoor toys should include not only teddy-bears and trains, dolls' houses and tea-sets, but also some sense-training toys, which fascinate and stimulate the

Fig. 33. *The provision of healthy and interesting outlets for the boundless energy of young children is a very pressing problem in congested cities. In some of the industrial districts of London this problem has been partly solved by the creation of "junk playgrounds" on bombed sites away from busy streets, where children can play in safety with bricks, timber and sand, in the care of voluntary supervisors.*

pre-school child. He likes to sort out shapes and fit them into their right places in a "formboard". He likes building up cones and towers of graded sizes. He loves to match colours and do animal jig-saws.

Young children need simple, primitive material like clay or modelling-wax, dough or mud; and they need opportunity to paint and crayon on large sheets of paper or blackboards. They are at the experimental stage, and they need plenty of room and large-scale materials with which to experiment.

Bright, simple pictures on the walls and clear, attractive picture-books are much appreciated.

Little children often have a keen sense of rhythm and enjoy free movement to music or taking part in a percussion band.

Many of these "play occupations" are not easily provided for in the average home, but a Nursery school has to provide for many children and so is "child centred" and has chairs and tables, and shelves, basins and toilets to fit the small child. There are many other advantages of the Nursery school which will be discussed later on.

Language Development. Between two and five years of age language develops rapidly. The two-year-old has usually about two hundred words at his command. The three-year-old has often a vocabulary of nearly nine hundred words, and by five years the child's vocabulary may comprise two or three thousand words. Of course, great variations occur among

individual children, depending on environment, intelligence, opportunity and encouragement, as has already been pointed out.

But the child of these ages is interested in speech and will imitate readily. He is still more interested in action than in words, but he uses the latter to communicate with others, to explain what he wants and to seek help or information. This is the Golden Age of the Question. Sometimes the child asks a question because he is genuinely puzzled and wants enlightenment. Sometimes it is to ensure that the adult will take notice of him. In the first case, his curiosity should be satisfied in simple and clear terms, so far as is possible; but often, if the question is returned to him, he will seek to supply the answer himself, and this will in turn stimulate thought and experimentation. In the second case, the intelligent adult will discern his craving for notice and will see that he gets sufficient of it in the right way and at the right time.

One of the normal questions of young children is "How are babies born?" The modern mother knows that when the three- or four-year-old asks this question, it is her duty to answer it accurately then and there, rather than to put him off with gooseberry-bush tales, or "I'll tell you when you are old enough, dear". It is not difficult to say, "They grow inside mummies' tummies. That is where the baby is kept warm and snug until he is ready to be born.

Daddy has to help Mummy by planting a tiny seed inside her body to make the beginning of the baby. When the baby comes out of his Mummy's tummy, she will feed him with the milk she has stored ready for him." Most children are quite satisfied with some such simple account. Many of them will have had opportunity to see baby animals, such as calves or kittens, suckling.

If this type of sex education is not given at this early stage, the child may show signs of anxiety or inhibition of curiosity because his questionings are sternly discouraged. There is evidence that young children weave strange fantasies around the whole subject; and unless these fantasies, which are

FIG. 34. *In the Nursery school or class, where the child has to compete with other children, the beginnings of social adjustment are learned more readily than in the more restricted atmosphere of the child's own home.*

often terrifying or distasteful, are not discredited by truthful explanations from the parents, the child's fears and feelings of disgust may have an unfortunate effect on his later development. Obviously, the parents are by far the best people to give the child sex education when he appears to need it; but if they cannot face the issue, a teacher, doctor or psychologist can supply it, with the parents' consent.

Children of between three and five years are normally curious about the how and when and why of everything. They need scope for experiment and discovery. They need opportunity to teach themselves by their mistakes and their mishaps. In every young child is the germ of the explorer and adventurer; it is the grown-up's duty to give him a chance to go on explorations and to seek adventures, whether on the rubbish-heap, in the coal-cellar or in the garden or attic.

Gradually, the child begins to verbalize his thoughts; he sorts out and checks his impressions, he takes note of differences and makes comparisons. One child stimulates another, and the value of companionship for intellectual development is very great.

FIG. 35. *At the age of three the toddler's interests are widening rapidly, and he requires more occupation and companionship than many homes normally provide. It is at this age, therefore, that Nursery education should commence, in a properly equipped Nursery class where even "messy" play is encouraged.*

Social Development. The pre-school period is the first real training-ground in social adjustment. It is a very difficult time for the young child in this respect. Gradually he gains in independence and is less dependent on his mother. Sometimes he is frankly hostile and unfriendly to her or to other grown-ups. Gradually, as he learns to master his feelings and discovers that grown-ups are reliable, kindly people, eager to help him, he becomes normally friendly and affectionate again. Some children, of course, do not have good experience of reliability and kindliness in grown-ups and consequently their outlook is different. They make new contacts with timidity.

A young child needs companions of his own age. He does not always welcome them at first. He tends to regard all other children first as rivals for his mother's affections—his brothers and sisters especially. He dislikes sharing his possessions or privileges, and his early days at the Nursery school are filled with battles for possession. These are hard fights, often fraught with disappointment and defeat, but it is valuable training for the battle of life. He must learn to defend himself and his own rights, but there are times, of course, when adult protection and intervention are necessary.

EARLY SOCIAL ADJUSTMENT

The great advantage of the Nursery school or Nursery class is that rudimentary social adjustment can be learned more readily than in his own nursery at home, where emotional attachments are stronger, feelings more intense, and rivalry and fear of deprivation more keen. The atmosphere at school is more impersonal, and it is a great advantage to a three- or four-year-old to have his family circle widened early.

Usually, children pass through a stormy phase of social adjustment, marked by quick quarrels and heated arguments. This is followed by an increase in friendliness and co-operation. Gradually the child learns the great advantages of co-operative work and play. He chooses his "buddies", and together they can build boats and battleships, aeroplanes and aqueducts, and devise endless imaginative games to suit their own purposes. They learn, too, that unity is strength, and can defend themselves against other children; while they encourage one another at times to be antagonistic to the teacher and the authority she represents. This is a healthy stage of social development.

Social experience, then, aids the young child in intellectual development, in language development and in learning social adaptability. There are, therefore, many advantages on the side of Nursery school education for the pre-school child. The writer's own view is that three years of age is a better time to start Nursery education than two years, for most two-year-olds need more individual attention and care than the Nursery teacher can always give. They need close contact with their mothers.

There are, of course, many cases where it is necessary for the mother to work, and it is better for the child to be under expert care than left to a minder, but the writer does not think that married women should be encouraged to relinquish their responsibilities for their young children too readily. Their first job is that of a good home-maker, and the proper care of the toddler is the hall-mark of the good home-maker. A mother who has been at work all day is often irritable, tired and impatient and her chief desire is to hurry the child off to bed and out of the way so that she can have time to herself. The two-year-old who has good play space in and out of doors and occasional young companions can be happily occupied at home. By three or four years of age he needs more occupations and more company and usually enjoyes life in the Nursery school very much indeed. His home still remains of great importance to him, however.

Emotional Development. Between three and five years of age the child probably experiences more emotional "growing pains" than at any other time, except perhaps during adolescence. There is considerable evidence to show that during this time the child is struggling to come to terms with inner feelings and to resolve emotional conflicts to some extent. He experiences dual feelings towards his parents—both love and hate. He learns to control or deflect his hostile feelings. He frequently feels jealous of the claims that his father makes on his mother, and jealous of his brothers' and sisters' claims on both parents. He has to learn to accept these claims, but it will be made more difficult for him if he is not assured of his mother's affection for him. Any circumstance which deprives him of his mother for a prolonged period is likely to prove disturbing to him. A period spent in hospital can disturb a child considerably, and he may return, after several weeks' absence, a fretful, timid child, who cannot bear his mother to go out of his sight. Wartime evacuation had this result.

The father's absence on active service, or for other reasons, is often keenly felt by the young child; children who are deeply attached to their father experience a genuine sense of loss at his departure. Some may feel responsible in some way for his going away—almost as if their naughtiness has something to do with it—and consequently feel guilty and anxious, and develop mild anxiety symptoms. The father's return brings reassurance and a reduction of anxiety almost immediately.

THE NEW BABY

One early experience which demands a difficult emotional adjustment is the arrival of a new baby. Some hostility and jealousy towards the newcomer are almost inevitable. The child feels that he takes second place in his mother's affections. He is no longer the centre of interest. The new baby is often noisy and its demands are very insistent. When it is ailing, the older child is hushed up and told to amuse himself. When his mother is feeding the baby, he is told "Don't bother me now". There are countless small slights and acts of negligence, which may be unintentional, but are nevertheless painful to the child. It is quite natural for feelings of jealousy to arise, and he may adopt devious ways to win his mother's anxious solicitude, such as contrariness, bed-wetting or stammering. Many parents nowadays have sufficient understanding of the difficulties the older child may experience to help him in two definite ways: first, by preparing him carefully for the baby's coming and, secondly, by making sure that he is not neglected or overlooked after the baby has arrived. In actual fact, he needs rather more of his mother's love and interest than before, when his feeling of security was not imperilled.

The question of children's fears at this age needs attention. Three years of age is the time when fears are most common. Children suddenly refuse to go to sleep in the dark, show unreasoning fear of animals, are unwilling to be parted from their mothers or refuse to go out to play with other children. It is obvious that the child feels a little insecure and unsure of himself and his surroundings. His relationship with his parents is all-important at this time. He needs comfort, reassurance and encouragement to be more courageous. Most children pass through some such phase, and they need careful treatment while it lasts. Young children should not be forced to face what is

FIG. 36. *The urge to self-expression and creation is strong in young children, and in the well-organized school or Nursery class it receives full encouragement. Clay and modelling-wax, paints and crayons—all have a valuable part to play in the child's adjustment to life.*

terrifying to them, however laughable their fears may appear to grown-ups. A light in the bedroom, a firm handclasp when a dog has to be passed, a promise of a speedy return when the child is to be left for a while, and an invitation to other children to come in and play are small ways to relieve large fears.

Little children adopt certain comfort habits when they are worried. They may suck their fingers or their handkerchiefs; they may insist on taking some insanitary toy to bed with them; they may masturbate—handle their sexual organs. Obviously, the only correct way to deal with their difficulties is to discover the real reason for worry and to put the matter right. Frightened, deprived, unhappy, bored children will resort to these methods of obtaining comfort. Punishment or restraint only exaggerate the trouble. Once the child has regained security and happiness, these difficulties will not occur.

Another difficulty may occur which is sometimes a reflection of inner emotional disturbance, namely, *enuresis*, or bed-wetting. Most children have gained bowel or bladder control by about 24 months, but this control is not as yet very firm and can easily break down. A very frightened or a very angry child may lose this control and experience toilet difficulties. This trouble should not cause much concern in these early years. Provided there is a good relationship between parents and child, and mutual willingness to put the matter right, careful training and encouragement will usually prove successful. Scolding usually aggravates the problem.

FOOD FADS

Difficulties over food occur from time to time and are usually a reflection of early feeding difficulties. Often these are emotional in origin; sometimes they have a physiological basis. The best method is to ignore food fads to a large extent, to avoid fuss or flurry, and leave the child's natural hunger to teach him common sense. Meals in the Nursery school usually help considerably in teaching the child good feeding habits.

Destructiveness and contrariness both occur during this period and may be regarded as a normal phase of development. The former may be due to carelessness, experimentation, or a rush of aggressive feeling which the child temporarily feels unable to control. The second indicates a growth of will-power and is often a testing-out of adult reactions. Outlets for destructive play in cutting, tearing, hammering, modelling and destroying activities help the child to overcome these impulses. Avoidance of excessive frustration or prohibition, while maintaining a firm, definite policy in disciplinary matters, will help the child to pass through his contrary phase.

The Value of Play. Free, spontaneous play is of immense value at this time. Frequently it is creative, imitative, imaginative and dramatic. The child may assume the role of the parent and act out his own feelings towards his companions or his dolls. It is nature's way of teaching the child to come to terms with reality, to master over-strong feelings, to gain relief from such feelings, and achieve a measure of emotional stability. In *The Psychological Aspects of Child Development*, S. Isaacs says: "The chief function of play in these early years is the active dramatization of the inner world of phantasy, as a means of maintaining psychic equilibrium."

The young child, therefore, needs opportunity and companionship for free play, and the minimum of adult interference. Although play is education in the widest sense in these years, and suitable play material should be provided, formal teaching methods should be strenuously avoided.

By five years of age the child has gained a number of skills and a fairly wide experience of his environment. His mastery of language has greatly improved, and a dawning interest in learning in the more formal sense is apparent. His social and emotional development has proceeded apace—he is more mature in his relationships with people and is less swayed by strong emotional impulses. A five-year-old's birthday is the right psychological moment for admission to school, provided that education leads through play to work and the teacher bears in mind the fundamental childishness of the five-year-old.

EARLIER SCHOOL LIFE

The five-year-old child develops before very long into the schoolboy or schoolgirl. Babyhood has become a time of the past, but sometimes mothers forget that it is not long past, and expect high standards of behaviour and thought too quickly. The writer knew one mother who was much ashamed because her nine-year-old boy asked for a cuddly toy to take to bed with him! He had been through several air-raids and suffered from night terrors. When given a purple, stuffed giraffe he was greatly content, talked to it in bed and settled down happily to sleep every night, and the night terrors disappeared.

Children who have never been to a Nursery school or a Nursery class are sometimes rather apprehensive about school at first. They set off bravely enough, bursting with pride, but the crowd of children, the taunting of a playmate, a sharp word from a teacher, can quickly reduce them to tears. Adjustment to school life takes time and patience. The impersonal atmosphere, the hurry-scurry, the new rules, new standards, and new instructions take time to get used to, and as the child's first acquaintance with school may colour his whole attitude, it is important to ease the situation in little ways whenever possible. Mothers who melt into tears at parting, or who have threatened the child with school punishments, or who criticize school methods continually, increase the child's first difficulties. Mothers who wave bravely from a distance, who have taught their children the first principles of school discipline, who inquire eagerly into all the varied activities and fun of school hours, are helping their children to take their first independent steps along the somewhat difficult road that leads eventually to maturity.

At five or six years old, the child is far better equipped to deal with the demands of his environment than before. He has greater skill in manipulation. He can handle a pencil and a paint-brush. He can hammer and saw. He can model. He can cut. He enjoys designing. He finds pleasure in all sorts of simple handicrafts. He is eager to make and do things all day long. This, then, should be the approach to formal learning—through play and through activity. His interests are many. His curiosity is keen. The clever teacher knows how to catch his interest, to stimulate his curiosity and gradually to introduce him to the fun of Reading, Writing and Arithmetic when he shows he is intellectually ready for these subjects. He should recognize that they are merely useful tools, whereby he can go farther on his explorations of the exciting world of people and things around him. It is outside our present purpose to elaborate this theme—the child's introduction to formal learning. Chapters VIII–X will deal more fully with this subject. It is sufficient to say here that the child's maturation rate is an individual one, that intellectual development is very variable, and that bright, average and dull children need differing methods and differing rates of education.

The five-year-old, then, shows a wider range of interests and greater concentration and a keener intellectual curiosity in his environment than the younger child. Emotionally he is gaining all the time in independence and self-control. He experiences the real pleasure of achievement, and is less dependent on adult approval. The firmer his hold on reality, the clearer his understanding of the real world, the less disturbing are his fantasies and the stress of his emotional conflicts. To a considerable extent these last are repressed during this period, but if the underlying conflict is violent, much mental energy is needed to repress his strong and urgent feelings, and he has less energy for learning and intellectual development itself.

SOCIAL ADJUSTMENT AT SCHOOL

Inhibition in regard to learning is fairly common. Some children cannot learn because they are too anxious, too afraid to make mistakes or to commit themselves. Such children need a longer period of play, because they are emotionally immature. They need to play out their fears and anxieties and to master their emotions. In such a way they gain greater stability and are more ready for school learning. It is, therefore, essential that opportunity for free play, for constructive and imaginative play rather than organized games, should be provided in the first stages of Infant departments. The Nursery stage should spill over into the Infant school, and in many schools nowadays this is widely recognized.

The school child's social life is a much more stable and satisfying one than that of the pre-school child. He learns to make real friends, to share experiences and joys and sorrows with them. He learns to co-operate with them in the fullest sense, and learns to be a follower or leader as the occasion merits. The opinions of his schoolmates sometimes weigh more with him than those of his parents, but everyone knows the child who cannot make friends, the child who always wants to boss or lead, the child who always wants the limelight and the child who always starts a quarrel, or who becomes the scapegoat and suffers more than his share of the teasing.

We will instance the case of a little girl of seven whose mother complained that she was always quarrelling with her younger sister and could never make friends unless she was allowed to be the leader of the group. Alice was acutely jealous of her younger sister, having been made so by her mother's open preference for the latter and clear rejection of Alice herself. She insisted that the little sister was "such a sweet little thing", and she could not understand why Alice never wanted to play with her. Alice would play with her if she could treat her as a baby and "manage" her completely. Directly the little sister rebelled, Alice would not tolerate the situation. The same trouble occurred with her friends, until she became more secure in her relationship to her mother, less jealous and more affectionate towards her sister, and

more willing to "give and take" with her friends.

The sensitive child, the one who cannot fight his own battles, is frequently the child who has never been taught self-reliance at home and has been brought up in the hot-house of maternal affection, without exposure to the cold blasts of everyday life. School is too great a contrast, and he has many painful lessons to learn outside the class-room before he can stand on his own feet.

During the ages of seven to eleven an important phase of social development usually takes place. Children learn to co-operate in larger groups. Gradually some form of gang or team grows up. Children of this age are usually full of

FIG. 37. *Most children take pride in their ability to invent or make something. It is through the medium of creative activities that the child should be introduced to the formal aspects of school learning.*

FIG. 38. *Children are fascinated by water; in the absence of a shallow brook or pool, there should be provision for water play in the Nursery class or school.*

adventurous spirit and independence which can readily become rebellion. They often develop a rigid though rudimentary social code, show strict loyalty to the members of their group and obedience to their leader, and strong antagonism towards a rival gang or to anyone representing authority. Obviously, such a group has great potentialities for good or for harm. A wise teacher or youth leader can direct the enthusiasm and energy of the children to some common, useful purpose—to collecting tinfoil or rose-hips, for example, or making something useful, such as a wigwam or log hut or model railway. Children are quick to recognize the real qualities of leadership and will accept the lead of a grown-up who understands their needs and provides them with the adventure and the activity which they crave. Cubs and Brownies appeal to many children and provide much better activities than delinquent adventures.

CAUSES OF "NAUGHTINESS"

The most common difficulty of this early school period is that of naughtiness or defiance. Much of this is merely another sign of emotional growing-pains. Instead of the screaming of the infant or the tantrum of the toddler, we have the truculence and the non-cooperation of the schoolchild. When the difficulties are very prolonged or persistent, inquiry reveals especially difficult or disturbing home circumstances.

Nancy's mother did full-time work. Her father was killed in the R.A.F. when Nancy was three years old. She was brought up by her aunt; her uncle was in the Forces. When the author first saw her she was seven years old and was said to be very difficult to manage at home, would shout and storm to get her own way and usually refused to do what she was asked. She had a dim memory of her own father, a vivid memory of her uncle, and a happy acquaintance with a soldier who was shortly to marry her mother. She had thus some unstable emotional relationship with three people, all of whom she called "Daddy". She was not sure of her mother's real affection and relied mostly on her aunt, who performed the most important functions of a mother for her. Her behaviour greatly improved when her uncle was demobilized and came home. She turned to him as to a father and accepted his authority fairly well. Her mother was urged to give up more time to her and to plan happily with her a home of their own and a new "daddy" all of her own. Reassurance of affection, gentle, tactful handling and a refusal to allow storms of tears to win the day gradually helped Nancy to build up happier relationships with the important grown-ups in her world, and then to make friends with children of her own age.

BACKGROUND OF TRAGEDY

Tommy, also seven years of age, is an example of a small boy with a tragic home background whose naughtiness would have quickly become delinquency if steps had not been taken to prevent it. His father, to whom he was devoted, joined the Royal Air Force when Tommy was four years old. Difficulties commenced immediately. His mother became interested in an American soldier and neglected the home. Tommy learned to run wild, to beg for pennies, to play truant, to visit department stores in order to appropriate small goods or sums of money. His mother did not attempt to prevent this. She became very much attached to the American, and when her husband came home on leave she refused to give up her lover. When her husband returned to the R.A.F., the emotional strain became unbearable and she committed suicide. Tommy was the first to find her with her head in the gas-oven!

He was subsequently taken to live with his aunt and uncle, but his wandering and pilfering habits were firmly ingrained. Added to this was his emotional unrest—unconsciously he seemed to feel vaguely responsible for his mother's death. Perhaps his continued naughtiness was an attempt to prove to himself that in reality he would not be punished in the cruel terms of his own imaginings. An attempt was made to reconstruct a happier home life with his aunt and uncle, and his father's help and interest were assured him. Play therapy provided him with outlets for his underlying aggressive feelings and anxieties, and school occupations and play activities supplied him with an alternative to delinquent adventure.

DELINQUENCY

A tendency to delinquency in children occurs fairly often during the last part of the period under review—from nine years to fourteen plus. The mischievous or high-spirited child may become a serious behaviour problem in the following circumstances:

1. When he has insufficient outlet for instinctive drives and energy.
2. When he is materially deprived.
3. When he is emotionally deprived, having insufficient affection (stealing is then symbolic of stealing love).
4. When his home offers poor ethical standards.
5. When he feels inferior in some way (for delinquency is often an attempt to regain self-respect).

6. When he is intellectually inferior, impulsive and readily suggestible.

A study of Child Psychology demonstrates this only too clearly, and psychologists have spent much time and energy in recent years in a study of this problem and in an attempt to provide remedies. Much has been written on the subject. In these pages we can only indicate the main direction which successful treatment should take. The child needs help in personality adjustment. His underlying feelings of inadequacy, deprivation and inferiority need ventilation. He needs assistance in recognizing his limitations and realizing his potentialities. He needs rehabilitation. This process can only be really successful if he can build up some strong emotional tie to some grown-up on whom he can rely, and in whom he can put his trust. He needs a satisfactory ego-ideal—a figure on whom he can model his life, so that his character development can proceed satisfactorily. His emotional deprivations must be made good. All this can be achieved by psychological treatment, but at the same time his environment must be improved, his old associations broken and alternative occupations suggested to him. Sometimes removal from home and neighbourhood is essential if re-education is to be successful, but adjustment within his own home is best if it can be achieved.

THE NORMAL CHILD

It must not be forgotten that the years between six and twelve are probably the happiest in childhood. Most children go frolicking through these years, finding fun and merriment in numerous childish ways. Most of them are full of adventure and eager to explore every possibility which promises well. They are usually heedless of grown-ups, careless of consequences, tireless in energy, clannish in the extreme, clownish in many ways, and often rather selfish. But none the less they are most lovable—being spontaneous and natural and altogether carefree. Their games and their secrets are their own, but, at bottom, they are devoted to their parents and surprisingly loyal to their brothers and sisters. They write ridiculous stories; they make endless useful things out of odds and ends; they collect anything under the sun, from conkers to caterpillars; they plot puerile pranks—in fact, to many a child life is one long April Fool's Day. Their parents and their teachers take responsibility for them, and children do not appear to worry greatly about their behaviour or their lessons. This is a description of the majority of children. But there is a minority of children who must be treated in further detail.

Worried Children. There are some children who cannot take things as they come and who are not happy-go-lucky or carefree. These children need more attention. Very frequently these troubles reflect their home atmosphere. If their homes have a disturbed, erratic or anxious atmosphere, it is difficult for children to possess real serenity of mind. Economic insecurity may be the cause of family worries. Parental disagreements may be another cause. Strain and stress at home frequently produce a worried child, one who is tense, timid, and constantly expecting difficulties which he cannot overcome.

Over-ambitious parents may urge their children beyond their normal powers. Such a child consequently dreads any failure at school, becomes

FIG. 39. *The five-year-old child shows a growing interest in the colours and shapes of objects, and loves making cut-out toys of paper or cardboard.*

over-anxious and cannot concentrate fully, and every examination becomes a nightmare for it.

Some children develop anxiety symptoms which are motivated to enlist the parents' anxious solicitude. A child who feels unwanted or deprived in some way may discover that any form of illness—vomiting, faintness, head-aches, or a nervous habit—will immediately bring forth a response from the parent, whether of irritation or sympathy. It is a pathetic fact that some children find this the only sure means of holding their parents' attention.

Wetting or soiling is frequently indulged in by an anxious child. Sometimes incontinence arises directly out of feelings of insecurity and fear—the loss of control being a well-known accompaniment of the emotion of fear. Sometimes incontinence may be a distorted form of aggression—a kind of attack on the parents in an infantile form. Immediately this symptom will cause concern and annoyance to the parents, which is usually the child's unconscious aim.

Anxiety neuroses in childhood are fairly common in a mild form. Normally, a good home and secure affectionate relationships are sufficient to counteract them. As the child gains real skills, can attain real achievements and win approval and appreciation, his symptoms disappear. But some children, who are not so fortunate in their home background as others, need expert help if they are to regain serenity and happiness. A child who is afraid of animals, afraid of sleeping in the dark, afraid of traffic in the street, afraid of a loud-voiced or scolding teacher, or afraid of playing in the streets, is a child who clearly needs psychological help.

Some children become like this by a chain of circumstances. An accident in babyhood such as a bad burn or a bite by a dog, circumcision, or tonsillectomy causing unusual haemorrhage and a slow recovery, a period of convalescence away from home among strangers, the mother's absence in hospital, wartime evacuation and unsuitable billets—any of these may have serious effects on a child's emotional development. He tends to feel that the world treats him with hostility and he has no reassurance that he can rely on safety and stability in his life.

Treatment for such a child aims at restoring a sense of security and stability and giving him some outside support and protection until he is rehabilitated. Much of this has been necessary for children who suffered the loss of home and parents during the Second World War.

Most children have a natural resilience and are well equipped to deal with difficulties as they meet them. Probably it is a mistake to under-rate children's powers of recovery from shock. Nevertheless it is important to prevent them from experiencing too frequent and too severe shocks during their childhood.

ADOLESCENCE

In babyhood the child learns to adjust to himself and discovers his own personality. In the pre-school period the child learns to adjust to his family. In the middle years of childhood he learns to adjust to his school. In adolescence he learns to adjust to society—perhaps the most difficult adjustment of all. His success will depend a great deal on the success of his earlier adjustments—to self, to family and to school.

Intellectual Development. The period of adolescence is the time when tremendous advances take place in the mental growth of the boy or girl.

FIG. 40. *Designing puppets and staging puppet plays are valuable creative activities and provide a wholesome outlet for the child's usually rich imagination.*

Naturally, this is the outcome of earlier experiences, and thought now is built upon the intellectual activities of earlier school days. In general terms, the young person shows:

1. Greater facility in abstract reasoning and logical thought, and

2. Greater powers of concentration, and a wider memory span.

Often he will suddenly realize the fascination of intellectual study, of scientific research, and he may become an avid reader. A boy will dream perhaps of becoming another Pasteur or H. G. Wells, while a girl may aspire to be a second Florence Nightingale or Madame Curie. This is a definite advance on earlier engine-driver or tram-conductor aspirations!

Young people need much opportunity for argument, discussion and debate. Most Youth Centres provide such an opportunity, and some of the radio programmes are very stimulating.

Naturally, young folk will tend to be rebels in their thinking. They will challenge tradition and established opinion and argue hotly and ignorantly

on many profound topics. But this is evidence of healthy intellectual growing-pains and should be encouraged rather than repressed. Literary, dramatic and debating societies are often very popular at this stage.

Another important characteristic is the widening and specialization of interests. Boys and girls usually show different interests. Musical, artistic, dramatic, linguistic, scientific and practical interests usually begin to show

FIG. 41. *Most children have a keen natural sense of rhythm and enjoy taking even a minor part in a percussion band.*

themselves between the ages of twelve and fourteen years. This is just the age when the child is to be transferred to that form of Secondary education to which he is most suited—academic, technical, or general and practical. Although the choice is not always easy, because children vary so greatly in their rate of mental growth and do not always show a definite bias so early, the majority tend to show evidence of particular talents and interests. The problems of Secondary education are discussed in greater detail in Chapters VIII–X.

Adolescents begin to take a more impersonal interest in affairs. This is more characteristic of the intelligent ones than the duller ones, and of boys rather than girls. Newspaper reading is more common. Interest in politics may begin to appear. Hobbies such as bird-watching, sketching, or camping bring the child in touch with Nature and with the world outside himself.

Physical Growth. The growth of the body is of considerable importance to the adolescent during this time. He becomes interested in his muscular development and his athletic prowess. He takes note of his height and weight. He shows tremendous enthusiasm usually for swimming, skating, tennis, hockey, football or riding. Parents, teachers and youth leaders realize only too well the value of this form of exercise, the opportunity it provides for social co-operation, and the outlet it allows for physical and emotional energy. Sport, especially boxing or football, is probably the best way in which a growing boy can relieve his agressive feelings.

"GROWING PAINS"

The physical changes of puberty, the glandular changes which cause new internal secretions, the onset of menstruation and nocturnal emissions naturally cause some mental and emotional disturbance. One cannot experience minor internal earthquakes—definite physical changes such as a change of voice—without some feeling of surprise, of alarm and interest. Some children become rather self-conscious, ashamed and anxious. They feel different from their fellows and strangely unsure of themselves. When they discover that these changes are universal and are an important step towards maturity, they regain much of their self-confidence and self-respect.

The clumsiness and awkwardness in gait, in movement and in speech so characteristic of adolescence must be tolerated by grown-ups. The fifteen-year-old is rather like a young colt, mightily uncertain of his new-found power, his increased strength and length; and if he appears like a "bull in a china shop" at an afternoon tea-party, it is wise to recognize that social ease is not acquired overnight.

Emotional Development. One can well compare the emotional upheaval which takes place in adolescence to the emotional disturbances in the pre-school years. Intensity of feelings, fluctuation of feelings, mood swings, instability, unreliability, anxiety, egotism—all these can be observed again.

113

If emotional conflicts of the early years have only been shelved rather than solved, difficulties may occur rather intensively for a time.

If a child has allowed himself to be dominated by his mother, if he always inwardly rebelled against his father's authority, if he has never been successful in making friends, these problems will arise again.

The adolescent will make another bid for independence. If he meets much opposition, he will either harden into a rebel or give in and remain dependent for much of his life. Parents have an important role to play at this stage. They must remain in the background, a tower of strength when needed.

Sometimes adolescents are rather apprehensive of their new-found powers and frightened of their independence. Obviously, they will hanker after childish things, adult protection and advice, and much of the carefree life of childhood. As adults gradually entrust them with more responsibilities, they learn to rely on themselves and their glorious independence.

Adolescents are also rather concerned with their strong feelings. At times they feel on top of the world and equal to any emergency. At other times they feel depressed, inadequate and most unequal to the demands of life. They are easily elated and easily deflated. This sense of inadequacy is a relic of earlier unconscious fears of unlovedness and of impotence. The young person needs much reassurance that he is loved and is powerful enough to face the new demands of life. He needs some opportunity for success, some real achievement which will bring him recognition, whether in the sphere of athletics or academics. Praise and appreciation are meat and drink to the young adolescent. If he constantly feels inferior, he will over-compensate by bombastic bravado, which is painful to everyone.

IMAGINATION AND IDEALISM

The adolescent's imagination is strong. He (or she) suddenly becomes interested in art or poetry, in dress-design or architecture. He builds ideals— imagines himself as a great hero, a film star or an explorer. He models himself on someone he admires greatly. This is a very healthy phase of development, and is, in fact, very necessary to his growing-up. The aspirations and day-dreams of youth are the forerunner of later real success and achievement, though probably not in such extravagant terms as envisaged by the adolescent. It is most important that the young person shall experience his dreams and hopes as well as his fears and doubts. It is the function of the adult to bring him back to earth now and again, to make sure that his feet are on solid ground, though his head may be in the clouds fairly often. But the grown-up who constantly scorns or criticizes or condemns or belittles is doing great harm to the adolescent, who is usually far too conscious of his failings already.

"Lena was a dark-eyed, serious-minded adolescent. Her father, whose reputation was far from good, had deserted the family. Lena had been brought up in a foreign country and was dependent on her mother for company at home, as she had no brothers and sisters. She was developing rapidly in looks, intellect, and in independence. Her mother, feeling a stranger in a foreign land, and unused to English ways, was afraid to let her go out alone in the country, and was much concerned about the company with whom she might mix. She was afraid to trust her and insisted on her having no secrets from her mother. Lena became rather defiant, truculent, argumentative and impudent. She insisted that she could look after herself. She started at a Technical school and found real delight in craftwork. She became interested in art and would spend hours copying famous pictures. Her ambition was to be a nurse. She found her mother obstructed her at every turn: her friends, her work and her career plans were all criticized. It needed much parental re-education to clear up the situation—to give Lena sufficient freedom and her mother sufficient reassurance."

IMPORTANCE OF FRIENDSHIPS

Adolescence is an important period in social development. The young person learns many painful lessons about the art of getting on with people —some, indeed, never learn the art at all. Friendships are characterized by strong feelings and firm loyalties.

The first stage is when friendships are formed with persons of the same sex and age. Cliques, rather than gangs, are the order of the day. Impassioned discussions, sentimental confessions and heartrending confidences are exchanged. The young people learn much from mutual criticism and become self-conscious about their manners, behaviour and personal appearance. Rivalry towards other groups is a common feeling of this period.

The second stage is characterized by close attachments to older persons of either sex. Again, this is a type of social growing-pain. The child learns much of value from the object of his adoration, and real inspiration and helpful guidance can be obtained. The danger is that he may become too dependent on his idol, and that his social growth may be held up. Sometimes his pride is wounded and his affections are treated lightly. This may cause serious emotional upset. We have the classical examples of *Young Woodley* and *Mädchen in Uniform*. Young folks' emotions must not be trifled with. The company of both sexes is usually the best antidote to these difficulties.

The third stage is friendship with a contemporary of the opposite sex. Whether these friendships are platonic or based on sexual attraction, they serve a most valuable purpose in helping the adolescent to make a satisfactory heterosexual adjustment. The young people learn much about each other—their tastes and interests, their differences and their similarities. By doing things together—walking, acting, dancing or playing—they begin to appreciate the value of good companionship. Sometimes these blossom into fleeting love affairs. Sometimes the friendship dies a natural death. But it has been a part of social education. Obviously, the adolescent needs plenty of society—mixed, cheery, active and energetic. This is the best safeguard against illicit love affairs and abnormal manifestations. An open house, good holidays, Youth Clubs, an active, busy life are what the adolescent requires most. He needs:

1. Satisfying work
2. Adequate recreation
3. Companionship of both sexes
4. Guidance from older persons when he seeks it.

Difficulties of Adolescents. Excessive strain during adolescence may precipitate a serious anxiety condition or even a minor nervous breakdown. For some children the physical and emotional strains are too great, and they find they are unable to face them adequately. Signs of tiredness, general apathy, persistent worrying, inexplicable outbursts of tears, or fainting spells should always be taken seriously. The child needs sufficient rest and relaxation and a reduction of strains. Too many responsibilities, too much importance attached to success in an examination, for instance, too many claims on the young person's energies or sympathies should be avoided.

Nervous breakdowns are only likely to occur if the child is already suffering from personality disturbances, and if family relationships are strained and difficult. Sometimes a boarding school or a holiday away from home can help a good deal in establishing mental poise.

DISTURBANCES OF PERSONALITY

Minor personality troubles, such as moodiness, self-consciousness, truculence or defiance, are very common. They have to be accepted as part of normal development during adolescence. The child needs tolerance and sympathy and a good deal of healthy neglect.

"Mary at twelve years old was like a fish out of water at home. She was always discontented, bored, critical and could 'never do anything right' in her mother's eyes. She suffered from asthma and enuresis. The former frequently occurred at examination time. She felt that her younger sister, of a charming, tractable disposition, was given preferential treatment. She felt that her parents were unjust and unduly restrictive. As soon as she was given one thing, she tired of it and wanted something else. 'She would ask for the moon if she thought she could get it' was her mother's comment. Her parents expected almost adult standards from her in the way of tidiness, reliability and good manners. They scorned her schoolgirlish interests.

"The friction in the family was intense. The mother was not willing to receive psychological guidance, and matters went from bad to worse. Mary will either become a confirmed rebel against authority, or she may well suffer a minor breakdown unless her parents can learn to modify their methods."

Delinquency at this stage must be taken seriously. Stealing is usually the outcome of emotional conflict. It may be the result of general restlessness, and an expression of independence. The need for money, for pretty things, for possessions of one's own, for sweets, cigarettes and grown-up things generally must be satisfied in some measure, or the young adolescent may help himself. The need for affection and appreciation is very real, and it is the unloved, unaccepted child who compensates by delinquent behaviour.

Sex delinquency may be a form of experimentation. It may be due to ignorance, temptation, excessive stimulation, or inner feelings of anxiety. The best safeguard is adequate sex education and wise companionship.

Adolescence is an interesting and exhilarating time. Many difficult adjustments have to be learnt before true maturity can be reached. Some persons never learn to make a good adjustment and remain children at heart. Growing-up children require much tolerance, kindliness and wise guidance if they are to reach a true and complete adulthood.

APPLICATIONS OF CHILD PSYCHOLOGY

One very important development in the field of Child Psychology during the last fifty years is the Child Guidance movement, of which the purpose is to diagnose and treat three classes of difficulties in childhood: (1) backwardness; (2) behaviour problems; (3) nervous disorders.

The aim of this work is primarily prevention—to treat mild symptoms

FIG. 42. *The adolescent's enthusiasm for open-air pursuits should be guided and encouraged as much as possible. These boys and girls, for example, have their own school "farm", complete with calf, and take a full part in all the necessary routine activities.*

at their inception and so avoid more serious forms of delinquency, mal-development and breakdown in later life. The approach to these problems is a three-fold one—social, educational and psychiatric.

The Child Guidance clinic is run by a team of specially trained experts, who combine to glean all the information possible about the child, in order to arrive between them at a diagnosis and assessment of his difficulties, whether personal or environmental, and to carry out the treatment most appropriate for the removal of these difficulties.

CHILD GUIDANCE

The team consists essentially of three specialists:

(1) A psychiatrist—that is to say, a doctor specially trained in mental diseases, with an extra training, if possible, in the mental abnormalities of children. He is usually the director of the team. His particular job is the investigation and, if necessary, the treatment of the child, with the co-oper-ation of the other members of the team;

(2) An educational psychologist, an Honours graduate in Psychology with some teaching experience. His particular interest is in the school environment of the child and the estimating of the child's mental—especially intellectual—capacity, which is arrived at by means of various intelligence tests. The educational psychologist will glean information about the child's school life and progress, will help in adjustments, and, in special cases, may give the child some remedial teaching to enable him to overcome special difficulties;

(3) A psychiatric social worker, possessed of a diploma in Social Science and a certificate which shows that she has attended a year's special course in Mental Health and has passed the final examination. She will be concerned with obtaining all possible information about the child's home environment and in guiding the parents in how to deal with the child and his difficulties.

PLAY THERAPY

The home background, the child's abilities and potentialities, and his personality and emotional relationships are studied by this team of workers and the form of treatment decided on. Sometimes readjustments in the home, in the school, or in the child's personality itself are brought about. The cause of the child's difficulty is discovered and suitable remedies prescribed, so far as is possible. Obviously, the co-operation of the child, the parent and the teacher is essential to this work, but usually this is readily available. It is also most important that the trained workers have a full knowledge of a child's normal development, so that they may recognize certain behaviour to be normal to a particular phase of development, and other behaviour to be unusual or abnormal and indicative of a disturbance of personality.

One of the members of this team will undertake what is called "play therapy", for which there is now a special course of training. This is very

118

useful in the treatment of small children, who are allowed to play, either by themselves or in a group with others, with "undifferentiated material", such as sand or modelling-wax, or with specially constructed toys designed to allow them to express their inner feelings. In the course of such play they may be observed to work off emotional exuberance expressed in the form of aggression, anger or fear, or "play out" situations which are troubling them by dramatizing, through dolls or figures, events in the family life. This observation is of great service in estimating the factors which are disturbing the emotional equanimity of the child, or hindering his proper mental growth and progress.

The members of the team meet at frequent intervals to discuss their cases, to decide on appropriate measures of treatment and to allocate to each member the tasks for which he or she is most fitted.

Closely associated with the clinic team there should be a children's physician, with access to full hospital facilities for diagnosing and dealing with any physical disabilities which may be discovered. A speech therapist, who can deal with the more detailed treatment of stammering and other speech defects, is a most useful addition to the clinic.

As a rule, these clinics are run as part of the school medical service, but they may be associated with a general or a children's hospital, or may be regarded as a special juvenile branch of the mental treatment service of the particular area in which they operate.

RECENT DEVELOPMENTS

None of these preventive measures can be expected to achieve a one hundred per cent success. In spite of all our efforts, psychological maladjustment will continue to exist, but if we can reduce it appreciably it will mean a great increase in the happiness of the individual and a marked contribution to the efficiency and economic soundness of the community. Every possible endeavour must be made to save our race from psychological abnormalities of every kind.

Another development in this field, which is likely to increase in Great Britain as a result of the 1944 Education Act, is the school psychological service. This service is organized by, and is responsible to, the local education authority. The service is very comprehensive and is in close touch with the schools. The staff consists of one or more educational psychologists, and trained social workers. The service is primarily an advisory one, designed to assist parents, teachers and medical officers in their treatment of backward, difficult and nervous children. The staff is responsible for selecting children for education in Special and Adjustment classes and schools, and ensuring that this form of education is suited to the age, ability and aptitude of the particular child. A certain amount of method work and organization within the schools is, therefore, undertaken. Teachers are quick to detect minor problems and early signs of retardation and refer them directly to the psychologist.

In the case of children presenting more serious forms of neuroses, the services of a medical psychologist are enlisted and treatment is arranged in a psychiatric clinic. In the case of those mentally defective children who cannot be educated in a Special class, the services of the school medical officer are required, and education in a Special school is arranged. The advantage of such a service is that "problem" children are recognized in the Infant and Junior departments before the "problem" becomes too complex. It is available for any or every child, and the approach is primarily an educational one in the broadest sense—re-educational, in fact—rather than a clinical one.

This does not imply that all problems can be solved by re-arrangement in the home or school environment, or by superficial psychological methods— suggestion, encouragement and persuasion—or by the provision of suitable outlets in play. A percentage of child problems requires far more intensive treatment—whether psychiatric or psycho-analytic—and it is the job of the psychologist to recognize the severity of such a problem and refer the child to the right specialist. Many simple preventive measures can, however, be taken with those children presenting minor deviations in development or behaviour; and the value of the general educational work in the schools and the homes, that is to say, applied Child Psychology, is very great.

Now that local authorities are impelled to make adequate provision for their maladjusted children, the extension of this school psychological service may be fairly rapid.

Test Yourself

1. Describe the special advantages of the Nursery school for the pre-school child, and show also its dangers.

2. Compare the social adjustment of the pre-school child with that of the schoolchild of from five to ten years.

3. Why is adolescence an important period in social development? Describe some ways of helping boys and girls to develop along healthy lines in the years of adolescence.

Answers will be found at the end of the book.

CHAPTER VIII

PSYCHOLOGY IN THE SCHOOL

EDUCATIONAL Psychology is not a new subject of study. In one form or another it has existed for centuries. The first important essay on education, which contained much shrewd psychological observation, was written by a Greek more than two thousand years ago. The main difference between present-day psychology and older studies is that psychologists nowadays use scientific methods of experiment to make their observations more accurate and their results more reliable.

Educational psychologists are interested in studying how children and grown-up people learn. They want to know the best ways to learn, and in what conditions learning can be most efficient. Children begin to learn some things very soon after they are born, and every parent knows how much children can learn merely by their play at home and by their ordinary life in the neighbourhood before they go to school to get regular teaching. Much learning, particularly in young children, goes on without any teaching or special training. The child seems to grow and develop through natural causes. Educational Psychology, therefore, must be concerned also with the study of development.

Here we shall discuss mainly the conditions in which development and learning take place in children of school age, that is, from about five years up to eighteen, and how this knowledge may be useful to teachers and parents.

We might say that Educational Psychology is concerned with bringing up children, young people and even adults in the way they should go. This is a very important process, particularly for the people who do the bringing up. It is not surprising, therefore, that some sort of Educational Psychology has been studied since very early times, and not only by professional teachers. In fact, professional teachers have contributed comparatively little to the subject. More often in the early days philosophers, politicians, priests and doctors did most of this work, helped occasionally by private tutors in wealthy families. The private tutors, since they lived in close contact with their pupils, had very good opportunities for observing the children's characters and habits of learning.

We can note roughly three stages in the development of Educational Psychology. In the first and by far the longest stage, the subject was based partly on observation, partly on guesswork, tradition and superstition—"old wives' tales". Some of this type of Educational Psychology is still popular.

In the second stage, attempts were made to observe accurately and describe in detail the growth and interests of children.

The third stage, which is not much more than fifty years old, was marked by the use of scientific experiments in order to get more reliable results.

Educational Psychology in the form of careful, systematic observation of children began with a dramatic outburst by the French author Jean Jacques Rousseau, in his book, *Émile, or Education*, published in 1762.

ROUSSEAU

Rousseau seems to have had an unhappy childhood. His mother died soon after he was born (a fact of great significance to the psychologist), and the unfortunate man spent the rest of his life in an endless and fruitless search for the affection he had craved in vain in his childhood. The book is not a treatise on Educational Psychology. It is an explosive attack against the contemporary ways of bringing up children by a man who had suffered much from them and was thoroughly exasperated as a result.

He violently opposed such beliefs as original sin, innate depravity and repressive discipline. "God", he said, "makes all things good: man meddles with them and they become evil. . . . Our wisdom is slavish prejudice, our customs consist in control, constraint, compulsion. Civilized man is born and dies a slave. . . . All his life long, man is imprisoned by our institutions."

FREEDOM FOR SELF-EXPRESSION

Rousseau believed in freedom for the expression of the natural propensities and interests of the child. He said:

"Love childhood, indulge its sports, its pleasures, its delightful instincts."
"Let the children run, jump, and shout to their hearts' content. All their activities are instincts of the body for its growth in strength."

For our purpose it is important to note that not only did Rousseau attack the ideas about human nature and teaching methods common in his time, but he drew the correct conclusion from his opinions. If we ought to use children's instincts, interests and natural activities as helps towards their development and education, then we ought to observe children and find out what their instincts and interests really are. In the author's preface to the book we find the following passage:

"I shall say very little about the value of a good education, nor shall I stop to prove that the customary method of education is bad: this has been done again and again, and I do not wish to fill my book with things which everyone knows. I will merely state that, go as far back as you will, you will find a continual outcry against the established method but no attempt to suggest a better. . . . *We know nothing of childhood* and, with our mistaken notions, the further we advance the further we go astray. The wisest writers devote themselves to what a man ought to know, *without asking what a child is capable of learning*. They are always looking for the man in the child, without considering what he is before he becomes a man. . . . Begin thus by making a more careful study of your scholars, *for it is clear that you know nothing about them.* . . ."

INFLUENCE OF CHARLES DARWIN

As a result of Rousseau's writings and those of his Swiss disciple Pestalozzi, more and more people gradually became interested in "child study", as it was called. In 1787, Tiedemann, a German philosopher-psychologist, published the first careful observations of mental development, observations of his own son from birth to three years. This work was almost completely ignored until it was translated into French in 1863. More observations of children appeared in Germany in 1851, 1856 and 1859, without attracting much attention. The period was not yet favourable. The necessary change of opinion was started by the publication of Darwin's two books, *The Origin of Species* (1859) and *The Descent of Man* (1871).

These books spread the idea of evolution, that is, the gradual development of forms of life from simpler forms. If this idea was true, it followed that development was a continuous process and went on according to rules which might be discovered by careful observation. At the same time, childhood acquired a new importance. Instead of being a useless period between birth and maturity, it was essential for full physical and mental development.

SCIENTIFIC STUDY OF CHILDHOOD

The stir caused by Darwin's theory of evolution spread to psychology. In 1878 Wundt set up in Leipzig the first psychological laboratory, and pupils trained there spread his ideas and methods throughout Europe and the U.S.A. In 1883 (Sir) Francis Galton, in England, began to study individual differences and natural inheritance. In 1890 an American, J. McKeen Cattell, was busy making and trying out mental tests. In 1893 a National Association for the Study of Children was started in America by G. Stanley Hall. This was followed in 1894 by the Child Study Association in England. Since 1900, Child Psychology has spread rapidly; it is now an important study, using modern scientific methods of observation and experiment.

Yet, even today, some people refuse to take Educational Psychology seriously. They say that bringing up children is a matter of common sense, without any need for books, theories, or specialized knowledge. Parents ought to know better than anybody else how to bring up their own children.

Others, again, believe that education consists mainly in teaching and learning school subjects; that if children are slow to learn it must be because they are lazy; and that what they need in that case is a "good thrashing" from time to time, not highbrow psychology.

Some people, again, are afraid of what they call "making experiments" on

123

children. Others dislike the idea of applying scientific methods to the study and control of human behaviour.

These beliefs may not have done much harm in simpler conditions, when most children learned at home, in the workshop, or on the farm what was necessary for their grown-up life and work. Nowadays life is much more complicated. There is more to learn. Everybody is compelled by law to go to school. And by the Education Act of 1944 every child above eleven years of age is required to attend a Secondary school until the age of fifteen at least.

OBSOLETE METHODS

In education, as in industry, the old-fashioned, easy-going, rule-of-thumb methods will not work in modern conditions. Just as it is becoming more and more necessary to use scientific methods in industry, so is it becoming more and more necessary to apply the science of psychology to the work of teaching and education.

We shall discuss some of the educational problems of the present time and try to show how the educational psychologists are helping to solve them.

Some people are suspicious of the psychologists' intentions. They are not quite sure what these experts are "up to", as they say. Not all teachers, either, regard educational psychologists with favour. They are looked upon sometimes as cranks or interfering busybodies, or regarded with amusement or mild contempt as mere theorists. Many teachers are doubtful about the practical use of Educational Psychology in schools.

What, then, are these educational psychologists "up to", and what practical help can they give to parents, teachers, social workers, directors of education and school inspectors?

SAFEGUARDING MENTAL HEALTH

Suppose we consider the intentions first. We said that the educational psychologist is interested in studying the processes of learning. In fact, all his problems are concerned with the conditions and methods which lead to the most efficient learning. But what do we mean by "most efficient"? Most efficient for what purpose?

Conditions and methods may be most suitable for getting as much work as possible out of children and young people. On the other hand, they may be most suitable for encouraging to the highest possible degree the learner's physical and mental well-being, personal development and happiness.

Educational psychologists study both these aspects, but they are concerned mainly with the learner's well-being, personal development and happiness. Some examples from different stages of schooling will make this clear.

One of the greatest trials of the teacher of elementary arithmetic is teaching the process of subtraction. At least three methods can be taught. Which is the best? That is, by which method will most children work subtraction calculations most quickly and correctly? With modern methods of investigation, this question can be answered with reasonable confidence. Three large groups of children approximately equal in general arithmetical ability will be arranged. Teachers of approximately equal competence and enthusiasm will teach each group one of the methods in question for a sufficiently long period. A final test will be given to all these groups, and the results of each method will be compared. This experiment can be repeated in various parts of the country as often as is necessary to establish a verdict.

DANGER TO DEVELOPMENT

However, in England and Wales since 1902, children of less wealthy parents could get into Secondary ("Grammar") schools only if they passed an examination in Arithmetic and English the age of about eleven years. Therefore, there has been a tremendous pressure on headmasters to begin training pupils for scholarships at the earliest possible age. Now, suppose that the psychologist investigating the teaching of subtraction finds that no child below a certain "Mental Age"[1] succeeds in doing subtraction sums correctly by any method. Suppose, also, he finds that ability to do subtraction sums improves as the children grow older. In that case the psychologist will say that it is a mistake to make children do subtraction before they are ready to learn how to do it. If they are made to do so before they are ready, then their future development may be damaged.

A psychologist, K. Jackson, reporting recently on a group of children backward in reading, said:

"My experience tells me that we begin formal teaching of reading at too early an age. Interestingly enough, all these backward readers had stuck, as it were, at two-letter words. They were frozen and blank if asked to name letters. I found my greatest difficulty was to help them forget their dislike of 'letters' and the first few pages of a book—the memory of the first pages of a 'reader' where they first stuck. It was a real effort to build up a belief that they could reach a second page, and a third and fourth.

"Many children of eight and nine years who did not know the letters, or who could not tell them if asked, could draw the letters if I named them. . . . They seemed unable to name the letters themselves because the task was toned with memories of defeat and frustration in the early years, the inevitable reaction to a demand which was made before they were able or ready to perform it.

"Few children of five years old are ready, physically or mentally, to sit and look at printed passages and realize that they hold a message. The eye muscles are not ready; the active impulses of their bodies resent the passive attitude; the eager curiosity of their minds yields unwillingly to 'sitting-still'

[1] For explanation of Mental Age, see page 139.

methods of satisfying it. We get the results we ought to have expected."

There are, here and there, welcome signs that parents and the general public are becoming aware that the pressure of academic examination work in Secondary schools is seriously hindering the personal development and mental efficiency of many pupils. Instead of driving pupils harder, some education authorities are now changing the examination system. There is, in fact, a general tendency to adapt school work to pupils' powers, rather than to insist on every pupil conforming to some academic standard. For most of the factual evidence which has encouraged this change we have to thank the educational psychologists.

The educational psychologist is concerned first and foremost with the child's mental health, and that is closely bound up with bodily health. In these days of high-pressure schooling, the psychologist may be the child's last defence against overwork and exploitation in the pursuit of academic honours.

SCHOOL ORGANIZATION

Educational psychologists can also take a hand in the practical affairs of school organization. This contribution can be better understood in relation to the Education Act of 1944 and the changes in school organization going on in Great Britain since that time.

State Schools Reorganized. Very briefly, the Education Act of 1944 proposed the following scheme (see chart, Fig. 43):

(1) The school-leaving age is raised to fifteen years. It is hoped to raise it later to sixteen years.

(2) The title "Elementary school" is abolished.

(3) The State schools to be organized in a single comprehensive system, in three successive stages:

Primary—up to age eleven plus (i.e. eleven years, but not yet twelve).

Secondary—eleven plus to fifteen, sixteen, or eighteen.

Further—fifteen or sixteen to eighteen.

The Act required education authorities to make adequate provision for Nursery schools or classes to take children from two to five years of age. Attendance at these is not compulsory. It also provided for Special schools designed for children up to the age of sixteen who, because of some special disability, cannot be taught satisfactorily in the ordinary schools. (In Scotland the State schools have been organized in Primary and Secondary stages since 1899.)

The Further Education stage needs a word of explanation. All pupils must remain at school until they reach the age of fifteen. After that, some will continue in the sixth forms of the Secondary Grammar schools until the age of eighteen or nineteen. There they will receive a more advanced type of scholastic or technical training to fit them for entrance to Universities, Training Colleges, Technical Colleges and professional work generally. On the other hand, the majority of the pupils will leave the new Secondary schools at the age of fifteen to work at various trades. The Further Education scheme is for these pupils who leave full-time schooling at fifteen. They will be required to attend a County College part-time, i.e. for one whole day or two half-days during forty-four weeks of each year. In some cases, such as occur in remote country villages where weekly attendance is difficult, the

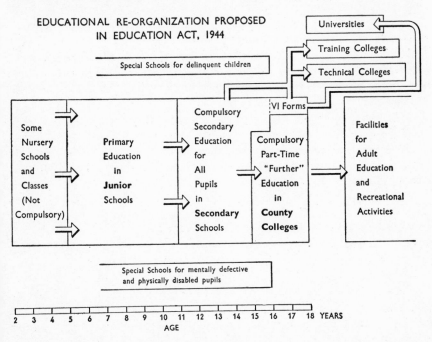

FIG. 43. *The State-school system* (England and Wales) *under the educational reorganization of 1944. The minimum school-leaving age will eventually be raised to sixteen years.*

young people may take their further education in one continuous period of eight weeks or in two periods of four weeks each. Some of the County Colleges, therefore, will be residential.

Some Problems of Reorganization. This scheme of reorganization raises problems which can be solved only with the help of psychological knowledge —such problems as the following:

What sort of schooling is best for the pupils in the Nursery stage (up to five years); in the Junior stage (from five to eleven plus); and in the Secondary stage (from eleven plus onwards)? Does each stage of schooling correspond to a stage of psychological development? If so, what are these development stages and what sort of interests do the children show in any particular stage?

In the Secondary school stage, can we treat all the pupils in the same way and try to make them all learn the same subjects?

This scheme was tried after 1902 and the results have been in many ways unsatisfactory. There are marked differences in ability and interest between one pupil and another, and these differences increase after the age of about twelve. It is becoming more and more certain that we cannot continue to give every pupil over eleven the same kind of bookish education as the Grammar schools have organized. In that case, what alternative kinds of Secondary education do we need? To answer this question we have to know something of the differences between pupils at the Secondary school stage, and what sort of schooling will suit each type.

Moreover, if we allocate pupils at the age of eleven plus, how are they likely to develop between eleven plus and fifteen or sixteen? Allocating children at eleven plus really means forecasting at that age what sort of young people they are likely to become four or more years later. Prophesying is never an easy task, and psychological prophesying is no exception to that rule. We shall need much more accurate knowledge than we now possess about mental development and abilities between the ages of eleven and sixteen years before we can satisfactorily solve this new problem of Secondary school allocation.

It is highly desirable to discover children who are backward and who will need special remedial teaching. The sooner these children can be discovered and segregated the more likely are they to respond to treatment. At what stage can backwardness and special mental defects be discovered? What sort of treatment is required for such children?

SOCIAL AND MORAL DEVELOPMENT

Delinquency. The psychological problems we have indicated above are concerned mainly with scholastic progress. In addition to this, the educational psychologist will be increasingly concerned with problems of social conduct and of moral development. These are, ultimately, problems of temperament, emotional balance and development of the personality as a whole. Problems of character, conduct and personality are always more difficult in an age of transition, when traditional ways of life and traditional values are breaking down and no new, thoroughly established values are available. Highly gifted, well-educated people may be able to find their way satisfactorily through periods of social change. For the average individual the task is much more difficult. In the smaller, more compact communities of the past, local custom and family life have been more settled and powerful in keeping discipline. Nowadays, the schools have to take over much of the social training formerly given in the family and the neighbourhood. What, then, are the conditions for successful social development? How can behaviour difficulties and delinquency be prevented or cured? Here again is a further set of problems which urgently need the skilled investigation of experts.

It may be argued that parents, clergy, teachers—the people in daily contact with children and young people in the circumstances of everyday life —are most able to solve problems of social development by common-sense methods, without the intervention of "theorists".

There are several obvious answers to this argument. "Common sense" is too often a matter of opinion rather than of factual evidence, too often self-contradictory. The trained psychologist uses improved methods of observation and measurement, and understands principles which help to make better sense of everyday experiences. Moreover, without any intention of malice, we may ask, "If common sense is such a satisfactory guide, why do the world's affairs in education as well as in other spheres get into such appalling tangles?"

The educational psychologist does not intend to by-pass parents, teachers, clergy or administrators, but to co-operate with everybody of goodwill in promoting the best conditions for learning and social development.

MORE PROBLEMS TO SOLVE

Relation between Growth and Learning. A new-born baby already possesses certain "ready-for-use" responses. If a pencil is placed across the palm, the hand immediately closes. If the cheeks are touched, the head is moved in order to bring the mouth to the object, and the baby begins to suck. As it grows older, some of these ready-for-use responses continue unchanged—sneezing, sucking and swallowing, for example. Others seem to disappear, the seeming disappearance being due in many cases to the fact that simpler actions have been absorbed into and made part of more complicated actions. Continually, from birth until development ceases, new and more complicated actions appear. For example, the eyes of the new-born baby do not move together, as do the eyes of older children and adults. A few days after birth, however, the two eyes begin to move together. At first both eyes fix on the same object, but the baby does not keep a *moving* object in sight. Later, the ability to follow a moving object appears. Still later, the baby begins to put out his hands to touch and grasp the object he looks at.

During the first weeks of life there is nothing we can call instruction, training or practice, as we usually understand these processes. Nevertheless, the baby's behaviour changes. The changes we mentioned in the preceding paragraph appear to happen spontaneously, in much the same way as the healthy child grows in height and weight. It seems, therefore, that growth itself plays a part in learning something new. We need to find out how this growth takes place and how it affects learning. It is absurd to try to teach a child before he can learn—yet many people make this absurd attempt.

Should Children be Seen but not Heard? The healthy child is active and inquisitive and, as he grows older, boisterous, sometimes destructive, often noisy. He may be obstinate at times. He develops well-marked likes and dislikes. What value shall we attach to this active, exploring, romping behaviour? Is it just a waste of energy, or is it necessary for the child's physical and mental development?

To what extent ought we to indulge the child's interests, as Rousseau suggested? Is child-play educationally valuable or just waste of time? Do we spoil the child if we spare the rod? Should little children be seen but not heard? Are children naturally lazy, or will they work at a task when they are interested in it?

The answers to these questions will make a vast difference to the sort of schools we build, and to the teaching methods we use. Contrast, for example, the methods illustrated in Figs. 56 and 57.

What is Ability? What is the relation between various abilities? Are all children who are dull more than usually clever with their fingers? Are very clever children always weaker and less healthy than the average? Both these views have been widely accepted as true.

What do we mean by ability? Do we find general all-round ability; or do we have to deal with a few, or with many, specialized abilities, e.g. mathematical ability, mechanical ability, artistic ability, musical ability, manual ability? Are these abilities related to each other, or are they independent? Do children who can do Arithmetic well always do well in Grammar or essay-writing?

PERCEIVING AND REMEMBERING

How does a child perceive or observe the world around him? Does he begin with a rough idea of a whole situation or pattern and then discover more and more details within it; or does he seize first upon little details and gradually put these together to make up a total experience? In teaching children to read, ought we to show them whole sentences or whole words before we teach them the letters, or should we start with the alphabet and then put the letters together to make syllables and then words, thus: a–t is "at"; b–a–t is "bat"; t–e–n is "ten"; b–a–t–t–e–n is "batten". Which method is more interesting and more efficient? This problem is most important in dealing with backward readers and spellers.

Memory and Memorizing. What is a good memory? How do we recall what we have learned? Which is the best way of memorizing: reciting, writing, reading aloud, reading silently? Do we remember all sorts of experiences equally well, or do we remember some experiences better than others? Is memory like a photographic plate, or is it more like a process of digestion? What is the effect of interest on memorizing?

Again, suppose we "train" our memory by learning Latin verbs; shall we be able to memorize telephone numbers, or chemical formulæ, or fat stock prices better than if we had not been made to study Latin?

Finding the Best Teaching Methods. Are some methods of teaching subtraction or spelling, or handwriting, or a foreign language, better than others? How can we find which are the best methods? Is there only one good method for teaching every child, or does the efficiency of a particular method depend on the teacher who uses it, and on the type of child taught?

METHODS OF EDUCATIONAL PSYCHOLOGY

Having looked at some of the problems, we ought now to ask about methods. How does the educational psychologist obtain the facts with which to answer these questions we have noted?

Like other scientific workers, he uses special methods of observation and he makes experiments. We will describe briefly some of the more common types of observation and experiment.

Methods of Observation. Two methods of observation are commonly used, namely, the "longitudinal" method and the "cross-sectional" method.

In the longitudinal method, observations and measurements are made one after the other *on the same children* over a long period. These reveal changes in behaviour, the times when new interests and activities appear, and when some earlier interests and activities disappear. They also show how fast children develop. The traits studied may be physical, e.g. growth in height and weight; intellectual, e.g. increase in powers of memorizing and reasoning, or changes in the length of sentences used in speech and writing; or emotional, e.g. changes in fears, in aggressiveness, in co-operative attitudes.

In the cross-sectional method of observation, groups of children all of about the same age and period of development are studied at the same time. This method reveals what characteristics children have in common. Cross-sectional surveys have dealt with what children know (or do not know) when they are old enough to go to an Infant school; what school subjects Junior and Senior pupils like best, and what children do with their spare time.

SCIENTIFIC ASSESSMENT

Scientists do not like arriving at their conclusions by guesswork. They want to measure accurately what they are studying. Guesswork is misleading. Too often we guess what suits our purposes (or prejudices) and ignore what does not.

We must make experiments and measure as accurately as possible in order to get rid of guesswork in observation.

It is not always easy to measure in psychology. We need some suitable "weights and measures". We can count how many words a ten-year-old boy or girl can say in three minutes and how many mistakes in spelling a typist makes for every hundred words she types. But it is not so easy to measure accurately how obstinate, co-operative, aggressive, or meek a child is. We may be near enough to the mark for ordinary affairs if we say that

131

MISSING WORDS

Read these, and put in the words that are left out. Like this :—

Grass......IS......green.   We hear with our......EARS......

Now do these. Put just ONE word in each space.

1. Mother...father have gone out.

2. A dog..four legs.

3. The moon gives...at night.

4. There are...days in one week.

5. A boy has eight fingers and..thumbs.

6. My teacher writes on the board with............................... .., but

7. uses a..to mark our books.

8. Six boys ran..of the room.

9. There are..months in one year.

PUT A LINE UNDER THE RIGHT WORD

Read these sentences, and put a line under the right word. Like this :—

Jack and Jill had a pail of (cheese, water, flour).

The boy ran (down, up) to the bottom of the hill.

Now do these. Put a line under just ONE word in each bracket.

10. A fire is (cold, hot, wet).

11. Children should sleep for ten hours every (night, week, afternoon).

12. A pen is used for (writing, sewing, swimming).

13. I am two years (younger, older, taller) than my mother's youngest child.

14. We found, on returning to the market, that prices had (dropped, risen) still (higher, wider).

15. He said that the (weight, length, cost) of the box was one (cubic yard, gallon, hundredweight).

[GO ON TO NEXT PAGE

FIG. 44. *Specimen pages from the Schonell Intelligence Test—a group test of*

Now answer these questions : Put your answers in the brackets.

88. A basket full of apples weighs 15 pounds. The basket when empty weighs 3 pounds. How much do the apples weigh? (............)

89. Three times an unknown number is one less than forty. What is the unknown number? . . . . . . (............)

90. I bought a number of books on Monday, four times as many on Tuesday and eight on Wednesday. In all I bought twenty-eight books. How many did I buy on Tuesday? (............)

Kitty was born three years before Peter. Peter is four years older than Jill, and two years older than Tom. Tom is seven years old.

Now answer the following questions :—

91. Who is the eldest of the four ? . . . . . . (............)

92. How old is Kitty? . . . . (............)

93. In how many years' time will Jill be as old as Kitty is now? . (............)

94. In how many years' time will Kitty be twice as old as Jill? . (............)

Mary, Jane and Dora had a bicycle race. Dora gave Mary 10 minutes start, and Jane 6 minutes start. Mary arrived at the winning post first, Jane arrived 3 minutes later and Dora 7 minutes after Jane.

Now underline the correct answers to these questions :—

95. Is Mary slower than Dora? (*Yes. No. I cannot tell.*)

96. Which of the three is the fastest? (*Mary. Jane. Dora.*)

97. How much longer than Jane did Mary take?

(**1** *minute.* **3** *minutes. Mary did not take longer than Jane.*)

I am twice as old now as I was three years before my twenty-first birthday. My father is 25 years older than I am.

98. How old was my father when I was born? . . . . (............)

99. How old is my father now? . . . . . . (............)

100. In how many years' time will his age be three times the difference between us? . . . . (............)

general intelligence devised by Professor Fred J. Schonell, of Birmingham University.

133

John is always co-operative, James sometimes, Robert scarcely ever. These vague guesses are useless for psychological purposes.

We want *units* of some sort before we can make accurate comparisons For example, we may need to compare the stimulating value of praise or blame and its effect on children's output of zeal and work. We could deal fairly easily with a problem concerning the value of different amounts of chocolate as rewards, since the incentive here, the chocolate, can be measured out accurately in units. The effect of a reward of one ounce of chocolate can be compared with the effect of two ounces, or with three or any other number of ounces.

It is difficult, however, to devise units of praise or blame, and we are not at all sure how many "units" of praise are equal in effect to a three-ounce bar of chocolate.

Approximate estimates of the "quantity" of praise or blame may be got by using standardized words or phrases indicating indifference, mild praise, warm praise, or very flattering praise. Absolute units and quantities of praise are at present impossible to define and arrange. Psychologists are continually trying to invent suitable units for improving their measurements.

COUNTING METHODS

It is possible to measure some traits of character, such as attitudes (e.g. co-operativeness, aggressiveness), by counting methods. A parent may say that his child is very co-operative, or only slightly aggressive, but the educational psychologist will want to know more exactly *how* co-operative or *how* aggressive the child is. Approximate answers to these questions may be got by putting the children concerned always in the same kind of surroundings and then taking samples of the behaviour in question. In some experiments, observers watch children through a one-way screen. They can see the children, but the children cannot see the observers. In the case we are considering the observers will count the number of co-operative or aggressive actions which the child makes in, say, half an hour, at different times of the day. In this way a rough estimate of the child's average co-operativeness or aggressiveness may be obtained. This counting method is illustrated in the following report (quoted by Kimball Young in *Handbook of Social Psychology*):

Two playground supervisors, A and B, were first observed in their management of a group of children at play. Both gave the children direct commands about 60 per cent of the time. For about 16 per cent of the time they gave a command only after a child had asked for a direction. They handled only about 12 per cent of the situations by guiding a child to an activity through praise, or by making their preference known in a friendly way. In only about 5 per cent of the situations did they give the child some responsibility for choosing what should be done. After instruction and training in democratic methods, A's use of the authoritarian method dropped from 77 per cent to

4 per cent, and the more democratic method of supervising play rose to 73 per cent. (The supervisor B was not specially trained in democratic methods of playground supervision, and his methods remained unaltered.)

Suppose we want to find out whether some new baby food on the market is really effective. Merely giving it to a few babies and observing their growth will not tell us much. If the babies are healthy and the food relatively harmless, they will grow by natural causes whatever the food may be. For all we know, the food may be keeping them back somewhat.

CONTROL GROUPS

In cases like these we have to use what are called "control groups". To find whether some kind of baby food is as good as breast milk we need one group of babies all fed on the food, and another (the control) group *as much like the first group as possible in every way*, except that they are fed upon breast milk instead. Any decided difference in this case is probably due to the food, particularly if we find that it occurs nearly always.

Similarly, we need control groups if we want to compare methods of teaching and learning. An experiment was performed some years ago to find whether special practice in one type of memorizing (e.g. memorizing multiplication tables) improved some other type of memorizing in which the pupils had no special practice (e.g. memorizing poetry).

Some London Primary school children were given a number of memory tests, and on the results of these tests they were divided into four groups equal in size and, on the average, possessing equally good (or bad) memories. Three of the groups had a period of special memory training every day. The fourth, the control group, carried on with the usual school work, and did not receive special training. The only difference between the trained groups and the control group was this period of special training. At the end of the training period all four groups were given some more memory tests similar to the first. But it was found that, although the three trained groups had improved in several other memory operations besides the one practised, so had the control group to about the same extent without any special practice. This meant that the special practice in memorizing "tables" or poetry daily for about three months had produced no effect on the other types of memory tested. In the absence of the control group, a part of the improvement observed in the practised groups would undoubtedly have been credited to the practice—but quite incorrectly.

"Scales" for Measuring Intelligence and School Attainment. One of the most important of recent problems in Educational Psychology has been the invention of reliable "scales" for measuring intelligence and attainment in various school subjects. The need for such scales arose in connexion with special educational methods for backward children. In the case of a child who is supposed to be backward it is desirable to know whether the child is, in fact.

135

7 YEARS

Kate is cleverer than May:
May is cleverer than Jane.

Who is the cleverest—Jane, Kate, or May?

8 YEARS

The person who stole Brown's purse was neither
dark, nor tall, nor clean-shaven.
The only persons in the room at the time were:

1. Jones, who is short, dark, and clean-shaven:
2. Smith, who is fair, short and bearded:
3. Grant, who is dark, tall, but not clean-shaven.

Who stole Brown's purse?

9 YEARS

In cold, damp climates, root crops, like potatoes and turnips, grow best:
In temperate climates, there are abundant pastures, and oats and barley
flourish:
In sub-tropical climates, wheat, olives, and vines flourish:
In tropical climates, date-palms and rice flourish.

The Ancient Greeks lived largely on bread, with oil instead
of butter: they had wine to drink and raisins for fruit.

Which climate do you think they had?

10 YEARS

The doctor thinks Violet has caught some illness.
If she has a rash, it is probably chicken-pox, measles, or scarlet fever:
If she has been ailing with a cold or cough, she may develop whooping-
cough, measles, or mumps.

She has been sneezing and coughing for some days: and
now spots are appearing on her face and arms.

What do you think is the matter with Violet?

FIG. 45. *An example of a Graded Reasoning Test, showing typical items selected from a group
test of reasoning power in children, devised by Sir Cyril Burt. The ages prefixed to each item*

11 YEARS

Father has just come home in a brand-new overcoat
There is clay on his boots and flour on his hat.
The only places he can have been to are Northgate,
Southgate, Westgate or the City: and he has
  not had time to go to more than one of these.
There is no clay anywhere in the streets, except where
  the pavement is up for repair.
There are tailors' shops only in Southgate, Westgate,
  and the City.
There are flour-mills only in Northgate, Westgate and
  the City.
I know the roads are not being repaired in the City,
  though they may be in the other places.

Where has Father been?

12 YEARS

I started from the church and walked 100 yards:
I turned to the right and walked 50 yards:
I turned to the right again and walked 100 yards.

How far am I from the church?

13 YEARS

A pound of meat should roast for half an hour:
Two pounds of meat should roast for three-quarters of an hour:
Three pounds of meat should roast for one hour:
Eight pounds of meat should roast for two hours and a quarter:
Nine pounds of meat should roast for two hours and a half.

*From this can you discover a simple rule by which you can tell from the
weight of a joint for how long it should roast?*

14 YEARS

John said: "I heard my clock strike yesterday, ten minutes before
the first gun fired. I did not count the strokes, but I am sure it struck
more than once, and I think it struck an odd number."

John was out all the morning from the earliest hours: and his clock
stopped at five to five the same afternoon.

When do you think the first gun fired?

are those at which the average English child is capable of answering questions of the type and
level of difficulty indicated in the example. For further details see pages 139 and 142.

backward and, if so, by how much; also whether the backwardness is general throughout all the child's work or only in some special ability, e.g. Arithmetic or Spelling or Reading. (See development charts in Figs. 53 and 54.)

Judgement of ability or attainment made on personal impressions may be very misleading, even when made by experienced teachers. So much depends on the standard with which the pupil in question is compared. A very clever person tends to underrate an average pupil. Adults of average intelligence tend to overrate children's abilities. A child of average ability appears to be backward in comparison with a group of clever children, whereas the same child would appear to be well advanced in comparison with a class of "duffers". Moreover, many teachers' judgements are based on what they, in their wisdom, believe that children at a certain age *ought* to be able to do if only they were not so lazy. The educational psychologist wants to know what children at a given age can actually do, apart from what adults believe they ought to be able to do. Standards and methods of testing which do not depend on individual teachers' peculiarities are required.

THE BINET SCALE

This problem was first solved satisfactorily by a French psychologist, Alfred Binet, between 1900 and 1905. He used a principle which may be called "achievement-for-age". This can be understood by reference to a practice well known in English Board schools in the 1890s. These schools were divided into "Standards", from I up to VI or VII. Usually, pupils entered Standard I at the age of seven and remained for one school-year in each standard. The syllabuses of work were prescribed for each standard by His Majesty's Inspectors, and teachers were expected to keep strictly to the schedule. In this way, a teacher knew what a child of any given age ought to be able to do if his progress had been "normal". If a child of nine to ten years could do no more than Standard I work, he was obviously two years behind the average attainment. If he could do Standard IV work, he was about one year ahead of the average. By this rough-and-ready scale the attainments of a pupil and his rate of progress relative to the average could be judged. This rough scale was made into a scientific instrument by using standardized test questions instead of a syllabus which merely represented the personal opinions of an Inspector of Schools concerning what ordinary children ought to be able to do successfully. Examples of "achievement-for-age" scales are to be found in Figs. 45 and 46.

Binet's original "scales" of intelligence have been revised and adapted since his death, mainly by Burt in England (1919) and by Terman (1919) and Terman and Merrill (1937) in the U.S.A.

Making a Standardized Test. To make a standardized test the psychologist first tries to get clearly in mind what he wants to test. It may be general intelligence or reasoning power. It may be school attainment in Reading or in

138

Composition, in Spelling, Handwriting or Arithmetic. The psychologist will then collect a set of problems or questions which appear likely to assess the ability or attainment in question. He tries out these preliminary questions on a large number of children in conditions like those in which he wants to use this test later. Some of the questions will be too easy, some too difficult for children of a particular age. Some will be found unsuitable for the special ability which is to be tested. By trying them out first of all on pupils the original questions can be arranged in order of difficulty. Some of them will probably be discarded and new ones brought in until the whole test is sufficiently reliable. By "reliable" we mean that if a test is applied twice to the same pupils it will arrange them in substantially the same order of merit on both occasions.

In all this preliminary work with tests, the psychologist is trying to discover what the *average* child of any particular age can actually do. Then the scores of the average children of three years, four years, five years and so on up to the top limits of the test become a standard scale for measuring the relative development or the educational attainment of a particular pupil who tries the test.

We shall have to refer later to different kinds of standardized tests and their uses. It is desirable at this stage, therefore, to look at some examples.

Individual or Group Tests. Some standardized tests are made to test individual children one at a time. Others can be given to large groups at the same time—a much quicker process, although perhaps not quite so accurate.

Intelligence or Scholastic Attainment Tests. Some standardized tests are made to test intellectual power; others put more stress on scholastic attainment. The pupil's score in a test of intelligence or intellectual power measures his Mental Age. The score in a test of school attainment indicates his Educational or Attainment Age. (To be strictly accurate we should say "Intelligence Age" or "Reasoning Age" rather than "Mental Age". However, this last phrase has now passed into common use.)

A GROUP INTELLIGENCE TEST

Part of a group test of general intelligence is shown in Fig. 44. To succeed in this the pupils must be able to read, write and do some simple arithmetic. In addition, however, they must be able to follow instructions, think clearly, reason correctly and know the meaning of what they read. The test requires the power to think and to apply knowledge rather than dependence on memorizing what has been taught. It is a test of *general* intelligence, since it assesses various kinds of intelligent responses.

This test is intended for pupils of between seven and twelve years of age.

An example of another kind of test is Sir Cyril Burt's Graded Reasoning Test, a few selections from which are given in Fig. 45. This is a group test of a more specialized mental power, namely, reasoning. Before each

Age last Birthday						Number of words
4	to	is	of	at	he	
	my	up	or	no	an	10
5	his	for	sun	big	day	
	sad	pot	wet	one	now	20
6	that	girl	went	boys	some	
	just	told	love	water	things	30
7	carry	village	nurse	quickly	return	

FIG. 46. *A test devised by Sir Cyril Burt which is designed to assess accuracy in reading. The test comprises one hundred and ten words, arranged in order of increasing difficulty. The child reads each word in succession until he can read no further. The number of words correctly*

140

50	60	70	80	90	100	110

scarcely belief steadiness labourers serious

9 projecting fringe luncheon nourishment overwhelmed
urge explorer trudging events motionless

10 economy formulate exhausted contemptuous renown
universal circumstances destiny glycerine atmosphere

11 perpetual emergency humanity **perambulating** ultimate
apprehend excessively domineer theory reputation

12 physician fatigue philosopher melodrama autobiography
constitutionally champagne encyclopedia hypocritical efficiency

13 melancholy exorbitant influential terminology palpable
mercenary contagion fallacious binocular microscopical

14 atrocious phlegmatic refrigerator unique alienate
eccentricity ingratiating subtlety poignancy phthisis

read represents his degree of reading ability. The figure in the left-hand margin indicates the age at which the average child may be expected to read the words adjacent. Results obtained with this test indicate that, age for age, girls are on the whole better readers than boys.

141

question we have added the corresponding "Reasoning Age". For example, it was found by trial with a sufficiently large number of pupils that 50 per cent of seven-year-olds could answer the first question correctly. That question represents the reasoning power of the *average* seven-year-old English child.

Examples of Scholastic Attainment Tests are: *Burt's Graded Word Reading Test* (see Fig. 46, on pages 140 and 141) and *Burt's Graded Handwriting Test* (see Figs. 47 and 48, on pages 144–147).

The test shown in Fig. 46 is printed on a card. This is handed to the child to be tested and he is invited to read the words until he is unable to read any further. From the position on the test at which he breaks down his "Reading Age" can be estimated. This Reading Age indicates the particular child's attainment in Reading as compared with the attainment of the average child.

HANDWRITING TESTS

It is possible also to construct standard scales for judging the quality of handwriting. Professor Burt describes the construction of his Quality of Handwriting Test thus: "The children were required to write, as carefully as possible, in ink on unruled paper, first, a prescribed sentence containing all the letters of the alphabet; and, next, all the capital letters in order. The scripts written by children of the same age were then, first of all, ranked in order of general legibility; where general legibility appeared approximately equal, they were ranked in order of general æsthetic merit; where both legibility and æsthetic merit appeared approximately equal, the samples were compared in certain detailed aspects taken one by one; and the sample excelling in a majority of these aspects was rated most highly.

"From the whole series thus graded nine specimens were then extracted (varying in order from best to worst). We thus secure scales for measuring individuals in terms of the average of their own age-group."

The samples shown illustrate the middle specimens (half-way between best and worst) for the ages six to seven, ten to eleven, and thirteen to fourteen (see Figs. 47 and 48).

Development and Attainment Quotients. If we know a child's Mental Age or his Scholastic Attainment Age, we can find his quotient for intelligence or for scholastic attainment. The Intelligence Quotient is found by dividing Mental age by birthday age and multiplying the result by 100:

$$\text{I.Q.} = \frac{\text{Mental Age}}{\text{birthday age}} \times 100.$$

This quotient is useful since it indicates how fast or how slow has been the child's progress in comparison with that of the normal or average child. For example, a child of ten years (birthday or calendar age) with a Mental Age of eight years has an Intelligence Quotient (called I.Q., for short) of 80 per cent. That means that he has developed in intelligence, up to the present, only 80 per cent as fast as the normal child (whose I.Q. is taken to be 100). On the other hand, if a child of ten years by birthday age scores a Mental Age of fourteen years in a standardized Intelligence Test, his I.Q. is 140. He has developed in intelligence 40 per cent faster than the average.

The I.Q. is important because, if it remains constant, it enables the psychologist to estimate in advance what the pupil's future progress is likely to be. Many experiments have been made to find whether the I.Q. does, in fact, remain constant. The results so far are not conclusive. If (and only if) the environment and general social conditions of the pupil remain the same, then in the majority of cases the I.Q. is relatively constant over a period of two or three years. In some cases, however, considerable variations have been known to occur, for reasons which are not yet fully understood. Predictions based on Intelligence Quotients need to be read with caution, and where there is any reason for doubt a pupil should be retested.

NEED FOR CAUTION

In view of a marked general tendency to interpret Mental Ages and Intelligence or Attainment Quotients too precisely, it is necessary to say, quite bluntly, that these "mental scales" are not like micrometer gauges, guaranteed to give readings within a few ten-thousandths of a unit. Mental scales give only approximate estimates, and that is all the competent psychologist claims for them at the present time. If in one test a pupil's Mental Age be given as thirteen years, it is quite possible that the same pupil may score, in a very similar test a month or so later, a Mental Age of twelve years eight months, or thirteen years four months.

In actual fact, the best available standardized tests do give reasonably consistent results if they are administered and marked strictly according to the prescribed instructions, in circumstances for which they have been standardized. Constructors of standard tests will not publish them until they have made sure by repeated trials that the tests are up to an acceptable standard of reliability. But no educational psychologist would dream of claiming that an I.Q. of 80 or 147 is as accurate a measure as a height of 5 ft. $7\frac{1}{2}$ in., or a weight of 7 st. $12\frac{3}{4}$ lb. When a psychologist who knows his business sees the statement that pupil A's I.Q. is 80, he assumes that if pupil A were tested *in standard conditions* by means of any reliable Intelligence Test his I.Q. would most likely lie between 70 and 90 and that it is most unlikely that he will ever score as low as 60 or as high as 100.

A second warning is even more necessary. Because a given item in a graded test has a Mental Age value of eight or of ten years, that does not mean that every child of eight or of ten years must be expected and made to answer it. The Mental Age value of any test item is the age at which that item is answered

FIG. 47. *In Burt's Quality of Handwriting Test, schoolchildren are required to write on unlined paper, first, a prescribed sentence containing all the letters of the alphabet, and, next, all the capital letters in order. The handwriting reproduced above, together with that on the next page, comprise one standard specimen of medium-quality handwriting, representing the attainment of an average child—in this case, one between the ages of six and seven years. A series of such standards, applicable to children of specified ages, is employed for assessing Mental Ages for Handwriting. Marking is carried out on a basis of legibility and æsthetic merit.*

144

successfully by the average or normal pupil. There is a deplorable tendency in some Primary schools, now that Intelligence Tests are being used in Secondary school entrance examinations, to attempt to coach children in answering test items; and the average age at which a test item is likely to be passed is taken to be the age at which any child, irrespective of his native capacity, must be *made* to pass that item.

This attitude is quite absurd. If we are told that the average height of English boys of eleven years is 4 ft. 6 in., we do not suppose that every English boy of eleven ought to be at least 4 ft. 6 in. tall. The very nature of the

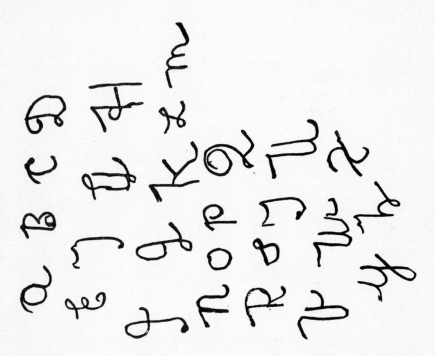

average means, in fact, that as many will be below as above that standard. And if we see some unfortunate individual of eleven years who is only 3 ft. 9 in. tall, we do not put him on to a stretching machine and try to pull him out by sheer force to a height of 4 ft. 6 in. Yet that would resemble what people who coach children in Mental Tests are trying to do. There are big differences in individual capacities and attainments. In any large unselected group of children aged eleven years, differences in Mental Age of from seven or eight up to fourteen or even fifteen years may be found.

Much care is necessary in the interpretation of mental test results. A good deal of the suspicion with which some people regard these measuring devices has been due to the irresponsible way in which the tests have sometimes been

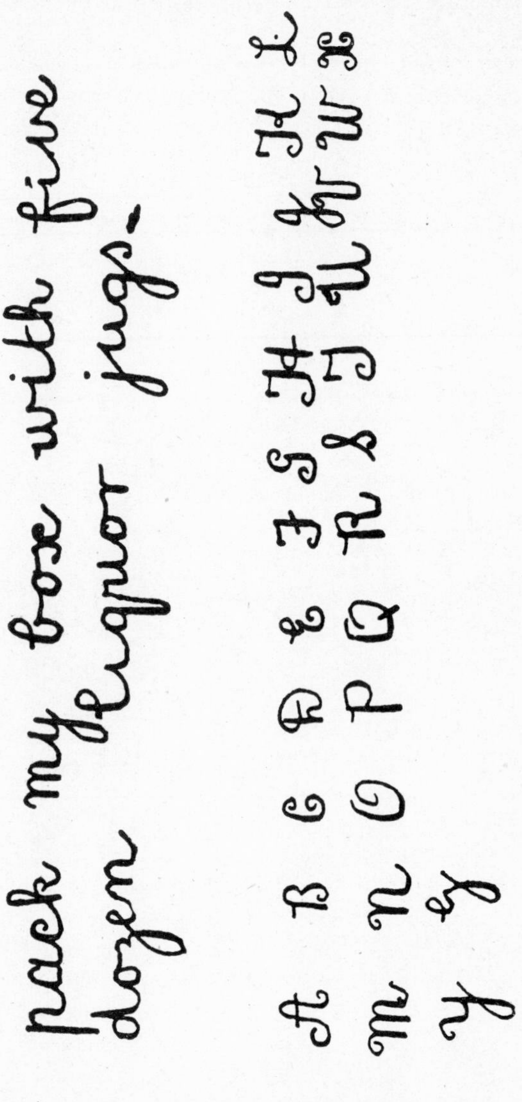

FIG. 48. *Further examples of schoolchildren's average, or middle-quality, handwriting, taken from Burt's Quality of Handwriting Test. These two specimens are employed as standards for judging the handwriting of children of* (left) *ten to eleven years and* (right) *thirteen to fourteen*

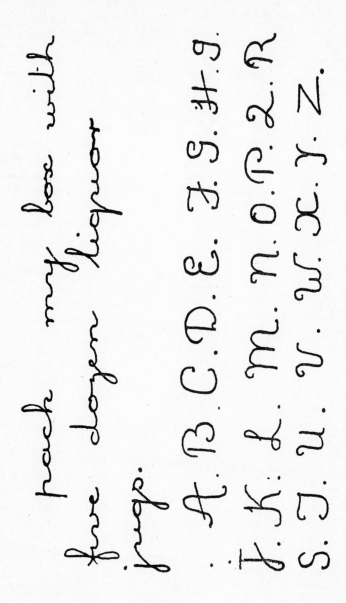

years respectively. In comparing specimens of children's handwriting with the standard specimens for their age, the principles upon which judgement should be based are, first, legibility; secondly, general æsthetic quality; and, thirdly, superiority in certain specified details.

used and the results interpreted. Nevertheless, when used with the necessary precautions and interpreted reasonably, these tests have proved indispensable for discovering above-average and below-average ability, and also in the treatment of children who have special disabilities.

CORRELATION

It is often desirable to know with some accuracy how different abilities are related to each other. This problem arises in the allocation of children to Secondary schools.

In choosing children from the State Primary schools for scholarships in Secondary schools it has been customary to arrange an examination at the age of ten to twelve years. This examination has consisted, for the most part, of two test papers, in Arithmetic and English Language. It is taken for granted that the children who succeed best at Arithmetic and English Language at the age in question will also succeed best in other subjects which they will later be required to learn in the Secondary schools. In other words, it has been taken for granted that the aptitudes required for success in Arithmetic and English are the same as, or closely connected with, the aptitudes required for Algebra, Geometry, Trigonometry, French, Latin, Geography, Chemistry, Physics, Biology, and so on. (The word "aptitude" is used here in much the same sense as when we say that "Mary has more aptitude for music than Jane, while Tom has no aptitude for it at all".)

This belief was accepted without much question by teachers mainly on account of a tradition that the mind (or intellect) was made up of a number of "faculties", each of which "looked after" certain types of performance. It was believed that there were separate faculties for memory, observation, imagination, reasoning and will. It was also believed that if these faculties were trained in any kind of work they would become *generally* more capable of dealing with many other kinds of work, without further training. Thus Science was supposed to train the faculties of observation, memory, reasoning, imagination. Latin was supposed to train all the faculties, including will-power, and therefore, according to the people who believed this, there was no need for a pupil to learn anything else at school but Latin. One well-known educationalist has said that if this principle was correct he could not see why the art of robbing orchards should not be preferred to Latin as a school subject; it exercised the same supposed faculties and, in addition, it was much more enjoyable for most boys!

It is possible that there may be some form of general aptitude which takes part in all intellectual operations, such as, for example, the general intelligence mentioned on pages 175-6. In that case, any examination which tested a pupil's degree of general aptitude (whatever that might be) would give some indications of his probable future success in any type of subject.

It is obvious that when entrance to Secondary schools, Universities, the

Civil Service and the learned professions depends so much on passing examinations we ought to know something about the nature of aptitude and abilities and about the relations between them. Up to quite recent times, this problem of mental abilities and their relationships has been settled merely by opinions, without reliable evidence. We need to know how closely any person's ability to pass a test in, say, Arithmetic or English Grammar agrees with his ability to pass a test in Science, Mathematics, History, or woodwork, for example.

Educational psychologists nowadays study this problem by measuring the degree of relationship between people's performances in various subjects or activities. This measurement of relationship can be done by means of a "coefficient of correlation".

The nature of the coefficient of correlation may be illustrated by the following example. Suppose we give a test in English Grammar and Arithmetic to a *large, unselected* group of pupils at various ages, then arrange the individuals concerned in order of merit according to their marks. If the teachers are equally good and the amount of time spent in study and practice is about the same in both subjects, we have three different possibilities: (1) the lists in Arithmetic might always come out in the same order as the lists in English, the top pupil in the one being top in the other, and so on down to the bottom of the list. In this case there would be a perfect *positive* correlation; (2) we might find that the top pupil in Arithmetic was always at the bottom of the English list and vice versa, in which case we should have perfect *negative* correlation; (3) we might find no more relation between the two examination lists than would have happened if we had drawn the candidates' names out of a hat at random. In this case we should have *zero* correlation.

Perfect positive correlation (the same thing as identity) is indicated by a coefficient of $+1$; perfect negative correlation by a coefficient of -1; and no correlation at all by a coefficient of 0. Varying degrees of correlation between 0 and $+1$ or -1 are indicated by fractions, expressed for convenience in decimal form.

Test Yourself

1. Does backwardness in reading imply a want of intelligence in a child?

2. A child on his tenth birthday reads successfully the first ninety words in *Burt's Graded Word Reading Test* (Fig. 46). What is his Reading Age? What is his Reading Quotient?

Answers will be found at the end of the book.

CHAPTER IX

INTELLIGENCE AND ATTAINMENT

WE HAVE reviewed briefly the educational psychologist's aims, some typical problems he is asked to solve, and some of the modern methods of observation and experiment by means of which he tries to collect reliable information. We must now consider some of the principles which have been established.

If the processes of development and learning in children were haphazard, not proceeding according to any plan, we could not possibly make predictions about any child's future development. We must have some idea of what we mean by normal development before we can say that any particular person is abnormal. We want to know whether there is a common order of development for the majority of children.

NORMAL DEVELOPMENT

Can we expect that most children will go through similar stages of development? When can we expect particular stages of development, interests and abilities to appear? We want a scale or "ladder" of development by which we can judge the relative standing of any particular child.

Actually, most parents use a rough scale of "normal" development by which they judge how forward their own children are and how backward the children of their neighbours. Some of the "marks" on this rough scale are quite familiar. Most children begin to cut their first teeth between six and eight months of age. If a child has teeth at the age of two months, or if no teeth have appeared by the age of twelve months, we begin to suspect that the child's constitution and development are not normal. The teeth appear usually in some kind of order—two front teeth at the top, two at the bottom; the back double teeth appear later. The first or milk teeth come out and the second set begins to appear at about six to eight years. The "wisdom" teeth do not usually appear until about the age of eighteen to twenty years.

Most children sit up at the age of about six months, then crawl, then pull themselves upright by the aid of the furniture, in that order. They walk at the age of about twelve to fifteen months. Most girls begin menstrual periods at about eleven to fourteen years, and in most women the periods cease between the ages of forty-five and fifty.

There are, of course, marked differences in *rates* of development; and in some cases the order of development appears to be distorted, usually to the detriment of the individual concerned. Nevertheless, much recent psychological study and experiment confirms the everyday belief in a common order of development. This is a principle of great importance. If there is a common order in physical development, there may be a common order in mental development. Detailed observation of children on a very extensive scale seems to show that this notion also is correct.

GROWING MUSCULAR CONTROL

Fig. 49 gives a summary of the order of development of certain forms of muscular co-ordination in children during the first year of life.

Inspection of this table shows certain interesting types of order: the muscles of the eyes, head and neck are first brought under control; then follow muscles of arms and upper trunk; hands and lower trunk; hip region, legs and fingers. Progress goes, that is to say, from the head downwards, and from the trunk outwards along the limbs, the muscles nearest the head and nearest the trunk being brought first under control.

Also, the actions develop from crude hit-or-miss movements to more and more accurate movements. This order of progression seems common to all babies. It is also found in lower animals.

Dr. Charlotte Bühler, after observing young children at play with various objects, says in her book *From Birth to Maturity*: "We were able to determine the following sequence. . . . From four to seven months the child handles only one toy; from seven months on, two toys. At first objects are shaken; then one is rubbed against the other; then hit against one another; then objects are thrown away. At ten months objects are put down with some care; at about one year forms (e.g. hollow blocks) are fitted into each other."

Each advance in muscle co-ordination means that the child has another way of getting new experience of his surroundings, which helps the development of his mind along a further stage of education.

MENTAL TESTS

Order in Mental Development. For our purpose here we need to know if there is also a common order of mental development. The extensive use of mental tests during the past few years seems to show that there is. As we have already said, mental tests are standardized by trying out the test items on a large number of children in order to find what the average child of any given age can do. Some standardized mental tests, therefore, like the well-known Binet Scale of General Intelligence, are really indicators of a natural order of mental development. By noting some of the sequences of test items we can see what appears to be a common order. The sequences can be followed more easily if we collect together test items of the same type, those for memory development, for example. The items in the following list are taken from Burt's revision of the Binet Scale (see *Mental and Scholastic Tests*). The examples show how the span of a child's memory increases with age.

Average Age	Test Items Which Ought to be Passed
Age 3	Repeats at least two of the following numbers correctly after the examiner: 3, 7 . . . 6, 4 . . .7, 2.
Age 4	Repeats six syllables: "I am cold and hungry." Repeats one of the following sets of three numbers correctly: 9 1 4 . . . 2 8 6 . . . 5 3 9.
Age 5	Repeats ten syllables: "His name is Jack; he's such a naughty dog."
Age 6	Repeats five numbers (one trial correct out of three): 5 2 9 4 7 . . . 6 3 8 5 2 . . . 9 7 3 1 8. Repeats sixteen syllables: "We are going for a walk; will you give me that pretty bonnet."
Age 8	Repeats six numbers (one trial correct out of three): 2 5 0 3 6 4 . . . 8 5 3 9 1 6 . . . 4 7 1 5 8 2. Reads without assistance a prescribed passage and recalls two items out of twenty.
Age 9	Reads without assistance a prescribed passage and recalls six items out of twenty.
Age 11	Repeats seven numbers (one trial correct out of three): 9 6 8 4 7 5 1 . . . 4 8 2 0 3 6 5 . . . 5 9 2 8 1 3 6.
Age 14	Repeats twenty-six syllables: "The other morning I saw in the street a tiny yellow dog. Little Maurice has spoilt his new apron."

Development of Word Ability and Comprehension. In Terman's Stanford Revision (1919) of the Binet Scale we find the sequence of test items, requiring ability to understand and use words, shown on page 154.

Inspection of this series of test questions will show certain sequences through which people pass in the development of their ability to understand and use words correctly:

(a) *Things* can be recognized and named before *qualities*, e.g. the average child of three years will name correctly penny, key, knife, etc., but cannot name ordinary colours correctly until five years of age.

(b) The average child can name certain *differences* at the age of seven years, but cannot state similarities until about a year later.

(c) The capacity to state correctly the meanings of *abstract* nouns, e.g. pity, revenge, charity, etc., does not appear in the average child before the age of about twelve years; and the capacity to state correctly certain differences between abstract notions such as "president" and "king" does not appear, on the average, until about fourteen years. (See accounts of the development of a sense of humour and the understanding of abstract statements on pages 162–5.)

In stating the meanings of words a common order of development is found. A definition test is included in the mental "scale" at the five-year level. At that age children will give definitions in terms of use, e.g.:

Chair: "To sit on"; "you sit on it".
Horse: "To drive"; "to ride"; "to pull the wagon".
Table: "What you put the dinner on."

At the eight-year level a second definition test appears, again requiring the meanings of common objects. At this age-level, however, a definition in the form of a description giving details of the shape, size, colour, etc., of the object is required, or a statement which tells the class to which the object belongs. The difference between the five-year and the eight-year level is shown in the following examples:

A Tiger

Eight-year level: "It is a wild animal of the cat family."
"It is an animal that lives in the jungle."
"It is a wild animal."
"It looks like a big cat."
Five-year level: "To eat you up"; "what eats people."

LANGUAGE DEVELOPMENT

Dr. A. F. Watts, who has made careful studies of language development in children, says that the order of appearance of the various parts of speech in children's talk is roughly as follows:

1. Proper names, e.g. Ma-ma, Dolly.
2. Common names, e.g. chair, bed, cup, ball.
3. Simple connecting words, e.g. and, but, so.
4. Verbs and verbal forms of naming picturable occurrences, e.g. push, drink.
5. Prepositions and simple relational words, e.g. in, on, under.
6. Pronouns, e.g. I, me, his, your, mine.
7. Adjectives for naming qualities, e.g. red, tall.
8. Abstract nouns, e.g. length (of the cat's tail), sharpness (of a knife), brightness (of a light).
9. Adverbs, e.g. slowly, quickly, very, nicely.

Any parents with enough patience to listen carefully to their children's talk, from the time they first begin, and note down new types of words as the

Average Age	Test Items Which Ought to be Passed
3 years	Points to parts of body when these are mentioned by the examiner: nose, eyes, mouth, hair. Names correctly any three of these familiar objects: key, penny, penknife, watch, pencil.
5 years	Names correctly four colours: red, yellow, blue, green. Defines the meaning of any four of the following words: chair, horse, fork, doll, pencil, table.
7 years	Explains correctly the difference in meaning between any two of the following pairs of words: fly–butterfly; stone–egg; wood–glass.
8 years	States correctly any similarities between the objects named in the following pairs of words: wood–coal; apple–peach; iron–silver; ship–motor-car. Defines correctly any two of the following words: balloon, tiger, football, soldier. Knows meanings of 20 words in a standardized list of words.
9 years	Makes sensible sentences by using three given words, e.g. boy, ball, river; work, money, men; desert, rivers, lakes.
12 years	Knows meanings of 40 words in the standardized list. Can explain correctly the meaning of three of the following abstract nouns: pity, revenge, charity, envy, justice. Explains in what way the three objects named in each of these groups are similar: snake, cow, sparrow; book, teacher, newspaper; wool, cotton, leather; rose, potato, tree; knife-blade, penny, piece of wire.
14 years	Knows meanings of 50 words in the standardized list. Gives at least two differences between "president" and "king".
Average adult	Knows meanings of 65 words in standardized list. Gives differences between the pairs of words in three of the following: laziness and idleness; evolution and revolution; poverty and misery; character and reputation.

child begins to use them correctly, can make their own tables of speech development and compare them with Dr. Watts' suggestions.

It is still more significant that when deaf and dumb children begin to talk they go through a sequence of development similar to that found in normal children, although the changes appear at a much later age.

Order in Emotional and Social Development. By emotion is meant here the primitive aspects of experience and behaviour usually called anger, rage, temper, fear, affection, love, and such modifications of these as hostility, aggression, jealousy, grief, remorse, pity, anxiety, despair, joy.

The term "social" refers to the behaviour of children and adults in company with others; their attitudes towards other people in the home or school or neighbourhood.

EARLY SOCIAL BEHAVIOUR

Obviously a child's temper and social behaviour will depend very much on how other people treat him, on the number of other children in the family, on the type of home and on his own physical strength and toughness. Emotional and social development are, therefore, likely to be more complicated and varied than physical and intellectual development. Nevertheless, psychologists have found signs of a common order of development among children, and certain types of behaviour tend to appear at characteristic ages.

This fact, again, is commonly recognized by parents and older children. They consider it quite natural for the baby to scream and kick and fly into a rage without much provocation. If a child of seven or older weeps, sulks, screams, knocks his head against a wall without a very good reason, it is taken as a sign of abnormal behaviour. The youngster is told with some contempt: "Oh! do stop being a cry-baby." We are still more surprised and disturbed when adults behave in these childish ways.

Dr. K. M. B. Bridges, who studied the development of Nursery school children, states that she observed three stages of development in young children's relations with adults. In the first, or *dependent*, stage the child relies on adults for attention and assistance. In the second, or *obstinate*, stage, usually between two-and-a-half and three years, the child resists adult influence and strives for power and independence. Later, at about the fourth or fifth year, the child normally reaches a more *co-operative* stage. He desires to gain approval and avoid disapproval. Conversation develops. Instead of protests and personal demands, the speech changes to descriptions of events and actions which the child is interested in sharing with friendly adults.

Quite frequently at puberty—normally between the ages of twelve and fourteen years—young people pass through an unsocial period. They withdraw into themselves and become moody and solitary.

There seems also to be a sequence of development in the children's relations with each other. Another keen observer of children, Susan Isaacs, has

I	II	III
AVERAGE AGE	EYE CO-ORDINATION	LOCOMOTION
6 days ...	Eyes follow a light ...	... ...
2 weeks ...	Eyes follow a person...	... ...
3 ,, ...	... ...	Holds chin up ...
5 ,, ...	Eyes follow a tape horizontally	... ...
9 ,, ...	Eyes follow a tape vertically	Holds chest up ...
10 ,, ...	Eyes follow a tape in a circle	... ...
14 ,, ...	... ...	... ...
15 ,, ...	... ...	... ...
18 ,, ...	... ...	Sits on lap ... ...
21 ,, ...	... ...	... ...
25 ,, ...	... ...	Sits alone, momentarily
28½ ,, ...	... ...	Rolls ... ...
30½ ,, ...	... ...	Sits alone for one minute
31½ ,, ...	... ...	Stands with help ...
41 ,, ...	... ...	Scoots backwards, lying prone
42 ,, ...	... ...	Stands holding to furniture
45 ,, ...	... ...	Creeps. Walks when led
47 ,, ...	... ...	Pulls itself upright by aid of furniture
56–62 weeks ...	... ...	... ...
62 ,, ...	... ...	Stands alone ... ...
66 ,, ...	... ...	Walks alone ... ...

FIG. 49. *The progressive development in eye, hand, trunk and leg co-ordination displayed by infants from six days after birth to the age of sixty-six weeks. Development proceeds from*

156

IV FINER MOTOR CO-ORDINATION	V MOTOR PLAY	VI PARTS OF BODY BROUGHT UNDER CONTROL
... ...	... ...	Eyes, head and neck
... ...	... ...	
... ...	... ...	
... ...	... ...	
... ...	Smiles at person ...	
... ...	... ...	
Reaches and touches	... ...	Arms and upper trunk
Grasps an object ...	Plays with own hands	
Holds an object ...	... ...	
Grasps a dangling object	Puts object to mouth	Hands and lower trunk
Transfers object from one hand to other	Plays with own toes	
... ...	Pats toy	
... ...	Rocks; shakes head	
... ...	... ...	
... ...	Pat-a-cake	Hip region, legs and fingers
Points with first finger	... ...	
... ...	... ...	
Opens simple boxes	... ...	
... ...	Puts fingers into holes	
... ...	... ...	
... ...	... ...	

the head downwards. This table is from a contribution by May M. Shirley to the Handbook of Child Psychology *(2nd edition, 1933), Clark University Press, Massachusetts, U.S.A.*

INTELLIGENCE AND ATTAINMENT

described the development of group feeling. At first children are individualists. "If there were, say, a dozen children playing in the garden or school-room, not more than three or four, occasionally five, would be taking any friendly notice of each other." Children under five or six cannot be said to play together. They play alongside others, sometimes demanding that the other children act as audience or assistants. At this age any group of children above three or four in number will not keep together unless an adult takes charge and organizes the play. Not until the Junior school period, between about eight and twelve years of age, do children spontaneously join together into larger groups or "gangs". Then, quite often, the group is formed, not so much because the children want genuine co-operation with each other, but rather because they band together to assert their independence of adult authority. There is a fashion at this stage for "secret societies" in opposition to the "government".

In her *Social Development of Young Children*, Mrs. Isaacs suggested that this "gang" stage is an important step forward towards mature adult co-operation. "The mutual support which the children give each other in this common action towards grown-ups is part and parcel of their growth towards co-operation and love within the social group. . . . Not until after six or seven years does it become stable. . . . Loyalty to his fellows becomes the child's chief virtue, and the grown-up is largely shut out of the intimate circle of feelings and values. Every group of boon companions of ten to twelve years of age will have its 'secrets' (and very often a secret 'language'), jealously guarded from the prying eyes of adults. Their morality is largely a morality of equals—but of equals banded together against the tyrant adults. These may be tolerated and respected, and may if they are sensible and 'decent' even be raised to the pedestal of heroes. But they will rarely be admitted to the inner fellowship of the children." (See also Kenneth Grahame's book, *The Golden Age*.)

PARENTAL UNDERSTANDING NEEDED

These broad stages of social development concern parents very closely. Normal parents want the love and devotion of their children. If a child is obstinate, defiant, or secretive the parent feels hurt or annoyed. Many parents, unfortunately, endeavour to bribe or coax the loyalty and devotion of their youngsters. Others treat any resistance as an affront to their dignity and authority, and try to enforce loyalty by threats or punishment. By doing this they make the child's allegiance to his gang stronger and more intimate than before. If parents can realize that there are these normal phases of social development which may involve obstinacy, resistance to authority or secretiveness, and can understand that the majority of children show them —and pass through them safely—they will find it easier to treat their sometimes exasperating family with more tolerance, goodwill and sympathy, and will reap the reward of a return to more active loyalty, affection and co-operation during the adolescent period.

If children of between nine and twelve years are wrongly handled, what would be in most cases a passing phase of "awkwardness" may become permanent hostility towards the parent or teacher.

EARLY SEX CHARACTERISTICS

Certain broad phases of development are noticed in sex behaviour. Up to about six or seven years, boys and girls will mix together in play and school work with little awareness of sex conventions. As the children grow older, the two sexes tend to separate. By the age of ten or eleven most boys show some antagonism towards girls and regard with profound contempt any boy who prefers girls and girls' occupations. He is a "sissy". At about thirteen to fourteen, girls (whose sexual development occurs earlier than boys') begin to show more interest in the opposite sex. They are more ready to organize dances, parties and other social activities. Most boys at this age have to be coaxed or wheedled into these activities with some difficulty. Their interest in girls begins a year or two later. This "experimental" stage is followed by more serious pairing-off and, later, by adult relations.

SIGNIFICANCE OF ORDER IN DEVELOPMENT

This order of development, of which we have given some typical examples, is important because it appears to be independent of particular environments.

From an educational point of view, this is a principle of first-rate importance. It introduces the problem of timing in educational practice. Anybody who measures at regular and frequent intervals a child's progress in learning realizes that it seems to go in spurts. There are times when the child improves very rapidly with a minimum of practice and special training. At other times much practice and training make little difference to the rate of improvement. Learning to walk, or talk, or understand jokes are cases in point.

"Thus," says Professor C. W. Valentine, in his *Psychology of Early Childhood*, "my little boy B was able to understand and use the number 'two' at the age of about two years to two years three months, but although I was constantly coaching and testing him, he could not use the number 'three' until about nine or ten months later, as was shown by his responses in practical tests. Preyer's son, after using two words together, was a year older before he used three words together." Dr. R. R. Rusk also has reported that he could not get his little daughter to use the number "two", despite constant encouragement, until nine months after she had used the number "one".

A striking experiment has been reported by an American psychologist, Arnold Gesell. He had in his clinic a pair of girl twins, whose physical characteristics—height, weight, illnesses, reactions to medical treatment and

159

general development—had been remarkably similar. One of these twins, called twin T, was given a course of special training in stair-climbing. The other, twin C, had some training at a later age. The course and results of the experiment can be summarized as follows:

The training of twin T began when she was forty-six weeks old. She practised ten minutes daily for six weeks in climbing a short stair. At forty-eight weeks she climbed the stair for the first time with slight assistance; at fifty-two weeks (i.e. after six weeks' training) she was fairly proficient.

PROPERLY TIMED TRAINING

Meanwhile, twin C had had no training. At the age of fifty-two weeks she could not climb the stair, even with assistance. At the age of fifty-three weeks, without training, she climbed to the top without assistance in 45 seconds, seven times during the first successful trial. She was then, at fifty-three weeks old, given two weeks of training. At the age of fifty-five weeks she climbed the stair in 10 seconds.

Twin T, at the age of fifty-two weeks, had climbed the stair in 26 seconds, that is, after six weeks of training.

The comparisons between the progress of the two twins are highly suggestive to educators. It is obvious that the training did produce some effect on twin T. She climbed in 26 seconds at the age of fifty-two weeks as a result of the training, as against twin C's time of 45 seconds at the age of fifty-three weeks without training. But two weeks of training at the age of fifty-three weeks to fifty-five weeks was much more effective on twin C than *six* weeks of training on twin T at the age of forty-six to fifty-two weeks. By waiting until twin C was ready for training the training time was reduced to one-third, with a higher efficiency. Moreover, even at the end of the training period, twin T's progress was largely crawling, whereas twin C climbed up. In other words, the premature training of twin T had fixed an infantile, inefficient method which was detrimental to the child's final performance. Note that from birth to the beginning of this experiment the development of these twins had been extraordinarily alike.

Of course, one short experiment on one pair of twins is not a sufficient foundation for a scientific principle. These results have been confirmed, however, by several other experiments on larger groups of children. It appears, therefore, that there is a best period of development, during which a certain amount of teaching and exercise will produce the greatest results in learning progress.

Why the Common Order of Development? The young of every species of animal, and not merely of mankind, seems to pass through a characteristic order of development. This fact suggests that the order in question is due to heredity.

Growth and development depend very much on the brain and nervous system, and on hormones—substances produced and secreted into the blood-stream by the ductless glands, e.g. thyroid, pituitary and adrenal glands.

The connexion between development of the nervous system and development of natural skills has been studied by means of surgical operations in certain lower animals. An American embryologist, Coghill, studied the development of a species of newt with microscopic accuracy. These newts first wriggle through the water by making a succession of C bends right and left alternately. Later they swim like little eels, with an S-like motion. Still later they leave the water, after growing legs, and walk. Coghill showed that in no case did any of these animals progress from one stage of locomotion to the next until the nerves responsible for co-ordinating the movement had reached a certain level of maturity.

BRAIN MATURITY

Psychologists believe now that the order in mental development depends to a very great extent on the "maturation" (that is to say, natural "ripening") of the brain and nervous system; and that what a child can learn, and the speed at which he can learn it, depend on the extent to which the maturation process is complete at that particular time.

We know that the brain and nervous system of human babies are not mature at birth. They continue to grow for years. One investigator studied the growth of brain and nervous tissue in lambs which walk at birth, puppies which walk at about three weeks, and human infants, in whom walking is usually well-established by the age of eighteen months.

A part of the brain called the cerebellum controls walking and balance. This anatomist examined specimens of lambs, puppies and babies at birth and, in the case of puppies and infants, at various ages up to the usual time of walking. He found that certain changes in the cerebellum associated with walking were complete in the lambs at birth, in the puppies within three or four weeks after birth, and in human infants not until about the age of eighteen months. On the other hand, the brain-centres for breathing, sucking, moving the eyes together instead of separately, and grasping matured much earlier.

In the report of the Consultative Committee on the Primary school it is said that certain facts which have emerged from comparison of the fetus (the baby before it is born), the new-born baby and the adult human being have an important bearing on the problems of education. In any particular part of the cortex (the outermost layers of the brain) the single layer of the fetus of four months develops into three layers. The three layers are distinct at birth and it is the outermost layer, the last to appear, which grows most noticeably during childhood. In any form of "amentia" (a condition in which the mind fails to attain normal development, e.g. idiocy, imbecility), it is the outer layer which fails to develop. In any form of "dementia" (a condition of mental decay) this outer layer, which was the last to appear, is the first to go. This layer, which seems to be associated with the growth of intelligence, increases in thickness in the normal child between birth and maturity by more than 50 per cent.

Moreover, this development of the original layer into three does not take place in all regions of the brain at the same time. It happens first in the part connected with movement, later in the part connected with seeing, still later in the part connected with thinking and reasoning. The part of the brain which, it is believed, takes care of the more complicated forms of learning and thinking is the last to be fully developed.

The connexion between this growth in brain and nervous system and the progress in Mental Age is too close to be due to mere chance. It explains such facts as those reported by Valentine and Rusk (page 159) and the increasing ability, as children grow older, to deal with abstract arguments and

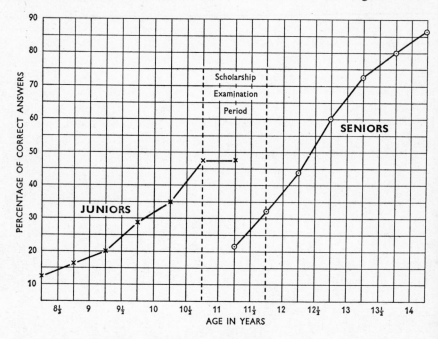

FIG. 50. *The rate of progress with age in understanding a joke.*

logical relationships revealed in the following tests by Watts, described in his book, *The Language and Mental Development of Children.* He says that the extent to which a reading performance depends on the maturity of the reader may be illustrated, perhaps, in another way. Occasionally a sense of humour is necessary for the full appreciation of what is read. With this in mind the following anecdote was read to about a thousand children.

UNDERSTANDING A JOKE

Two men once met in a narrow passage where there was not enough room for both of them to pass each other easily.

"Will you please make way?" said Mr. A, who had got there first.

"Certainly not," replied Mr. B. "I'm not going to make way for a fool."

"Very well," said Mr. A, "then I will."

And he at once stepped aside.

The children were then asked to say which of the following answers is the best reply to the question, "*Why did Mr. A step aside?*"

(*a*) Because he knew that he was a fool.

(*b*) Because this was a good way of showing that Mr. B was a fool.

(*c*) Because he saw that Mr. B was angry.

(*d*) Because he did not know better.

The results are shown in the table below:

JUNIORS		SENIORS	
Age	*Percentage of correct answers*	*Age*	*Percentage of correct answers*
8 to 8½	12	11 to 11½	21·5
8½ to 9	16·1	11½ to 12	32·1
9 to 9½	20·3	12 to 12½	43·7
9½ to 10	28·7	12½ to 13	60·1
10 to 10½	34·8	13 to 13½	72·4
10½ to 11	47·2	13½ to 14	80·1
11 to 11½	47·8	14 to 14½	86·0

The apparent discrepancy between the results of the juniors and of the seniors is due to the fact that the junior group had not yet sat for the entrance scholarship examination for the Secondary schools. The senior group consisted of older pupils left after the brightest juniors of eleven-and-a-half years had been "creamed off" and sent to Secondary schools.

The *rate* of increase in percentage of correct answers can be judged more readily if the results are set out in the form of a graph, where this rate is indicated by the steepness of the line (see Fig. 50).

Several significant facts are indicated by this graph.

(1) Some bright children of eight-and-a-half can see the joke—about one in every eight. They have developed faster than usual.

(2) In the juniors, before the brightest pupils are "creamed off" by the Secondary school entrance examination, the *rate* of increase in this ability begins to rise more sharply at the age of ten-and-a-half years.

163

(3) In the less bright seniors the period of most rapid increase in the ability occurs at the age of about twelve-and-a-half years.

(4) The ability is correlated (see pages 148–9) with Mental Age, which is a measure of brain development rather than of school attainments as such. (Note also the fact that there is practically no improvement in the ability to see a joke between the ages of ten-and-three-quarters and eleven-and-a-quarter. Is this due to the stultifying effect of "examination pressure"?)

Thus it would seem that the natural aptitude for this type of ability approaches maturity in the brighter pupils at the age of about twelve years and in the average pupils at about fourteen years.

In another experiment Watts tested the increase-with-age of ability to understand abstract statements. The test was arranged as is shown below, but the reader will understand that only a part of the test is reproduced.

Do You Understand What You Read?

1. Each of the sentences in the left-hand column can be matched with one that has nearly the same meaning in the right-hand column.
2. See if you can arrange them all in pairs by giving each sentence in Column 2 the same number as the sentence in Column 1 which is most like it in meaning.

	1	2
1	It was an eloquent testimony to their organizing ability.	The doctor can sometimes prevent you from getting certain diseases by vaccinating you.
2	Compulsory morality is no morality at all.	They did not want to face the facts, it was quite plain.
11	For the educated all phenomena are inter-related.	It spoke well for their power of getting things done.
20	Immunity from infection may be developed artificially by inoculation.	Wise men tell us that everything which happens is somehow connected with everything else.
	(*20 statements in Column 1*)	(*20 statements in Column 2—in random order*)

This is a searching test of understanding what is read. Obviously, success will depend upon schooling, and opportunities for reading and discussion—that is, upon environmental advantages. Nevertheless, in the same type of schooling and environment we find a wide range of ability to score in a test like this—a fact which indicates that inborn capacity and the natural growth of brain are also involved.

Watts found the following average scores (at different birthday ages) in the pupils he tested:

Age	$11\frac{1}{2}$–12	12–$12\frac{1}{2}$	$12\frac{1}{2}$–13	13–$13\frac{1}{2}$	$13\frac{1}{2}$–14	14–$14\frac{1}{2}$	$14\frac{1}{2}$–15
Average score	5	6	7	9	11	14	17

The trend of this development shows up more clearly in the graph (Fig. 51). Again we find the ability to understand abstract ideas increasing more rapidly at about the age of thirteen and still more rapidly after fourteen. Incidentally, the relation between these test results and raising the school-leaving age to fifteen or sixteen is too obvious to need emphasis. If the majority of pupils in the country leave organized schooling at the age of fourteen years they leave just at the time when the power to understand logical relationships is developing most rapidly. This is a shocking waste of teaching time and our national intelligence, and is nothing less than an educational calamity.

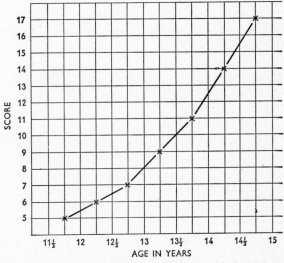

FIG. 51. *Graph showing the development of the ability to understand abstract statements.*

Learning-Readiness. The probability that there is a common order of intellectual, emotional and social development is a matter of first-rate importance to educators.

All the evidence accumulated during the past few years shows that children and young people between birth and maturity pass through certain phases (or stages) of development. If we study the progress of learning in any child, we find that there are certain periods in which the child shows strong interest in certain types of activity, and learns those activities much more rapidly and with less training than at any other time. In other words, children show periods of "learning-readiness". This idea has been illustrated by Gesell's experiments with the twins (pages 159–60), Valentine's attempt to teach his son numbers (page 159), and Watts' experiments on seeing the point of a joke and understanding abstract statements (pages 162–5).

We believe that this learning-readiness is connected with the growth of brain and nervous system. On the evidence now available, it seems that the periods during which learning takes place most easily are the periods when certain powers of mind and body are approaching their full maturity. Some powers ripen earlier than others. Common sense suggests, therefore, that we shall get the best results with the least amount of teaching and practising if we time the introduction of school studies to suit the stage of maturity of the pupils. It is exactly the same principle as that of regulating a child's food.

Educational psychologists now believe that we must adapt school work to children's mental development, just as we adapt their food to the state of their digestive organs. We can do this only if we know what powers are most likely to mature at any particular time in the majority of children.

MAIN STAGES OF DEVELOPMENT

Much of the work recently done by educational psychologists with standardized Intelligence and Attainment Tests has helped us to map out the common course of development into mental and educational ages, and to find out what sort of learning and school work is best suited to each Mental Age. Without going into any great detail, we can sketch out the main stages of development and the ages at which they are reached by average children. The course of development is roughly as follows:

From Birth to One Year. The child gradually comes to direct the movement of his hands in accordance with what he sees; but success in this takes some time to develop. He uses mouth and hands to explore objects surrounding him by means of the sense of touch. He begins to move about, mainly by creeping. (See Fig. 49.)

From One Year to Four or Five Years. The child explores a gradually widening neighbourhood as ability to walk develops, at first by using his newly acquired hand-control to grasp supporting objects, such as chairs, tables, rails, etc. He begins to speak, and talking gradually develops into conversation. The child's senses are not yet fully developed (e.g. he cannot read small print without eye-strain): he notices situations as a whole rather than small details. Hence he is willing to accept a broomstick as a "horse", a row of wooden blocks as a "train", a clothes-basket as a "ship", and so on. Much of his play thus consists of "make-believe". The girl "mothers" her dolls as though they were live babies.

From Five to Eleven or Twelve Years. The sense organs approach full maturity: the average child of seven to eight years can see, hear, touch,

166

taste, smell, and use his sense of muscular movement as accurately as the average adult. The child improves rapidly in controlling the smaller muscles, such as those which produce the delicate movements of the fingers and eyes in writing, first with a pencil and later with a pen. He also begins to be able to read smaller print, to draw details more accurately, to use crayons and water-colours, and to delight in constructing things with simple tools (hence the popularity of, at first, modelling-wax and, later, constructional toys). Owing to his increased powers of observing, the child now takes more interest in real things and explores his neighbourhood thoroughly. He likes to experiment and to "help" (not always successfully!) with routine jobs in the kitchen, the garden, the workshop, and the garage. He hangs wistfully around tradesmen doing repairs or redecoration in his home.

PERCEIVING RELATIONSHIPS

The child now realizes that fairy stories are fantastic, and demands true stories. He is inquisitive about number, size, measurements, and collects all kinds of odds and ends, useful and otherwise (e.g. cigarette cards, postage stamps, and nowadays even film-stars' photographs). He takes an increasing interest in Nature, especially in animals, and tries to keep tadpoles, minnows, white mice, rabbits, guinea-pigs, pigeons or bantams. Girls gradually abandon dolls in favour of kittens or a puppy. In short, this is a period of interest in the real world.

Towards the end of this period, as we saw when dealing with the capacity to see jokes and to understand logical (or abstract) relationships, the child begins to ask about cause and effect. He now begins to classify and arrange, in some "system" or other, things and events which up till now he has collected (either actually or in his memory) as separate items; he arranges and rearranges his stamps, cigarette cards, postcards, etc., and the mere process of classifying them in some order seems to give him satisfaction.

He also comes to judge time, and the relations between different periods of time, more accurately. This means, of course, that by the age of ten or eleven he begins to be able to grasp historical sequences and even to tolerate a few historical dates.

APPROACH TO MATURITY

From Twelve to Fourteen or Fifteen Years. This is a period of rapid change, during which most children grow in height—sometimes by as much as five inches in a single year. Children approach sexual maturity—girls somewhat earlier than boys. They acquire what are called "secondary sex characteristics" —breasts and broader hips in girls, beard and breaking voice in boys, pubic and axillary hair in both. These changes are accompanied by the growth of new interests, especially in social relationships rather than in material things. Many young people now become interested of their own accord in social,

167

moral, and religious problems, and choose ethical standards for themselves deliberately.

These profound changes in emotional development and social outlook seem to interfere, for the time being, with the course of intellectual development.

From Fourteen or Fifteen Years to Adult Maturity. When the bodily and emotional changes just described are complete, there follows a period during which the advances and gains of the preceding period are confirmed, reinforced, and made secure and stable, i.e. it may be called a period of consolidation. Each individual reaches the limit of his maturity in muscular development, physical strength, intelligence, and power of self-control. The young adult's interests turn to the choice of a career and the acquiring of the necessary qualifications (if any); to marriage, perhaps; and even, in some cases, to the exercise of his rights and duties as a citizen.

Significance of the "Ladder" of Development. In organizing school work along psychological lines the most important consideration arising out of the "ladder" of development sketched in the preceding pages is the relation between practical activities and book learning, or between doing things and imagining, thinking and reasoning about them.

It is a mistake to suppose that younger children cannot imagine, think or reason. They can, in their own simple ways. But—and this is the important matter for the parent and teacher—the young child's imagining, thinking and reasoning are always closely bound up with experience of real things which he can actually see, hear, touch and play with. As a result of actual first-hand experience with real things in play or in helping older people to do the everyday jobs of the neighbourhood, the youngster learns names; he talks about his experiences; he asks questions. Learning by doing is the proper sort of learning for children up to a Mental Age of nine or ten years.

LEARNING TO READ

It is only when the child has learned the names of familiar things and activities, qualities and processes, that he can begin to think and to "reason in his head" by using words instead of going through the actual experiences. Psychologists believe that a grave mistake has been made in teaching Reading, Writing, Grammar, and Mathematics in the Junior school period by means of words and books alone, before children are mature enough to deal with abstract words. Children will not learn to read readily, with interest and understanding, until it has dawned on them that the printed or written signs in the books actually stand for the objects and creatures they can see and touch, the food they can taste, the flowers they can smell, the sounds they can hear, the actions they themselves perform or watch other people perform. And all this does not dawn on them until they reach a Mental Age of about six years. At the same time, or possibly a little later, they begin to realize the meanings of numbers and understand the processes of simple Arithmetic. The time for formal Grammar and Mathematics comes later, somewhere about a Mental Age of eleven or twelve.

Of course, if children are made to work hard enough for a long enough time, all but the very backward can be taught to repeat bookwork by memory. That, however, is no guarantee that they understand and can use it intelligently. Knowledge which cannot be applied is all but useless. True knowledge requires understanding and appreciation as well as memory, and it is well known that the quickest way to memorize is to understand.

THE CURVE OF LEARNING

To make the best use of the facilities promised in the Education Act of 1944 we must press on resolutely with two reforms. We must provide more practical experience and activity for pupils in the Junior schools during the Mental Age period of from seven to eleven years. We must do the same for the pupils in the new Secondary school system whose Mental Ages are below average. The quickest way to realize the kind of schoolrooms we need for this purpose is to study carefully Fig. 56, and compare it with the other illustrations in Chapter X.

It would be wrong to suppose that these "stages" of development are clearly marked off one from the other. Children do not pass through one stage and then suddenly and abruptly jump into the next. If the reader will look back at the "progress charts" (Figs. 50 and 51) he will see that the graphs take the form of smooth curves or slopes, not that of steps or stairs. Progress is nearly always gradual and often intermittent. Some new reaction may appear on one or two occasions, and then it may not be observed again for months. Professor Valentine, in his book, *Psychology of Early Childhood*, reports several instances of this intermittent onset of development. He states: "A function ('function' here means an ability of some sort) will appear once or twice as though mature and ready for practice, and then will disappear for days or weeks before its next appearance . . . for example, a question by a child under three years would reveal a flash of the idea of physical causation, and then months go by without the idea appearing again." The same thing happens in the case of physical skills. The periods we have indicated in the various "ladders" of development (pages 166–8) are those in which, in average children, interests and aptitudes have matured sufficiently for successful steady exercise.

Moreover, the actual appearance of some particular ability or interest depends also on the opportunities offered by the environment. If conditions prevent the child from exercising an *aptitude* he will not be able to develop the corresponding *ability*.

Again, as we shall see when we come to discuss individual differences, some persons never reach full maturity. Their development may cease at a childish level. Because the power to think in words and in logical ideas appears most strongly after a Mental Age of eleven to twelve years, it does not follow that every child will think in abstract terms. Some persons do not reach a Mental Age of twelve years, even though they may live to be seventy or more.

Furthermore, even a well-developed, intelligent adult does not think and act always at the adult level. If, for example, a University professor is thinking about some theoretical problem or is addressing a rather solemn audience in a learned society, his thinking may be very logical and highly abstract. On the other hand, if he is enjoying a social half-hour around the common-room fire and discussing sport or politics or swapping stories, he may, and usually does, think in quite other than abstract, logical or scientific terms.

Finally, we have to take note of the fact of "regression". If an individual of almost any age above twelve months suffers a shock (grief, disappointment, terror), or loses his status (and at a later age his self-respect), or gets extremely angry, he may go back for the time being, or even permanently, to behaviour belonging to an infantile level of development.

In thinking about maturity and levels of development, these possibilities we have just mentioned must be kept in mind.

INDIVIDUAL DIFFERENCES

Hitherto, we have emphasized the existence of a common order of development and the psychologists' attempts to map out its normal course in terms of mental or development ages. Now, still keeping to the principle of adjusting learning tasks to the learners' capacities to deal with them, we have to take account of well-marked differences between one learner and another.

For practical purposes we can consider these differences within a few broad classifications:

1. Rates of development.
2. Level of development finally reached.
3. Types of ability—what we may call "talents" or "flair".
4. Temperament.
5. Character.
6. Physical strength, quickness, endurance and general health.
7. Home conditions.

People who study catalogues will be familiar with the notion of a "specification". All the bicycles in the world are built according to one general pattern. Within this general pattern, however, there are many variations in details of construction and in the qualities of the materials used. These variations must be understood by the prospective buyer if he wants to get a machine for a particular purpose.

Similarly, in organizing educational facilities, we can suit the facilities to the needs of individual pupils only if we have the individuals' specifications.

Such specifications can be set out conveniently in terms of classifications (1) to (7) above.

1. *Rates of Development*. Birthday age may be a very misleading indication of mental development. Mental Age is more satisfactory. By comparing Mental Age with birthday age we get a development quotient which indicates relative *rates* of development.

Thus, some children of ten years (birthday age) score a Mental Age of five years only, in a standard test of general intelligence. A small proportion of the child population—the feeble-minded and the idiots—score even less. Other children of ten years (birthday age) score up to fifteen or even more years of Mental Age in the same test. This means that, with respect to the capacities measured by the test in question, some children in ten years develop up to the level of the average adolescent of fifteen or sixteen years; others in the same time develop no farther than the average child of three, four or five years. The same principle holds good for other types of mental and educational development.

WIDE VARIATIONS IN PERFORMANCE

The very great differences in educational attainment which can be observed among school pupils of the same birthday age have been illustrated by Sir Cyril Burt with respect to English Composition. All the children between ten and eleven years old in the Primary schools of a London borough were asked to write an essay about G. F. Watts' well-known picture "Hope". What was judged to be the best essay out of about three thousand examined read as follows:

" Sublimely, majestically sorrowful she seems. Yet her name is Hope. Cowering low, not in submission to Fate, but longing for happiness, she sits, blindfolded; and fingers, lovingly and musingly, the one vibrating string of her lyre, striving to create sweet melody. The first beam of sunshine is kissing her feet; and in her inmost soul she wonders whether the time will come when it will kiss her drooping head.

"She is the good spirit of the world, and the ruler of the minds of those who dwell in it. In the darkest hour of night she visits us, and helps us to wait patiently for dawn and the light.

"Hope cannot read the future. But the morning star, the eye of Heaven, is a prophet; and though Hope cannot see it, she feels its light shining in her heart. It puts into her soul dreams of happiness, thoughts of the realization of her ideals, and the winning of eternal bliss.

"In the most unhappy moments of the life of man, she comes to him, drives away despair, and teaches him patience. She is like a sparkling and refreshing fountain to a thirsty flower, or a light seen in the darkness by some weary footsore traveller."

This essay was written by a girl aged ten years eight months (birthday age).

171

In the same test, the poorest essay, written under exactly the same conditions as the one just quoted, went as follows:

"Wos a pon a tim a putr of a lrg sitndan was out a bot ro stne no."

Translated into intelligible English, this would read: "Once upon a time a picture of a girl sitting down without any boots or stockings on."

This second "essay" was the work of a boy of about the same birthday age as the girl! So wide may be the variations of performance in children of the same birthday age.

What can be accomplished by exceptionally clever children is indicated by the following example reported by an American psychologist: A boy, eight years four months (birthday age); Mental Age, fifteen years seven months; Intelligence Quotient, 187. In addition to his ordinary school work, he had covered, with the guidance of his mother and the help of a tutor, some Geometry; Algebra as far as equations; reading of easy Latin passages; about two years' work in ordinary school French; simple conversation in Spanish and Italian. He had also made a beginning in Anglo-Saxon and Hebrew. At the age of thirteen this boy had already completed three first-year College courses. He became a Doctor of Philosophy at eighteen.

At the other extreme end of the scale of human development, we find imbeciles and idiots who never get beyond a Mental Age of two to four years.

INBORN ABILITIES

2. *Final Level.* The cases which have just been mentioned illustrate not only differences which can be observed in rates of mental development, but also differences in the upper limits or "ceiling" to which development attains. In some cases mental development proceeds at a rapid rate and rises to a high level. In other cases it proceeds very slowly indeed and ceases at levels representing the development we should normally find in young children.

These wide differences can be observed even in similar social environments. They must be due, therefore, mainly to differences in the inborn quality of brain and body tissues. Good education will enable the dull child to make the most of his limited intelligence. It cannot turn the dull child into a genius or even into an average pupil.

In organizing educational facilities to suit individual pupils we have to take account of these differences in rate of development and in upper limits of capacity. In the past there has been a marked tendency to neglect bright children who will pass their examinations in any case and to drive along the duller pupils in a desperate attempt to make them work beyond their natural abilities. We ought to ensure that every pupil, bright as well as dull, has the opportunity to work up to his limit.

General intelligence plays a very important part in a child's scholastic progress, particularly in the Junior and early Secondary school periods. It is important in allocating children to different branches of Secondary education, and for success in a job later. If we are interested in adjusting school work to pupils' abilities we ought to know approximately how many pupils we are likely to find in any large random group. By "random" it is meant that we take the children as they come, without specially selecting them.

This knowledge is a desirable check on personal impressions. After an exasperating struggle to explain some problem in Mathematics or Grammar, a teacher is strongly tempted to believe that at least three-quarters of the human race are congenital idiots. The temptation is particularly strong if the work is beyond the pupils' stage of maturity.

As a result of testing many thousands of children (in one Scottish experiment all the children born in Scotland in 1921 were tested), psychologists know how general intelligence is "shared out", so to speak. The numbers most likely to be found at each I.Q. level are shown in Fig. 52.

In any *small* group, such as the pupils in one school or in one classroom, we could not expect to find exactly these proportions. The children in small groups may have been specially selected. The results are affected also by the type of neighbourhood, the excellence or otherwise of the teaching, and the kind of test used. In very large groups, however, we can expect something like the distribution in Fig. 52.

A glance at this figure shows us that nearly half the total population will possess I.Q.s of between 90 and 110. These are the "normal" or average people. Also, we can expect about as many cases above 110 as we find below 90. Further, the proportions in each I.Q. level fall rapidly as we go farther from the average.

As we have said before, Intelligence Quotients must not be taken too

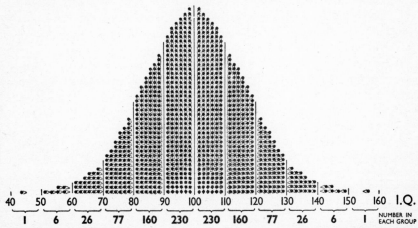

Fig. 52. *The distribution of general intelligence among schoolchildren. This graph-like figure shows how a group of one thousand British children, selected at random, would appear to an observer in the air if they were lined up in rows according to their Intelligence Quotients. These Intelligence Quotients are represented by the upper row of numbers.*

173

literally. Not all the children with I.Q. above 110 will do better in school than children in the 90–110 group. Physical health, regular school attendance, and temperamental qualities such as ambition, industry, persistence, cheerfulness and freedom from anxieties all count for much in school success. So do the personality of the teacher and the efficiency of teaching methods. A steadfast, persevering, ambitious child with a good home background and I.Q. of between 100 and 110 may do better in the long run than the happy-go-lucky, changeable or lazy child with I.Q. of 120 or more.

TOWARDS A RATIONAL CURRICULUM

Allowing for these factors, however, we find on the whole that children in the higher I.Q. levels (say, above 110) learn more easily and make more rapid progress in school work than children with I.Q.s of below 95. Those children who possess I.Q.s of 125 and above are likely to reach entrance scholarship standard for Secondary schools if they have suitable temperament and character qualities; those with I.Q.s of 145 or more are likely to reach high Honours standards in the University, given the opportunity. In particular, those pupils with high I.Q.s seem most capable of dealing successfully with abstract ideas, bookwork and "theory".

A word of warning is desirable here. It is sometimes taken for granted that people with low I.Q.s are abnormal, in the same way as a neurotic or lunatic is abnormal. This assumption is quite wrong.

A person with an I.Q. of from 80 to 95 may be a cheerful, sociable individual who can keep going with reasonable success in an ordinary, everyday environment where habitual experience in routine jobs only is necessary. If we keep in mind the notion of a common order of development, the lower I.Q. means that the person concerned has advanced along the common course of development more slowly than is usual and has ceased, at a comparatively low level, to develop any further.

These people break down when they have to tackle more complicated jobs requiring quick adaptation and theoretical knowledge. Since all pupils above the level of the certifiably feeble-minded will now proceed automatically to Secondary school education at the age of eleven or twelve years, it will be necessary to make Secondary education more practical and less bookish for a half to two-thirds of the total Secondary population. That reorganization is a practical problem of first-rate importance for the next generation. There are among the population of average I.Q.s important reserves of practical intelligence, initiative and good citizenship which we have not developed because schools have been preoccupied with "theory".

TALENTS

3. *Types of Ability.* People differ not only with respect to rate of development and the upper limits of capacity reached; they also differ with respect

174

to the kind of work they can do best. They differ with respect to what may be called talents.

Experts have been arguing for years about the real nature of human ability. The problem the psychologists have to solve may be put as follows: Have we only one general ability which takes part in every kind of activity? Or have we a few different abilities? Or do we use a special ability for every different performance? It may be, of course, that our total ability consists of a combination of all three types.

This problem has been attacked by the use of coefficients of correlation (pages 148-9). We can argue as follows. If all our performances whatever are due to one single general ability, then there should be a close connexion (i.e. a high correlation) between all of the same pupil's performances. If he does well (or badly) in Arithmetic, he should also do well (or badly) in Composition, Spelling, Drawing, Science, History, Geography, Handicraft, and other subjects.

If his performances depend on a few abilities, we should expect him to do well in one group of activities such as numerical calculations, or English Composition, Grammar, Spelling and Reading, or Handicraft and Drawing, with little or no relation to his success or failure in any other group of activities.

If we have a large number of separate special abilities, we should expect low correlations between any one performance and each of the others.

Thousands of trials with many kinds of test performances seem to show that all activities which require conscious attending, as distinct from rote-memory and purely automatic habits, are positively correlated, but in varying degrees. Some performances are highly correlated with each other. In other cases the correlations are low.

THREE KINDS OF ABILITY

The simplest explanation of these results is to suppose that human abilities are of three kinds:

(a) General ability, which takes part in every conscious activity.

(b) A few group abilities, each of which takes part in a certain group of activities. For example, there is evidence for a number ability, a verbal ability, a mechanical ability, and a manual ability. (Some psychologists have claimed to isolate other talents or group abilities, such as speed of action, reasoning, and judgement of space. There is less agreement about these than about the first four.)

(c) A large number of separate and independent specific abilities, each of which is concerned with only one kind of performance. Certain kinds of manual dexterity, judgements of tone, musical pitch, colour, taste or smell may involve these specific abilities.

The exact nature of the general ability (sometimes denoted simply by the letter "g") is not clearly understood. It may represent the readiness with which various parts of the individual's nervous system can work together as a team in any type of performance. Whatever may be the real explanation, there is no doubt that people with a high endowment of "g" possess the power of thinking for themselves. They can solve new problems and do not have to depend as much as the average person does on imitation and traditional knowledge. In particular, they can deal successfully with abstract ideas and logical relationships. They do not confine their thinking to the use of practical examples. They can also carry along as a system a large number of ideas at the same time, and apply these ideas quickly and accurately whatever the task they happen to be engaged upon. They can put two and two together easily and make four, as we say.

The Growth of General Intelligence. Making out a specification for an adult is not the same problem as making one for a growing child. General intelligence does not keep on growing. On the average it grows steadily up to a Mental Age of about fourteen. Then its further development slows down and quickly reaches its upper limit. That is true for the majority of people with I.Q.s of between, say, 90 and 110. In intellectually dull people, however, general intelligence ceases to grow sooner and stops at lower levels of capacity. In people with very superior intelligence, development may continue until twenty-one or more years of age. Nevertheless, the general intelligence—like height, for example—does not in any case increase indefinitely.

For educational progress during the growing years, general intelligence is more important than group talents or specific abilities. Tests show that the younger a child is the more closely correlated are his abilities. Group talents and specific abilities become increasingly important after the age of twelve or thirteen.

In many cases, specific abilities are not noticeable before Secondary school age. Yet talents and specific abilities will determine to a marked degree the type of career in which a particular individual is likely to find the best use for his abilities. Testing for talents and specific abilities is, therefore, particularly important in vocational guidance. (See Chapter XI.)

EXTROVERT AND INTROVERT

4. *Temperament.* We have already said that progress in school work and success in vocation and social life depend on qualities (or "traits") of temperament as well as on sheer intellectual ability. At the same time, it has been found much more difficult to invent any reliable tests for particular temperamental traits. Consequently, there is at the moment much less agreement among psychologists regarding the details of temperament than there is about the nature of intellectual abilities.

However, some important temperamental differences are easily noticeable in everyday life. In sizing up people for various types of occupation we invariably take these traits into consideration. A timid, anxious, cautious person is not likely to make a good commander of a tank squadron; nor is a carefree, reckless, happy-go-lucky individual likely to make a good research scientist. It is equally ludicrous to make a melancholy, pessimistic, bad-tempered, unsociable individual undertake the job of salesman or commercial traveller during a trade depression; or enrol a rash, hot-headed, highly-strung or "practical joker" type as a policeman.

We can get some insight into the meaning of "temperament" by considering certain typical pairs of opposites, e.g.

melancholy, pessimistic	cheerful, optimistic
sociable; easily gets on with people	shy, reserved, withdrawn, suspicious; finds personal relationships difficult
aggressive	meek
anxiously cautious	recklessly bold
excitable, irritable	placid, serene
shows quick reactions	shows slow deliberation
flexible, accommodating, adaptable	rigid, has fixed ideas

Most people nowadays are familiar with the terms "extrovert" and "introvert". These are traits of temperament rather than of intellect. They are often identified, quite wrongly, with gaiety and sociability or their opposites. Strictly speaking, the extrovert is a person whose interests are directed spontaneously towards the external environment of people and things. The introvert, on the other hand, is more interested in, and more clearly aware of, his own inner life—his thoughts, feelings and attitudes. These two traits are important for the choice of a career, for deciding what a person prefers to learn, and the adjustments he will make in marriage and other social circumstances.

CHARACTER

5. *Character Qualities and Traits.* Psychologists disagree about the exact meaning of "character". The term will be used here to mean power of self-control (or lack of it)—particularly power to put aside some immediate pleasure, either for the sake of a principle or ideal or to get some future advantage which seems more valuable than the immediate pleasure.

For the psychologist, character is strong or weak according to the degree of control. In everyday life, however, we often think of character as good or bad, depending on how far we agree with what the person in question does. If we combine these two judgements we get four character types: good strong—good weak—bad strong—bad weak.

Strong characters show the following traits:

Reliability—the person acts according to some principle rather than according to the whim of the moment. Reliable people always, or nearly always, act in the same way in similar circumstances. Their actions are predictable, whether we call them good or bad.

Persistence of action—the person keeps on with a task until it is finished, even after the original novelty interest has faded. Such people are not easily put off. They normally get what they want in the long run.

We normally include among the good character qualities industry and conscientiousness. The conscientious, industrious person will work seriously even when he is not being supervised.

These character traits and qualities are obviously very important, both in school work and social life. The "good" strong aspects of character make up most of what we should include in the "attitude of responsibility", so desirable in business and public life. The same aspects are favourable to educational progress. Pupils who show them will make the most use of whatever intellectual powers they happen to possess.

Character traits and qualities, therefore, must be included in our specifications. However, we are faced at present with the difficulty that there are few really reliable standardized tests of character. The traits in question can be estimated most readily by observing a person in everyday life, particularly when he is not under supervision.

HEALTH AND HOME ENVIRONMENT

6. *Physical Strength and General Health.* Our specifications must include estimates of health and physique. For many vocational purposes we need details of how tall, short, slim, or good-looking a person is. For educational purposes we require to know the level of vitality, energy, endurance, the susceptibility to disease, and the actual presence of a particular weakness or deformity. A weak heart, defective breathing (due, for example, to adenoids), tuberculosis, chronic catarrh, under-nourishment, lack of sleep or of fresh air and sunshine, defects of eyesight, or of hearing and muscle-sense, epilepsy—each of these will interfere seriously with educational progress.

Moreover, by putting a child under a continuous disadvantage compared with his more vigorous and fortunate fellow-pupils, such defects may have a serious effect on disposition, outlook on life, and social relations. It is by no means uncommon to find anti-social behaviour, even downright delinquency, due not to some original depravity or childish "cussedness", but to an attempt on the part of the victim to offset the feeling of inferiority or helplessness induced by a physical defect. In particular, if the defect is made a matter of public comment or ridicule, or if proper allowance is not made by parents or teachers, the pupil in question is very liable to become embittered. Then he seeks to "get his own back" on society in general by making himself a nuisance.

7. *Home Conditions.* We cannot complete our specification of an individual pupil unless we take account of home conditions. It is well known

that pupils from good home conditions, irrespective of sheer intellectual ability, succeed better on the average than less fortunate pupils (page 188). This is particularly the case in Reading, Composition, Vocabulary, and Oral Speech. The fortunate child travels more, gets more stimulating and varied experiences, discusses more, reads more, takes part in more practical everyday activities and games. In consequence he acquires better poise, more self-confidence, greater adaptability. His social relations are more satisfactory. There is more co-operation between home and school.

The children of well-to-do families have space at home in which to play, quiet rooms in which to read, books, paper, paints, modelling materials, tools, with which to express their ideas; and their time is less occupied with household tasks, particularly in the case of girls.

Obviously, then, in order to deal justly with a child's difficulties in school a teacher must know how much is due to inborn disability of intellect, and how much to home conditions over which the child has no control. It is deplorable to blame or punish a child because of something for which his parents or the general social system should be held accountable.

Moreover, we are beginning to realize nowadays much more clearly how important for a child's social and personal development are his relationships with his parents and the parents' relationships with each other.

The young child must have adequate affection. Mere regular feeding and hygienic conditions are not sufficient (see pages 190–2). The care which a child gets in a good home satisfies this craving for affection, and it helps to establish in the child a feeling of psychological security. It gives the child an assured status.

On the other hand, if the child is treated as if it were not wanted (its parents may have wanted a child of the opposite sex, for example), if parents quarrel persistently, if parents are separated, divorced or dead—these conditions tend to produce emotional tensions and conflicts which interfere with the normal development of the child's personality.

IMPORTANCE OF ORDER OF BIRTH

Other home factors which are known to be important for the development of personality are the number of children in the family and the order of birth. Most people realize well enough the effects of size of family and of the proportion of boys to girls, but effects of the order of birth are not so readily admitted. They are important, nevertheless. The eldest child has a different status from the intermediate children and the youngest. The eldest girl, particularly, may have to take on responsibilities beyond her years. The youngest of either sex tends to be treated by everybody as the "baby" until marriage; and then quite frequently these grown-up "babies" expect their spouses to carry on the tradition. The effect of order of birth and distribution of the sexes may be appreciated if one compares an only son who has three or four younger sisters with an only son who has several elder sisters. A person not acquainted with psychology may ask: "How on earth can it matter in school whether a child is on good terms or not with his parents?" It *does* matter, by reason of a psychological principle known as "transfer" or "displacement". If a child fears or dislikes a parent, he often adopts the same attitude towards other adults who in any way resemble the parent in question—if only by being in a position of authority over the child. The original emotional attitude is transferred or displaced from a parent to teachers, for example. Very often the displacement is quite unintentional. The pupil may not realize consciously what is happening. He merely feels that he fears Mr. X or loathes Miss Y, and he may imagine quite honestly several wrong reasons for this unfortunate state of affairs.

This psychological connexion between conduct and progress at school and conditions at home is the reason why it is necessary to specify home conditions, such as those mentioned above, in a pupil's records. Again and again it has been proved that home conditions are the most important factor in pupils' difficulties in school. Unless these home conditions are known and taken into account, little can be done to remedy matters within the school. The greatest possible co-operation between parents, educational psychologists, social workers and teachers is necessary. It is essential that these facts be stressed at the present time, in view of the unfortunate emotional attitudes taken up by many people. Any inquiry about home conditions may be called "snooping" and may be resisted on the assumption that parents have the right to do whatever they please with their own children.

EDUCATIONAL DIAGNOSIS

We can now discuss in greater detail two very important practical problems of school organization, namely, what type of Secondary school will best fit a given pupil on reaching the age of eleven or twelve years; and how to discover and remedy any special disabilities that may reveal themselves.

Types of Secondary Education. It is of interest to note that Secondary (Grammar) schools, which have a history of nearly a thousand years in Western Europe, were organized in the first place to train an intellectually clever minority of boys in Latin Grammar. To Latin Grammar have since been added from time to time Mathematics, Modern Languages, Geography, History, Literature, and Science. More recently, practical activities such as Handwork, Needlework, Housecraft, Gardening, Art and Music have been given a place in some Grammar schools, together with commercial and business training.

In spite of this apparent modernization of the curriculum, Latin and Greek and Grammar subjects generally still have a very high prestige in the majority of Secondary schools. The practical subjects are considered as extras to help duller pupils to pass the time and keep them out of mischief.

This system and this attitude are quite clearly unsuitable if all pupils over eleven must proceed to Secondary education. The new system of Secondary education for all will fail unless Secondary schools are organized deliberately to cater for all types of pupils according to their psychological needs. The pupils in the high I.Q. levels will still thrive on Mathematics, Grammar, theoretical Science and bookwork generally. It does not follow inevitably that these provide the best subject-matter, even for all the pupils with high I.Q.s. Nevertheless, they will be able to cope with such studies with adequate success.

The pupils in the average and lower I.Q. grades will not. It will not be satisfactory merely to give them the same educational fare as the high I.Q. pupils but in smaller doses. It is essential that their education shall contain more concrete activity, more closely connected with the interests and needs of everyday life. In addition, pupils with low I.Q.s and with special disabilities must have special skilled remedial treatment.

HOW TO SELECT?

First, then, how can we allocate children of from eleven to twelve years to the type and intellectual level of Secondary education best suited to their capacities and interests? This job has been done hitherto mainly by selecting pupils according to their success or failure in an examination consisting of one test in English and one in Arithmetic.

There may be some justification for this scheme. We have said above that there does seem to be some form of general ability. Moreover, English (in English-speaking areas) and Arithmetic are both general basic subjects which are needed in the mastery of several other subjects of the curriculum. And there is some evidence for supposing that a well-designed test in English and Arithmetic will pick out pupils of from eleven to twelve years with a relatively high endowment of general ability. In so far as the Secondary school studies follow the same plan and need the same general ability as the Primary school work, then the customary scholarship examination at these ages is likely to select the most promising candidates for Secondary education. If a well-designed and standardized test of general intelligence is included with the tests in English and Arithmetic, the three together may be a still more satisfactory method of selecting pupils with high *general* ability.

REVERSAL OF "FORM"

It has been found, however, by means of careful "follow-up" surveys, that by no means all the pupils who appear in the top sections of the entrance scholarship examinations at the age of from eleven to twelve years remain at the top during their Secondary school and subsequent careers. Matters are quite the reverse in some cases. There are several fairly obvious reasons for this reversal of "form". Some examination successes at the ages of eleven to twelve years are due to systematic and concentrated coaching in the Primary schools—"spoon-feeding" or "cramming", as it is called. The conditions of the examination tend to favour the older pupils. They have had a longer experience of being fed with a spoon, and more time to memorize.

GENERAL ABILITY NOT ENOUGH

We have also to take account of the other specifications discussed in previous pages. Total ability includes a good deal more than the general ability, even if that general ability is what we call general intelligence. There are also the group and specific abilities, and these group and specific abilities become increasingly important as the pupil reaches the birthday age of thirteen and upwards, that is, during the Secondary school period. It does not follow that the child of eleven who is particularly gifted at arithmetical calculation will be equally gifted at the higher stages of Algebra, Trigonometry, Geometry, Co-ordinate Geometry and the various other departments of higher Mathematics. In fact, some brilliant mathematicians are by no means clever at simple arithmetical calculations; and "lightning calculators" who can perform astonishing feats of mental arithmetic are not by any means always good mathematicians. Geometry, Trigonometry, higher Algebra —all demand special abilities, as well as general intelligence, for success.

Still more strongly does this argument apply to experimental Science, mechanical ingenuity and practical dexterity.

The fact is that a test in English and Arithmetic, even if supplemented by a general intelligence test, will give a sound prediction of future intellectual progress only with respect to the basic abilities which these examinations "sample". If one were a buyer for a wholesale clothing merchant, it would scarcely be logical to judge the styles and qualities of all the complete outfits of clothing by testing samples of hats and boots only, even if all the clothing had been made by the same manufacturer.

In addition to the problem of predicting intellectual progress, we also have to take account, in our specification of the eleven- to twelve-year-old pupil, of temperament, character, health, physique and home conditions.

The fact is that the more varied the scope of Secondary education, and the more diversified the "population" of children who go into it, the more comprehensive must be our specifications of individual pupils, if their allocation to the type of schooling best suited for them is to be made correctly.

On account of the principles just described, the evidence for which has been accumulated in the past forty years by educational psychologists, education authorities are now tending more and more to abandon single entrance examinations and to substitute for them methods of allocating pupils to Secondary education on the basis of cumulative record cards. It is desirable for the general public to understand clearly the reasons for this change, since their co-operation will be necessary to make the new system a success.

THE CUMULATIVE RECORD

The records are called cumulative because they will contain details entered yearly covering the whole of the Junior school period—some four or five years at least. Psychologists nowadays are very reluctant either to make or to accept predictions about scholastic ability and future progress, on the evidence of one examination only, in any subject, at the age of eleven. Mental development is not absolutely constant in individuals, although averages worked out for large groups may show constant trends. Variations which may be of great importance in judging individual cases are cancelled out when averages are taken. It is probable that much more accurate estimates of a child's abilities, interests, and most likely future progress can be made from the results of four years' observation than from one set of examinations lasting perhaps three or four hours on one day.

There will probably be differences in detail in the record cards made by different education authorities, but they will all need the following types of information:

1. Health and school attendance records.
2. Any special home conditions which may affect a pupil's educational development.
3. Results of standardized tests of general intelligence.
4. Estimates of group abilities based on school work and standardized tests, e.g. number, reasoning, verbal, artistic and manual abilities, and speed of work.
5. Records of attainment in the usual school subjects, e.g. reading speed, reading accuracy, reading comprehension; arithmetical calculation, arithmetical problems; spelling; handwriting; drawing, handwork.
6. Temperamental traits, particularly sociability, co-operativeness, quickness of response, readiness to anger or fear, excitability, recklessness, caution.
7. Character qualities, e.g. trustworthiness, persistence, conscientiousness, industry, self-control.
8. Outstanding interests, if any.
9. Noteworthy disabilities, if any.

SPECIAL DISABILITIES

People who cannot read, write and do simple Arithmetic are severely handicapped. Progress in school and in occupations later depends on ability to read and understand what is read. We cannot afford to let the backward readers jog along anyhow and take their chance. On the other hand, we shall not cure backwardness in Reading and elementary Arithmetic merely by making the pupils concerned spend more time learning their alphabet and multiplication tables. That is as stupid as is putting a sufferer from some obscure internal disease to hard manual work. We can help the backward children properly only if we know the causes of their backwardness. The treatment of a backward child calls for as careful diagnosis as does the treatment of a sick patient.

Uneven Development. The efforts of educational psychologists to map out the course of mental development in terms of Mental Ages and Development Quotients have brought out very clearly the fact that different mental powers and abilities develop at widely different rates in the same person, and the upper limits of ability reached by the same person may vary considerably according to the subject-matter concerned.

We have already discussed the different factors in total ability—the general factor ("g") which is closely connected with general intelligence, the group factors or "talents", and the many specific factors. This means that a pupil may have high general intelligence coupled with medium or low endowment of one or more talents, and medium or low endowment of several of his many specific abilities; or a pupil with medium or low general intelligence may have at least average or even higher development in some talent or specific ability. Development nearly always proceeds along a "broken front".

General intelligence is, of course, a decisive factor. The very intelligent person has a great advantage in that he can adjust himself better to difficulties and overcome any special disability. Moreover, high general intelligence is nearly always closely connected with reasoning power. The highly intelligent person, in other words, can make the most of what special abilities he does possess, and he can usually choose an occupation in which his special

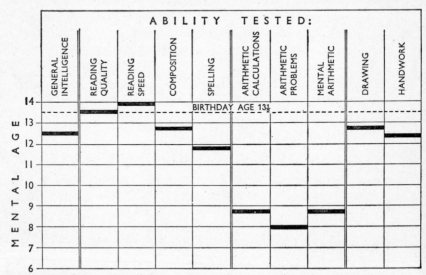

Fig. 53. *Development specification of a girl (birthday age,* 13½ *years), showing specific backwardness in Arithmetic. From "The Testing of (Intelligence", Schonell—Evans Bros.)*

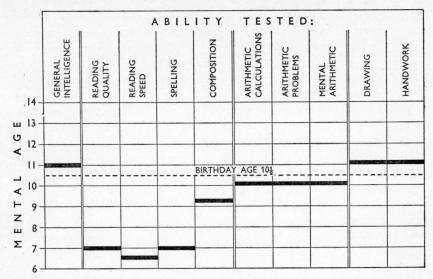

FIG. 54. *Development specification of a boy* (*birthday age*, 10½ *years*), *showing specific backwardness in Reading and Spelling.* (*From "The Testing of Intelligence"—Schonell.*)

disabilities, if any, do not matter. For example, the young genius mentioned on page 172 was weak in handwriting, but this did not trouble him very much. He soon learned to use a typewriter and he also dictated his homework to a secretary, even at the tender age of about nine years! A clever scientist, mathematician or administrator may be, and often is, quite bad at spelling and an abominable writer, but he can usually employ assistants to spell and write for him.

The person below average in general intelligence is in quite a different case. Even if he has a fair degree of some special aptitude, his lack of general intelligence prevents him from using it efficiently.

Professor F. J. Schonell classifies backward children into three types:

(*a*) Dull[1] pupils, whose backwardness is due mainly to intellectual deficiency. These children are invariably *generally* backward, incapable of making normal progress in most or all of their school subjects.

(*b*) Generally backward pupils who are not dull. These pupils are backward in most subjects, but the difficulty is not due to intellectual weakness, but to absence from school, frequent change of schools, bad teaching methods or adverse emotional attitudes.

(*c*) Specifically backward pupils, who are up to normal standard in most

[1]A pupil is considered dull when his I.Q. falls between the range 70–85; if it is below 70 he is considered to be mentally defective.

of their work, but very weak in one or two subjects. There may be about 11 per cent of these specifically backward children in the whole of the school population.

Figs. 53 and 54 illustrate two of Professor Schonell's cases of specific backwardness, the first in Arithmetic, the second in Reading and Spelling. (In the diagrams, the steps of the "ladders" represent Mental or Attainment Ages as measured by standardized tests in each of the subjects specified.)

Fig. 53 illustrates the case of a girl (birthday age, thirteen-and-a-half years; Mental Age for general intelligence, twelve-and-a-half years) whose ability in reading speed is that of the average fourteen-year-old pupil, but whose ability in arithmetical problems reaches no higher than an eight-year-old level.

In Fig. 54, the pupil, a boy (birthday age, ten-and-a-half years; Mental Age for general intelligence, eleven years), is normal for Arithmetic, Drawing and Handwork, but very backward in Reading and Spelling. In speed of reading this pupil could do no better than the average child of six-and-a-half years.

These two cases also illustrate very well the notion of relatively independent group abilities or talents (see page 175).

Finding in which subjects the pupil is backward is only the first stage in diagnosis. The next problem is to discover the precise causes of the backwardness. The difficulty may be due to faulty eyesight, hearing, or muscle sense. It may be due to defective perception or a poor memory. It may also be due to bad teaching, absence from school or emotional disturbance. Educational psychologists are now trying to perfect tests which will reveal the specific causes of backwardness. These are known as "diagnostic tests".

Test Yourself

1. Describe the games and social development of children in the "gang" stage.

2. Distinguish between a mental test, an attainment test, and a diagnostic test.

3. What is meant in Educational Psychology by "maturation" and "learning-readiness"? What is the probable relation between them?

4. Distinguish between general intelligence (g) and special abilities (s). State some ways of measuring (a) general intelligence, (b) one particular ability.

Answers will be found at the end of the book.

CHAPTER X

ENVIRONMENT AND DEVELOPMENT

S O FAR we have stressed the importance of the process of maturation, or ripening, of a child's capacities and the fact that all children appear to show a common order of development, irrespective of the particular environment. We cannot conclude, however, that environment has no influence on development. To do so would be a serious mistake.

In the experiments with identical twins already noted, the training did, to some extent, improve the performance of the trained twin. Those experiments did not indicate that teaching and training have no value. They indicated that teaching and training produce the best results, in quality of performance and amount of improvement, if they are applied when the pupil is mature enough for that particular type of exercise.

Good food, fresh air, sufficient rest and sleep, freedom from anxiety, exercise and training in efficient methods, are all necessary for full development. This has been well known to physicians and educators for many years.

SOCIAL ENVIRONMENT

Lately, we have begun to realize more clearly the very great importance for development of a stimulating social environment and, in particular, of a child's emotional relationship with the adults in his neighbourhood. These social conditions affect not only a person's social adaptation, manners and attitudes, but also his intellectual development.

During the Second World War, British Army authorities noted a rather alarming proportion of semi-literate young men and women among conscript recruits. The problem was not the completely illiterate recruits; these were few in number, and usually there was some special reason in their history which would account satisfactorily for the difficulty. It was, rather, the number of younger recruits who could read and write only very simple exercises; whose comprehension was poor; whose general knowledge and interests were very limited. Yet the majority of these semi-literates had had at least an Elementary school education up to the age of fourteen.

The first scapegoats for this rather alarming condition were, as usual, the schools and the teachers. Most thoughtful people agree that British Elementary education has been very inadequate. At the same time, this did not seem to be a sufficient explanation. The significant fact emerged from investigations that the degree of disability increased with the length of time which had elapsed since the people in question had left school. The most likely explanations are : (a) Elementary school education has been badly adapted to the needs of many young people; (b) their circumstances, both economic and social, after leaving school have been such that they have had no adequate opportunity or stimulus to use their mental capacities constructively. Part of the illiteracy seems likely to have been caused by mental disuse—by brains becoming rusty, as it were.

Standardized tests of attainment in spoken and written speech, in reading ability and in comprehension have shown that, on the average, children from the more well-to-do economic and social levels are nearly always more advanced for their age in the abilities named than children from poorer homes. The following table (quoted by Dr. C. Bühler in *Handbook of Child Psychology*) indicates the differences in rate of learning new words found in two groups of young children, selected from good and from poor home environments respectively, in Vienna.

AGE	NUMBER OF WORDS USED	
	Children of good environment	Children of poor environment
1 year	7	0
1 year 3 months	49	1
1 year 6 months	91	4
1 year 9 months	121	8
2 years	216	27
2 years 6 months	—	92

Thus, on the average, the children from the poor environment at the age of two-and-a-half years were one year behind the other children in vocabulary.

In this connexion, Sir Cyril Burt, on the basis of much experience in testing mental development, says: "Imagine two children aged seven and seventeen years respectively, both possessing an intelligence equally normal, neither having passed an hour in school. The younger might show a Mental Age equal to six, the older, despite ten years actual seniority, might show a Mental Age of barely nine years. So barren is growth deprived of opportunity".

We should expect that the more varied a person's experience, and the more opportunity he has for reading and conversation, the greater will be his general knowledge and, therefore, the better will be his score in a standard-

188

ized intelligence test. Actually we find that although the inventors of mental tests try hard to exclude the effects of special schooling and training, nevertheless children from good environments do better on the average, in verbal tests of general intelligence, than children from poor environments—"good" and "poor" meaning not so much sheer economic wealth as opportunity for experience and social life. A neglected child of wealthy parents who spends most of his time with servants may have an educationally poorer environment than a well-cared-for child of artisan parents.

INTELLECTUAL DEGENERATION

Now an important question arises. Does the lack of experience and social stimulation in a mentally poor environment affect merely the child's knowledge and adaptability, without causing any real deterioration of his intellectual capacity, or does it affect the quality of intelligence itself? The opinion is growing stronger among educational psychologists that a very poor social and intellectual environment may lead, in some cases at least, to intellectual degeneration.

Several investigators have called attention to the cumulative effects of poor or isolated environments on the growth of intelligence. It has been found, for example, that of children admitted to certain State orphanages in the U.S.A. from the lowest income levels of the population, the older the children (that is, the longer they had been exposed to the influence of the poor environment) the lower were their Intelligence Quotients, on the average. (See, in this connexion, Sir Cyril Burt's statement quoted on page 188.)

An English investigator, Hugh Gordon, who tested the intelligence of canal-boat and gipsy children, found that up to the age of about six the I.Q.s were, on the average, what might be expected of normal children. However, the I.Q.s decreased progressively as the children grew older, and in many cases approached a level which would be labelled "feeble-minded" in an ordinary environment.

This progressive deterioration in intelligence has been found also in institution (for example, foundling hospital) children.

Deterioration with increasing age is found in children of the same family. If the difference in I.Q. were due to hereditary causes it would be evident at earlier age levels. The fact that the eldest children in these deprived families show most retardation in I.Q. relative to their birthday age suggests that the poor environment is the more likely cause. Thus, although the process of maturation, previously discussed, provides a powerful influence in determining the *order* in which the various capacities and types of behaviour will appear, at the same time a good stimulating environment with adequate opportunity for exercise, experience and social activity is essential for full mental development.

Effect of Emotional Disturbance on Development. In a very significant series of experiments an American investigator, Rene Spitz, has tested the general development of two groups of children between birth and the age of one year. This investigation is sufficiently important to warrant a detailed description.

The two groups in question were called the "nursery" group and the "foundling" group.

The mothers of children in the nursery group were delinquent girls who had been committed to prison. "When, as is often the case, they are pregnant on admission, they are delivered in a neighbouring maternity hospital, and after the lying-in period their children are cared for in the nursery from birth to the end of their first year. The mothers are mostly delinquent minors as a result of social maladjustment or feeble-mindedness, or because they are psychologically defective,[1] psychopathic[2] or criminal."

The foundling group were in a foundling home. Some of the children concerned had a background not much better than that of the nursery children, but a sufficient number came from socially well-adjusted, normal mothers whose only handicap was inability to support themselves and their children.

For purposes of comparison a third ("control") group of children was tested. These babies had been brought up in their own homes in an isolated fishing village of about five hundred inhabitants, where conditions of feeding, housing, hygiene and medical care were very poor indeed.

All the babies were tested at regular intervals by means of development tests standardized for very young children. The average development quotients for the first and last four months of the first year of life are shown in the following table:

GROUP	AVERAGE DEVELOPMENT QUOTIENTS	
	First four months	Last four months
Village Group	107	108
Nursery Group	102	105
Foundling Group	124	72

It can be seen that, although the foundling group started with a development level markedly better than that of the other two groups, the level at the end of the first year of life had fallen to nearly half its original value. The other two groups maintained their original level and developed normally. The foundling group were also very much more susceptible to disease.

[1] Highly neurotic, hysterical, unstable, etc.
[2] Tending towards insanity, but not actually insane.

Worse still, this development quotient of 72 had fallen to 45 at the end of the second year.

The foundling group were reared in excellent hygienic conditions, with modern standards of nutrition. The only significant difference between this and the other two groups was the absence of the babies' mothers. In the nursery institution the babies were cared for by the mothers throughout the whole period.

The mothers of the foundling group children left when their babies were about three months old, and thereafter the children had no human contacts, except when the institution nurses went into the wards to feed and clean them. Their emotional needs were starved. By the end of the second year it was found that such of these babies as survived had an intellectual development which was no better than that of feeble-minded children.

MOTHER LOVE AND MENTAL GROWTH

The investigator states that when the babies in the foundling group who were still alive were re-tested at a later date she found that in the ward of the children ranging from eighteen months to two-and-a-half years old only two of the 26 children could speak a couple of words. The same two could walk. A third child was beginning to walk. Hardly any of them could eat alone. Cleanliness habits had not been acquired, and all were incontinent.

Experience with English children during the mass evacuation of 1939–40 showed that emotional factors, including affectionate attachment to the mother or mother-substitute, are as important as the maturation of muscular control in the development of habits of cleanliness. Children who were known to be clean and continent relapsed into bed-wetting and soiling of clothes when separated from their mothers and homes. These lapses ceased in many cases either when a child rejoined its mother, or when a satisfactory emotional relationship was established with a foster-mother.

Reports of the Care of Children Committee (the "Curtis Report") bear on this connexion between emotional condition and mental development. Thus: "Although these children had the freedom of the garden, they were not playing with the resourcefulness characteristic of their ages. This may partly have been due to lack of material, partly to lack of individual interest. They gathered immediately around the visitor, showing that intense desire for individual attention which is characteristic of children with some 'emotional hunger'.

Most of the children seemed immature for their ages. There did not seem to be much warmth between the matron and the children, but there was no constraint or fear. They are probably reasonably happy, but undeveloped."

These cases illustrate the important psychological principle that the human organism works as a whole. We cannot separate development of intelligence and scholastic progress from the effects of anxiety, lack of satisfaction, or lack of security and of affection, particularly when children are young. Educators as a whole have been singularly unwilling, or unable, to realize the importance of this principle. It is encouraging, however, to note that the Home Office, as a result of the Curtis Report and the Children Act, was in 1948 training 100 specially selected young women to be "house-mothers" (not "matrons") in children's institutions. (See also *Oliver Untwisted*, by M. A. Payne.)

EFFECTS OF SUCCESS AND FAILURE

Here we have another important example of the influence of emotional conditions on scholastic progress and learning efficiency.

Success helps learning. It energizes the whole organism. Freed from anxiety, worry, and the gnawing unpleasantness of the feeling of inner insecurity, the learner eats with better appetite, digests better, takes more exercise, sleeps better, attacks new problems with zest and a feeling of adventure, anticipates the future with lively interest, and concentrates whole-heartedly on the task in hand. The whole organism, physical and mental, feels in good fettle—"on top of the world", as we sometimes say.

On the other hand, repeated failure depresses bodily processes, damps

Fig. 55. *One of the means used in the modern school for developing originality and independent thinking is the painting class, where imagination and self-expression are encouraged. Few children are devoid of creative ability, and in most of them it is abundant.*

down endeavour, interferes with feeding, exercise and sleep. It produces a continual subconscious distraction. The attention of the learner is occupied with the depressing consequence of failure rather than with the task in hand. Persistent failure may, and often does, lead to physical, mental and moral degeneration due to refusal to face the future. As a result development may be stopped at a premature stage, or distorted into abnormal side issues which can best be understood as attempts on the part of the victim to compensate for lack of the satisfaction of success.

People often misinterpret this principle. They talk about "soft pedagogy", sloppiness, spoiling the children, and so on, and praise the supposed bracing effects of difficulty.

It is desirable, therefore, to make the position quite clear. We do not suggest that occasional failure is harmful or that children should not be required to work for their successes. Difficulties properly adjusted to a child's maturity and level of mental capacity may stimulate him to greater effort. Failure may act as a challenge, especially to the more intelligent pupils—it shakes them out of any feeling of smug self-satisfaction which may have been caused by successes too easily won.

On the other hand, repeated failure caused by making children attempt what they are incapable of doing successfully is dangerous. The pupil concerned loses confidence and self-respect. This is the worst possible condition for efficient learning and further development. This is the reason why educational psychologists attach such great importance to suiting school work to the child's capacity and level of maturity.

Exactly the same arguments apply in the case of adults.

ORGANIZING SUCCESS IN LEARNING

In education, the psychologist will tell you, as in other aspects of everyday life, nothing succeeds like success. Organizing successful learning should be made into a universal principle in all education and school work. We should base our curricula and teaching methods on it. We must do so in order to meet the needs of the very varied capacities of the pupils in the Secondary schools outlined in the Education Act of 1944.

How can we organize success? Two methods are obvious: (a) grading the work to suit the learner's maturity, intelligence and special abilities; (b) teaching efficient methods of learning.

Of these, grading the work properly is particularly important.

Two American psychologists gave a group of children of from four to five years of age three tasks which they knew would be too difficult for some members of the group (that is, they deliberately organized failures). The children who gave up trying, who asked for help more than half the time, who excused themselves frequently, and who showed destructive temper as a result of failure, were then picked out to take part in a second experiment.

193

For these pupils who failed, the psychologists then proceeded to organize success. The new tasks they asked the children to do were graded in difficulty, the easiest being put first. In this way the pupils enjoyed the satisfaction of success early in the exercise and worked up gradually to the harder problems. The later tasks were adapted so that immediate success was not likely, but success was possible if the pupils persevered. The experiment was arranged so that the children could recognize their successes and keep some record of their own progress.

In these conditions, the group chosen in the first place on account of their poor reaction to failure showed marked improvement. Sulking and crying ceased entirely; there was much more interest, and the children made much greater efforts to solve their problems for themselves.

"INTEREST" IN LEARNING

An investigation was made in England into the relative popularity of Secondary school subjects. Some eight thousand pupils of between eleven and sixteen years, in 47 Secondary schools, were asked to say which of their school studies they liked most, and which least. They were also invited to explain the reasons for their preferences. Precautions were taken to make sure that the pupils did not choose subjects of study because they liked or disliked the teachers concerned.

Two main reasons for liking or disliking school studies stood out quite clearly: (a) the subject-matter itself was interesting or dull; (b) the pupil could or could not succeed in mastering the subject-matter. This latter may be called "power" interest, as opposed to "content" interest.

The investigation showed that pupils of Secondary school age can enjoy doing a subject, even if it is not in itself interesting, provided that they can master it. Two subjects were frequently disliked because of lack of success —Latin and Mathematics. The author of the report suggested that much of the unpopularity of Mathematics is due to the fact that the abstract theoretical aspects of the subject are taught too early, before the children are sufficiently mature for the work. With this opinion the present writer heartily agrees. He has known cases of pupils who seemed quite hopelessly incapable of doing elementary Mathematics, and they obviously detested the subject. When these pupils have been allowed to make a fresh start with work graded to their capacities, they have made marked progress and their attitude has changed in proportion.

Further evidence of the soundness of this principle of organizing success in learning has emerged from modern investigations into the causes and cures of special educational backwardness, particularly in Reading and Arithmetic.

Inability to read may be due to general mental defect. Much more frequently it is due either to some special difficulty and/or to lack of success in the first stages of reading. Reviewing recent researches into the psychology of reading, Dr. C. M. Fleming says in her book, *Research and the Basic Curriculum*: "Poor readers as a group are not markedly distinguished for inferior intelligence. . . . Emotional maladjustment is observable in almost every case of Reading disability. . . over-protected children may be unwilling to take the step toward maturity involved in learning to read independently. Spoilt children may be unable to adjust themselves to the orderly routine of school life, and children who suffer from unwise parental ambition or unhappy rivalry with older brothers or sisters may accept the position that they are 'word blind' or 'cannot read'. . . . Encouragement is one of the first needs of the child who has met defeat, and confident expectation of success is one of the best means of eliminating failure."

These statements apply equally well to any other field of learning. Confident expectation of success is essential, not only for efficient mastery of a task at the moment, but also for the advance from one phase of development to another. If the learner has nothing to expect but more failure and more humiliation, no matter how hard he may try, then he will soon give up trying and be driven to seek satisfaction in another way.

IMPORTANCE OF CONFIDENCE

Particularly he will strive to take refuge in the past and avoid the future. Some people appear to love difficulty for its own sake—so long as others have to tackle the difficulty! They are horrified at the suggestion that we should make it possible for young learners to succeed. These arguments are beside the point. No competent psychologist has suggested that teachers or parents should make everything easy for children. If we did so, the children would be the first to grumble. We should deprive them of the great pleasure of successful effort. Children despise too easy successes. In any kind of exercise in which they are interested, the majority of children will deliberately set themselves more difficult "targets" when they reach a given level of mastery. Even young children do this. When the one-year-old can walk on two legs he wants to stand erect on one leg. When he can run he wants to hop, or skip, particularly if he is in contact with older, more mature children who have already mastered these skills. And if he does not succeed at the first trial he keeps on trying, *so long as success seems to be within reach*. Moreover, it can be shown by experiment that the nearer the learner approaches to this "target" the more intensely he strives to perfect the learning. But if and when the pupil becomes convinced that success is impossible, then not even driving or severe punishment will make him keep on trying with the zest which is necessary for efficient learning.

The essential condition for progressive development is not immediate success, but confident expectation of success. To those people who persist in talking about the need for difficulty in order to promote self-discipline or improve will-power it is necessary to point out that progress in self-discipline and improvement in will-power will depend, not on difficulty as such, but on difficulty successfully mastered.

What are schools for? There are several answers. Their purpose is to teach useful subjects like Mathematics, Grammar, foreign languages, History, Geography, or the technical subjects necessary for competence in a trade. From this point of view the schools help the children and young people to pass examinations, get better jobs and succeed in life. However, in our preoccupation with getting on in life we should not forget the other duty of schools, which is to encourage the child's mental and social development.

THE AIMS OF EDUCATION

In educating children we are continually being forced to make choices. Which should we emphasize more—the examinations, the subjects and getting a job, or the best possible development of the individual pupil?

The sensible parent and teacher will keep both of these aims in mind. They must not be kept separate. The practical problem is: where shall we put the emphasis at any stage in the child's schooling?

In the past there has been far too much eagerness to emphasize subjects,

FIG. 56. *A class in a girls' school at the beginning of the present century. The enormous advances achieved in the school environment and in teaching methods during the past four decades stand revealed when this photograph is compared with the other illustrations in this chapter, which show examples of the newer tendencies in school activities and atmosphere.*

examinations and technical skills. The schools have taught subjects rather than pupils; and if the pupils did not fit the subjects, then so much the worse for the pupils. The teachers' job was to make the brats learn by hook or by crook. It is useless to put all the blame for this on the teachers. Parents have been as much to blame, if not more. They have egged on the teachers to do it.

The educational psychologist, on the other hand, is most interested in mental and social development. He wants to fit subjects and tasks to the pupils' interests and powers. This is quite possible nowadays, particularly in the primary stages of schooling, up to the ages of twelve or thirteen. Moreover, the psychologist claims that if we look after the mental and social development in the earlier stages, the pupil will be better able to deal competently with his examinations and with his job afterwards. Therefore let us try to adapt the schools and teaching methods to the interests and capacities of the pupils.

We cannot do this, however, unless we know some details about learning-readiness. By their investigations into stages of development, the growth of general intelligence, Mental Age, talents and special abilities (and disabilities), the educational psychologists are making it possible for inspectors and teachers to adapt schools and school work to the pupils' powers and interests at each stage of their schooling, ranging from the Infant school right up to the top classes of the Secondary schools.

WORK AND PLAY

Motive—Incentive—Interest—Play—these topics are important in many branches of Applied Psychology, and they are the concern of parents as well as teachers. We have already referred to them indirectly, and now we shall confine ourselves to a short review of the ideas about these topics which are now agreed upon by the majority of educational psychologists.

(*a*) Children attend most easily and steadily, learn most quickly, and remember what they have experienced most clearly and tenaciously if they are thoroughly interested in what they are doing. In addition, when children are interested in their school activities, difficulties of class order and social conduct do not arise.

On the other hand, if children are bored and "fed up" they will not learn; even punishment will not make them learn. Very often the punishment is associated by the suffering pupil with his school work, and that makes him even more "fed up".

(*b*) Schools, as well as homes, are social institutions. They cannot be managed successfully unless all the people concerned, old and young, obey certain rules which regulate individual conduct in the public interest. For example, the members of any community must respect and care for the property of the community. They must also pay due regard to the property and persons of the other members. Community life requires self-restraint and mutual co-operation. Good manners are essential for civilized social life.

(c) Schools are expected to train children and young people in citizenship, honesty, punctuality and conscientious industry; and to encourage in them high standards and ideals. Even parents, business men and politicians whose own standards are by no means ideal expect the schools to keep the children "on the rails".

Thus teachers (and parents) are concerned with two aspects of interest, namely, interest in learning in the usually accepted meaning of the term, and interest in social conduct and good citizenship. The practical problem is how to encourage these interests to the highest possible degree of which the child or young person is capable, and how to remove, or at least keep within bounds, interests which may interfere with school work and sound social development.

FEAR AS A MOTIVE

Of course, children can be stimulated to put some effort into their work, or can be prevented from serious misdemeanours, through fear of punishment. Fear, however, is not the most healthy or useful educative stimulant to work or safeguard against misdemeanours. Children may become hardened to punishment. More and more severe punishments are then necessary to produce the effects desired. And if the only reason for zeal or good conduct is fear, then the youngster will shirk his work or commit the misdemeanour as soon as he believes that he can do so without being found out.

Fear alone is not a satisfactory motive. We need to manage children and young people in such a way that *positive* motives for work and good conduct are encouraged. If people work or behave well because they want to do so, they will carry on satisfactorily even when nobody in authority is watching.

Satisfying Needs. Perhaps the best way to regard this topic of motive and interest is to think of motive in connexion with satisfying needs.

Every human individual has needs which must be satisfied in order to keep life going. Some of these needs are sufficiently obvious. We need food, drink and fresh air. We need conditions of comfort and general well-being. We need to avoid extremes of heat and cold, pain, disgusting tastes and smells. We seek sunlight, comfortable temperatures, and pleasant sounds, tastes and smells. We need to get rid of waste products of the body.

Normally-constituted people crave the physical experience of sex. Interest in sex matters begins quite early in life, contrary to general opinion. It becomes most insistent during and after puberty, when the sex functions reach full maturity. (We should note, however, that if early curiosity about sex has been abruptly suppressed or otherwise unwisely dealt with by parents, the interest may be concealed, even at the adolescent stage, and become furtive and unhealthy.)

The Need for Stimulation, Exercise, Experience. The reader may ask: "how on earth can the needs mentioned in the last few paragraphs concern education and the teacher?" They do, nevertheless, in an indirect way which we will point out later. Meanwhile, we must take note of another set of needs for which we crave satisfaction, which do concern us directly in education.

When we discussed order of development and the successive maturation, or ripening, of various powers of body and intellect we mentioned periods of learning-readiness and noted the strong interest of children in certain types of experience and exercise during these periods. One cannot fail to note the intense interest which nearly all young children show in touching, handling, sucking and biting any objects within reach. They bang together sticks and spoons with great enthusiasm and intense interest. They appear to find the noise quite fascinating, whatever adults in the neighbourhood may think of it.

There is an equally unmistakable interest in making noises with the vocal organs, tongue and lips. Most children pass through a "ba-ba-ba, ma-ma-ma" period, in which they seem to find satisfaction simply in exercising the organs necessary for speech development. Later in life we find a similar intense interest in exploring the neighbourhood; in using the developing sense organs for looking, listening, smelling, tasting; and in trying out tricks of muscular dexterity.

We suggested that these periods of learning-readiness and intense interest in certain experiences and activities corresponded with the approach to maturity of powers of body and intellect. Any powers of body and intellect which are approaching maturity appear to set up cravings for exercise. Enjoying the experiences and doing the exercises in question bring massive feelings of satisfaction. On the other hand, it is well known that muscles and nerves which are deprived of exercise for long periods waste away.

We also noted evidence that children deprived of normal stimulation and exercise for too long periods become intellectually backward, to the level of feeble-mindedness.

Stimulation and exercise, therefore, appear to be primary needs which must be satisfied in order to get full development of body and intellect.

NEED FOR REST

Although stimulation and exercise are primary needs, however, we can have too much of them. If the stimulation is too insistent or too intense it becomes a form of torture from which we crave relief. To have to stare at a bright, unshaded light, or listen to a high-pitched tearing or screeching sound for any length of time is most uncomfortable. However, regular *slight* stimulations are soon ignored and forgotten—such, for example, as the ticking of a clock.

Repeating the same action over and over again can be a very tiresome process. So can standing or sitting rigidly still for any length of time. In fact, any activity, in any part of the body or bodily organs, sets up conditions

199

which tend to slow it down and finally stop it altogether. After vigorous exercise or strong stimulation of the sense organs we want to relax or even to sleep. Relaxation and sleep are as necessary for health as food and exercise.

Critical readers may object at this point, on the grounds that the muscles of heart, lungs, stomach and other involuntary organs keep on without stopping from birth to death. This is no exception to the principle of fatigue, however. In actual fact, the involuntary organs work at full pressure only in very occasional emergencies, and these extreme efforts cannot be kept up for long periods without complete collapse. In normal exercise some parts of the involuntary muscles and glands are always held in reserve in a resting condition. Moreover, no muscle or nerve ever works continuously. It takes a short rest pause in each cycle of activity. It is estimated that the heart, when beating at the rate of 70 pulses per minute, is actually contracting for only 9 hours in the 24; that is to say, the rest periods after each contraction amount to 15 hours every day!

Thus the craving for stimulation and exercise, together with the "brake" of boredom and fatigue which sets up counter-cravings for change, relaxation and sleep, serves to regulate the activity of the individual within healthy limits.

Social and Psychological Needs. The needs already mentioned are connected mainly with physical comfort and bodily wellbeing. We now realize also that human relationships are essential for full personality development. We have emotional and social needs to be satisfied. Of these the most important and insistent are the needs for companionship and affection, for status, and for security.

"Affection", as used here, means something quite different from, though not inconsistent with, sex desire. It implies mutual liking and respect, willing and enjoy-

FIG. 57. *With such common materials as cardboard and modelling-wax, matchsticks and cotton-reels, these boys are building a model of part of Southampton Docks, as a highly realistic feature of their Geography lesson.*

able co-operation between two or more people. It is expressed in its clearest form in the concern and tenderness of a mother for her child.

"Status" represents the relative standing of a person with respect to other people in his environment. We all want to stand well in the estimation of our fellows. We are intensely interested in any activities or positions which satisfy this craving. We also want to stand well in our own estimation. People who pay very little attention to public recognition may have—usually do have—a good deal of self-respect.

By security we do not mean absence of physical danger and fear, but rather a feeling of emotional security—self-confidence, freedom from anxiety, the assurance that we are capable of meeting successfully any emergency which may happen. The calm, serene, cheerful, optimistic, equable-tempered, self-confident person is the representative of this condition of emotional security.

Inter-relation of Needs and Satisfactions. From the point of view of Educational Psychology (school work, home conduct and personality development), we have to note certain inter-relations between these needs:

1. When any need becomes very strong it seems to take possession of, and control in its own interest, any physical activities and ideas which may be useful in satisfying it. Very hungry people are restless. They readily notice any signs of food or preparations for a meal. They talk about food, think about it, even dream about it. Similarly, any craving for drink, sex activity,

exercise, sleep, affection, status, security, etc., disposes us to attend to, to be interested in, and to seek whatever objects and activities are appropriate for satisfaction. We learn knowledge and skills most readily in the service of satisfying our needs.

2. Two or more needs may reinforce each other. To eat in good company, in pleasant, tasteful surroundings, is more satisfying than merely to eat. Status, affection, security help to increase the satisfaction of eating.

3. Needs may conflict with one another, e.g., desire for social status may conflict with the desire to grab food. This fact is important in dealing with learning situations. When conflict arises, the stronger and usually the more primitive hunger wins. If we desperately need food, drink, fresh air, change of position, exercise, sex experience, freedom from pain, then we find it impossible to concentrate fully, or even at all, on any other occupation until this craving is satisfied. If any reader doubts this, let him try to concentrate on a rather dry book when he is desperately hungry for food or sleep.

Incentives. An incentive is any object or condition for which people strive consciously. In other words, it is any object or condition which will satisfy directly or indirectly a need which we feel. This can be illustrated in the economic world by reference to profit or money incentives. Money may satisfy directly the craving for status. Having more money than other people may be considered as a sign of status, whether we spend the money or not. But money is desirable also because it is the readiest means of obtaining other satisfactions, e.g. food, drink, freedom, experience, better houses, more power to control other people, status, security.

Interest. Interest is a state of mind in which we attend to and strive to get some object or condition. Interest is essential for fully efficient learning.

Most of the practical skill in teaching and child management lies in stimulating interest, or in keeping alive and increasing interest already aroused and guiding it into constructive activities.

REMOVING DISTRACTIONS

The real problem, so far as school and home conditions are concerned, is not to interest children simply. Most children are interested in something or other most of their time, and if the child is interested in doing what parents or teachers want him to do, no problem arises. The problem arises either when the child does not attend to, or is actively hostile to, parents' or teachers' desires, or when an interest considered appropriate by the authorities fades out, and the child wants to do something else. How is it possible to deal with these situations?

If we want to direct children's interest we must first satisfy any competing interests. It is useless to expect a child who is hungry, thirsty, wet, cold (or hot), stiff after sitting too long, who has toothache, stomach-ache, eye-strain, catarrh, or who wants to pass urine or fæces, to attend to his lessons. The primitive bodily hunger or pain must first be relieved and the child made comfortable. Similarly, if the child is anxious, afraid, disappointed or resentful he will not be able to attend well. We have to relieve these distracting feelings.

We can try to encourage an indirect interest in educational activities by offering prizes, privileges, praise, or "marks", or by using blame and various kinds of punishments in the hope that the child will work harder to avoid punishments. By these methods we try to enlist the aid of cravings for status and security. These methods, however, may and often do create as many problems as they solve. The main interest of the children, in such cases, may be concentrated on the prizes, privileges and marks, or on evading the punishments. When this happens, we have the all-too-familiar situation in which a child will not work (or behave himself generally) unless there is a sufficiently big prize, or a sufficiently severe punishment which he knows he cannot avoid. Unwise use of external rewards and punishments sets up false values in the child's estimation and directs interests towards undesirable objectives.

SUCCESS THROUGH SELF-EXPRESSION

The best way to maintain and guide interest is to try as far as possible to make the educational activities of school and home into direct satisfactions of needs. This principle takes us back to the discussions on development, maturation and learning-readiness. When some bodily or mental faculty is approaching maturity it appears to set up a craving for the appropriate exercise. Thus one important clue to the control of interest and behaviour is correct timing of the work to suit the pupils' level of maturity.

We can add to this the child's craving for status and success. We must grade the work to ensure confident expectation of success. It may be necessary in some cases to organize a child's work around his strongest interest and his best ability. Mr. P. I. Kitchen, in his book *From Learning to Earning*, describes two cases (a boy and a girl, each aged about fifteen years) in a Continuation school. Both these adolescents were resentful and obstructive in their attitudes to the school and the work done there. Both of them gave much trouble to the teachers, until it was discovered that the boy was an interested and successful breeder of prize rabbits and that the girl had a flair for organizing social activities. The boy was invited to give a lecture to the school on the breeding of rabbits and to show his best specimens; the girl was made a member of the school social activities committee. In both cases there was a surprising improvement in attitude and co-operation, which extended even to the school "lessons". Both children had acquired status through the expression of their strongest interests.

Modern educators are trying to utilize learning-readiness and to organize school work in terms of experiences to be enjoyed and activities to be pursued. Even Arithmetic can be made interesting. (See Figs. 58 and 59.)

203

However, even with the best will in the world it is not likely that we can make all the work suit all the pupils all the time. Sooner or later everybody has to do something or other which does not exactly suit his interest at the moment. What can we do to encourage zeal in uninteresting work? Experiments have shown the value of the following methods:

(a) Mark and criticize a child's efforts rather leniently than severely at first, until his self-confidence is established.

(b) Praise improvement and good work. Successful effort is doubly satisfying when it is publicly recognized.

(c) Teach pupils efficient methods of work, instead of letting them get along as best they can. This encourages success.

(d) Make the pupils' success *visible* by grading the work in difficulty and by keeping, or allowing the child to keep, some records of performance. By this means the child competes against himself, as it were.

(e) Set definite "targets" to be attained. Make these targets for individual children and base them on each child's actual ability and previous attainment. Keep the "target" just ahead of the child's present performance.

(f) Do not prolong any spell of work until the child is weary. Stop, if possible, while some interest still remains. This is particularly important in dealing with younger children.

Discerning readers will have noted that these really essential recommendations cannot be carried out fully unless classes in school are reasonably small. Even in Secondary (Grammar) schools in 1948, one could find classes of thirty-five or more pupils. A skilful teacher can do much to encourage and direct interest even in these conditions, but at the cost of exhausting effort. (And good teachers are not superhuman. They also can become bored and tired. It must be remembered that the rules for motivation and interest apply to teachers as well as to pupils and factory workers.)

TEACHER AND CHILD

One further clue to encouraging and directing interest may be sought in the personal relationship between teacher and pupil, or parent and child. The child craves affection and regard for his personality. If the relationship between adult and child is one of affectionate regard, the child will work readily and spontaneously for the adult's approval. The approval is the child's guarantee of the adult's affectionate regard, and the work done is the child's willing token of his own regard for the adult.

This situation has its possible dangers. If not managed with common sense, it may happen that a child will work for one teacher quite willingly, but will not do a stroke of work for somebody else. Moreover, teachers or parents, starved of affection themselves, may be tempted to pander to a child's whims in order to secure his affection. In any case, as a child grows

FIG. 58. *By skilfully presenting school work in terms of experiences to be enjoyed, the so-called "activity method" succeeds in making attractive even traditionally dull subjects, such as Arithmetic. These Primary schoolboys are learning toymaking as part of Applied Mathematics.*

older and is more capable of responsibility, he must be encouraged to do necessary work even though it is not immediately interesting. The youngster will do this partly in so far as he realizes that the work *is* necessary, partly in so far as his self-respect is bound up with completing the job satisfactorily.

Penalties and punishments are sometimes necessary. They should be used as a last resource, and then made sufficiently impressive to act as a "brake" on future occasions.

Judicious, sympathetic guidance rather than mechanically efficient teaching methods is the mark of the really good teacher. The good teacher does not so much teach his pupils as make it possible for them to teach themselves—a process which has more lasting results and a deeper influence on personality. The mechanically efficient teacher may defeat his own efforts (he does so very often, in fact) by imposing a strict regime on all his pupils, irrespective of their individual characteristics and needs. Moreover, in his zeal to impose his own rules of efficiency such a teacher allows no freedom of choice to the pupils and deprives them of necessary exercise in self-government.

The Best Conditions for Persistent Interest. We have stressed the connexion between interest and satisfying needs. Learning takes place most rapidly in the process of satisfying needs. At the same time we have to remember that when any need, whether it be for food or status or security, is satisfied the interest and striving—and therefore further learning—in that direction cease.

Somehow, therefore, we have to keep the interest expanding. To some extent this will happen of its own accord in a favourable environment through the process of maturation. As the new powers of body and mind ripen, they set up a craving for their appropriate exercise. In a good home or school, parents and educators will try to provide constructive toys, apparatus and material for expression, and some freedom of choice, so that as the powers of the children mature opportunity for the appropriate exercise is ready at hand.

The natural progression of interests will be strengthened if the children form a mixed group with respect to age. The younger ones want to grow up. They identify themselves with adults and older children. The prowess and learning of admired adults—parents, teachers, local celebrities, national figures—and of older children set the targets for the youngsters, as well as providing models for imitation.

Self-image, Self-valuation and Level of Aspiration. Continued interest and progress depend upon the relationship between a person's self-image, self-valuation and level of aspiration.

At a relatively early age, at least as soon as the child begins to talk about himself correctly, he begins to develop a "self-image". This represents the

FIG. 59. *Six-year-olds "shopping" at their own "stores" and so becoming familiar with simple calculation and the reckoning of money—another aspect of the "activity method" of teaching Arithmetic. Children learn more easily when their interest is held.*

individual as he sees himself. He can develop this directly by observing his own appearance (and what he cannot actually see he can view in a mirror). He will also be assisted in the process by what other children and adults say about him, and by how they treat him. He will compare himself and his attainments with those of his fellows. To this self-image a value is attached. Some children set a high value on themselves; others do just the opposite. The actual value adopted will depend partly upon inborn constitution and endowments, partly on critical power and intelligence, and partly on the circumstances of the environment in which the child finds himself.

SELF-IMAGE AND SELF-VALUATION

Together with the self-image and the self-value goes a level of aspiration. This represents what the person desires to do or to become at some time in the future. The level of aspiration, again, depends on the proportion of success over failure which has been experienced in actual performance, on intelligence and temperament, and particularly on the general standards in the school, home and neighbourhood. If the level of aspiration is low and self-valuation high, we get the easily satisfied, complacent person who can see no reason for exerting himself further. If self-valuation is moderate and level of aspiration unduly high, we get the over-anxious, tense person who is continually driving himself to (or beyond) the limit of his capacity, with the risk of breakdown. If self-valuation is low, and level of aspiration too high, then we usually find feigned indifference, or apathy, or blank despair, with a persistent refusal to make any positive effort.

For persistent, healthy effort and balanced personality development we need to keep the self-valuation realistically related to the self-image and the level of aspiration realistically related to the self-valuation. This can be done partly by judicious advice and encouragement, partly by putting the youngster into situations where he will have sufficient opportunity to compete against people at least equal to or rather better than himself.

Parents have great responsibilities in this connexion. By flattery and by keeping a child in too easy circumstances the self-valuation, self-image and level of aspiration may all be set absurdly and impossibly high in relation to the child's real capacity. On the other hand, by setting too high a target and then sapping the confidence and self-valuation by constant nagging, fault-finding and unfair criticism, parents may reduce the child to angry, frustrated impotence and prevent him from even trying—to say nothing of succeeding—in the endeavour to make the most of what abilities he possesses.

Good management of these three factors is most important in dealing with cases of specific backwardness. Before the backward child will make the necessary effort to improve, his self-confidence and self-respect must be restored. Before this can happen he must experience success until he loses the fear of failure. This is well put by Dr. C. M. Fleming: "Remedial tuition

207

is best given when the pupil is not fatigued, and it should never carry with it the association of punishment or separation from fellow pupils." (This is equivalent to loss of status.) . . . "Practice for brief periods at intervals of a day or two is more effective than longer periods at intervals of a week or more. Treatment should be definite in aim and adapted to the level of the learner." (Organizing success.) . . . "Generous praise should be given and learning take place in an atmosphere of happy confidence." (Satisfaction of need for affection and security.)

Dr. Fleming goes on to suggest that pupils with special disabilities are usually taught best by methods which utilize whatever special ability they may possess (building up self-valuation and self-confidence). Only after confidence has been re-established should attempts be made to supply corrective material to deal with the defect. Children with speech defects should learn to read by methods which do not require spoken answers to meanings. Pupils who cannot control their movements should learn through sight or hearing rather than through tracing methods. Pupils with manual dexterity should learn through script writing, drawing or tracing. In other words, in dealing with a backward pupil every effort must be made to encourage the child to "put his best foot forward".

CHARACTER-BUILDING

For the most complete development of zeal and social conduct it is necessary for the individual to set up "ideals"—that is, high standards of efficiency in work and social responsibility—and then to associate his self-valuation (or self-respect) with the achievement of these high standards. In other words, the person must identify himself with the high standards and incorporate them as part and parcel of his personality. How can this identification of the self with the ideal and its incorporation within the personality be achieved?

It is not done by logical argument or by preaching, at least not in the first place. Many sinners know very well what is the right thing to do, but this knowledge does not prevent them from sinning again on the next occasion. It is true that discussion, intellectual guidance, critical thought will make clear the nature of the ideal and help the aspiring youngster to see how best to shape his conduct. It is doubtful, however, whether these intellectual processes have much value unless and until the youngster *wants* to learn.

The first process in the establishment of aspirations and high ideals is emotional rather than intellectual. The child wants to be like some person he admires. The admired person is usually a parent (or parent substitute) in the first place. As the child grows in body and mind his social connexions extend. He wants to be like older brothers or sisters, like local celebrities and popular national heroes.

The connexion between the child and his aspiration is almost always predominantly emotional until adolescence. Adolescence is a critical phase in social development in which the emotional allegiance of the child to a person may develop into the conscious recognition of a moral principle. Literature, Biography and History will always be important subjects of study for adolescents, because in these subjects they will find exemplified the personalities and characters they can incorporate into their own personalities.

It is because the beginning of aspirations towards high standards is always to be found in the affectionate regard of the child for a parent, teacher, or adult acquaintance that parents and teachers should strive continually to establish good relations between themselves and the children. Given the basis of affection, the child will tend to share the likes and dislikes of the admired adult or older boy or girl, and will strive to imitate their behaviour and acquire their attitudes. There is good reason to believe that many children grow into delinquents or acquire anti-social attitudes because they have not had the opportunity in early childhood to set up this relation of affectionate regard with some admired parent, teacher, or other adult.

PLAY

To the average adult, "play" suggests relaxation, or rest from serious work. Many people also have a feeling that playing is really wasting time which might be better given to useful work.

The educational psychologist regards play in rather a different way, particularly in the case of children and young people. To the psychologist, play is any activity taken up for the sake of the satisfaction felt in the activity itself.

FIG. 60. A "special difficulty" class for children who are backward in specific subjects. Designed to capture interest, the activities include "shopping" and the making of toys and models.

If this is accepted, it follows that if the child is in circumstances in which he has some freedom of choice he will play spontaneously at those activities which best satisfy his growing needs. It is found, in fact, by careful studies of children's play that their games and other activities are characteristic of their stage of development. The strong desire to play has the effect of inducing children to exercise the powers which are ripening at that particular moment.

No child should be controlled so strictly that he cannot play freely at some time during the day. In play the child exercises his growing powers when they most need exercise. In play he makes experiments and tries out methods of acting and living. In play he is free to exercise his own judgement and to learn initiative. All the evidence now available suggests that if a child is not allowed to play he will not develop fully. Facilities for free play, therefore, are essential in the home, at school and in the neighbourhood. The proportion of free play to "serious work" will vary according to the age of the child; the younger the child, the greater the proportion of free play.

The educational psychologist's aim is to study the child of school age (and the adult also) in order to find how people of various types and ages learn best and how their personalities develop. On the basis of this knowledge he hopes to improve the organization of school work and of educational conditions generally, and bring them into line with the requirements of learners at different stages and levels of development. A thorough overhaul of traditional school methods and subjects is vitally necessary, if for no other reason than to prevent waste of time and money in futile schooling. New social, no less than new educational, conditions need new methods in the schools, and it will be well if such methods are founded on the very valuable scientific evidence which Educational Psychology has accumulated.

Test Yourself

1. What features of home environment would you look for as being suitable for a child between the ages of three and six?

2. What might be drawbacks in a school of the type illustrated on page 196? Try to write your criticism in the light of historical perspective.

3. Discuss the attitudes of the two boys illustrated on page 201. What impression of their school would you gather from these two pupils?

Answers will be found at the end of the book.

CHAPTER XI

VOCATIONAL PSYCHOLOGY

"IT IS NOT society's fault that most men seem to miss their vocation. Most men have no vocation."

This opinion of George Santayana (quoted from his book *The Life of Reason*, Vol. II) must have been shared by many parents as they wondered what in the world their young sons could possibly take up as a career with any chance of success. Yet Santayana, although wrong in his views on this point, had some excuse. When he wrote these words in 1905, it was a bare fifteen years since the first serious effort had been made to measure and compare the mental and physical powers of different individuals, and society as a whole had no knowledge of what has since grown into a vast combination of science and art. Moreover, he probably suffered from the prejudice common to philosophers of that period, who condemned experiments which, they believed, tried to apply a foot-rule to the human soul.

Parents today, however, can have little excuse and those of tomorrow will have still less. Hundreds of thousands of people have been helped into suitable work by the use of the modern selection or guidance procedures which are now being used more and more extensively in Britain, in North America and in Europe. Millions in the armed forces during the Second World War saw the effectiveness of selection tests in placing men in units where their individual peculiarities were of most benefit to the service of which they were a part. And after the war many of them asked why similar methods could not be used to place them in the right civilian jobs.

Just as an architect in planning a building takes into account the natural advantages of the site on which he is to build, the nature and position of other buildings and the cost of the work in relation to the resources of his client, so the modern architects of careers, the vocational psychologists, take into account the natural abilities of the people they advise, the types of jobs available in the country or district and the amount of money parents can be expected to spend on education and technical training.

Psychology has as one of its aims the study of human behaviour. A vocation is a calling, and is usually understood to mean one's business, trade or profession. Hence it follows that Vocational Psychology is the study of human behaviour in relation to human occupations. This involves, as a preliminary, the study of individual human beings while they are actually engaged in their work.

How does the vocational psychologist attempt this study of a person's behaviour while at work? To obtain a true picture he will have to study both the individual's reactions to the work he has to do, and the quality of the finished product. He will have to watch the worker while at work and judge whether he is quick or slow, neat or clumsy, interested or not; and he will have to examine the actual product being made in order to judge the degree of the worker's success. Having made this critical examination, he can then make suggestions for improving the worker's efficiency and his consequent satisfaction in his job.

This study obviously implies that the worker has already entered the occupation under consideration. In practice, however, the vocational psychologist is more concerned to see that an individual enters a suitable occupation than in improving his lot once he has entered, and he approaches the problem from two angles—Vocational Selection and Vocational Guidance.

SELECTION AND GUIDANCE

When an employer wishes to engage work-people to perform a particular task, he will naturally wish to select, or have selected for him, those workers whom he considers most suitable from one or another standpoint. The study of methods for selecting workers for a given occupation is known as Vocational Selection.

When people are seeking employment, they should naturally have some idea as to the kind of work for which they are likely to be suitable, and young people should be given some guidance in the choice of a career by those in a position to judge their capacities. The study of methods for determining the sort of employment best suited to an individual is known as Vocational Guidance.

Vocational Selection and Vocational Guidance are both concerned with individuals and their occupations after, or immediately prior to, the completion of their school education. The same methods can, however, be applied to selection and guidance during the school career and are referred to as Educational Selection and Educational Guidance. During the middle years of a child's school life it is necessary for decisions to be made as to which type of school he should proceed to on leaving his Primary school. Secondary schools of different types exist to cater for the children selected for them. Also, during the later years of school life, decisions have to be made regarding courses of study, additional subjects, and subjects to be discontinued.

The study of Vocational Psychology may, therefore, be divided into four sections—Vocational Selection, Vocational Guidance, Educational Selection and Educational Guidance.

Vocational Selection is the attempt to choose for a given occupation those who have the aptitudes and temperaments to succeed in it.

There is often much misunderstanding about the difference between

Vocational Guidance and Vocational Selection. The former implies a careful study of the individual with a view to advising him about the work for which he is best fitted.

It follows that in order to give proper guidance the psychologist must have a detailed knowledge, not only of the individual's capacity and personality, but also of industrial operations and the requirements of the various professions and businesses. Vocational Selection, on the other hand, necessitates a careful study of a particular industrial operation or the needs of particular occupations or professions, so that the most suitable people may be selected for the work. Again, it follows that, in addition to understanding the requirements of the work, the psychologist must also be able to form a correct and comprehensive assessment of the individual.

Vocational Guidance is the attempt to advise a given individual in the choice of an occupation which will give him the most favourable chance of developing his innate capacities to their utmost extent, and for which he will be temperamentally suited.

It is by no means a modern innovation, but only within comparatively recent years has any attempt been made to give it a scientific basis. The choice of an occupation must rank as one of the most important decisions that has to be made in a person's lifetime. It is of importance to the person himself, affecting, as it may well do, his present and his future happiness. It is of importance also to his employer.

It is, furthermore, of very great importance from a national point of view, since the standing and the development of a country are bound to depend ultimately on the efficiency and contentment of each individual.

CONTROLLED EXPERIMENTS

In the past twenty-five years, considerable investigation has been undertaken by means of controlled experiments in an effort to develop a reliable system of Vocational Guidance for children leaving school. The purpose of this section is to examine briefly what has been attempted in the past in this direction, in Great Britain and other countries; how far the science has developed at the present time; and, if possible, to suggest ways in which our methods may be further developed so that every child leaving school may receive the help and advice to which he is entitled.

Obviously, Vocational Guidance and Vocational Selection are very closely related and must be studied along similar lines. This means that some attention must be given to Vocational Selection in this chapter, although the subject is chiefly a problem for employers and as such is more fully discussed in Chapter XIV.

It sometimes happens that Vocational Guidance is confused with Child Guidance. No attempt is made to deal with Child Guidance in this section, as it is dealt with in some detail in Chapter VII. It will be generally accepted, however, that in dealing with the difficult child, the choice of his employment or of his course of education must often play an important part; indeed, the choice of wrong employment or of a wrong school or course of instruction may well be partly responsible for some of the difficulties experienced with adolescents.

RESEARCH WORK IN BRITAIN

Much research into the problems of Vocational Psychology has been conducted and is still being conducted in Great Britain. A considerable amount of useful work has been undertaken in the Universities, but these investigations have been rather of a preparatory and theoretical nature, and their main concern has been neither with the practical task of giving Vocational Guidance nor with the use of psychological techniques in industry. The Industrial Fatigue Research Board (later to become the Industrial Health Research Board) set up by the Government in 1918 has carried out many investigations into the value of psychological methods in industrial operations and into problems relating to Vocational Guidance and Selection. It is impossible to give descriptions of all these investigations, but accounts of them may be found both in psychological journals and in the reports issued by the Board.

Here attention will be directed to some of the research directly concerned with the practical problems of vocational and educational guidance and selection.

Any account of the early research work in Vocational Psychology in Great Britain must consist largely of a summary of the development of the National Institute of Industrial Psychology, which was founded in 1920, largely by the efforts of Dr. C. S. Myers, Director of the Psychological Laboratory in the University of Cambridge. Much of its work at the start, and during its development, has been concerned with utilizing psychological and physiological knowledge in relation to problems affecting industrial and commercial life.

In 1921 work in connexion with Vocational Guidance was begun by Dr. Cyril Burt, who began to prepare a series of tests for typists and shorthand writers.

These consisted of special tests of general intelligence, of educational attainments, of linguistic ability and general knowledge, and of speed and accuracy in shorthand writing and typewriting ability. From the data collected after testing a large number of shorthand typists Dr. Burt standardized the tests in order to differentiate those capable of clerical work demanding high intelligence, those capable only of routine clerical work, those unfit for clerical work at the time but likely to become capable after further training, and those wholly unsuited to any clerical work.

In 1922 the Vocational Section was established at the National Institute, with Dr. Burt in charge, and research work was put in hand relating to the development of tests for selecting dressmakers and apprentices to engineering. In the same year the Institute, in co-operation with the Industrial Fatigue Research Board, began a joint investigation into Vocational Guidance. The occupations of two thousand consecutive school-leavers in a London district were carefully analysed; and then an intensive study was undertaken of one hundred children due to leave school. These children were given Vocational Guidance based on psychological principles, and their careers in industry were then watched for two years. At the end of this period it was found that of those who had entered occupations of the kind recommended, over 80 per cent were satisfied with their work, prospects and pay. On the other hand, of those who had obtained employment other than of the kind recommended, more than 60 per cent were dissatisfied.

FAVOURABLE EVIDENCE

A further experiment was begun by the Institute in 1924. The subjects for this experiment were twelve hundred London Elementary school-leavers, six hundred of whom received special Vocational Guidance based on a psychological procedure, the other six hundred being given advice of the kind usually dispensed at terminal school conferences. During the first three or four years after the children had left school the career of each one was carefully followed and records were kept. The criterion of success was based on the number and length of tenure of the posts held, the reports received from employers and children on the children's suitability for the employment, and the reasons for leaving posts as given by employers and children respectively. The evidence in this inquiry was clearly in favour of those children who accepted the Vocational Guidance after the special psychological procedure. This investigation afforded a valuable opportunity for further systematizing and improving methods of assessing qualities of temperament and character.

Another experiment in Vocational Guidance was conducted by the National Institute of Industrial Psychology in the County of Fife, Scotland, during the years 1928–1932. This investigation was planned to compare the conditions affecting Vocational Guidance in a rural and an urban area respectively, and to throw light upon the constancy of the results given by psychological and other tests when applied to the same individual at different ages. In addition, it provided opportunity for examining further the value of the Institute's general procedure in Vocational Guidance. Very detailed information is given by Earle and Kilgour in the report on the investigations (*A Vocational Guidance Research in Fife*). The general conclusion reached was that the vocational study (in its widest sense) of a child should begin as soon as he or she reaches the age of 11+ or thereabouts, and that it should be undertaken from two points of view, educational and occupational.

It is suggested in the report that at a first stage, between the ages of eleven and twelve, attention should be given to the choice of an advanced course of studies, having regard to the level of general ability already shown, the special interests and aptitudes (if any) already shown, and the age at which it is the declared wish or intention of the child and his parents to attempt to find him employment. At a second stage, either between the ages of thirteen and fifteen or between thirteen and seventeen, according to the age at which it is intended the child should enter employment, the exploration of vocational aptitudes should be made by examination of the pupil's progress in study, tests of specific aptitudes, and tests of the abilities and attainments necessary in particular occupations for which the course of study is a suitable preparation. For example, the tests of the abilities and attainments necessary for office clerks would be arithmetic, book-keeping, composition, and the like.

The result of the research showed that children attending rural schools were rather less proficient in abstract subjects than those attending town schools, while on the other hand they were rather more competent in dealing with practical problems.

As for the tests, the results of these demonstrated that the consistency of the results given by tests of intelligence applied to the same individuals after a prolonged interval of time was sufficiently high to warrant "long-range" forecasts. An equally high consistency of the results given by tests of scholastic attainments was not, however, maintained over periods longer than one year.

It was considered to be impossible to predict the quality of a child's performance in his future school work from data consisting solely of results in tests of scholastic attainments with that degree of confidence warranted by the data consisting of results of intelligence tests. The consistency of results obtained from tests of mechanical ability applied to the same individuals over an extended period was sufficiently high to warrant forecasts from the age of thirteen, perhaps even from the age of twelve-and-a-half. In regard to tests of manual dexterity, some of the results could be depended upon only for "short-range" forecasts, at any rate until the ability had become stabilized. The age at which this stability occurred varied from one individual to another. The final conclusion was that the general procedure of the psychological examination in Vocational Guidance was both valid and reliable.

FURTHER INVESTIGATIONS

For many years the Birmingham Education Committee had been keenly interested in Vocational Guidance, and by 1924 a scheme had been developed whereby, prior to leaving school, each child was seen individually at a choice-of-employment conference by a Juvenile Employment officer. The Committee decided, in 1926, to investigate the use of a psychological procedure. Six reports have been published on these investigations, three being concerned with the value of vocational tests as aids to choice of employment (Vocational

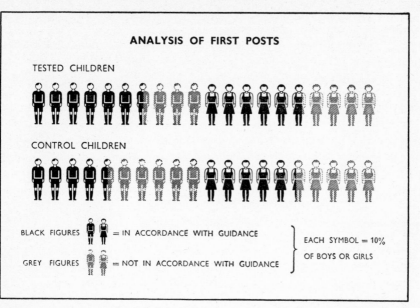

FIG. 61. *An analysis of first posts carried out by educational experts in Birmingham. Of the tested children, 65 per cent of boys and 57 per cent of girls (or 61 per cent of both sexes) found first posts in accordance with Vocational Guidance. Of the control (untested) children who obtained "accordance" posts the proportions were: boys, 45 per cent; girls, 53 per cent (or 49 per cent of both sexes). For further explanation, see text.*

Guidance) and three with the selection of skilled apprentices for the engineering trades (Vocational Selection).

The first Vocational Guidance investigation related to 328 children, who comprised all the boys and girls leaving three Elementary schools in a central area of Birmingham during some eighteen months. Each term the leavers from each school were divided into two unselected groups. The children in one group were given Vocational Guidance at the usual employment conferences and were regarded as a control group. The advice to those in the other group, which was known as the "tested" group, was determined after a psychological procedure which consisted of a series of tests, temperamental and personality ratings, special medical examinations and home visits. For both tested and control children full information from their school records was available. The tests used were chosen to assess intelligence, performance ability, manual dexterity, mechanical aptitude (boys), dressmaking aptitude (girls) and clerical ability (boys and girls of more than average intelligence). After the Vocational Guidance had been given, if desired by the parents, efforts were made to find for both tested and control children employment along the suggested lines.

The children who were left free to choose for themselves with the advice of their parents were able to avail themselves of the services of Juvenile Employment officers and, finally, four categories emerged. These were: tested children in posts in accordance with the guidance; tested children in posts not in accordance with the guidance; control children in posts in accordance with the guidance; and control children in posts not in accordance with the guidance. Fig. 61 gives an analysis of the first posts obtained by the children in the "tested" and the "control" groups.

Evidence as to the relative value of the two methods of advice was obtained by following up both the tested and the control children in their industrial careers. This "follow-up" period lasted for two years and reports were obtained by home visits, "open" evenings at school, letters to children and letters to employers, and from the official records at the Juvenile Employment and Welfare Department at the Education Office.

An analysis was made of the data obtained during the "follow-up" to show the numbers in accordance and non-accordance posts; the duration of the different posts; the reasons for leaving posts; the views of the employers as to the efficiency of the children; and the opinions of the children themselves as to the suitability of the posts. In each case the statistics were analysed into

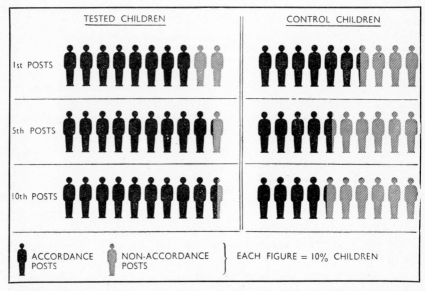

FIG. 62. *These figures illustrate trends shown by "tested" children and "control" children when transferring from one post to another during the four years after leaving school. As regards the tested children (80 per cent of whom had chosen their first posts in accordance with Vocational Guidance), "accordance" employment was chosen by 91 per cent and 95 per cent for their fifth and tenth posts respectively. For the control (untested) children (only 63 per cent of whom had chosen first posts in accordance with guidance) the figures for fifth and tenth posts were 46 per cent and 42 per cent respectively.*

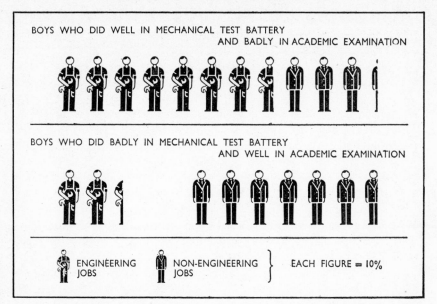

BOYS WHO DID WELL IN MECHANICAL TEST BATTERY
AND BADLY IN ACADEMIC EXAMINATION

BOYS WHO DID BADLY IN MECHANICAL TEST BATTERY
AND WELL IN ACADEMIC EXAMINATION

ENGINEERING JOBS   NON-ENGINEERING JOBS   EACH FIGURE = 10%

FIG. 63. *In order to compare the efficiency of psychological tests with the usual academic entrance examination, an investigation was carried out among Technical School boys. The results showed that of the boys who subsequently proved successful in engineering jobs only 23 per cent had secured good marks in the academic examination, whereas 77 per cent had done well in the battery of psychological tests. Of the boys who proved satisfactory in non-engineering occupations however, it was found that 67 per cent obtained good marks in the academic examinations, as against 33 per cent who achieved good results in the test battery.*

the four categories, and from whatever angle the evidence was studied the same indications appeared. Tested children in accordance posts were more satisfactorily placed than were children in any of the other three groups that were investigated.

The inquiry definitely corroborated the results of the experiment conducted by the National Institute of Industrial Psychology in London, and the Birmingham Education Committee felt it necessary to consider the practicability of using vocational testing and a psychological procedure as aids to the Juvenile Employment officer in his work. If the very large numbers of children leaving the Birmingham schools were to be given the benefit of these new procedures, it would be necessary to have a staff capable of applying them, and so a second inquiry was instituted to explore the matter on a more extensive scale.

In conducting the inquiry already described, the application of all the vocational tests and the psychological procedure was undertaken by the two investigators responsible for the research. To deal with a considerably larger group of children it was decided to enlist the co-operation of members of the teaching staff and of members of the organizing staff of the Juvenile Employ-

219

ment Department. Before these teachers and officers could begin to do any testing, however, it was essential for them to receive a course of instructions in the required technique. Comprehensive training courses, the first of their kind in this country, each lasting an academic year, were organized.

In the earlier experiment all children were "followed-up" for two years in order to obtain information about their industrial careers; in this larger experiment the "follow-up" continued during four years for more than six hundred of the children concerned and during two years for more than one thousand six hundred children. The results of this experiment are given in great detail in the published report. From every aspect from which the "follow-up" data were studied, the evidence showed very definitely that those children who, having been given Vocational Guidance following a psychological procedure, took the advice given to them, were better and more securely placed in employment than children who did not accept the advice. They were also better placed than children who did not follow the special psychological procedure in the first place.

During the "follow-up" period many children changed their employment, often from work in accordance with the guidance to work not in accordance with advice, and vice versa. An attempt was made to study the trends in this process of transference, and Fig. 62, based on the report, gives an indication of these trends.

The analysis in Fig. 62 shows that tested children were not only more ready to accept the Vocational Guidance than were control children, but that the tested children also showed a preference for changing from non-accordance posts into accordance posts, whereas the control children showed a marked trend in the opposite direction.

The Birmingham Education Committee also instituted special research into the selection of skilled apprentices for the engineering trades. This research centred chiefly around apprentices at a Technical College and pupils at a Junior Technical school. A battery of fifteen tests based on psychological principles was chosen with a view to assessing qualities of general intelligence, mechanical aptitude and ability, and manual dexterity. This battery of tests was given to third- and fourth-year apprentices at the college and to boys leaving the school after a two-year course. All of these were rated for "engineering apprentice ability" by the instructors at the college and the headmaster of the school respectively.

SUPERIORITY OF TESTS

Comparison of the test results and these ratings showed that seven of the fifteen tests taken in conjunction had high diagnostic value, so that youths doing well in the test battery were likely to make successful engineering apprentices. A further comparison was also made between the test battery and the existing form of entrance examination to the Technical school, which

AIR MECHANICS AND FITTERS IN FLEET AIR ARM

AVERAGE *FAILURE RATE* DURING TRAINING

BEFORE NEW SELECTION METHODS USED

AFTER NEW SELECTION METHODS USED

EACH FIGURE = 1%

FIG. 64. *During training, special tests based on psychological principles reduced the failure rate for mechanics and fitters in the Fleet Air Arm from nearly 15 to less than 5 per cent.*

was of the usual academic type. Fig. 63, based on the report, clearly shows the value of the tests as compared with the academic examination.

A considerable amount of research work has been undertaken with a view to exploring the methods of determining the types of post-primary courses to which children should be directed. The Scottish Council for Research in Education appointed a committee to ascertain the attainments expected of a normal child at the time of his transition from primary education to advanced or secondary education. This demanded the preparation of standardized tests in primary school subjects.

As a result of these investigations it was found that a diagnostic study of individual pupils from the scholastic angle is not merely possible but well worth while; and that when a decision is required at the commencement of a secondary course of studies, specially devised tests would appear to be potentially more valuable than entrance examinations or teachers' reports. Teachers' estimates of ability, while often showing considerable agreement with the test results, are subject to unknown and unpredictable variations and are not by themselves sufficient to justify forecasts of future proficiency.

No statement of the vocational and selection work carried on in Great Britain would be complete without a reference to the extensive investigations conducted in the Services during the Second World War. It is not yet possible for the full tale to be told, but the great importance and far-reaching consequences of this wartime work are gradually becoming known. For

221

instance, more than eight hundred thousand candidates for the Royal Navy were dealt with by a special procedure, and as an indication of the value of these new selection methods it may be mentioned that, so far as the selection of mechanics and fitters for the Fleet Air Arm was concerned, the average failure rate during technical training was reduced from 14·7 per cent to 4·7 per cent after the introduction of these methods (see Fig. 64).

PSYCHOLOGICAL TESTS

The term "psychological tests" has not much meaning, except to differentiate tests so described from other types of tests and examinations. When ordinary people talk of examinations they are generally referring to examinations set by schools, Universities, the Civil Service or other bodies to test candidates in particular subjects, and most people have a fairly clear idea in their minds of what such examinations consist. But when we think of psychological tests our ideas are by no means so definite; we are not sure that we know what they really are and may be more than a little suspicious of them.

The kind of person who thinks, quite rightly, that psychological tests will be of value in his (or her) work, but who also thinks, quite wrongly, that anyone can use such tests and obtain reliable results, is not only misguided but may even be dangerous. For the fact that a man or woman is a capable or even a brilliant teacher, doctor, personnel manager or Juvenile Employment officer is not a cogent reason for thinking that he or she will necessarily understand the new technique of testing or, without any form of specialized training, be capable of applying it.

The purpose of the academic type of examination is to measure a candidate's store of acquired knowledge in a particular subject, whether he has reached a required minimum level of knowledge in that subject and, if so, by how much he has exceeded that level. These examinations are, in fact, tests of attainment and measure the amount of knowledge and skill gained as a result of education, training and experience. Psychological examinations, on the other hand, may or may not be tests of attainment, and when they do happen to be tests of attainment, they differ from the normal type of examination in a way which will shortly be explained.

DISCOVERING APTITUDES

Psychological tests are so called because they are devised, given, and scored according to a psychological technique which has been carefully built up and tried out by fully qualified psychologists. They include in their scope tests of intelligence and tests of such special aptitudes as manual dexterity, mechanical aptitude and clerical aptitude. The term "aptitude" as used here refers to the "innate or inborn capacity possessed by an individual for any particular activity, whether that activity be verbal or practical".

Apart from the evidence produced by special tests, it is not always possible to tell whether a child has a particular aptitude, unless that aptitude has already shown itself through its corresponding ability. To distinguish between the innate aptitude and its outward manifestation we call the latter an ability. An innate aptitude may perhaps never have shown itself, because of lack of opportunity in the candidate's environment, and the object of psychological tests of aptitude is to discover to what extent it may exist.

So far as possible, these tests are so devised as to avoid testing knowledge acquired by experience or training. It is, however, obviously impossible to eliminate entirely these two factors; one cannot ignore every fact and skill that a person has acquired in ten, fourteen or eighteen years and devise tests which will treat his whole past as though it had never existed. It is here that the interview plays its part in throwing light on how much experience and knowledge a candidate has had a chance to acquire.

METHOD OF TESTING

A psychological test may have any number of questions up to fifty or a hundred, and the candidate is expected to answer as many as he can. There are usually many more questions than can be answered in the time allowed. This method is adopted so that the examiner may measure exactly how much the candidate is able to perform in a given time. The method of answering the questions in the psychological test is different from that in an ordinary examination. In the academic examination the candidate is expected to supply fairly lengthy written answers, whereas in the psychological test, more often than not, alternative answers are supplied and the candidate indicates the answer by a tick, by underlining or by some similar device.

If the main object of an examination at the end of an educational course is to discover the extent of the candidate's acquisition of the facts presented during that course, a truer result is to be expected from an attainment test of the psychological type than from an academic examination. The greater the number of questions, the less likely is it that questions about any particular part of the course will be omitted. Less, also, is the chance that the candidate may have made a lucky last-minute revision of that part of the subject from which a high proportion of the questions asked is drawn; for in the psychological test the answers to such questions are still only a few out of many. Only candidates with extensive and accurate knowledge of facts can be expected to reach a high score in a psychological test.

Another point in favour of the psychological type of test is that the slow writer, as distinct from the slow thinker, is not penalized. The slow thinker is bound to be handicapped by the time element in any type of examination, but even he will not be at such a disadvantage in the psychological test, where the answers are given and have to be picked out from among others.

A quick thinker may, however, be a slow writer and in the essay form of answer, so usual in the academic examination, his slowness in putting words on paper is a brake on his output. This handicap will not affect him in the psychological test, in which he merely indicates the answer in some short, easy way.

When it comes to correcting or scoring an examination paper there is no doubt as to which is the easier and more accurate method. In academic examinations the examiners have to read through the written answers; the answer of each candidate to any given question will be different from all the others, and the candidates will inevitably be rated largely according to the personal judgement of the examiners. In the psychological test, the examiner has only to pick out, and to count up, the right answers. Each answer must be entirely right or entirely wrong, and the personal judgement of the examiner (sometimes called the "subjective" element) is completely eliminated. In the essay type of answer required by the academic examination it is obviously unlikely that the candidate will be able to include all the relevant facts or detailed interpretations, and the examiner will have to decide whether the candidate made deliberate omissions for a good reason or whether he really did not know. Thus, chance may play a bigger part than either judgement or ignorance in settling a candidate's total score in the examination.

VARIATIONS IN JUDGEMENT

A remarkably interesting investigation, now widely known, was carried out by two Americans, Starch and Elliott, on the variation in judgement shown by different examiners. One candidate's answers to an examination in English were reproduced and sent to 142 teachers for marking. Of these 142 teachers, 14 marked the paper below 80 per cent and 14 marked it 95 per cent or over, the remaining 114 ranging their marks between 80 per cent and 95 per cent. This investigation was challenged on the ground that English or any literary examination papers are always especially hard to mark accurately (an interesting self-condemnation on the part of examiners), so the investigation was repeated with a Geometry examination, as this more exact subject was regarded as easier to mark. The results were very similar. Copies of the answers were sent to 116 teachers, whose marks ranged from 28 per cent to 92 per cent, 20 of the teachers marking the paper below 60 per cent and 9 marking it above 85 per cent. Many other investigations of this type have been carried out and the results have nearly always been similar, showing that this "subjective" form of marking, which is bound to depend largely on each examiner's own judgement, is, to say the least, a somewhat unreliable means of assessment.

A more recent verification of "the part played by chance in the verdicts given at different examinations" is found in the report entitled *An Examination of Examinations*, issued by Hartog and Rhodes in 1935, in which they give many examples of extraordinary and, to the lay mind, almost unbelievable variations in marking. From another source comes what is perhaps one of the happiest stories on this theme of unreliability of examination scores. A certain University examiner, one of four in his subject, for his own convenience wrote model answers to his questions. These were inadvertently included with the candidates' scripts and sent to the other three examiners. Each of them failed him!

When the psychological type of examination is used the examiner can be certain that his own personal judgement will play no part in the marking. Provided that a key to the answers is available, any careful person can correct the answers given by the candidates; and there will be no doubt that any other careful person will award exactly the same marks to each candidate. In this sense the marking is entirely objective.

LIMITATIONS AND ADVANTAGES

Admittedly, the psychological test of attainment has its limitations. It cannot measure a candidate's originality of thought or his fluency and style of expression. The essay type of answer will always be necessary for this purpose, and it is only fair to say that more objective methods of marking such answers are being developed. To obtain a true picture of a candidate's grasp of a year's work in any non-mathematical subject, the ideal would seem to be a combination of the two types of examination: an examination of the essay type to assess understanding and fluency and originality of expression, and a psychological or objective examination to measure purely factual knowledge.

There is yet another advantage which the psychological test has over the academic test in this matter of scoring. The latter can only determine the position of each candidate in a group relative to the position of all other candidates in the same group, that is to say, the group taking the same examination. The particular examination paper will not have been given in its entirety to any other group and, therefore, it is hardly possible to compare scientifically and accurately the results of one group with the results obtained by candidates in any other group. But a psychological test, before being given to the candidates for whom it is intended, will already have been given to many other people as similar as possible to them in age, education and environment. The average scores of these preliminary trial groups can then be calculated, and the result of any new candidate doing the test can be compared with these scores. He can be ranked or placed accurately in comparison with people who are reasonably comparable with him. It is essential that these scores are obtained from comparable people. It would be of little use to compare the score obtained by a British child of fourteen years of age with the score gained in the same test by a Polynesian of twenty years of age, or even with that gained by a Polynesian of fourteen years of age. The differences between such candidates are obvious. It is, however, very nearly as foolish to expect a reliable assessment from the comparison of the test result of a British child of ten from a highly cultured family with that of a British child of fourteen (or even of the age of ten) from a low-grade slum home. In actual practice it has been shown that when norms (that is, average scores for comparison) are prepared they have to be based on groups not merely comparable in a broad sense but also comparable locally: that is to say, the scores of London children must be compared with norms prepared from London children; it may be very misleading to compare them with norms prepared from, say, Aberdeen children. Furthermore, norms prepared from town-dwellers will not necessarily serve for children living in the country

PREPARATION OF TESTS

This proper preparation of tests is commonly known as "standardization", and psychological tests differ from the normal examination because the material of the tests, the giving of them and the scoring of them are standardized. The simplest way to understand what this standardization means is to imagine that a psychologist has been asked to devise a test of intelligence for fourteen-year-old children, and then to observe his methods.

He has first to devise numerous questions and problems, which then have to be graded in order of difficulty. To do this accurately involves the giving of the questions to large groups of children of fourteen, in order to find the proportion of such children able to answer each question correctly. This will enable the investigator to rearrange the questions in order of increasing difficulty. The newly-arranged test must now be given to yet another large group of comparable children to discover whether the final mass of scores follows a "normal distribution". This is a technical term which, briefly, implies that a few of the children should do very well on the whole test and a few should do very badly, but most of them will be fairly equally spaced around the average score for the group and not too far from it. Unless the spread of individual scores conforms reasonably closely to this ideal, the test cannot be regarded as reliable; any significant divergence from it indicates that some factor is playing a disturbing part and must be eliminated. Such a factor may be the arrangement of the questions, the time allowed for answering them, or perhaps the way in which they have been scored. The psychologist, therefore, tries out the test on other groups until he has eliminated, as far as possible, the disturbing factors, so that the scores conform to the normal distribution. When this point is reached he may regard the rest as reliable. He still does not know whether it is valid, however—that is, if it is really a measure of intelligence, as distinct from scholastic attainment. To find out whether his test is valid he has to compare it with another test which is already accepted as a valid test of intelligence. If the comparison is satisfactory and each child occupies approximately the same position in each set of results, he can assume that the new test is measuring intelligence and is ready for use.

The preparation of a test of this type is, therefore, a long-drawn-out process, and even at this stage something still remains to be done. The scoring has to be standardized, and tables of norms or average scores have to be prepared. The scores of sufficiently large numbers of comparable children have to be converted into an easily used table so that, on future occasions, any individual score obtained in the test by a comparable fourteen-year-old child can be compared with this standard table and his intelligence appropriately assessed.

Unfortunately, all this careful preparation by the psychologist can easily be vitiated by careless and uninformed use. "A psychological test (whatever it may be designed to measure) is a means of gauging an individual's aptitude by measuring his ability to perform a *standard* task of graded difficulty under *standard* conditions. Too much emphasis cannot be laid on the importance of the standardization of the test, the standardization of the conditions of giving it and the standardization of the scoring. With regard to the standardization of the test, it is essential that each candidate shall have exactly the same operation to do or the same problem to solve. The conditions under which the test is given must be as nearly similar as possible, and the instructions accompanying the task must never vary. . . . The scoring of the test is of paramount importance, and whatever system has been adopted by the originator of the test must be adhered to rigidly. This system of standardization underlies all psychological testing and differentiates it from the usually accepted form of examination. If it is not adhered to, it is of little use giving the test, as norms cannot be used for comparison."

INTELLIGENCE AND SPECIAL APTITUDES

The various kinds of tests of general intelligence are described elsewhere in this book. It must be emphasized, nevertheless, that tests of general intelligence also play a very important part in Vocational Guidance, and no such guidance would be satisfactory unless an assessment of the candidate's intelligence were available.

It is necessary, therefore, to consider this "general intelligence" that the vocational and educational psychologists aim at assessing. The average man may think he is fairly clear in his own mind as to what he means by "intelligence", but how would he describe it if he were asked to do so? Most people use the word loosely and in a variety of situations. Adults, babies and animals are universally described as "looking intelligent" if they happen to have a certain superficial brightness of expression, which, however, need not necessarily mirror an equal brightness of intelligence beneath. Mary's parents think that she is very intelligent because by sheer hard plodding and a good memory she manages to keep a fairly high position in her class at school; but a good memory is by no means an infallible indication of intelligence. Most people have heard of "lightning calculators", but few people are aware, perhaps, that some of these prodigies are in institutions for the feeble-minded and mentally deficient.

The search for a correct definition of intelligence has led to much argument and disagreement among psychologists. Some have defined it as the power to adapt oneself to new situations; others as the capacity to learn; one group regards it as the power of mental analysis and synthesis; another, as the power of thinking about abstract conceptions, as distinct from things which are concrete.

Others, again, have described intelligence in physiological terms as, for example, "a function of the central nervous system". Indeed, so many and diverse have been these definitions that in 1921 several famous psychologists contributed to a symposium on the nature of intelligence. This symposium did not do much to clarify the situation, as each psychologist produced his own definition and no common agreement was reached. The various theories are clearly summarized by Knight in his book *Intelligence and Intelligence Tests*, but in recent years there has been a fair measure of agreement with the view that some degree of "general intelligence" is bound to be present in, and to underlie, all mental activity, whether that activity is directed to an abstract or to a practical end. The nature of intelligence is discussed in Chapter I.

Our social system is such that a low degree of intelligence is regarded as a greater stigma than a low degree of, say, mechanical ability or dressmaking ability, and the results of an intelligence test ought never to be considered apart from completely documented information regard ng the individual's make-up, such as his temperament, interests and physical condition.

If it is true that nothing is achieved in the realm of mental activity without intelligence, it appears equally true that some achievements are not due to intelligence alone.

If this be the case, then, before satisfactory Vocational Guidance can be given to anyone, the psychologist must be able to assess, not only that person's intelligence, but also any other innate aptitudes that he or she may possess.

If there existed reliable tests for each group of innate aptitudes, this assessment might be a comparatively simple matter, but this is unfortunately not the case.

A few decades comprise only a very brief period in scientific research, and this field of inquiry has been cultivated for only forty years or so; consequently, with a few exceptions, aptitude tests are still in the experimental stage, and must be used with caution.

in this short survey we can do little more than look at a few typical tests of

228

special aptitudes, with some pictorial examples, in the hope that these will indicate the underlying principles.

Performance Tests consist of problems which are presented to the candidate in such a way as to eliminate almost entirely the difficulties that usually arise from the use of language. The test "material" really is material, as distinct from printed or spoken words, and this material has to be manipulated in some way or other in order to solve the problems. These tests can be given to only one candidate at a time and are, therefore, "individual" tests; the instructions are usually given orally, but they can, if necessary, be given in "dumb show", the examiner showing the candidate what he has to do instead of telling him. The solving of the problem, however the instructions may have been given, does not call for the use of words at all. The candidate thinks out the problem and manipulates the material in silence.

ELIMINATING LANGUAGE BARRIERS

Performance Tests were originally devised to meet a special need in the sphere of mental testing. After Binet's series of Intelligence Tests had given such an impetus to mental testing throughout the world, it was found that there was a serious practical defect. As the Binet tests, and all the others based on them, depended on the use of language, both by the examiner and by the candidate, they were of no use when the candidate was illiterate, spoke a language foreign to the examiner, or had some physical defect such as deafness. Consequently, it was impossible to assess the Mental Age or Intelligence Quotients of such people, and tests for general intelligence were devised eventually which eliminated the use of language from the test "situation". The first of these tests was published in America, for it was in America that the language problem proved especially difficult.

Performance Tests, as originally devised, purported to be tests of general intelligence. The early ones were perhaps a little naive, but they were regarded at the time as being reliable tests for what their originators wanted to test, namely, general intelligence. Consequently, all earlier references to them describe them as "Performance Tests of Intelligence". Subsequent experiment and research, however, have shown that the various forms of Performance Tests give very different and inconsistent assessments of a candidate's intelligence. They do, however, fill a definite want and, provided that the assessment of intelligence is based on the results of a combined series of at least half a dozen tests, and not on one only, or even two or three, they can be regarded as giving a fair assessment of a candidate's general intelligence or Mental Age. They are especially valuable for use with young children, partly because of their non-verbal character and partly because they appear to them as very attractive puzzles or toys.

The following are some typical Performance Tests:

Mazes. A series of thirteen straight-line mazes was devised by Porteus at

Vineland, New Jersey, U.S.A., and graded in difficulty for children from three to fourteen years of age. Fig. 65 provides an example of one of these test mazes. The candidate begins at the letter S and traces his way out with a pencil.

Cube Construction Tests. Two well-known tests of this type are the Cube Construction test, devised by Yoakum and Yerkes in America, and Kohs' Blocks.

The first has for its material three model wooden blocks. Model I is 3in. square by 1in. deep, is marked into 1in. cubes, and is painted red on all sides except the top and bottom. Nine separate 1in. cubes, with some sides painted red, are given to the candidate, who has to make them up into an exact copy of the model. Models II and III involve the same principles, but are progressively more difficult.

Kohs' Blocks consist of sixteen 1in. cubes all painted alike, the six faces being respectively red, blue, yellow, white, yellow-and-blue divided diagonally, and red-and-white divided diagonally. Various designs in the same four colours are painted on cards. The candidate has to arrange the blocks so as to reproduce the design. Kohs devised seventeen designs of this type; but whatever the number, the designs are graded in difficulty. Two designs are shown in Fig. 66, one easy, the other more difficult.

Formboards. There are many varieties of this type of test, but the underlying principle is the same in all: variously shaped pieces have to be fitted into a frame in such a way as to fill the frame exactly. Three examples are shown in Figs. 67, 68 and 69—a simple one, an amusing one and one of the more difficult sort respectively.

Mechanical Models. An exhaustive investigation into the existence of a mental power which can be termed mechanical aptitude has been made by Cox. For assessing this aptitude he has devised various tests. These consist of small wooden mechanisms, each of which is so constructed that the can-

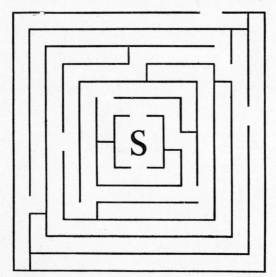

FIG. 65. *An example of a Porteous Maze. Beginning at S, the candidate must trace his way out of the maze. These tests are designed for children between the ages of three and fourteen years, and are graded in difficulty.*

FIG. 66. *Kohs' Blocks. In this type of test the candidate is given a number of variously coloured blocks, with which he is required to reproduce a prescribed design.*

didate can see only the first and last links in a chain of mechanical events which occur when the model is worked by hand. He is required to show how the observed movements are brought about. These models all conform to the same general design, but vary in details and difficulty. Two of them (a simple and a more complex one) are illustrated in Fig. 70.

PRECISION AND SPEED

Most tests of this type attempt to assess the precision and speed of hand and finger movements. Many of them require the candidate to put together, or to take apart, some small object such as an electric lamp-holder or the hub of a bicycle wheel. Others require an aiming movement such as dropping little balls into holes, sticking pegs into holes, or threading a cord through eyelet-holes. In nearly all these tests the candidate's score is assessed according to the time taken by him to perform the required operation. The examiner times the performance with a stop-watch and the score is usually given in seconds. This brings to notice an interesting difference between the scoring of some psychological tests and the marking of the usual type of school and similar examination papers. Whenever the score of a test is gauged by

231

FIG. 67. *This is an illustration of one of the simpler types of formboard test.* The separate pieces seen lying at the side of the frame must be fitted by the candidate so that they fill up exactly the square and the triangular shape in the board.

the time taken to perform it, the larger the score the worse the result, the lower the score the better the performance. The candidate with the lowest numerical score heads the list. Among the most satisfactory tests of manual dexterity are those devised by the psychologist Cox; they are described in his book, *Manual Ability*.

Space and Form Perception. In one sense formboards test the appreciation of space and form, but they test it in a moderately easy manner, because the candidate who does not see the solution "in the flash of an eye" (which some people do in a marvellous way) can resort to the trial-and-error method, trying out one piece and then another until the right one is found. More difficult tests of this kind merely show the picture of the shapes on paper and the candidate has to do all the fitting in his mind's eye. In such tests sometimes the perception of "solid" pieces is introduced. In Fig. 71 is illustrated one of these pencil-and-paper tests of appreciation of space and

form. Five of the fifteen pieces shown in the lower part of the diagram have to be selected to fit the five spaces in the squares in the upper part of the figure. The quick-witted reader will notice that the "pieces" will fit the spaces only if they are turned over like the leaves of a book, some side to side, and others head to tail.

These, as might be

FIG. 68. *These eight wooden shapes must be fitted together in such a way as to form the likeness of a human profile.*

232

FIG. 69. *The Dearborn form-board constitutes a more difficult test than those shown on the previous page, although the principles involved are the same. The empty spaces must be filled precisely by the pieces outside the board. In order that this can be done, some of the pieces already in place must be rearranged. Each piece is provided with a knob so that it can more easily be lifted into or out of the frame.*

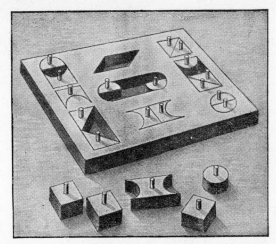

expected, are always tests of the pencil-and-paper type and involve problems of filing, classification, memory and other mental activities which play a part in most clerical work.

The tests that have been described in this chapter are but a few of the many aptitude tests in existence. A large number of them began as selection tests, that is to say, they were first devised to aid in the selection of people for certain types of occupation, and, having proved their worth in this sphere, they were used as guidance tests for people seeking advice on the sort of occupation they should choose.

Unfortunately, many of these special-aptitude tests are not properly standardized and are, therefore, of little value at present. In Britain the best are those devised or sponsored by the National Institute of Industrial Psychology.

Notwithstanding the present somewhat experimental state of many tests of special aptitudes, these can, if used and interpreted properly, provide a useful indication of a candidate's capacities; they are also extremely valuable as "pointers" when the vocational psychologist is observing indications of the candidate's temperamental make-up.

ASSESSMENT OF TEMPERAMENT

The elusive and difficult aspect of Vocational Guidance known as the assessment of temperament, personality and character must be approached with, if possible, even greater caution than has been exercised hitherto. Although many of us are prepared to agree that it is generally unwise to rely on the judgements formed by others of the characters of those with whom we come into contact, yet most of us have the feeling that our own opinions in such cases are quite reliable. We are ready to form opinions of our friends, our neighbours and our chance acquaintances, and are fairly certain of the correctness of our views, even when those views have been formed only

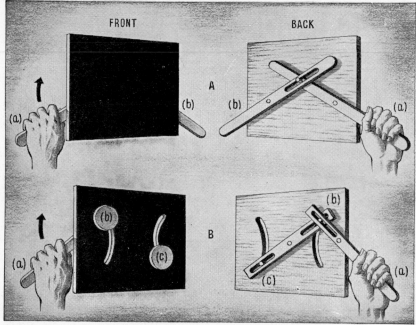

FIG. 70. *Such models as these are designed to test mechanical aptitude.* A (left) *gives a view of the front of the model as seen by the candidate. The examiner holds up the model with the back hidden from the candidate, and pushes up handle* (a) *in the direction of the arrow. Handle* (b) *moves up simultaneously.* A (right) *shows the mechanism at the back of the board.* B (left) *shows the front of another model and* B (right) *shows the back of it. The buttons* (b) *and* (c) *move up and down in their respective slots when the handle* (a) *is pushed up or down. In all the models the board is black, and the movable parts—handles, buttons, etc.—are white.*

superficially. Why, then, should we not find the assessment of personality the easiest, instead of the most difficult, factor in the study of the individual?

Let us try to give a carefully considered answer to this question. Except in regard to a few people very well known to us, few of us can say that we have anything more than a very superficial knowledge of the personalities of those whom we meet in our everyday life. We may know that Brown will readily lend us his lawn-mower—but do we know whether he is happy doing routine work or whether he would prefer work demanding originality of outlook? Do we know whether he is a careful worker or rather "slap-dash"; whether he fears, tolerates or actively seeks responsibility; whether he gets on well with his fellow-workers or whether he is a "lone wolf"; whether he is submissive to those over him or aggressive to those under him? Thinking on these lines soon leads us to realize that the vocational psychologist begins with a very great handicap in dealing with a stranger to whom he is expected to give guidance about a career. The psychologist is presented with a difficult problem; to solve it he has to make use of many different methods of obtaining the information needed, and, before arriving at his conclusion, he has to be extremely careful to assess this information accurately in the light of its relative importance.

It has been agreed that the theories concerning the nature of intelligence are many and varied: the theories concerning the nature of temperament and personality are at least as multifarious. This is not the place for a detailed discussion of these various theories, but it is important that at this stage we should glance briefly at some of them.

THEORIES OF TEMPERAMENT

Certain psychologists and physiologists have propounded theories based on physiological knowledge according to which variations in temperament have a material basis in the endocrine glands. It is certainly true that abnormalities in these glands produce variations in temperament: for example, the normally calm and balanced person will become abnormally excitable and irritable when the thyroid gland is over-active. But too much weight must not be given to the operation of these glands on temperament, since the science of endocrinology (as the study of these glands is called) is comparatively young and much research still waits to be done before sufficient positive facts are generally available. (See pages 19 and 307–8; also Fig. 7.)

There are also the theories based on anatomical considerations, of which Kretschmer is a leading exponent. He distinguishes two main forms of physique: the thick-bodied, short-limbed, thick-necked type, which he names the "cycloids", and the lean, long-limbed, small-waisted type, which he names the "schizoids". These are thus described by Miller: "To them (the cycloids) the spirit of the age is more real than the spirit of the ages; they occupy themselves with social schemes, not because they are schemes but because they are social. Fussy busybodies are found among them, but rarely cold calculators. Such men laugh heartily and eat with relish. They are epicureans without fastidiousness, humorists but rarely wits. . . . (The schizoids) are the eminent Georgians, who foregather in Bloomsbury's green and pleasant squares. They are singularly feminine in physique and voice. The beard frequently adopted is fine and etiolated as plants grown in sunless cupboards. Their views are precious and *raffiné*. Every idea is carefully chosen so as to be devoid of any suggestion of vulgarity. They despise the Victorianism of their fathers, and replace the spinsterism of those days with a variety of their own."

The psycho-analytic theories of Freud and Jung are perhaps those most familiar to the general public, although knowledge of them is usually very superficial and incorrect. Freud's name is connected with the conception of "complexes"; to Jung we owe the division of temperaments into introverts and extroverts. "Complex", "inferiority complex", "superiority complex", "introverts", "extroverts", all these terms are as well known as they are ill used. Of all the recently popularized additions to our language they are probably the most glibly used and the least understood. It is so very easy to label people in accordance with certain "types", but it is dangerous and misleading, because the normal people of everyday life are very rarely, if ever, clear-cut "types": they are nearly always a mixture of many types, of which one type may predominate.

Fortunately, the vocational psychologist, though he must certainly be familiar with the various theories regarding the basis of temperament, does not need to be expert in evaluating them in order to make a sound assessment of the temperamental characteristics of those whom he is advising on the choice of a career. His business is not to choose between the different theories, but rather to devise and use methods of assessing the temperamental factors in a candidate's character.

The methods of assessing temperament and personality will be discussed under the following four types: tests, the questionnaire, the interview and rating scales. It should be noted, however, that rating scales are not so much a method in themselves as a part of the technique for recording information which has been collected while using the first three methods.

TESTS OF TEMPERAMENT AND PERSONALITY

Many attempts have been made by a number of psychologists to devise tests of temperament and personality, so that objective and quantitative assessments of these factors in a person's "make-up" may be made, but none of these attempts has so far succeeded in producing any really reliable tests.

Tests of emotional reactions and of temperament can undoubtedly provide illuminating and helpful data to the experienced psychological adviser, but the value of the assessment will arise indirectly from the manner in which the candidate does the test rather than directly from the quantitative "score" which he may achieve.

Hence it follows that many performance tests succeed in eliciting interesting information about a candidate's temperament. The trained observer will always take note of any indications of temperamental traits that may occur during the performance of a test. The candidate's reaction to success or failure, his perseverance in the face of difficulties, the presence or absence of self-criticism or of self-confidence, are a few of the factors which may reveal facets of his personality. The Cube Construction Test (which we considered earlier in this chapter) is especially enlightening, as it is very prone to produce exasperation in the candidate.

To sum up the present position, it may be said that while some existing tests of temperament are certainly of value, much research still needs to be done: in any case, such tests should only be used and interpreted by the trained diagnostician, be he psychologist or psychiatrist. Anyone who wishes to read further on this subject will find useful and helpful material in *The Study of Society*, edited by Bartlett, and in Vernon's articles on the subject.

THE QUESTIONNAIRE

It will not be necessary to provide here a very detailed description of the questionnaire, as in one form or another it has become a popular "self-quiz" in magazines and newspapers. The questionnaire, properly constructed and interpreted, has both advantages and disadvantages as compared with tests. One of the advantages is that it can be used for very large groups of people who need not necessarily be seen by the psychologist. Moreover, when the psychologist is using the questionnaire with people whom he is actually interviewing, much of his time is saved, as the giving of individual tests of temperament is always a lengthy procedure. Another advantage is that the questionnaire forms an admirable basis for the interview. Before the interview takes place, the candidate fills in a questionnaire concerning his own personal characteristics and interests, and at the interview the examiner is able to discuss with him the answers he has given and his reasons for giving them. This discussion can produce very illuminating results.

A disadvantage of the questionnaire is that the psychologist cannot be sure

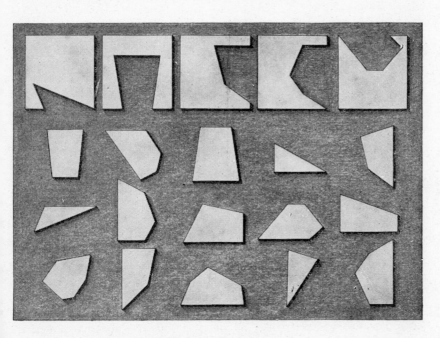

FIG. 71. *In this test (see pages 232 and 233) the candidate is shown the shapes on paper. In his mind's eye he has to fit five of the fifteen small pieces into the broken squares above.*

237

of the reactions of the people answering it unless it is followed by an interview. Was the subject being flippant, or was he conscientious? Was he happy or depressed (for reasons quite unassociated with the questionnaire) at the time of completing the form? Was he really trying to be co-operative? It is obvious that these and many other questions may seriously affect the reliability of the answers.

Vernon points out that, as the questionnaire method is more often used to obtain replies from groups of people than from individuals, some of these difficulties cancel themselves out: the flippant will be balanced by the conscientious, the optimistic by the pessimistic, and so on. Furthermore, when a questionnaire is used for one individual during a Vocational Guidance examination, the examiner can be fairly sure that the candidate will answer to the best of his ability, because, in his own eyes, so much is at stake. When the examiner discusses certain of the answers with the candidate after the form has been completed, he is also able to estimate to some extent the reliability of the replies.

The devising of a really good questionnaire is not easy. Many "snags" may crop up in the wording and in the formation of the questions, since what appears clear to the deviser may convey quite a different idea to the candidate, or, indeed, different ideas to different candidates. To obviate this, questionnaires are presented in as simple a form as possible. In the usual type the candidate is asked to make a choice between alternative answers, thus:

$$\text{Do you regard yourself as:}\begin{cases}\text{Industrious} & \text{or Lazy}\\ \text{Careful} & \text{or Careless}\\ \text{Popular} & \text{or Unpopular}\\ \text{Ambitious} & \text{or Unambitious}\\ \text{Talkative} & \text{or Taciturn.}\end{cases}$$

Another type of questionnaire relies upon a three-point scale on which the candidate is required to rate himself on a number of qualities.

THE INTERVIEW

It is, perhaps, not too sweeping a statement to say that from time immemorial the personal interview has been the accepted method by which an employer has selected suitable applicants for a vacant position. An interview has also frequently played an important part in examinations, and it is probable that the general form of the interview in either case has not changed very greatly until recent times. This type of interview, which may be called the traditional interview as contrasted with the modern psychological interview, has two characteristics in common with its modern counterpart, namely, personal contact and the resulting personal interaction. There cannot be a real interview unless the interviewer and the person interviewed are face to face; and whenever two people come face to face there are bound to be personal interactions. In the interview these interactions occur on two planes: the intellectual plane (or perhaps it should be termed the factual plane), through the medium of oral questions put by the interviewer with a definite end in view, and the corresponding answers by the candidate; and the emotional plane, in which occur the reactions of each of the two persons concerned to the physical and psychological qualities of the other. In the "employment" interview of the usual type the question whether or not the prospective employer likes the applicant is usually a most important factor.

With these two characteristics, the similarity between the old type, or traditional, interview and the modern psychological interview ends. Later, an attempt will be made to show how the latter differs from the former, but before doing so it is necessary to explain how the traditional interview fails. Much investigation has been carried out in recent times into the reliability of results gained from the interview of the traditional type, not only in the educational world but also in the professions and industries.

In the educational world the interview is usually synonymous with the oral examination or "viva voce", of which Vernon says: "Theoretically they should constitute a valuable supplement to written examinations, since they provide a fresh medium of expression of ability. But investigations have shown that judgements based on interviews tend to be still less reliable than those based on essay-examination answers". In one case, two boards of interviewers, having previously agreed together on the questions they would ask, interviewed the same sixteen candidates. On comparing the results, it was found that, whilst the individual members of each board tended to agree with each other, the two boards as separate entities most emphatically disagreed. The final marks differed by 12 per cent for average candidates; the widest difference was 31 per cent and the narrowest only 1 per cent.

In the table printed below, figures are given which illustrate that in the industrial world, where investigations along the same lines have been very

Applicant	SALES MANAGERS											
	1	2	3	4	5	6	7	8	9	10	11	12
A	33	46	6	56	26	32	12	38	23	22	22	9
B	36	50	43	17	51	47	38	20	38	55	39	9
C	53	10	6	21	16	9	20	2	57	28	1	26

numerous, results have been very similar. This well-known instance is given by Hollingworth. Fifty-seven applicants for sales positions were interviewed in the traditional manner by twelve sales managers recognized as well experienced in the selection of salesmen. Typical results are given in the table, which shows the respective positions of three of the candidates as placed by each of the twelve sales managers.

It seems unfortunate that one applicant, A, could be rated sixth by sales manager No. 3 and fifty-sixth by sales manager No. 4; but it is almost incredible that applicant C should be placed first by sales manager No. 11 and fifty-seventh by sales manager No. 9.

The interview plays such a very important part in Vocational Guidance and Selection that improvements in its technique have been attempted in order to make it a useful tool in the hands of the vocational psychologist. Gradually, therefore, the "psychological" interview has been evolved: it has not yet reached perfection, but it is certainly a great advance on the traditional interview as regards the objectivity of its findings and is consequently far more

	1	2	3	4	5
PERSONAL APPEARANCE				✓	
PERSEVERANCE			✓		
CO-OPERATIVENESS	✓				

FIG. 72. *Rating by Defined Groups. This form of rating scale was used in early research work, but has now been replaced by more satisfactory methods.*

successful than its somewhat erratic predecessor. The main difference between the two is that the psychological interview is planned in advance; the psychologist carefully maps out the information he wishes to obtain and devises questions which are likely to elicit this information. Thus the interview becomes semi-standardized, but it must never be fully standardized: the rigidity of the test situation must be avoided. It is impossible to foretell how an interview will develop, and a certain amount of freedom is essential; but this freedom is controlled under the psychological technique to the extent that inconsequential chat is avoided, except in so far as it helps to put the candidate at his ease.

Having planned his interview chart, the psychologist has a difficult technique to follow and many pitfalls to avoid.

An interviewer must have a mature outlook and a wide experience of human nature in its many manifestations; he must possess the two qualities of insight and detachment; and he needs good intelligence and powers not only of inconspicuously persuading the candidate to talk freely and frankly, but also of being able to reconstruct, from the fragments emerging during the interview, a true picture of the candidate's personality. Bias of any kind must be studiously avoided, for in an interview it is liable to produce what is commonly known as the "halo" effect—that is, bias in one direction may spread and colour all other judgements. It is against this possibility that the good interviewer is constantly on the watch. The ideal arrangement is for the candidate to be interviewed separately by more than one interviewer and for the interviewers to meet afterwards and discuss their various assessments. In such discussions, bias on the part of one interviewer is often cancelled out by an opposite bias in another interviewer.

The interviewer must get the full co-operation of the candidate, without which all else is of little avail. He has, as Macrae says, to "think himself into the position of the person being interviewed". He has to be natural and friendly without being effusive; he must be constantly encouraging and never adversely critical; he must never be critical in any moral sense; and he must never adopt in the slightest degree a patronizing attitude or give the impression that he is "talking down" to the candidate.

To conclude, it must be emphasized again that the interviewer should have at hand a carefully prepared chart which he should fill in during or immediately after the interview, and that the talk with the candidate should have been carefully arranged so that the necessary information will be forthcoming in a natural manner without the unnatural emphasis of question and answer.

RATING SCALES

The fourth aid in the assessment of temperament and personality is the rating scale, although, as we have already emphasized, it should not be considered alone. Rating scales are very helpful in controlling the "halo" effect; moreover they help to provide an "objective" form of assessment which can, if required, be converted into a quantitative measure. This means that, when considered necessary, a score can be given to the candidate for each quality rated.

There are a number of forms of rating scales, but the three described here are those in most general use, namely, the Order of Merit, Rating by Defined Groups, and the Graphic Rating Scale.

The Order of Merit. This can only be used when people in a group have to be rated for one or more qualities: it is not a method that can be used for isolated individuals. Each quality is considered separately by the rater, and the individuals are then arranged in order from the highest to the lowest, according to the assessment of the quality for each person. This method suffers from two weaknesses: it can only operate within the one particular group of people, and it relies on purely subjective estimates on the part of the rater, who provides his own standard for the purposes of comparison and has no outside or independent standards against which to check his judgements.

Rating by Defined Groups. In this form of rating, each quality is rated against a scale consisting usually of five, sometimes of seven, points. These may be marked numerically, as 1, 2, 3, 4, 5, the lowest value being 1 and the highest value being 5; or they may be labelled as "very good", "good", "average", "poor", and "very poor" respectively. The rater puts a mark against each quality at the appropriate point in the scale (Fig. 72).

This form of rating scale was used in early research work, but it was found to be unsatisfactory for two reasons. In the first place, raters varied considerably, not only in their interpretations of what constituted each quality, but also in their assessments of what were good, average, and poor values of each quality. Secondly, it was found that the limitations of the scale imposed too great a rigidity in the marking. This method has now given place to a more elastic form of rating scale.

The Graphic Rating Scale. In the graphic rating scale a straight line represents the distribution of a particular quality from minimum to maximum or *vice versa.* Each quality is given a title and a general definition, with further definitions at each of the main points along the scale, thus:—

INDUSTRIOUS-
NESS

| (Consider to what extent he "sticks" to the job) | Gets down to the job and doesn't slack. | Shows a desire to complete the job. | Works fairly steadily. | Requires frequent "prodding." | Idles unless watched continuously. |

ACCURACY

| (Consider whether work suffers owing to carelessness) | Extremely careless. | Careless. | Normally careful. | Usually very careful. | Never shows signs of carelessness. |

POPULARITY

| (Consider the subject's standing with his fellows) | Arouses definite dislike. | Somewhat disliked. | No definite indication. | Liked: a good mixer. | Popular favourite. |

LEADERSHIP

| (Consider ability to direct others) | Seems to take lead unconsciously. | Capable of leading others when asked. | No particular indication. | Seems incapable of leading others. | Definitely proved incapable of leading others. |

The rater can place his tick at any point along the line, and the grading can be reduced to numerical values which need not be limited to the five main points of the scale.

When devising a rating scale, every effort must be made to prepare for the various qualities definitions which can be readily understood and followed by all raters using the scale. With this object in view, while the scale is being prepared the definitions should be submitted to the criticisms of as many competent people as possible. It will be found extremely difficult, or even impossible, to devise a scale entirely above criticism, but when it has once been standardized it must be adhered to rigidly. Unless raters subdue their personal opinions and accept the definitions given, no objective standard of rating can be achieved.

There are dangers in the use of rating scales, and these must be avoided as far as possible. The first danger is the tendency to avoid the extreme rating, whether high or low, and to "bunch" all the ratings around the average. The second danger is a tendency to avoid the lower ratings altogether in an effort to be "kind and sympathetic" to the candidate. Where Vocational Guidance is concerned, such soft-heartedness is no kindness at all, because a knowledge of the candidate's weak points is as important as a knowledge of his strong ones. A third danger is the "halo" effect already mentioned. This effect can be counteracted to some extent by occasionally reversing the order of the descriptions, as has been done in the examples given above. It will be seen that, reading from left to right, two of the examples range from high standards to low, the remainder from low to high. Thus it will be essential for a rater to read each separate definition carefully. Consequently, he will not be so inclined to place his marks more or less automatically at the same end of the scale, as a result of an early favourable impression.

Practical experience teaches that of all types of rating scales the graphic type is the most satisfactory that has yet been devised. This method has proved especially valuable when several raters are making independent assessments of different groups of candidates.

THE VOCATIONAL PSYCHOLOGIST AT WORK

The methods which the vocational psychologist uses in his attempts to give guidance both of an educational and a vocational character have now been briefly described. We shall now explain how the psychologist makes skilled use of these various methods.

A boy of sixteen who has come for guidance in the choice of his future career may be taken as an example. The first and most important thing is for the psychologist to get on good terms with the boy. Unless the boy feels that the psychologist is taking a really friendly and personal interest in him and is trying to help him in every possible way, he will never extend to the psychologist the co-operation which is so essential to a successful interview.

Prior to the interview, certain groundwork should have been prepared. A report should have been obtained from the headmaster of the boy's school. If this report is in the form of a cumulative school record, the psychologist will have at hand an extremely valuable aid. Much improvement is being effected in the preparation of school reports, and the value of the cumulative school record is now generally appreciated. Such a record should begin when the child enters school and should continue throughout his school life. It should contain all fundamental educational information about the child at regular intervals, such as his intelligence level, his abilities in school subjects, his interests and hobbies, qualities and defects of his personality, and other facts of importance in regard to his "make-up". A medical report and some indication of the home background may also be included in the school record.

After a short introductory talk, the boy may be asked to complete a self-rating personality chart, which will form an excellent basis for the remainder of the interview. The psychologist will use an occasional test, possibly of the performance or non-verbal intelligence type, partly to obtain additional assessment and partly to assist him in filling up the temperament and personality chart which he is gradually completing.

By this time the psychologist will have in mind certain aptitudes (for example, mechanical, clerical or manual) in connexion with which he would like to have definite assessments. If the boy has attended a school where there was a teacher trained in testing technique, useful data regarding these qualities may be found in the school record. If this is not the case, the psychologist will have to give the boy tests of special aptitudes.

Information regarding the boy's educational history and his abilities in school subjects—including, of course, his weak subjects—should be included in the school record, which should give, in addition, an account of his behaviour.

It is useful to know how he gets on with his fellow pupils, how he reacts to authority, whether he shows powers of accepting responsibility, and so on.

During the course of the interview the psychologist will have learned a good deal about the boy's interests and hobbies, in addition to the information included in the school record, and he will know what views are held by the parents. In short, he should by now have prepared a complete analytical picture of the boy. This information may be summarized on a single sheet.

CHOOSING THE RIGHT CAREER

It now remains to match this analytical picture of the boy with a suitable career. In order to do this the psychologist must have at his command analytical surveys of various trades and professions. He must know the level of intelligence needed in various forms of employment, the qualifications required, the special abilities, the type of personality, and so on. He must also be informed about the methods of entry and training before and during employment.

Obviously he cannot possibly have a personal knowledge of, or even a working acquaintance with, all professions and trades, but he must at least have lists and detailed particulars at hand for immediate reference.

The next step is to decide on general guidance. In order to do this, a process of elimination may be followed. Most jobs can be roughly divided into groups according to the intelligence needed, and the first stage is indicated, therefore, by the boy's mental level. Aptitudes will now come under review in order to decide whether his work should be of a practical nature.

Then it will be useful to decide whether he makes contacts easily and to what extent he should meet others in connexion with his work. It should now be possible for the psychologist to give general guidance, and afterwards he will proceed to consider specific forms of employment. In this connexion it should be emphasized that Vocational Guidance does not consist of assigning one particular job to each person. Every one of us is competent to do more than one particular job, and many jobs call for very similar qualities.

In the first report published by the City of Birmingham Education Committee on the value of vocational tests as an aid to choice of employment, actual examples are provided of guidance given to boys and girls leaving Elementary schools.

The following two instances will indicate the form which this general guidance and specific guidance may take:

(1) (Boy) *General Guidance*

Suitable for work needing superior intelligence and very good manual dexterity, but only average mechanical ability. Clerical ability very good.

Specific Guidance

(a) General Post Office Stores
(b) Clerical
(c) Superior Warehouse

(2) (Girl) *General Guidance*

Suitable for any work requiring very good intelligence; very good dressmaking ability and social qualities.

Specific Guidance.

(a) Shop Assistant (good-class)
(b) Dressmaking
(c) Superior Warehouse, involving clerical work.

REACHING A CONCLUSION

A very considerable development of Vocational Psychology may be anticipated in the coming years in the fields of both education and industry. It is proposed now to consider the lines along which this development is likely to proceed, and it will be found convenient to divide the study into the following four main divisions, namely, Educational Guidance, Educational Selection, Vocational Guidance, and Vocational Selection.

The Education Act of 1944 has attempted to place on a systematic basis the educational system of Great Britain. The details of this have already been discussed in Chapter VIII. In this chapter it is proposed to consider the methods which should be adopted in order to direct children into the appropriate courses of secondary education.

EDUCATIONAL GUIDANCE

It is quite obvious that all children will not be suitable for the same Secondary school course; some should continue their education along scholastic lines, such as is provided in the Grammar schools; others should attend courses which have a definite bias in a technical direction (e.g. engineering or commercial courses); while others again should receive their education along more general lines, as provided in the so-called Modern school. It may be that these different courses of instruction will be found in the one building, in a multilateral school, or in different schools of the unilateral type. It may be more convenient for one type of school to be in one area and for another area to be supplied with the other type. These are questions for the educational psychologist and the educational administrator. The question of how the children are to be chosen for the different types of instruction must be considered here, for it cannot be divorced from Vocational Psychology.

It is difficult to see how any reliable system can be evolved which does not provide for the use of tests of a psychological character. These tests should be given in school, and it will be necessary, therefore, for each school to have on its staff at least one teacher trained in the technique of psychological testing. When a child has reached eleven years of age, it will be possible to decide, by the proper use of intelligence tests and aptitude tests, whether he should continue his education along general lines or whether he should take a Grammar school course. At later stages other reliable tests should be used to give guidance regarding technical courses and technical subjects. In this way each child will be guided into the educational stream best suited to his intelligence and his aptitudes, as is envisaged in the Education Act.

EDUCATIONAL SELECTION

Although it has been found convenient to separate Educational Selection from Educational Guidance in this chapter, there is no clear line of demarcation between the two. At the present time the Grammar and the Technical schools select their entrants by some form of competitive examination. It is important that the entrance examination for a particular school should be designed to select those children who are able to profit from the type of instruction provided. When the Education Act of 1944 comes into full operation all children will receive expert Educational Guidance. Whether the matter is considered from the point of view of guiding the child into the appropriate educational stream or with the object of selecting the appropriate children for a particular course of instruction, the fundamental principle must be scientific guidance or scientific selection.

VOCATIONAL GUIDANCE

At this point it is of interest to refer again to the large experiment conducted by the Birmingham Education Committee, already described.

The official report on this research work states that definite evidence was produced that the adoption of scientific methods in Vocational Guidance improves very considerably the advice that can be given to children leaving school.

Children who are given vocational guidance by these methods and who follow the advice given are much more happily placed in employment, are more permanently settled, and are of greater value to their employers than children who are specially guided but do not follow the advice, or children who are given the sort of advice which is not based on scientific methods.

This evidence definitely corroborates earlier research in Birmingham and also similar investigations conducted by the National Institute of Industrial Psychology.

The writers of the report proceed to make suggestions as to how these scientific methods may be put into general use. Attention is directed to the position which will arise when the Education Act of 1944 comes into full operation, and the report continues:

"All children at the age of eleven+ will begin a secondary course of education, but naturally the secondary course of instruction will vary according to the abilities and aptitudes of the different scholars. Possibly, for a few years, the course will be on general scholastic lines, but as their capabilities are assessed, so the children will be guided into particular streams, for example, scholastic, technical, commercial, artistic and practical. The possibility of using tests of the type used in these Vocational Guidance experiments, including tests of scholastic aptitudes, will no doubt be borne in mind. The information obtained should be collected on cumulative record and progress cards and at a later stage there should be added other data obtained for Vocational Guidance purposes. These records would then be available at the appropriate stage for the Juvenile Employment officer.

"Steps should be taken to arrange training courses for selected teachers in senior (secondary) schools with a view to ensuring that there shall be on the staff of each school at least one teacher competent to apply psychological tests and trained in the collection of relevant data. . . . These teachers should be required to give selected tests at appropriate stages in each child's school life, and to record the data on cumulative record cards with other information regarding the child's progress, attainments and history.

"These records should be used from time to time to enable decisions to be reached as to the course of instruction each child should receive.

"Towards the end of the child's school life the Juvenile Employment officer should study these records, co-operate with the Head and with the trained teacher, and give Vocational Guidance."

A point which frequently causes criticism may be put in the form of a question.

What is the use of giving Vocational Guidance to a pupil leaving school if there is a dearth of employment, and it is not likely that he will obtain the work recommended?

This is a point which deserves very careful study. In the first place, it must be remembered that Vocational Guidance should not mean the labelling of a boy with one particular job for which, and for no other, he is regarded as suitable.

Vocational Guidance at its best should primarily be of a general character and should consist of an indication of the aptitudes and abilities of a particular child. He may be, and usually is, capable of tackling fairly successfully a number of different jobs, all of which, in varying degrees, will call for the aptitudes he possesses. The next step should be to consider, in relation to the child's characteristics, the openings which may suggest themselves and which are available; in such a case it will be helpful to the child, even if he is advised to take up other work temporarily, to have been given expert advice as to his capabilities, so that he may continue his studies to fit himself for opportunities when they arise.

This having been accomplished, there can be no doubt that such a child will not be so easily discouraged as one who, without Vocational Guidance, is left alone to withstand the buffets of employment or the disadvantages of wrong placing and who has no encouragement and no future opportunity for which he can continue to prepare himself.

VOCATIONAL SELECTION

In the main, the employment of Vocational Selection is the responsibility of industry and is dealt with in another chapter. However, it is appropriate to call attention here to the importance of using scientific methods in selecting young workers for particular jobs. More and more firms are employing trained personnel staffs for this work, and there can be no doubt that the industrialist who is to succeed will in the future make the fullest use of the methods described in this section and in the section dealing with Industrial Psychology.

Vocational Guidance should not be regarded as an attempt in a short interview to give advice to a child on a question which will affect the whole of his future life. Rather should Vocational Guidance be regarded as a gradual process which is being developed throughout the whole of the latter part of the child's school career and should be a natural sequel to—or perhaps even a part of—Educational Guidance. Records carefully prepared on a scientific basis should be kept during the child's school career. At certain stages, tests should be given by teachers who are competent to apply them, and the results should be added to these cumulative record cards. The heads of the schools, in consultation with the trained teachers, should from time to time use these records to guide the children into appropriate educational streams. Towards the end of the child's school life, the Juvenile Employment officer should co-operate with the school staff in order that expert guidance and help may be given in regard to the choice of a career.

Only in this way will it be possible to ensure that each child has the education for which he is suited and to which he is entitled; only in this way will it be possible to assist each child to obtain the employment for which he is capable and from which he will derive the greatest happiness; only in this way will industry, and indeed the nation, be able to face the future with confidence and security.

Test Yourself

1. What methods does the vocational psychologist use to aid him in assessing personality and temperament?

2. Give headings of the information needed concerning a boy of sixteen years of age to whom Vocational Guidance is to be given.

3. Discuss the relationship between Vocational Guidance and Vocational Selection.

Answers will be found at the end of the book.

IV. PSYCHOLOGY IN PRODUCTION

CHAPTER XII

INDUSTRIAL ENVIRONMENT

IN THE course of a century there has been a very striking change in the attitude of employers towards their employees. A hundred years ago workers were referred to as "hands" and were generally regarded as something rather less important than the new machines that were coming into use. In general, no heed was paid to the physical conditions under which men worked and some of the drab factories which still survive bear witness to this outlook. Hours of work were practically unlimited, and the conditions of workers' homes were such as would horrify us today. It was usual for young children to work 15–16 hours a day and 90–100 hours a week.

The accepted attitude of the average employer was that the amount of work done, the output, was in direct mathematical proportion to the number of hours worked. If a worker was occupied at a machine for 96 hours, he would produce exactly double what he would produce in 48 hours.

Despite this grim state of affairs there were a few employers who shone out as notable exceptions, and Robert Owen was foremost among these.

Owen was a Manchester cotton mill owner, who, inspired by a generous humanitarian outlook, adopted a remarkably different attitude towards factory workers. Applying his ideas to his mill in New Lanark, he abandoned the usual 15- or 16-hour day and limited work to 10½ hours a day. He made other changes which shocked his fellow employers and earned for himself a reputation for something akin to madness. But Owen found that output did not suffer and that there was a remarkable improvement in the health and cheerfulness of his operatives. He had disproved the accepted beliefs and at the same time built up a flourishing and successful business. He had made the first departure from the mechanical outlook which regarded men only as an unfortunate necessity if machines were to be worked.

HOURS OF WORK

The next important experiment which challenged the old conceptions regarding the hours of work was undertaken towards the end of last century. By that time, hours of work were substantially less than they had been, but they were still in the neighbourhood of 54 a week. In the 1890s, a Manchester

FIG. 73. *Squalid conditions and the use of child labour are both apparent in this picture of matchbox-makers plying their trade in the East End of London. Such workshops were commonplace during the greater part of the nineteenth century. Infants, too young to be left at home, often accompanied their parents at work, amid harmful surroundings.*

engineering firm, Messrs. Mather & Platt, embarked upon the experiment of reducing hours and starting work at 8 a.m. instead of the usual 6 a.m. These changes resulted in an increase in production and a reduction in time lost through absenteeism.

Although the success of this experiment was sufficiently notable to encourage the British Government to adopt a similar scheme in certain dockyards and munition factories, industry as a whole did not follow the lead. Evidently the Government itself did not have the courage of its convictions, for when the First World War broke out the first method adopted to speed up production was a general increase in hours of work. Then, as twenty-five years later, women streamed into the factories. The lessons of the past were ignored and hours were increased until they became more or less unlimited.

In 1916 the problem of munition production was so acute that the Minister of Munitions appointed the Health of Munition Workers Committee, which was invited to "consider and advise on questions of industrial fatigue, hours of labour and other matters affecting the personal health and physical efficiency of workers in munitions factories and workshops." From this beginning, it may be said, Industrial Psychology as we know it today had its origin. For the science of Industrial Psychology is essentially a study of man in relation to his industrial environment.

Between 1915 and 1916 the Health of Munition Workers Committee carried out research in munition factories into the effects of long hours upon output, upon accident incidence and upon sickness and lost time. The investigations were, of course, carried out during the war period when abnormal conditions prevailed, but the results obtained were striking and indicated that there was a wide potential application to industry in general. When the committee was finally disbanded in 1917, a new organization, the Industrial Fatigue Research Board, was formed with a wider scope to carry out similar and extended investigations. The titles of the first six reports published by the board indicate the type of work undertaken in the early days. The titles were as follows: "The Influence of Hours of Work and of Ventilation on Output in Tinplate Manufacture"; "The Output of Women Workers in relation to Hours of Work in Shell-making"; "A study of Improved Methods in an Iron Foundry"; "The Incidence of Industrial Accidents, with special reference to Multiple Accidents"; "Fatigue and Efficiency in the Iron and Steel Industry"; and "The Speed of Adaptation of Output to altered Hours of Work". After a few years, further reports showed that the field of investigation was widening.

In 1921, Dr. C. S. Myers was largely responsible for founding the National Institute of Industrial Psychology, an independent, non-profit-making organization which for the first time enabled any individual firm to avail itself of the knowledge and experience of industrial psychologists who had made a study of industrial conditions and problems.

In the period between the wars, the Industrial Fatigue (now Health) Research Board carried out a large number of investigations and published some seventy reports on its work, and by 1939 the work of both this body and of the National Institute of Industrial Psychology had become widely known.

At the same time, the attitude of the employer towards the worker was undergoing a profound change. The obligations that industry had towards the employee were recognized, and a few individual firms and some industries employed their own staffs of industrial psychologists.

During the period of the Second World War the importance of the work of industrial psychologists was clearly recognized by the Service departments, particularly in the field of selection of suitable personnel for various jobs. In Time and Motion Studies, too, much valuable work was done. It is possible that the work done by the motion study unit of the War Office in Britain played no small part in determining the design and efficiency of various weapons and hence made its direct contribution to victory in the field.

THE PSYCHOLOGIST IN INDUSTRY

Psychology itself has been described by William McDougall as "the science which claims to formulate the body of ascertained truths about the constitution and working of the mind, and which endeavours to refine and add to this knowledge". Industrial psychology concerns itself with these same problems against a background of industrial activity.

Perhaps today the fact of the interaction between mind and body is widely accepted. It is, therefore, not surprising to find considerable stress laid upon bodily as well as mental reactions to the external environment. We shall, therefore, have to consider the problems associated with the cause and effect of fatigue, and indicate various ways in which it can be alleviated, as well as the physical environment and its effect upon our reactions. Factory lay-out and Time and Motion studies have to be considered as means of increasing human efficiency by the reduction of unnecessary mental and physical effort.

Moreover, it is important to place each individual in work for which he is suited and to select for each particular job a person capable of performing it with efficiency. Industrial Psychology, therefore, is concerned with Vocational Selection and Vocational Guidance, which have already been discussed.

We must accept the fact that, unfortunately, industrial activity cannot take place without a certain toll of human life and health, and the Industrial Psychologist must be interested in such questions as well as in the larger question of human welfare in relation to work—whether, in fact, the factory worker is to have the chance of full development of his personality, or whether he is to feel stunted and restricted, a creature incapable of giving of his best or of enjoying life to the fullest extent of his capacity.

PROBLEMS OF FATIGUE

We all know what it feels like to be tired, but few of us have thought about the actual nature of fatigue. Fatigue may be considered to be of two different kinds.

There is actual physical fatigue, about which physiologists know a good deal, and there is mental fatigue, caused sometimes by monotony or boredom. Let us consider first the physical state known as fatigue.

In muscular activity energy is supplied by a substance in the body known as glycogen, which is used up during such activity. The waste products of the reaction are normally dealt with by the blood circulation and through the action of the lungs and kidneys. If the muscular activity is excessive or prolonged, as during violent physical effort, the waste products may accumulate, giving rise to the experience of fatigue.

By a simple experiment it can be shown that an individual muscle or set of muscles may very quickly become fatigued and be incapable of further activity. Even the simple task of raising oneself by the arms on a horizontal bar cannot be done for more than a limited number of times. The muscles then become fatigued and require a period of rest in order to recover.

In the normal life of the individual there are sufficient opportunities for rest to prevent such a state of exhaustion, and during the normal working day there are various pauses which allow recovery from the less extreme forms of fatigue.

At night there is a period of rest and recovery, and a healthy individual is able to start the new day fresh and alert for the tasks that lie ahead.

The subjective side of fatigue is more complicated, and the problems of boredom and monotony will be considered later.

The method that psychologists have adopted to measure fatigue involves the use of the work curve; this method necessitates a study of the actual amount of productive work done at different periods of the day. If asked, the average worker will say that he works at the same rate throughout the day, and that his production does not vary from hour to hour or from day to day. The measure of truth in this belief may be judged from facts that have been actually recorded.

A study was made in a factory of the production of a given article throughout a working week and the results were carefully analysed. The following table shows the average time taken to produce a single article at different times of the day and the average hourly rate of production at these times.

Time of day	Average time in seconds to produce one article	Average hourly rate of production
8.00– 8.30 a.m.	12·5	288
10.30–11.00	10·5	342
12.30– 1.00 p.m.	12·5	288
2.00– 2.30	11.5	314
4.00– 4.30	10·5	328
6.30– 7.00	16·5	213
Average for week	11·6	310

These figures, typical of many others that have been recorded, indicate that production throughout the day is not at a uniform rate. At the beginning of the day there is a period during which the worker is "warming up" to his task. About the middle of the morning he is working at his best, and mind and body are tuned up to maximum efficiency. As the morning draws to its close, however, the worker begins to feel the effects of fatigue, and, whether consciously or not, the rate of work begins to fall. In the last hour of the morning the output is the same as during the first hour.

After the interval for dinner the worker returns refreshed from the rest, and during the first hour of the afternoon production has improved on the last hour before dinner. Again a warming-up period takes place and at about four o'clock production reaches another peak.

Fatigue now begins to set in again and the rate of work rapidly declines. Between 6.30 and 7 p.m. the rate of production is lower than at any other time in the day.

It is clearly of the utmost importance to know, not only how production varies during the course of the day, but also how it varies with different periods of employment. Thus the old theories, which held that production was directly proportional to the number of hours worked, have been proved to be false.

An inquiry instituted during the First World War carried this work further by studying the effects of varied hours of work on the production of fuse bodies.

A group of women engaged on this work were observed and exact figures of their production were recorded. The hours were nominally high, though actually, owing to bad time-keeping, they were slightly less than was officially presumed. When the hours were nominally 74·5 per week (actually 66·0), the average hourly production was 108 units and the weekly production 7,178 units. When the hours were reduced to a nominal figure of 63·5 per week (and were actually 54·4) the hourly production rose to 131. This hourly increase was not quite sufficient to counterbalance the smaller total of hours worked, and the weekly production fell to 7,126 units. Finally, the hours were reduced to 55·3 per week (47 5 being actually worked). The hourly production then rose to 169. This remarkable improvement in the hourly rate of work increased the weekly output to 8,028, an increase of 13 per cent over the weekly production when the hours were longest.

Similar investigations have been made for other operations, and in general it has been established that the more the production is governed by the human factor the less profitable is it to work excessive hours.

PERIODS OF WORK AND REST

During the Second World War further detailed studies of the effects of long hours, fatigue and boredom on production were carried out by the Industrial Health Research Board, and similar results were obtained, thus establishing beyond any doubt that fatigue has the effect of producing a decline in production. It must not be assumed, however, that there is one and only one optimum period of employment that will give the best production results from all people in all jobs. This is not the case, and in a report published by the I.H.R.B. (Conditions for Industrial Health and Efficiency Pamphlet No. 2, H.M.S.O., 1944) it is stated that the evidence suggests that weeky hours for men should not exceed 60 and for women 55. Even this may be too long, and particularly so in the case of persons engaged in heavy manual work.

The length of the working day is not, however, the only matter that requires a close study. It is also necessary to examine the best way in which the day should be split into periods of rest and work.

The old idea was simple. Work started at 8 a.m., or even earlier, and continued until the dinner hour at 1 p.m. At 2 p.m. work was resumed until the hooter went at 6 or 7 p.m. and everyone hurried home. Experience now has

FIG. 74. *A spinning room in a modern Lancashire cotton mill. In addition to the modernization of equipment, greatly improved working conditions—including excellent lighting arrangements, humidity units, air-conditioning plant and locker seats—are important factors in maintaining a contented atmosphere among a healthy staff, and moreover, in achieving a considerable increase in efficiency and a greater output in consequence.*

shown that this is by no means the best way of dividing up the working day, and it is quite usual nowadays for rest breaks to be given in the course of the morning or afternoon spell, or both. The benefit that may be derived from such rest pauses, as they are usually called, is illustrated by an example taken from a laundry.

During the period of the rush season it had been found that one department could never get through the pile of work before 7 or even 8 at night. At the time, the hours of work were 8 a.m. to 1 p.m. and 2 p.m. to 7 or 8 p.m. If work continued after 7 p.m., an interval of half an hour was allowed. The long hours were continued week after week, and in course of time the workers were all thoroughly tired and dissatisfied. The following year the management decided that they must endeavour to prevent these long hours, so, as an experiment, they altered the arrangement of the working day. Work started at 8 a.m. as before, but at 10 a.m. a break of 15 minutes was allowed. Many of the workers had come to work after having breakfasted on little more than a cup of tea, so they used the interval for a light snack of sandwiches or cakes and tea, which could be obtained in the canteen. At 10.15 they returned for another two hours' work, much refreshed and ready to get on with the job.

At 12.15 they had a dinner break, half an hour, during which a meal was available in the canteen. At 12.45 they resumed work for another two hours until 2.45, when another tea break of 15 minutes was allowed. Finally they returned to work from 3 p.m. to 5 p.m., when they finished for the day and went home. The combination of reduced hours and short working spells had the effect of enabling them, week after week, to go home at 5 p.m. with a full day's work done.

Not only was the work completed in a very much shorter time, thereby saving the employer considerable overhead costs, such as lighting and power, but the workers had many more hours of leisure, which they were well able to enjoy, as they were less tired at the end of the day.

TIMING THE REST PAUSES

The introduction of rest pauses is not always so straightforward and so simple as this example might suggest, and before introducing them it is wise to study the particular circumstances of the work being done. The Industrial Health Research Board's Report No. 42 (Rest Pauses in Industry) surveyed the problem of rest pauses and pointed out that widely different results have been obtained, making it impossible to generalize. Before rest pauses are introduced the conditions prevailing and the state of the output curve should be studied in order to indicate at what point a rest is desirable. The pause should then be introduced at that period when output has reached its maximum and before it begins to fall. The introduction of a pause at this point will then retard the onset of fatigue and other factors which are detrimental to production.

Following the pause, a high level of production may continue for the rest of the working spell. After the introduction of the pause, further records should be kept in order to assess its effects.

The length of the pause needs similar consideration. The goal to be aimed at is that it should be sufficiently long to allow recovery from, or the prevention of, fatigue, but not so long as to offset the advantages thereby gained.

Long before industrial psychologists studied these problems the Army had discovered the value of rest pauses, and when on the march a rest of ten minutes was allowed in every hour. The housewife, too, has accepted the idea, even if she does not understand the principles underlying it, and the break for a cup of tea in the morning is often part of her daily routine.

An objection to rest pauses sometimes raised by workers is that they lose money by the enforced break. In order to overcome this objection some firms pay their piece-rate workers on a time-rate basis during the interval. In 1938 the new Factory Act in Britain laid down that if a spell of more than four and a half hours is worked a break of at least ten minutes must be given, and after five hours work at least a half-hour meal break allowed.

Thus the rest pause has become established and the bad old days of long periods of work without a break have passed away, but there remains plenty of opportunity for further investigation in particular cases, so that the duration and position of the break may be based on sound judgement, backed by full knowledge, rather than be left to chance.

While the preceding paragraphs have considered physical fatigue, there is also the mental aspect. Subjective factors, such as boredom, are no less important than the objective ones.

Experienced workers engaged on light repetitive work may suffer little from physical fatigue, but the monotony of repeating the same thing over and over again may induce a feeling of boredom that is no less wearying than a hard day's physical exertion. While it is difficult to "explain" boredom, the bored person is quite able to state that he is bored, and the degree of his boredom is something that he alone can estimate.

In the Industrial Health Research Board Reports Nos. 52 and 56, Wyatt and Fraser describe their investigations into the problems of boredom in work.

Investigations were carried out in various repetitive jobs, including jobs such as tobacco weighing, chocolate packing and soap wrapping. It was found that the output curves of some of the workers followed the pattern described at the beginning of this chapter, that is to say, a period of warming up was followed by a period of maximum production, followed in turn by a drop in production due to fatigue. Some of the workers were, in fact, conforming to the normal. Others, however, were working irregularly. Production varied apparently indiscriminately from hour to hour. On questioning these workers, it was found that those who worked normally expressed no feeling of boredom, while those who produced irregular variations of work made frequent complaints about boredom. They appeared listless and showed great difficulty in concentrating on their work. Particularly was this the case in the middle of the morning, at the time when production was lowest.

Typical of the bored workers was a variability in their rate of work, and a low output rate in the middle of the work spell, just when it was anticipated that it should be at its maximum. It was said by the workers that this time seemed to pass more slowly than any other period.

An experiment was carried out to examine the effects of varying the work of cigarette makers. This showed that the best results were obtained if making and cutting alternated every one and a half hours and the lowest production resulted from performing only one operation throughout the day.

It was also found that many workers who expressed feelings of boredom for certain jobs found others preferable, though there was no obvious difference between the jobs. Interest in the work was able to dispel boredom.

Where workers were engaged in filling chocolate boxes, different individuals preferred different-sized boxes. A relief from boredom is commonly found in the indulgence in daydreams.

The most bored worker is often an intelligent person whose job does not demand the exercise of his intelligence. Such persons are liable to be discontented and unhappy in unskilled repetitive work, and their potential ability is wasted in such work.

Dr. May Smith, an eminent industrial psychologist, suggests six ways in which boredom can be mitigated:

(1) By letting the worker feel that the work matters. In Britain, despite the monotony of the long industrial hours following the Dunkirk evacuation in 1940, there was little evidence that workers were bored. The sense of excitement and the feeling of the importance of the work enabled workers to carry on without the listless feeling associated with boredom.

(2) By a system of payment having a personal interest. Provided it is properly understood, a piece-rate system of payment tends to produce less boredom than a flat time-rate for the same work.

(3) By allowing adequate rest pauses. When work spells are broken up by rest breaks the time seems to pass more quickly and boredom is less common.

(4) By arranging the work in small units so that it does not seem like a never-ending stream. This is the old story of discerning the goal ahead.

(5) By allowing talking and singing when other people are not disturbed by it. Soldiers on the march have found this to be true, and apart from the stimulus of the rhythm, singing helps to dispel the boredom of a dull occupation and thus makes the time pass more quickly.

(6) By the use of music. "Music While You Work", introduced by the British Broadcasting Corporation, has proved universally popular. Music is played in factories even though it may be inaudible to the visitor owing to the noise of machinery.

The modern industrial age has produced many routine occupations which may give rise to boredom, but if we study the individual and try to find what type of job suits him best, the problem of alleviating, or eliminating, boredom can be faced without undue misgiving.

WORKING CONDITIONS

Just as the type of occupation and the length and arrangement of working hours will affect the worker and may have a good or bad influence upon the amount and quality of work of which he is capable, so will the physical environment in which he works. The nature of this atmosphere is often taken for granted, and beyond lighting a fire when it is cold and wearing different clothes in summer and winter, we do little more to control or improve our physical surroundings. Research has shown that where unsatisfactory atmospheric conditions prevail, not only is there a feeling of discomfort, but production is diminished and sickness and accidents are likely to be increased. It is well known that on a hot sultry day we experience a lack of energy and an inability to get on with the job in hand.

From the air that we breathe we make use of oxygen, and if the quantity of oxygen is seriously reduced the vital functions may become impaired. Unless, however, conditions are exceptional, as, for example, in high flying or in a hermetically sealed space such as a submarine, the quantity of oxygen in the air seldom reaches a level so low as to be seriously deficient. There are, however, other factors that are likely to cause a feeling of discomfort.

Whether at rest or in motion, the body produces heat, and it is the function of good heating and ventilation to ensure that there is a proper balance between the heat generated by the body and the heat lost to the surrounding atmosphere. If health and comfort are to be maintained, the body temperature must remain more or less constant, and this can only be achieved if the heat produced by the body is lost at the same rate at which it is produced.

It is evident also that the temperature which is comfortable depends partly upon our occupation. Extensive observations have shown that the temperature at which persons engaged in light or sedentary work are most comfortable lies between 60 deg.F. and 68 deg.F. For such workers a temperature below 60 deg.F. gives a feeling of cold and anything above 68 deg.F. is regarded as too hot. For more active occupations the figure can be lower, and 55 deg.F. may be satisfactory for workers engaged upon manual tasks.

VENTILATION

In addition to temperature there are two other factors which have a considerable bearing upon the feeling of comfort. These are the humidity, or amount of moisture in the air, and the air movement. It is well known that hot thundery weather is one of the most uncomfortable types that we meet. This is because one of the means by which the body loses heat is by evaporation from its surface. Thus the humidity of the air affects the rate of evaporation from the body, and consequently the rate at which the body may lose heat. At ordinary room temperature the moisture content of the air should certainly not exceed 70 per cent of the saturation figure, and even this figure is too high for comfort. Under ordinary conditions of weather, unless there are hot and wet processes going on, an adequate supply of fresh air is sufficient to ensure that the humidity is not excessive.

The third factor is the amount of air movement. Here again the reason is associated with the capacity of the body to lose the heat that it is generating. We know that wet garments on a clothes-line dry better on a day with a breeze than on a perfectly still day. As the moisture evaporates from the clothes, the air immediately surrounding them becomes more heavily saturated with moisture. If there are adequate air currents, this moist air is blown away and less saturated air takes its place; if there is no air movement, the surrounding air, laden with moisture, is incapable of receiving more from the clothes. Similarly with the human body, if there is no air movement, evaporation, with its consequent cooling capacity, is hindered. For this reason, when the temperature is high considerable improvements can be effected in the feeling of comfort if air movement can be maintained. The use of desk fans in an office, or larger fans in a workroom, ensures that the air is moving and alleviates conditions that might otherwise become unpleasant or even intolerable.

In winter the velocity of the air in an ordinary workroom, generally around 30 ft. per minute, is satisfactory, but in summer higher velocities are desirable. Generally the correct placing of windows is sufficient to ensure adequate air movement, but care in the design of windows is necessary, as well as their proper use, if unpleasant draughts are to be avoided.

Today the desirable atmosphere is regarded as being:

(a) Cool, rather than hot.

(b) Dry, rather than damp.

(c) Diverse in its temperature in different parts and at different times, rather than uniform and monotonous.

(d) Moving, rather than still.

Various experiments and observations have been carried out to determine the effect of temperature and air movement on industrial efficiency. In the tin-plate trade, where very high temperatures are experienced, it has been found that there is a considerable seasonal variation in output. Where there was no artificial ventilation it was found that in summer production was 12 per cent less than in winter. In a factory ventilated by means of a fan system, causing considerable air movement in the vicinity of the men's workplace, the fall of output in the summer was found to be only 3 per cent of the winter figure.

Similar inquiries made by industrial psychologists in the glass-bottle and coal-mining industries have resulted in similar findings.

LIGHTING

The eyes are capable of serving us and giving us information only if there is light. Thus the importance of knowing something about lighting is beyond dispute. It is the intention here to answer the questions: How is light measured? How much light do we need? What is the difference in the effect of good and of bad lighting?

The degree of illumination on a surface is generally measured in terms of foot-candles. One foot-candle is the illumination falling on a surface placed 1 ft. from a standard candle. On a clear moonlight night the illumination is perhaps equal to half a foot-candle, while on a bright sunny day it may be as much as 10,000 foot-candles. Light is easily measured by means of a light-meter, a small pocket instrument of which there are a number of varieties.

FIG. 75. *This is one of the workshops in the modern factory illustrated in Fig. 84. The photograph shows clearly the excellent arrangements made for lighting and spacing.*

By means of a photo-electric cell a direct reading in foot-candles can be made of the amount of light at any place.

The amount of illumination necessary varies according to the particular job. Where vision is important to the operation under consideration, a figure of 20 foot-candles or more may be advisable. In passages and stairways and where good general lighting is less important a lower figure will be satisfactory. The war-time black-out has made us more susceptible to lighting conditions and has perhaps emphasized the cheerless feeling of badly-lit and dingy surroundings. Good lighting makes us cheerful and alert.

In order to be satisfactory, it is not only necessary for the intensity of illumination to be adequate; lighting should also be uniformly distributed and fittings so placed as to avoid dark areas. Dark corners and badly-placed light fittings may be responsible for accidents.

A very common defect is that light sources are so placed as to give rise to glare. Everyone is familiar with glare in its most common form. If, on a bright summer day, one glances from a printed page to the sun, on looking back at the page the print is for a moment invisible. The glare of motor-car headlights at night has a similar effect of causing momentary blindness. This is caused partly by the fact that the pupil of the eye automatically adjusts itself to the brightness of light falling upon it. The pupil contracts in bright light and grows larger in dim light. To a certain extent this occurs if the lamp fittings in a room are so placed that their light falls directly upon the eye. Thus, for example, a badly-placed light in a kitchen may lead to breakages and other accidents resulting from sudden changes in light intensity.

Glare may also arise from a reflecting surface. The effect is similar to that described above, but the irritation may be greater since it is often more insidious and more difficult to escape. Glare may be reflected from any bright, polished surface and care should be taken to avoid it. The golden rule to observe is "Light on the object and not on the eyes".

Glare is often due to badly designed lampshades. Shades should be so designed that they prevent vision of the electric bulb upon a casual raising of the eyes. The old-fashioned lampshades of the shallow, conical type fail hopelessly in this respect. The bulb hangs below the level of the shade and is visible to anyone who chances to look up. Such unshaded lamps are common both in factories and homes. Not only do they cause unnecessary fatigue, but they are liable to be directly responsible for accidents and breakages of all kinds.

If special lighting is required for some particular job, for example, for embroidery or needlework, additional lighting may be obtained by an individual light directed on the work. Such individual lights must also be provided with suitable shades or their value will be entirely offset by the detrimental effects of the glare they cause.

The advantages of well-placed and suitable sources of light, whether natural or artificial, may be lost if windows, lamp fittings, walls and ceilings are not kept clean.

Today we have considerable knowledge of vision and suitable types of lighting to ensure the best use of our eyes. Much of the knowledge is available to all of us, and we should make use of it in our daily affairs.

Test Yourself

1. Give three main points of interest to the industrial psychologist in his study of the relationship of human welfare to efficient work.

2. If you were faced by an increase of absenteeism due to influenza in a factory of which you were a welfare officer, what remedies would you apply?

3. Illustrate from the experience of your daily work the importance of maintaining a right rhythm in everyday life.

Answers will be found at the end of the book.

CHAPTER XIII

ADJUSTING THE INDUSTRIAL PROCESS

I F WE have a task before us there are two ways in which we can approach it. We can either go straight ahead and get on with the job, tackling each problem as it arises, or we can think out the way we propose to work and prepare in our minds a plan of action. Which of these methods is likely to prove the more efficient? How can we ensure that the method that we select is put into operation in the best way possible? Let us consider a homely example to illustrate the two alternatives.

Nearly every housewife undertakes the "spring-cleaning" of her house at least once a year. What would we think of the housewife who, having suddenly decided to spring-clean the sitting-room, first cleaned the carpet and then the walls, and finally remembered the chimney and called in the sweep on the following day. This would be unplanned work with a vengeance, and we should wonder whether such a woman was in her right senses. The right approach is simple, but can only be carried out in practice if due thought is given to it. First the chimney must be swept, so arrangements must be made to call in the sweep either the day before or early in the morning. But even before the sweep starts his work the carpet can be removed. Planning is essential. In the same way it is necessary to plan the work in a factory.

It is a historic fact that many present-day factories have grown up piece-meal from small beginnings. Growth has taken place by extensions and additions which catered for immediate needs. New plant and machinery have, in many cases, been put into any available space regardless of their position relative to other machines and processes.

PRODUCTION PLANNING

The problems of routeing and lay-out are problems of planning production in the most logical way. Where circumstances permit—for example, when a new factory building is planned—the entire lay-out can be planned on paper before it is put into effect. Usually, however, this is impossible. Even so, much can be done if thorough information is obtained regarding the conditions as they actually exist. In order to obtain such information it is advisable to trace the path taken by individual articles in the course of their manufacture.

Examples from various industries have shown how articles may pass up and down from floor to floor of the factory as though a deliberate effort were being made to see just how long could be taken in getting work from one place to another. The first object of production planning is to ensure that this type of wasted effort does not occur, and the first step to take to achieve this is to prepare a detailed plan of the factory. On this plan can be marked the path taken by the articles as they proceed through the works, and also the paths taken by the workers as they carry out their tasks. By such means the extensive or major movements of materials and workers can be surveyed.

There are many examples of considerable saving of effort being effected by rearrangement of the position of machinery so as to give a smooth flow of work. Experiments of this nature are within the reach of each one of us. In ordinary everyday affairs both men and women could save themselves much unnecessary labour if they would examine the reasons for the way in which their things are arranged, and if they would ask themselves whether it were not possible to improve the arrangement.

For example, in the kitchen both the position of cupboards and shelves and the way in which the articles are placed upon them are matters that can either be thought out with proper attention to economy of effort or can be left to chance. The old practice of keeping tea, coffee, sugar, rice and the like in tins often necessitated opening several tins before the right one was selected. Even when the name is printed on the tin some malignant force seems to ensure that the name is turned to the back, and each tin has to be turned round before the name can be seen. Glass jars overcome this difficulty and save time and much irritation. Shelves should not be so deep that articles in the front obscure those at the back, but where such shelves already exist it may be possible to arrange an intermediate one at the back, so that the articles at the back are more easily seen and reached. Such a device may save breakages due to the awkwardness of reaching the wanted article.

PLANT LAY-OUT

An example of the value of adopting the ideas described above was met in a laundry where the ironing and folding of shirts was carried out by a team of four girls. The first girl operated two machines, one for drying and pressing the neckband and cuffs and the other for drying the sleeves. The second girl operated one machine, a steam-heated press, on which she dried and pressed the body of the shirt, while two other girls did the final folding.

Fig. 76 shows the lay-out of the unit as it was first found. The detail of the work was examined and the path taken by the shirt from start to finish of its operation was noted. This path has been marked.

It can readily be seen that there was a good deal of unnecessary movement and that improvements were possible. On the basis of the facts revealed by the plan, a change in the lay-out of the machines was proposed and soon adopted. The intention of the new lay-out was to eliminate the wasted efforts and unnecessary work, and Fig. 77 shows the way in which this result was achieved.

The result of the change could be measured by the rate at which the team produced finished work. Before the change, average production was 37 shirts per hour, while afterwards it was 41, so that the removal of the unnecessary obstacles and hindrances resulted in an increase of production of over 10 per cent. Let it be stressed that there were no other changes apart from those described. The workers were not encouraged or compelled to exert themselves any more. No additional rewards were offered. The increase in production resulted solely from removing the sources of unnecessary effort and thereby making the task simpler.

Many similar examples have been met with in numerous industries and there is little doubt that a careful study of the existing methods in almost any activity would reveal much unnecessary and wasted effort.

The underlying principle towards which industry should aim is the con-

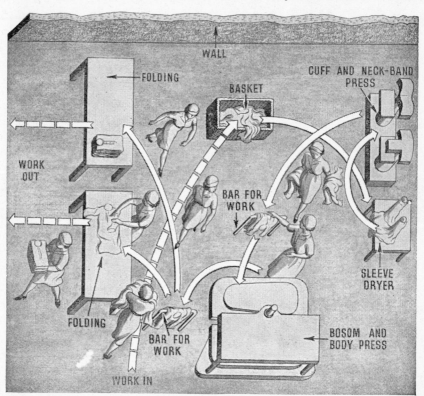

FIG. 76. *This plan of part of a laundry lay-out shows how the haphazard placing of equipment caused much unnecessary labour in the room where shirts were ironed and folded. The arrows indicate the complicated route followed by the shirts during the process of the work.*

266

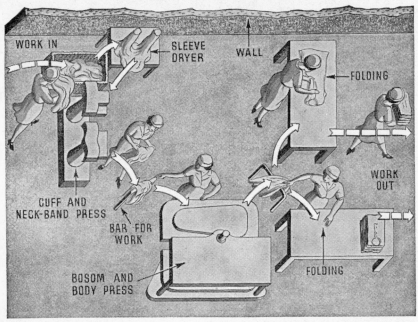

FIG. 77. *Compare the lay-out of equipment in Fig. 76 with the more scientific arrangement shown above. After rearrangement, each article now proceeds from one stage to another by the shortest route, and movement of the operatives is reduced to a minimum.*

version, through the united efforts of all concerned, of raw materials into the finished product in the shortest time with the minimum effort and the minimum wastage. In order to obtain these conditions there are four objectives to be attained. These are: to avoid wasted movement of work and of workers in the course of the work; to secure effective control of production; to prevent wastage of time due to waiting for the supply of work; and to avoid obstructions and congestion which hamper the free movement of workers in the performance of their task. The means by which wasted movements may be avoided have already been indicated. This can only be done if there is exact knowledge of what is actually going on. Thus the first step must be to obtain actual information about the plant under consideration. By means of such examination it is probable that the sources of inefficiency may be revealed.

A further example of the value of an exact study of conditions occurred in a laundry. When sheets have been washed they are dried by means of a machine known as a calender. When each sheet is dried it is folded by two girls. In this example the manager was dissatisfied with the production of the machine. It appeared to be considerably below what was expected and no explanation was forthcoming. The machine and the workers were, therefore, observed over a short period and exact information was obtained. From this study it was seen that every time a sheet was folded it had to be put down on a table a few paces away from the machine. The exact position of this table was fixed by the position in which the two girls stood when starting to fold the sheets. By the time the folding was completed their positions had changed and they were now three or four paces away from the table. Times and distances were measured and calculations were made from the known number of sheets folded each week. From these figures it was found that the placing of folded sheets on a table obliged one of the two girls to walk some twenty miles a week, while the other girl waited for some five hours. Such wastage of effort and of time could only be eliminated by first discovering its existence; and when discovered its elimination was extremely simple. The above examples illustrate two of the objects of planning production, namely, the avoidance of unnecessary movements, and the prevention of loss of time through waiting for work.

CO-ORDINATION OF EFFORT

The second object of planning production is to secure effective control of production. If there is no central control, each department may be working without regard to the work of the other departments. Work finished in one department might pass to the next despite the inability of the latter to absorb it, or conversely one department might be wasting valuable time waiting for work to arrive. Without central control of production, without production planning, the whole intricate structure of modern industry can be reduced to a chaotic muddle. The landing on the shores of Normandy in 1944 would not have been successful if the national effort leading up to it had not been scientifically planned. What is true in war is also true in peace. Planned effort is essential if an article is to be successfully produced and sold.

One of the ways by which control is maintained is by the keeping of records of what is happening in the works. There are those who believe that records are more trouble than they are worth. Such people have seldom made the effort to put their theories to the test. Others who actually keep records suggest that their value cannot be overestimated. In one instance workers in a group engaged on sorting work were asked to keep records of their work as they did it. At first they protested that they had no time to spare for something so unnecessary, but eventually they agreed. It was found that the immediate effect of the record keeping was to send up the output. The mere fact that they now knew how much they were doing and knew that their work would be checked had the effect of increasing production without any sense of increased effort. No doubt this result was partly due to the removal of the element of boredom that is associated with working in ignorance of results. A degree of interest results from gaining information about performance which acts as a valuable spur to endeavour.

Another reason why accurate records should be kept is that they afford a measure by means of which improvements can be assessed and the results of changes checked.

There are few things more irritating than to be kept waiting, whether for work or for pleasure. The cost of waiting for work has not been estimated, but it is probably very considerable. Very often waiting is due to no other cause than badly-planned production. In one factory the time spent by one girl waiting for her supply of work to arrive was calculated and it was found that she was kept hanging about, growing more and more impatient, for more than six hours a week. The arrangements for supplying her with work had never been properly studied; they were left to chance and were consequently inefficient. Due regard should be given to ensuring that work is available as required. The unnecessary waiting about for work produces considerable disharmony in the mind of the worker and proper production planning should ensure that it does not occur.

Finally, production planning sets out to avoid congestion caused by obstructions which prevent the free movement of the worker in the course of his work.

Obstruction and congestion do not necessarily result from insufficient space. They are caused just as often by the misuse of space available and the lack of any clear plan as to how it should be used.

Just as a building has to be planned on paper before it is erected, so the lay-out of the contents should be planned. Sufficient gangways must be provided and are best maintained by white lines of demarcation. When the position of plant and gangways is fixed it must be strictly held to.

The purposes of production planning are thus designed to enable work to be carried out with the utmost ease and efficiency and with full knowledge of what is being done and why it is being done. The management must never sit back, content that everything is just as it should be. It must be dynamic and challenging, always asking whether things are being done in the right way or whether there are any means by which improvements can be made.

TIME AND MOTION STUDY

In order to appreciate the position which the science of Time and Motion Study holds in Britain today, it is necessary to trace briefly its history since the early days of the present century.

There appears to be no record of any conscious study of the movements of men at work until F. W. Taylor made his famous studies.

F. W. Taylor came from Philadelphia. Owing to a breakdown in health when he was a student, he was forced to take up work in an engineering works where he learned the trade of pattern-maker and machinist. He studied engineering and in due time rose to the position of chief engineer in an iron works.

Even at this time he seems to have had an inquiring mind that was prepared to challenge accepted practices. It is reported that he was the first person to introduce the overhand method of pitching in the game of baseball. Whereas others had readily accepted the standard underhand method, Taylor had the courage and scepticism to question it. When his ideas were opposed and it was pointed out that the new method was contrary to the rules, Taylor replied that the rules should be altered. This attitude of mind was to serve Taylor in good stead in later days. His inquiring mind was not one to be hedged in by tradition and if he thought a new way better than the old he was not to be put off on the plea of "rules" or "convention".

In the field of engineering Taylor was equally prepared to challenge accepted practices and traditions. If he thought that greater efficiency was possible he examined means by which such increased efficiency could be obtained. He became convinced that there was a right and a wrong way of doing everything. If the wrong way were to be replaced by the right way it would be possible to increase production and consequently reduce costs. Taylor's close contacts with workers had convinced him that their fixed habits and standard methods of work constituted an obstacle to maximum efficiency. Like the baseball players, they accepted the method of work that had been handed down to them, thereby preventing them from making any radical improvements.

But if the workers were restricted by traditional practices, Taylor found that management was restricted no less, and that it would be necessary to convert both management and labour if his ideas were to bear fruit.

SELECTION, TRAINING AND INCENTIVES

When Taylor began to investigate the problem that he had set himself, he was immediately struck by the fact that the management not only had no idea of the worker's potential capacity, but that no effort was made to train the worker in his work. In consequence of this, capable men were working in inefficient ways. Traditional methods were readily accepted and perpetuated without any reference to their efficiency.

The only way to determine the best methods of work was to make a minute study of the job and thereby to ascertain what was essential and what was unnecessary. But Taylor knew the average worker, and realized that it was useless to expect him to change his methods unless some incentive were provided. The incentive that Taylor supplied was the opportunity to obtain a higher wage by a higher output.

Then, Taylor was determined to ensure that as far as possible the men selected to do the work in the new way should be thoroughly trained. There was to be no more "picking up" of traditional methods.

The experiment in which he first put his theories to the test was concerned with the selection, training and methods of work of men engaged in loading pig-iron (that is to say, iron bars) into trucks. He found a mixed crowd of untrained labourers working at the job with little interest and with little opportunity of promotion. There had been, therefore, very little attempt to adopt any of Taylor's fundamental principles, namely, the correct selection of workers, their correct training and the provision of suitable incentives to encourage them.

Taylor watched the men at work and studied the detail of their movements. The job consisted essentially in stooping to pick up a pig, carrying it a short distance, placing it in position in a truck and returning to repeat the operation. When Taylor first started to study the work he found that 75 men averaged about 12½ tons a day. By his calculations Taylor concluded that it should be possible for the right men, under the right conditions, to handle nearly four times this amount. He questioned the foremen and managers to see whether they thought this possible. Not one of them believed that even with the most compelling incentives, the most rigorous selection of workers and the most thorough training a figure of 20 to 25 tons could be exceeded.

MEETING THE CHALLENGE

Faced with such a challenge, Taylor proceeded to apply his principles. In the first place, he selected a worker who seemed to him to fulfil his requirements. He must be physically capable of what was expected of him, and one to whom a financial reward would act as an incentive. For this purpose one, Schmidt, was selected. He appeared to be fresh at the end of a normal day's work; he was conscientious and appeared to be anxious to earn more money. Taylor suggested to him that he should take the opportunity of becoming a "high-priced" man and so be able to earn 1·85 dollar a day instead of his present wage of 1·15 dollar. Schmidt agreed to co-operate and to do exactly as he was told throughout the working day. So under Taylor's guidance and direction Schmidt surrendered his personal initiative and worked as he was instructed. At the end of the first day he had loaded 47½ tons of pig-iron, a figure that he maintained for the next three years. As promised, his wages averaged 1·85 dollar a day.

Following Schmidt's example, other men were trained to adopt the new methods and enabled to gain the advantages of the additional pay, but it was found that of the original gang of 75 only one in eight was physically capable of doing the work.

Taylor's work continued and other operations were studied with similar results. He was repeatedly able to increase the earnings of the few workers, to eliminate others and to reduce the costs to the company. It was estimated that in handling material alone he was able to save the firm some 75,000 dollars a year.

Whatever the defects of Taylor's system—and it has been severely criticized—he must be recognized as a pioneer. He started a movement the importance and the potentialities of which are today only just beginning to be realized.

271

In fairness to Taylor it should be said that whatever use has been made of his work, he himself was convinced that not only the efficiency of the worker but also his prosperity and happiness could be enhanced by the application of his methods. Even in his own time he was often thoroughly detested by workers, and today the word "Taylorism" is often used as a term of abuse for a system of scientific sweating of workers.

MOTION STUDY

If F. W. Taylor is regarded as the earliest pioneer of Time Study, F. B. Gilbreth and his wife, Lilian Gilbreth, are equally the pioneers of the allied subject of Motion Study. The Gilbreths' work dates from 1885.

In the analysis of the job, Taylor placed his emphasis on the time taken to perform its constituent elements. The Gilbreths, on the other hand, considered that the most important aspect of job analysis was the study of the movements involved. The Gilbreths formed a happy combination, for while F. B. was an engineer, his wife was a psychologist. By close study of the movements involved in any activity many unnecessary movements may be revealed. By eliminating unnecessary movements and by arranging that each necessary one leads logically to the next, the time taken is reduced to a minimum and unnecessary effort and fatigue may be eliminated.

Time Study is the study of the time taken to perform each particular operation in an industrial task and, from the data thus obtained, endeavouring to fix the proper time the whole task should take. Motion Study is the study of movements involved in a task, with a view to eliminating such as are unnecessary and improving those that are necessary. It may be divided into "Extensive Motion Study", which is concerned with the arrangement of apparatus and the larger movements of the body involved in its use, and "Intensive Motion Study", which is concerned with the smaller movements of the hands and fingers. These definitions are sufficiently wide to be acceptable today.

Time Study has been widely adopted as a routine method of fixing rates of pay in industry. Motion Study was almost entirely neglected until the impetus given to it by the Production Efficiency Board of the Ministry of Aircraft Production in Britain during the Second World War.

STANDARDIZING MOVEMENTS

The Gilbreths set out to discover a standardized method of performing a task, by splitting it up into constituent parts which were then subjected to a close study, including a time study.

The time taken by the different elements was compared as between one worker and another. Thus for each element of the operation there might be a different time taken by each worker under observation. The first element might be performed fastest by worker A, the second by worker B and the

272

third by worker C, and so on. The sum of these fastest times, made up from the different workers' performances, was regarded as standard for the operation.

Similarly, the standard movements were arrived at by combining the movements of each worker for that element at which his time was the shortest.

As with the Taylor training, the training in the new method is accompanied by various incentives such as additional pay.

Whatever criticism may be levelled at this method, many remarkable results have been achieved, and Gilbreth's study of bricklayers has become famous. By rearrangement of the bricklayer's apparatus, the bricks, the mortar and the scaffolding, and by providing an unskilled labourer to supply the bricks ready to lay, he found that movements could be substantially reduced. Where possible, two hands were used instead of one and unnecessary movements eliminated. The result of these studies enabled a trained bricklayer to lay nearly three times as many bricks as he had done previously.

It is from these early studies that the whole modern science of Motion Study has been built up, and today it embraces a wide field, including such problems as the elimination of unnecessary movements; the correct rhythm of movements to ensure that one movement leads logically to the next; proper posture whether standing or sitting, including alteration to the design of workbenches, seats and machines; lay-out of the workshop; and, not least important, the technique of obtaining the willing co-operation of the workers concerned.

In the preface of Frank Gilbreth's book, *Motion Study*, which was published in 1911, the following words appeared: "Some day an intelligent nation will awake to the fact that by scientifically studying the motions in its trades it will obtain the industrial supremacy of the world."

PRINCIPLES OF MOTION ECONOMY

Perhaps this point has not yet been reached, but during the Second World War remarkable developments took place in Britain. The Ministry of Aircraft Production was faced with the problem of trying to get the maximum production of aircraft. Miss A. G. Shaw, who had studied under the Gilbreths and had since been employed in a large engineering works, was appointed to the Ministry's Production Efficiency Board and given the job of developing the application of Time and Motion Study in the factories concerned.

In her book, *An Introduction to the Theory and Application of Motion Study*, published in 1944, Miss Shaw sets out some of the "general principles of Motion Economy". These principles may be paraphrased as follows:

Minimum Movements. Materials and hand tools should be placed within an arc in front of the operator, this arc covering the area most easily reached and thus ensuring easy hand and arm movements. Unnecessary bending and stretching can be prevented by placing everything required in the position easiest to reach.

Symmetrical Movements. So far as possible, movements of workers should be symmetrical about an imaginary line through the centre of the body. Thus balanced posture can be maintained. When movements are not symmetrical there is unnecessary fatigue from the muscular exertion required.

Simultaneous Movements. Simultaneous hand movements should be arranged, both hands, if possible, doing the same thing at the same time. In assembly work this means that complete assembly should be carried out simultaneously by each hand, two parts being assembled simultaneously.

Rhythmic Movements. A definite rhythm of movement should be established. Faulty material or a bad placing of work causes a break in such rhythm, resulting in loss of efficiency. The parts of the body should be able to move freely in a balanced pattern which is exactly repeated with each successive cycle.

Natural Movements. There are certain movements of the body that come more naturally and easily than others. In working out the movements for a given operation such movements should be adopted in preference to those that are awkward or unnatural.

Habitual Movements. Habit formation is an unconscious and automatic operation. For this reason workers should be trained in the right methods from the very outset, before bad habits have the opportunity of creeping in, with the consequential difficulty of "unlearning" them.

This characteristic can be turned to advantage if a rigid rule with regard to the correct placing of tools and materials is enforced, so that they are always in the right place and so that they can be picked up without thought.

Change of direction of bodily movements inevitably involves a slowing

down. Such changes in direction should, therefore, be reduced to a minimum. Where possible arc movements should be made to serve more than one operation; for example, more than one part to be assembled may be picked up in the course of a single major movement.

The above principles are basic and fundamental and must be

FIG. 78. *Proper posture and movement make any task easier. This gardener will almost certainly be very tired at the end of the day. Compare with Fig. 79.*

FIG. 79. *This man's fully extended arms relieve strain on the muscles and ensure that he is pushing the handles of his barrow forwards and not downwards.*

considered in relation to one another. Wherever a repetitive job is carried out without due regard to them there will be waste of effort and unnecessary fatigue.

Despite the enormous importance of the work of Taylor and Gilbreth, at one time it appeared that they and their successors were tending to neglect a most important element in their studies. In attempting to standardize the human element they perhaps neglected the psychologist's axiom that individuals vary one from another and, indeed, the same individual varies from day to day and from week to week. Farmer stresses the dangers that may arise from over-standardization, and writes: "It is doubtful if a set of movements, however good they may be, can necessarily be regarded as the best movements for every person concerned. Personal differences must be allowed for and the possibility admitted of the worker's discovering a method better suited to his requirements than the prescribed one."

USE OF MOTION PICTURES

So far no mention has been made of what must seem to be the most obvious instrument for studying motion, namely, the camera.

In the laundry trade it has been used with considerable success. The ironing of sheets on a calender is a process common to every laundry, and both the production of work and its quality vary enormously from one laundry to another.

In the course of a long study of calender feeders, a team of two girls was found which reached a production rate unequalled in any other laundry. Films of these workers were made and it was noted that they achieved their high rate of production by means of a remarkable economy of effort.

In another laundry a team of calender feeders was observed whose movements were clearly far from satisfactory. Although the rate of production was high the quality of the work was poor.

This team was taken apart and the girls were asked if they would co-operate in an experiment. The idea appealed to them, particularly when they learned that it would mean that films would be taken of them. They were shown the films of themselves, and the unnecessary movements and wasted effort were

275

pointed out. They then saw, over a period of several weeks, the films of the expert operatives. By a simple device it was possible to repeat the same operation over and over again on the screen. The advantages of the improved method of work were pointed out and they co-operated enthusiastically in the experiment. Before long their own methods of work underwent a marked change. The old mistakes were gradually eliminated and the new technique adopted.

When the experiment was embarked upon, the idea of improving production had not been raised, but in a short time there was an increase estimated at 10 per cent. There was unanimous agreement that the quality of work had undergone a marked improvement, a factor which considerably eased the work of the folders.

A few days after the last training class a girl whose fingers had been sore when working the old method was asked how she liked the new method of work. With a triumphant gesture she held up her hand—for the first time for many weeks her fingers were no longer sore.

We have seen that the principles of Time and Motion Study can be applied to a very wide variety of operations. The principles are fundamentally similar to those of production planning. Their objects should be to make work easier and reduce unnecessary fatigue. So far as Time and Motion Study are used to speed up and mechanize the individual they are being misused and may give rise to resentment on the part of the worker, and possibly lead to nervous strain. When applied with proper understanding and with real insight into the psychological needs of the worker, full co-operation can be expected and benefits both lasting and real can be achieved.

Test Yourself

1. If you wished to reduce the time spent in the carrying out of some piece of mechanical team-work, what chief points would you investigate?

2. Name some arrangements made in modern industry to ensure a definite rhythm of movement.

3. Why do the studies in Time and Motion sometimes give rise to resentment on the part of the worker and how may they be made more acceptable?

Answers will be found at the end of the book.

CHAPTER XIV

PERSONNEL PROBLEMS

LET US assume that we have a factory building, we have the plant and we have the work to do. Without the staff to work the machinery this potential wealth is of no use to us. How then are we going to staff the factory? Certain principles are quite clear. We will want an office staff and a works staff. We will want managers and labourers, skilled machinists and unskilled "hands". It is quite clear that we will make sure that the typist can type, that the costing clerk can read and write and that the engineer knows something of his job. The more skilled the job the more do we expect particular qualifications from the person we employ. But there is more than this that we can do. If we are wise we will make use of the principles of Vocational Selection and select our staff on a scientific basis.

The science of Vocational Guidance and Vocational Selection is concerned with the problem of placing the individual in a job for which he is suitably equipped. Vocational Guidance sets out to find a job or occupation suitable for a given individual. This has been discussed in the chapter dealing with Vocational Psychology and little more will be said about it here. Vocational Selection, however, takes a rather different viewpoint. The job is given and the problem is to select the person most likely to prove capable of performing it successfully.

In the days before the First World War the usual method by which a factory engaged labour was by putting a notice outside the entrance: "Hands wanted". There were generally more people looking for work than there was work for them to do, so in due course a number of applicants would come forward. They would probably be seen by the foreman, who would have his own method of selecting the one who seemed to him to be most suitable. Very likely the foreman would know that his friend Bill had a nephew looking for work. Bill was a good chap, so his nephew would get the job. If there was no personal reason the foreman might be influenced by other irrelevant ideas.

Many trivial factors tended to influence the foreman's choice. Seldom were the questions asked: "What are the requirements for doing this work successfully?" and "How can I find which applicant fulfils these requirements?"

As has been pointed out, the object of Vocational Selection is to select for a given job, by means of tests, the person best equipped for it. How then do we know that some people will do better at the job than others and how are we to set about finding the one who will do best?

The question of different abilities is answered by that experienced psychologist, Mrs. Raphael, who writes: "A careful study of the relative ability of the various workers will often show that there exists an almost astounding diversity. In the course of psychological investigations it is necessary to measure the difference in output of workers of equal experience, over a long period. Quite frequently it is found that men sitting side by side, identically equipped and with equal opportunities for work, will show a difference in output of 50 per cent, and it is no unusual thing to find differences of as much as 100 per cent. In most cases these differences are found on investigation not to be due to variations in willingness or keenness, but in actual differences in intellectual or manual ability."

The writer refers here primarily to manual work. That the same applies to intellectual work is axiomatic. No one would expect a dull or backward person to compete successfully with a distinguished scholar in a job demanding a high degree of intellectual ability.

THE MAN FOR THE JOB

We can, therefore, accept the fact that all people are not alike in their abilities and that some are better equipped than others for particular occupations. The problem is, then, to discover what ability is required for a particular occupation, and to find a simple method of picking out the people possessing such ability from a mixed group of candidates.

Before accepting that there is any need to use tests for selection, we must prove that the rule of chance is wasteful and unsatisfactory.

The results of employing an unsuitable person are detrimental both to the person himself and to the employer. The man himself may become a misfit, dissatisfied with his work and unable to settle down to it. He may, from fear of unemployment or from inability to take the fatal step of resigning, attempt to carry on, discontented with his occupation and not doing justice to his own abilities. Alternatively, he may drift from one unsuitable job to another, unable to remain anywhere for long.

For the employer the consequences may be equally harmful. In due time he may find it necessary to discharge those whose performance is not up to a required standard. If the work is skilled the cost of training may be considerable, and money is wasted if those trained do not prove satisfactory. It would be cheaper and more effective to train only those who have a reasonable chance of proving satisfactory at the end of the training period.

During the Second World War the whole problem of selection received considerable attention, particularly in the Royal Air Force. A pilot in control of a heavy bomber has in his hands not only the lives of his crew but also the safety of a machine costing many thousands of pounds. A bad choice of pilot might result in the needless loss of both machine and crew. If such losses could be prevented by ensuring that only those suitable for the job were trained to perform it, the saving in lives and machines would be considerable.

In time of war the cost of mistakes may be literally a matter of life and death, not only to the person who makes the mistakes, but to many other people.

The case for right selection is indeed a strong one. During the later part of the war every recruit was given a series of tests in order that a rough estimate of his mental capacity could be made at the outset. Before he was allocated to any special training, however, additional tests were given, and selection made from the results.

Although, perhaps, many details will always remain secret, it is fair to assume that the Service chiefs would not have given the scheme their approval unless they were satisfied as to its value.

ACCIDENTS AT WORK

In 1942, a peak year, the number of accidents that occurred in premises under the Factories Act throughout the country was 313,267. In addition to this, 1,363 workpeople were killed.

The accidents referred to in the former figure are only those which have, by law, to be reported to H.M. Inspector of Factories; that is to say, accidents which incapacitate a person from continuing his normal work for more

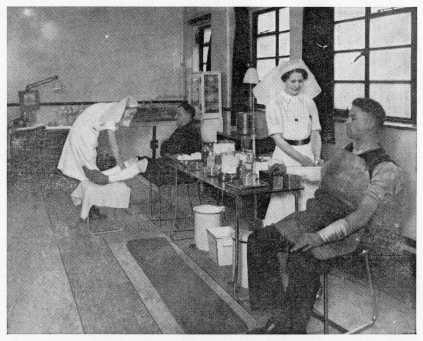

FIG. 80. *Many industrial concerns provide emergency medical attention for their workers. These men are being treated for injuries at a first-aid post in a Birmingham factory.*

279

than three days. The number of accidents of a minor nature that do not result in such incapacity can hardly be estimated accurately. Vernon quotes various estimates and known figures which suggest that the average ratio of the minor accident to the reportable accident is about 40 to 1. If this figure is accepted we must conclude that no fewer than 12 million minor accidents occurred during the year just mentioned. For the same year an analysis of the reportable accidents according to their cause showed the following percentages:

Cause	Percentage
Power-driven machinery	17·1
Use of hand tools	8·0
Struck by falling body	12·0
Persons falling	13·3
Stepping on or striking against objects	8·2
Handling goods	25·7
All other causes	15·7

Although the actual number of accidents occurring in 1942 was the highest figure for many years, due to a variety of causes associated with war conditions, the percentage due to each specific cause was practically unaltered over a number of years. An estimate of the accident rate, that is, the number of accidents per 1,000 persons employed, is shown in the accompanying table:

Males		Females	
18 years and over	53	18 years and over	28
Under 18 years	59	Under 18 years	22

It is clear from these figures that the problem of accidents is a tremendous one, affecting the lives and happiness of a large number of workers and their families.

The word "accident" seems to suggest that something unavoidable has occurred, which is unrelated to the victim of the accident. At the same time it is recognized that some people seem to have more accidents than others. They are sometimes described as being "all thumbs", and when they do not injure themselves they seem to be dropping the crockery or breaking things in the house.

Before the First World War no proper study was made of individual susceptibility to accidents. During that war, however, Professor Greenwood and Mr. Udney Yule examined accident records and subjected them to a statistical analysis.

They found that certain people have more accidents than others. This could have been due to one or more of three causes: (a) chance, pure and simple; (b) that the fact of having one accident increases the chances of having another (biased distribution); or (c) that some people are more liable to accidents than others (distribution of unequal liabilities). The anticipated

280

FIG. 81. *Note the contrast, in this cotton-spinning mill, between the ragged workers and the master. Little children were considered essential for cleaning—and mending broken threads— as they could creep under the machinery where adults could not go. Note also the uncomfortable posture of the woman leaning over the machinery.*

distribution was worked out for each of these possibilities and then compared with figures from actual records. The evidence from this examination showed conclusively that certain individuals, comprising between 10 and 25 per cent of the population, were more "accident-prone" than others. This group sustained an undue number of major and minor accidents of every kind, both at work and at home.

It is clear that, with these facts proved, we can consider the problem of accident prevention from a new viewpoint. We can study all factors that contribute to accidents and as far as possible try to obtain those environmental conditions that are least liable to produce them, and we can also attempt to exclude the accident-prone person from those jobs where accidents are most likely to occur or where the consequences of accidents are likely to be serious.

For instance, an accident to a man engaged in ticket collecting is likely to be less serious than an accident to an omnibus driver.

Before it is possible to assign an accident-prone person to a suitable occupation we must devise some means of identifying him.

Tests devised by Farmer and Chambers related to factors such as intelligence, temperament, neuro-muscular co-ordination and so on. Among a group of apprentices tested it was found that those who did worst at the tests suffered, over a period, two and a half times as many accidents as the remainder of the group. Thus by means of these tests it was possible to pick out the accident-prone person before he started work, and to direct him to work of a "safe" nature.

Further studies by Farmer and Chambers were able to relate industrial proficiency with accident-proneness. Those who failed in trade tests were found to be more susceptible to accident and sickness than those who passed

FIG. 82. *A scene in a flax mill in the late eighteenth century. Children and adults alike were exposed to the risk of serious injury as they worked, often in badly lighted premises, among unguarded machinery. There were no laws then to protect factory workers.*

the tests. They concluded that certain people react unfavourably to industrial conditions. They react by inefficiency and by having an undue amount of sickness and accidents.

While we have shown that some people are more susceptible to accidents than others, it must also be realized that the conditions in which work is done will also affect the frequency of accidents. Certain conditions are more liable than others to produce accidents, so that, whether the individual is accident-prone or not, it is possible to reduce the likelihood of accident by ensuring an environment in which it is least likely to occur.

Investigations by Osborne and Vernon showed that the number of accidents experienced by workers at three munition factories were influenced by the temperature. It was found that at a temperature of 52 deg. F. the accidents were 35 per cent more numerous than at a temperature of 67 deg. F. At temperatures above 72 deg. F. accidents to men increased very rapidly.

In the same investigations it was shown that the rate of accidents was low at the start of the shift, rose to a maximum in the middle, and fell at the end of the shift.

The influence of fatigue in causing accidents was indicated in a fuse factory. It was found that in a 12-hour day the accidents sustained by women were nearly two-and-three-quarter times as numerous as for a 10-hour day. The same group of women working the 12-hour day had accidents more frequently in the afternoon spell, when they were tired.

Similar evidence has been obtained to relate accidents to lighting. Results from certain industries have shown that a particular type of accident, namely, persons falling, was nearly twice as frequent during winter when artificial light was necessary as in the summer when daylight was adequate.

IMPORTANCE OF STATISTICS

The facts stated above have become known, and could only have become known, by the examination of accurate statistics. Unless records are carefully kept it is impossible to say whether the accidents occurring in an individual firm compare favourably or unfavourably with those in another firm. It is impossible to say, except by guesswork, whether one industry is more or less "dangerous" than another. It is not possible to say whether accidents are increasing or decreasing. In short, without accurate and reliable statistics the whole study of accidents and their prevention would be a hit-or-miss affair of pious hope. The Royal Society for the Prevention of Accidents has published a pamphlet in which the case for keeping accurate records is put forward, and in which a standard system, based on recommendations made by the International Labour Office, is set out.

In the past, very little attention was paid to the question of sickness absence or labour turnover. It was taken for granted that people would from time to time be ill, and that the staff of any business concern changed from

283

FIG. 83. *The industrial accidents rate is still far too high. Carelessness is a prime ca*

year to year, but little was known about the causes or measurement of either. A report of an investigation by the Industrial Health Research Board calls attention to the fact that even firms that have had health departments for years differ in their opinion as to whether there has been an increase or decrease in the standard of health of their employees. When records are compared as between one firm and another it is found that there is no stan-

many potential accidents can you find in this picture? See list on page 378.

dard by means of which can be judged whether the amount of absence is high or low, having regard to the particular type of work. Nor are the factors known which contribute to the figures. The report stresses, therefore, the desirability of arriving at a standard method of recording the facts of sickness and absence.

A war-time report by the Industrial Health Research Board discusses the results of two investigations into the sickness absence records of about 4,500 women employed in five munition factories. While the results of the inquiry should not be used as a basis for wide generalization, the following facts were revealed. Half of the total time lost from work was accounted for by sickness. This represented nearly four hours per worker per 48-hour week. Furthermore, it was found that a small proportion of the workers (16 per cent) were responsible for two-thirds of the total sickness absence, a fact that bears out previous findings both in Britain and in the United States. Analysing sickness according to its cause showed that the greatest loss was caused by sickness classified as respiratory, "nervous", and fatigue and digestive diseases. Up to the age of 30 years, illness was increasingly frequent, but after this age, though it became less frequent, it involved longer periods of absence.

Two groups of the women, one selected for its good record of little or no sickness and the other for its long or frequent absences, were interviewed. The interviews revealed that workers who had personal worries had a higher sickness absence record than those with no worries, and the report suggests that the whole problem of the health of individual workers should be approached from a much wider angle than has been customary in the past. The health of the individual is a product of his whole background, including thoughts and feelings as well as his working and living conditions.

A similar relation between the worker's health and the general social and economic background is noted in an American inquiry. In this instance it was found that during the summer of 1944 many government employees were experiencing considerable unrest owing to the apparent insecurity of their jobs. Various symptoms of nervous disorders became increasingly common. This was at a time when it appeared that the war would soon be over and consequently many of the temporary war jobs would come to an end. When later the situation changed and it was evident that the end of hostilities would be delayed the incidence of breakdown in health diminished.

Absence from work on account of sickness was thus definitely related to factors which are outside the usual field of the general medical practitioner.

FACTORY "ATMOSPHERE"

In the preceding pages we have attempted to describe the conditions of work and industrial environment in which the worker will carry on his work with the maximum efficiency and with the minimum of obstacles. Are we to conclude, then, that if all these principles are carried out the workers will be happier and healthier than under any other circumstances? An answer to this is given in the results of an experiment carried out some years ago at the Hawthorne works of the Western Electric Company in the United States.

The reasons for the inquiry were twofold. In the first place there was a general interest in problems of fatigue, monotony and kindred subjects in the factory. This interest had its origin in a study of the work carried out by the Industrial Health Research Board in Britain, much of which has been quoted.

In the second place the management of the company felt that though their policy with regard to machines and materials was quite clear, with regard to the employees it was indefinite. The former was based upon exact scientific facts, whereas the latter was something that had grown up without any definite or conscious direction on the part of anyone.

A CLASSIC EXPERIMENT

With these facts in mind a certain job was selected as suitable for close study. The work consisted of assembling telephone relays, a simple repetitive task, the normal time taken for each assembly being about sixty seconds. A small group of workers was selected to act as subjects for the inquiry and in April 1927 this classic piece of research began.

During fifteen experimental periods, varying from about two to thirty weeks, various changes were made in the environment conditions and the hours of work.

At the start the conditions were steadily made easier for the workers. Hours were reduced, rest pauses were introduced and refreshments were provided. At an early stage the method of payment was changed from one based upon the output of a group of a hundred workers to one based on that of a group of five.

At first the reduction of hours resulted in increase in total output, but at length the stage was reached where further reduction in hours, although increasing the hourly rate, could not increase the total output.

At a later stage in the investigation the conditions of an earlier stage were again introduced by cutting out rest pauses and lengthening the working day. It was anticipated that this would bring the output down to the figure it had previously been under similar conditions, but contrary to this anticipation output rose to a point above its previous peak. When the rest pauses were re-introduced the output continued to rise.

It was now clear that the output was related to something other than the conditions which had been changed. Output could not be regarded as a measurement of these physical circumstances. Its upward trend ignored them altogether. At the same time it was noticed that there was a decrease in absenteeism of about 80 per cent. These results puzzled the management considerably and led to the second phase in the experiment. This second phase consisted of an interview programme. On being questioned the girls them-selves showed surprise at the increase in production. They did not feel that they were working any harder or faster than they had been in the past. They did, however, say that they noticed certain differences. They noticed a far freer and happier atmosphere and enjoyed the absence of the old type of

287

supervision. They related the increase in production to these two factors rather than to anything else.

In reporting the progress of the experiment it was observed that the changed conditions had resulted in creating an eagerness on the part of the workers to come to work in the morning. The important factor contributing to the better mental attitude and greater enjoyment of work had been the greater freedom, less strict supervision and the opportunity to vary from a fixed pace without reprimand from the "gang boss".

The "interview programme" which was now introduced was the outcome of the management questioning the merits of the supervisory methods of the past. It was thought that if all employees could be interviewed and their honest comments secured, it would not only give a comprehensive picture of the existing supervisory practices, but would also give an assessment of the desirability and effectiveness of such practices.

The purpose of the programme was summarized under the following headings:

To learn from employees their likes and dislikes relative to their working status.

To provide a more definite and reliable basis for supervisory training and for added control of proper working conditions, placement and efficiency.

To supplement and verify the conclusions that had been reached from the study of the small group of workers.

The first attempt at this "interview programme" was carried out in a group containing about 1,600 workers, skilled and unskilled. At the outset the interview lasted about thirty minutes, but as the programme developed the

FIG 84. *Congenial and healthy working conditions result in an all-round increase in efficiency. In this Swedish factory modern design has provided a maximum of light and air for the worker. Figs. 75 and 85 show interior views in this factory.*

interview gradually lengthened. By the end of three years over 21,000 employees had been interviewed.

Among other things the interviewers attempted to ascertain the factors which are the basic forces of motivation in industry. A large number of items were distinguished—payment, hours of work, noise, monotony, and so on. The investigators came to the conclusion that "the relationship between first-time supervisors and the individual workman is of more importance in determining the attitude, morale, general happiness and efficiency of the employee than any other single factor".

The same opinion was expressed some years ago at the annual general meeting of the National Institute of Industrial Psychology. "When the worker is able, to some extent, to 'identify' himself with his work and with the firm that employs him; when he feels that his work is of value; when he works under a supervisor who is just and sympathetic; when he is reasonably secure in his employment, and feels that he will get a 'fair deal' from the management; then, and only then, is he likely to do his best—and may indeed achieve high efficiency even under physical conditions that are far from perfect. When, on the other hand, he believes, rightly or wrongly, that the management are concerned merely with profits and care nothing for the worker as an individual; when he is on bad terms with his supervisor; when he feels that good work is unappreciated, promotion going by favouritism and dismissal by prejudice; then he will be unhappy and inefficient, and the strictest discipline, the most elaborate of bonus schemes and the best of welfare services may count for little or nothing."

An inquiry conducted by the British Institute of Public Opinion illustrates a similar outlook. In reply to the question: "Which do you think is more important in a job, wages as high as possible, or security of employment with lower wages?", the following percentages were given: 23 per cent said "High wages"; 73 per cent said "Security"; and 4 per cent said

"Don't know". They were also asked: "Apart from wages and security, what do you need most in a job for making you feel contented whilst at work?"

The replies fell under three main headings. Congenial working conditions were mentioned by 26 per cent, with 6 per cent specifically referring to the necessity for a canteen or recreation- and rest-rooms; 24 per cent wanted a friendly atmosphere in their workplace, 10 per cent stressing that they desired to have an appreciative employer; 16 per cent talked of their need for shorter hours of work or good holidays with pay, while another 16 per cent desired, above everything else, interesting or worthwhile work.

Many investigators have expressed this same opinion and every factory worker knows what is meant by the "factory atmosphere", even though he cannot define it or explain what goes to make it up.

While high sickness rates and labour turnover are indicative of a poor atmosphere in which the individual's needs are not met, there is little doubt that even technically efficient works will not get the best results from either their plant or their workers, if the latter have the sense of frustration resulting from those factors which lead to the "bad atmosphere".

GOOD MANAGEMENT

A comparison was made between two small factories, the work and plant of which were closely similar. In the one case there was perpetual friction and discontent, the quality and quantity of the work was poor and the firm was making, for the particular industry, poor profits. When the workers were interviewed they all told the same tale. In essence it was that whenever the manager was present they became very nervous, hot, and weak at the knees.

Despite excellent intentions he had not the nature that enabled him to establish a sympathetic understanding with his employees. They looked back to the days of his predecessor, who appeared to have been a bit of a rogue, but who had the capacity for making his workers feel their own sense of importance and value and who always started the day with a cheery "good morning" for everybody. The consequence of the unfortunate relationship between his successor and the workers was expressed in terms of poor production, numerous mistakes and high absence rate.

In contrast to this, a similar works was fortunate in the personal charm of its manager. With a good word for everybody he acquired for himself the genuine affection of all his workers. In times of shortage of employment a youth in a nearby town deliberately turned down the offer of a good job elsewhere in anticipation of a chance to get work at this factory. His comment was that "once you got there you were made for life". In the same works an employee was asked who was the owner of a field adjacent to the factory. "That's our field," he replied, and the very choice of words showed how

FIG. 85. *A dining room for all grades of workers—office and workshop—in a modern Swedish factory. Individual seats are provided. There is no overcrowding, and everyone can enjoy a good and inexpensive meal in comfort. Light, heating and ventilation have been carefully considered. The exterior of this factory is shown in Fig. 84.*

closely one worker was able to identify himself with his place of work.

The developments of modern industry, with its huge factories, its mass production and its repetitive work, may have provided for the masses a standard of living that was unattainable in the old days of village crafts and man-power rather than machine-power. In recent years there has been a cry for greater efficiency, and perhaps the science of Time and Motion Study was the outcome of this cry. The industrial psychologist does not decry efficiency. On the contrary, he sets himself to discover and remedy those human exertions which produce fatigue without producing the desired results. It has been suggested that the pioneers of Time and Motion Study failed in part to appreciate that the subjects of their investigations were human beings, and in so far as they did this they failed in their objectives. The industrial psychologist, on the other hand, while of necessity making an exact study of the physical and measurable environment of the worker, must always have in the forefront of his mind the knowledge that it is the individual who is the object of his study.

He must remember that no two human beings are alike; that all are made up of a complex system of feelings and emotions, and that unless these feelings and emotions are allowed and encouraged to express themselves in a natural and healthy manner they will become dangerous forces, liable to upset the delicate balance of the individual.

If the preceding pages in this section put the main stress on the external environment in which the industrial worker finds himself, the reason is that the whole study of Industrial Psychology cannot be separated from the other aspects of psychology.

Each particular branch of psychology is closely linked with the others, and if this section was not limited in its scope there would be serious overlapping with the other sections. The adult has developed from the child, the abnormal is a divergence from the normal.

The psycho-neurotic types discussed in the last three chapters in this book are not laboratory specimens. They occur in industry as elsewhere and the foreman and manager must recognize them and treat them accordingly.

A passage was quoted from Frank Gilbreth's book, *Motion Study*, in which it was claimed that the first country to appreciate the significance of Motion Study would obtain the industrial supremacy of the world. Whatever the truth of this, we would rather suggest that if happiness is wealth, the first country to accept and apply the principles of Industrial Psychology throughout its factories may indeed become the wealthiest in the world.

Test Yourself

1. Show some of the disadvantages which may result, both to the employer and the employee, if a person is selected for work unsuitable to him.

2. What, in your opinion, is the most important factor in the building up of a right relationship between employers and workers?

3. Describe some measures that can be applied in a factory with a view to preventing accidents.

Answers will be found at the end of the book.

CHAPTER XV

MIND AND BODY

WHEN Sir George Savage, a famous psychiatrist of an older generation, was asked, "Don't you find it very difficult to certify people as insane?", he replied, "Not in the least, but if I was ever asked to certify a person as sane, then I would indeed have grave doubts and searchings of heart."

What, then, are we to call normal and what abnormal? Everyone presents some sort of abnormality some of the time; we are anxious, depressed, excited, suspicious, angry, morose, stupid and dull from time to time, and from place to place. Abnormality is more a matter of degree than of quality, and we have a right to consider ourselves normal only if we claim that for most of the time and in our usual circumstances we adjust sufficiently well to be able to get on with our jobs with reasonable efficiency and are not an intolerable nuisance to ourselves and others.

The old idea of the phrenologists that certain parts of the brain are associated with certain "faculties", such as understanding, affection, morality and the like, must now be abandoned. In its higher functions the brain works as a whole and, so far as mental deficiency is concerned, there is evidence that the cells of the highest levels of the brain (cerebral cortex) are poorly developed or irregularly arranged. But we must admit that, while we can speculate that irregular connexions between nerve cells, abnormalities in electrical discharge, deficiencies or superfluities of certain glandular secretions, of vitamins or of salts conveyed to the brain by the blood may be responsible for the production of psychopathic personalities, we have no exact knowledge of the subject. It may be that all people who behave abnormally have something wrong with their inherent constitution; but if these people are to some extent born, not made, in a great many cases the interplay of the individual with his environment during the course of his life is chiefly responsible for the psychological abnormalities which he exhibits.

The causes of psychological abnormality may be briefly summarized under three heads: (1) abnormalities arising from heredity and from defects of physical constitution; (2) those due to environmental influences; and (3) those resulting from degenerative changes in the tissues of the body and brain. A brief outline of these causes of abnormality will now be given.

1. Heredity and Constitution. It is not uncommon for people seeking to find an excuse for what they know to be abnormal or undesirable behaviour to blame their parents or their "birth". "Mother never could tell the truth", "Father had a horrible temper", "I was born like that", they may say; or, as an exasperating neurotic used to say when her behaviour was particularly outrageous, "Oh well, it's my nature." How far is such an excuse valid? The answer must be that, so far as real biological heredity is concerned, this excuse has very little weight.

Mind depends on the structure and function of brain; and if the brain is not sufficiently developed, this will have mental repercussions. Failure of full development of the brain is in some cases hereditary; in other cases, fewer in number, it is due to injury at birth; and in others, to defects in constitution, which are not handed down from one generation to another, but would seem to be caused by some fault in the make-up of the body.

True hereditary transmission through the germ-plasm probably accounts for a certain number of mental defectives (some people say as many as 80 per cent). Most of these are of the rather higher grades. Heredity also accounts for about 30 per cent of insane persons, mostly of the so-called manic-depressive type (see Chapter XVII), and some epileptics.

Birth injury accounts for a number of mental defectives, chiefly of the lower grades, and for a group of epileptics.

Constitutional defects probably account for a good deal of psychological abnormality, so the excuse "It's my nature" may be permissible in some cases, at least up to a point. However, the question as to how far education, training and the individual's own will-power can overcome the defects of a bad constitutional make-up is an interesting one, and we cannot pretend that our knowledge so far allows us to form any final conclusions on this subject.

It is quite certain that some mental defectives, particularly among the "mongols" (page 334), are the result of bad constitutional make-up.

MENTAL DEFICIENCY

"Mental deficiency" is generally used as a term to denote deficiency in intelligence, perhaps because our knowledge of intellectual defect is so much more extensive than that of any other form of defect in the mental field. This is because intellectual deficiency is of prime importance in education, and many batteries of tests have been devised and extensively employed to assist teachers. Thus the intelligence grading has been sufficiently standardized to allow children to be grouped in accordance with their fitness for particular levels and methods of education. The nature and the method of application of these tests have been described elsewhere in this volume, and further discussion of them here is unnecessary. (See page 135 *ff.*)

More recently, methods of testing temperament and personality have been devised, whereby we are gaining much more insight into development of capacity in the emotional field and in the power of performance. This may throw light on constitutional factors in other forms of mental illness.

There is a small group of persons described as "psychasthenics" (page 331), who are usually included among the "psychoneurotics", but who most certainly owe their disability to constitutional factors. These people are not characteristically deficient in intelligence, all grades of capacity in this respect being met with, but they are deficient in the power of decision. They are the people who, in extreme cases, waste hours in deciding which boot to put on first, how to tie their tie, or how to begin a letter.

EPILEPSY

Another large group, described as "psychopathic personalities", owe their disability to abnormalities of constitution. These include epileptics and some defectives who are described in law as moral defectives.

Epileptics often show a special type of personality, which will be described later (page 339). These people are characterized by having an abnormality of the brain which can be demonstrated by special apparatus. Experts in this field hold that quite a large section of the population shows this unusual electrical activity of the brain. It is thought that, while all those possessing this characteristic are not epileptics, all epileptics may possess this abnormality. Further studies of this may throw great light on the constitutional factors which underlie epilepsy and possibly other varieties of psychopathic behaviour.

The law recognizes a group of moral defectives, but many people have thought that this is an artificial division of mental defectives, the moral defective not being essentially different from others suffering from mental deficiency whose chief characteristic is the defective intelligence which makes it impossible for them to learn to adjust to the needs of society. The more recent conception of psychopathic personality has, however, brought back the conception of an "inherent lack of moral sense" in another way. It is no longer thought that there is any lack of a particular part of the brain associated with morality, but that in the general make-up of the personality there is something which makes it difficult for the individual to achieve the necessary adjustments in order to understand the demands of society and act in accordance with them.

If the true nature of the psychopathic personality is obscure, the problem of how far and in what way inherent constitutional abnormality is responsible for the psychoses, or true insanities, is still less understood. Most experts are now agreed that this is an important factor (the temperamental factor) in the withdrawn, the elated and depressed, and the suspicious types, all of whom will be described in later pages.

2. *The Effect of the Environment.* In considering the causes of psychological

abnormality, there is a factor of the greatest importance which is often confused with heredity, but which, however, owes nothing to genetic transmission. This has been described as "social heritage" and comprises all the customs, traditions and attitudes to life not only of the parents of the individual, but of his whole family, social group, community, class and nation. Impinging upon him from the very moment of birth, social heritage is bound to have a tremendous influence in moulding his attitudes, opinions and actions. (See pages 77–8.)

In the development of each individual there are influences which are essentially part of him, founded on his heredity and constitutional make-up, while others essentially belong to his environment. There is always interaction between these two groups of factors, and it is not easy to determine which is the more potent. In some cases the inherent factors are so feeble or so indeterminate that the environment or the social heritage obscures them and represses them, so that the person seems to have no individuality of his own. In other cases the inherent factors are dominant, and the person becomes an independent original. In most cases, however, there is some sort of a working compromise, and the character of the person can be shown to owe something both to inherent individuality and to environment. The sum total of these resultants, working through the person's lifetime, is the personality, and all such varieties of interaction as are described above are capable of producing "normal personalities", i.e. personalities not departing so much from the average mean as to create difficulties or to attract special notice.

If the personality does not achieve a clear dominance of one or other group of factors, or a working compromise between them, conflicts will arise, and conflict is the cause of many manifestations of abnormal psychology. It is obvious that conflicts may occur between elements of inherent constitution—the instincts—especially when these are modified by the processes of education in its widest sense.

MAINSPRINGS OF BEHAVIOUR

McDougall, in his *Social Psychology*, has shown that the human being starts with a certain limited number of instinctive reactions which are the mainsprings of all behaviour. These are gradually modified in the course of mental and physical growth to determine the more complicated emotions and modes of behaviour of the person, but as they develop they may come into serious conflict with each other. McDougall describes the ultimate configurations as sentiments, such as love, hate, religious beliefs, business interests or sporting enthusiasms. It is easy to see how these may conflict from time to time, or even for long periods, in a person's life.

Freud, who is generally recognized as having influenced modern medical psychology to an important extent, maintained that the chief basis of abnormal psychological experience and manifestation was a conflict between the demands of sex in its widest sense—ranging from the primitive, crude mating appetite and instinct to the fully established love sentiment—on the one hand, and the moral demands, not only of social heritage, but of the individual's own ethical and religious sentiments on the other. He held, further, that this conflict is often so difficult of solution and so distressing that it becomes "repressed", that is, it sinks below the level of consciousness, so that the person avoids its unpleasant consequences by being entirely unaware that such a conflict exists. It is seldom, however, that the repression is completely successful, and manifestations of its existence and dynamic process become evident in the form of abnormal, often asocial, behaviour and in dreams. Freud held that it was by a study of such apparently irrational actions and of the person's dreams that knowledge of the underlying conflict could be obtained. If such a conflict could be discovered, and the patient could grasp its implications, it was often found that with the passage of time not only were the force and insolubility of the conflict mitigated, but the person's power of adjustment was improved, with the result that the conflict itself and its unwelcome results disappeared.

CLASH OF SENTIMENTS

There is little doubt that in ordinary circumstances the demands of sex in its varying manifestations are more difficult to harmonize with other demands of the personality and of society than any other group of instincts, but other instincts are often involved in conflict. For example, in wartime the instinct of self-preservation conflicts with sentiments of pride in courage, patriotism and the like. In the investigation of psychological abnormality, difficulties and conflicts in the sphere of sex will often (indeed, most often) be found, but too much insistence that sex lies at the bottom of all such abnormality is unwise.

There has been considerable divergence from the original teaching of Freud. The Swiss physician Jung laid chief stress on the aims of life for the future, and on the effect of ancestral memories on the attitude of the individual towards these aims. The psychologist Adler thought that the conflict was chiefly concerned with will-power and domination, and others have stressed several variations in the mechanisms of abnormal mental processes.

It may be that the interest aroused during the last thirty years in the psychological explanation of all sorts of abnormalities, not only mental but also physical—which has, indeed, been most fruitful—has obscured the undoubted influence of bodily and environmental factors, which previously had been given as the only explanations for everything. We must not forget, however, that a human being has a body as well as a mind, and a mind as well as a body. Mental causes will operate on both mind and body, and

297

physical causes on both body and mind. While, therefore, we may allow that in the study of psychology, whether normal or abnormal, the chief stress should be laid on mental factors, we must not forget that fatigue, poisons, germs, injury and new growth can cause changes which at first sight seem to be entirely psychological in origin.

It is clear that a very great deal could be written on the subject of the responsibility of the environment in determining abnormality of mind, and indeed a vast literature has grown up on this subject; but our purpose is to

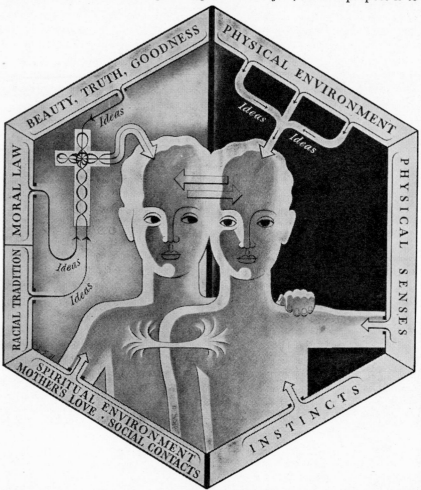

FIG. 86. *A symbolic representation of the dualism inherent in human personality—the Carnal Man and Spiritual Man of St. Paul, the Ego and Super-ego of Freud. Harmony and co-operation between these two elements mean health and happiness. Disagreement between them on the conscious plane gives rise to most of the difficulties with the self that normal people experience; while serious conflict at a deeply unconscious level implies mental disease.*

give indications rather than details, for the details of the subject may be studied more profoundly in further reading.

3. *Degenerative Changes.* As life proceeds, the various tissues of the body first grow, then reach a stage of equilibrium in which it is only possible to replace or compensate for wear and tear, and finally the tissues grow old and degenerate. All the tissues, however, do not grow old at the same rate; the nervous system and the brain are specially prone to degenerate earlier than the rest of the body. In the first place, nerve-cells are very delicate and easily killed by poisons, injury or new growth; and in the second, once a nerve-cell has been killed it cannot regenerate.

CONSTANT WASTAGE

All the nerve-cells that are ever going to be possessed by a person are developed by the time he is sixteen, but fortunately there appears to be a considerable reserve, except in mental defectives. Therefore, for a time there is no appreciable deterioration in mental capacity, in spite of the constant wastage of nerve-cells, because, so far as we can understand, others can carry on their work. Nevertheless, sooner or later the reserves will be exhausted and capacity will decrease.

This degeneration is seen not only in the intellectual sphere—that of memory, concentration, originality of thought, or soundness of judgement—but also in the emotional sphere. Old people are apt to be morbid or sentimental or, as it is often called, childish. Moral control is often reduced, and many unexpected delinquencies, especially in connexion with sex, may be committed by people who have previously been upright, conscientious and controlled. The "nasty old man" may not be so personally responsible as is sometimes thought, and his conduct under the influence of degenerative changes in his brain must not be judged by his previous record, when he had full control of all his lower-level thoughts, emotions and actions.

SEX—NORMAL AND ABNORMAL

Between the mental life of men and women and their bodily health and constitution there is a close and fundamental relationship, which will be discussed in greater detail farther on in this chapter. It is in the important field of sexual activity that this relationship is displayed in one of its most vital aspects.

The sensations of human beings may be roughly divided into pleasurable sensations and painful ones. In the young infant, gentle touching and handling of any part of the body seems to induce pleasurable sensation. Soon the intensity of such pleasurable sensation seems to be specially developed in certain parts—the mouth, the genital organs and the opening of the bowel (the anus). Some psychologists refer to these areas as "erogenous zones", implying, if they do not categorically state, that the pleasure experienced is of a sexual nature. It seems unnecessary to insist on the specific sexuality of such pleasures in very early childhood, but still it must be noted that sexual sensation which is experienced after puberty is not any particular form of common sensation, such as those of touch, heat, cold or pressure, but is a very intense general pleasurable sensation, perhaps similar to that gained by the infant from all parts of his body.

DEVELOPMENT OF EMOTION

As to the so-called erogenous zones, after sexual life is established the genital organs are obviously concerned with sex, the mouth (though primarily concerned with nutrition) has a sexual connotation in kissing, while sensation at the anus may have a sexual function in very special circumstances. There is also a sexual stimulus involved in the handling, feeling and contact of the whole surface of the body, and so there can be no doubt that general pleasurable sensation becomes very much involved with the sexual experience of the individual once puberty has been reached.

Sexual Emotion. Apart from sensation, there is an emotion specifically concerned with sex which undergoes development with the growth of the individual. For some time before puberty, there is a growing but ill-defined tension in the body which demands relief. At or about puberty, it is found that stimuation of the genital organs, until a point of intensity of pleasure known as the orgasm is reached, results in a sort of explosive easing of tension, which for the time relieves the need. With the establishment of puberty this is associated with a discharge of seminal fluid in the male, and with the secretion of certain glands and contraction of certain pelvic muscles in the female. Since the urinary openings and the openings of the genital ducts are identical in the male and closely adjacent in the female, it may be that in both sexes the "genital" erogenous zone is really a combined genital and urethral zone. It is noteworthy that in the female intense sensation is only transferred to the vagina much later, and is confined at first to the clitoris and the urethral opening.

Masturbation. An orgasm can be produced by any sufficient stimulus of the genital organs, however caused. As a rule the adolescent, by accident or instruction, learns to produce this orgasm by himself, and this masturbation (or "self abuse," as it is unfortunately called) should not be regarded as abnormal at or about puberty. At this age the relief of inner tension is all that seems to be required, and gives full satisfaction. The sensation involved in the manipulation needed to produce the orgasm is in itself highly pleasurable and, if indulged in occasionally, does no harm; but it is when this manipulation is repeated over and over again simply in order to produce this pleasurable sensation that it becomes an undesirable habit.

With increasing age, changes come in the nature of sexual feeling. There now begin to develop not only sensations and feelings of tension in the subject himself or herself, but also affection for another person, who becomes the object of rather vague desire. At the same time an inclination to altruistic and really unselfish behaviour begins to develop. This is an important development, for it means that the personality of the child is unfolding and expanding, so that from an individualist he becomes a social being with a real desire to promote the welfare of others. Towards this expansion of the personality sex is undoubtedly a strong stimulus; and if sex is gratified and satisfied only by self-manipulation, then this expansion and socialization is checked, if not prevented.

Undifferentiated Extroverted Sexual Impulse. To begin with, this sexual urge, as distinct from the inner tension, is directed outwards towards some individual other than the self in an undifferentiated way, leading to attachments to members of either the same sex or of the opposite sex. The main attachment at this stage is emotional—the adolescent "crush"—often for a member of the same sex, because there is as a rule a certain amount of segregation of sexes in school or work in mid-adolescence.[1] This emotional "crush" may or may not become associated with mutual gratification of the physical sensation and tension by manual manipulation or other methods.

Directed Sexual Impulse. Still later, this sexually undifferentiated love for someone else is normally canalized to the opposite sex. At first, in late adolescence, these emotional attachments are intense, but of no long duration, and their rupture causes no lasting emotional disturbance, though temporarily the reaction may be considerable ("calf-love").

Finally, this attachment to the opposite sex is still further canalized into fully-developed love for one mate, and this normally should lead to marriage and the foundation of a family.

MALADJUSTMENT

Against the background which we have briefly sketched of the normal development of sexual feeling and emotion, it is now possible to explain the main varieties of sexual maladjustment.

Auto-eroticism (Love of the Self). Masturbation, as has been indicated, may be regarded as a normal event and little notice need be taken of it, provided it is not indulged in too often so that it is used as a means of gratifying a pleasurable sensation rather than as a way of relieving tension which has become unbearably pent up. Nor should it be continued too long, into later adolescence, when it will not release tension sufficiently, since at a later stage more than this is required—namely, some emotional relationship with another person. At this stage continued masturbation may delay or even prevent the

---

[1] The "crush" for a member of the same sex is not only a result of segregation, for there is a natural shyness of, and withdrawal from, the opposite sex in adolescence; and in co-educational schools close friendships and emotional friendships are still formed between members of the same sex.

outfolding of personality towards wider social contacts and riper interests.

Masturbation may sometimes occur in female infants, but this again is an accidentally acquired means of gratifying general pleasurable sensation in a specially sensitive part of the body and, as the child develops other interests the habit usually passes away quickly, provided that too much attention is not directed to it by the parents so that the infant feels that she is achieving an all-too-pleasant notoriety.

The proper treatment of masturbation at any age is a wholesome indifference to it on the part of the adult and a diversion of the child's interest by toys and games and, at an older age, to intellectual interests and sport. At the same time, a straightforward explanation should be given of the reasons why masturbation is indulged in and why it is undesirable to establish it as an uncontrolled and even uncontrollable habit. Above all, there should be no threats, no bogey stories, which only fix the child's attention on the habit and fill his mind with fears and conflicts accompanied by anxiety. This is far worse for the child than the original masturbation, and such anxiety may cause mental and bodily illness. It cannot be sufficiently stressed that masturbation uncomplicated by anxiety is never responsible for mental or bodily illness, stunting of growth, impotence or frigidity in later life, or any of the other bogeys with which the masturbator is so frequently intimidated.

UNNATURAL ATTRACTION

Inversion, or Homosexuality. This is emotional "love" for a member of the same sex, with or without physical gratification. There are a few people of both sexes who by reason of glandular abnormalities are not properly differentiated into one sex or the other. These "feminine" men and "masculine" women may have the physical sexual formation of one sex but the emotional disposition of the other, and so may be manifestly homosexual. It should not be thought, however, that all men who look feminine, or all women who look masculine, are homosexual, for this is emphatically not so. Much more commonly, homosexuality is determined by obstruction of emotional growth at the undifferentiated and adolescent stage, or regression (a harking back) to that stage of the development of sexual emotion. As has been pointed out, there is a tendency for the sexes to be segregated at this mid-adolescent stage, so attachments to persons of the same sex are easily established. Homosexual tendencies may start at this stage because of obstruction or regression which are determined by conflicts and guilt feelings. As a rule, these are due to bogey teaching, or absence of teaching, on sexual matters, or to terrifying experiences before the child has reached an appropriate stage of sexual maturity, so that the patient fears the next advance towards the full development of his, or her, sexual life.

The treatment of the inherent or glandular form of homosexuality is difficult, if not impossible, in the present state of our knowledge, but the

302

obstructed or regressed form can be treated (if it has not been established for too long), if the situation is fully investigated and the patient can clearly understand the nature of the conflicts involved.

Perversions, or Misdirected Sexual Impulses. "Pederasty" is a diversion or misdirection of the normal sexual impulse generally met with in male homosexuals. This diversion is due to some conflict in relation to normal sexual development which may be more or less unconscious and require analytical treatment, or may in some cases be due to lack of opportunity to enjoy normal sex gratification.

The concentration of sexual desire upon some part of the body or article of clothing not directly connected with normal sexual satisfaction is called "fetishism". This again is due to obstruction or diversion of sexual development caused by conflict, but in this case the conflicts may be very complex and very difficult to elucidate. As a rule, the normal gratification is prevented by guilt or fear, and the desire is displaced from the natural object of such desire to the desire of some symbolic substitute. This transference may mean that the desire may be unusual or bizarre, but no longer charged with guilt. The mechanism is thus similar to that underlying the genesis of obsessions (page 322 *ff.*).

Sexual satisfaction by wearing the clothes of the opposite sex ("transvestitism") depends on conflicts involving dissatisfaction with the patient's own sex. These may be determined by the knowledge that the parents desired a child of the opposite sex and so actually, or in the imagination of the patient, resented his or her existence and deprived him of love. Or there may have been real or fancied disadvantages in childhood attached to his or her sex as compared with those enjoyed by brothers or sisters, as the case might be. Or again, there may be fear or anxiety over the real or fancied responsibilities of his or her own sex in adult life—such as going out into the world, money-making, child-bearing, parenthood, and so on.

SATISFACTION DERIVED FROM PAIN

Sexual satisfaction by the display of the naked body or genitals is known as "exhibitionism". Some degree of this is a common factor of all sexuality, but if the sexual act and the normal interest in it are displaced and a desire to exhibit the body is substituted, such exhibitionism becomes a perversion.

Sexual satisfaction in being hurt ("masochism") is usually a perversion of the female or of the "feminine" male. In ordinary sexual activity the female obtains some pleasure from submission to the dominance of the male, and even has no objection to the infliction of a mild degree of pain. If the subject, owing to anxiety or guilt, has a desire for punishment or to make restitution through her own suffering, the sexual urge may be deflected from its normal outlet into satisfaction in self-abasement and suffering, mental or physical.

Sexual satisfaction in inflicting pain is known as "sadism". This is the obverse of masochism, and is usually a perversion of the male or of the "masculine" female. It is a perversion into self-assertion, possibly intensified by a tendency towards the explosive or the over-excitable types of behaviour, both of which may be induced by "conditioning". If the sex act, which is fully pleasurable, be habitually accompanied by the experience or infliction of pain, such experience or action may itself become sexually pleasurable. Something very similar is to be observed in the frustration of the female, who may "revenge" herself on children by inflicting mental and sometimes physical pain on them.

Impotence and Frigidity. The inability of the male to perform the sexual act is termed "impotence". This may in a few cases be due to physical causes such as great fatigue, very debilitating illness, or injury, disease or malformation of the genital organs. In the vast majority of cases, however, it is due to conflict, with consequent anxiety, relating to the moral issues or physical effects of masturbation, the sexual act or the responsibilities of parenthood. Treatment of the physical causes depends on the curability or otherwise of the underlying causes. The cure of those causes which have been determined by anxiety depends on the possibility of resolving the conflicts involved.

The inability on the part of the female to experience—and, what is just as important, to give to the male—any satisfaction in the sexual act is known as "frigidity". The causes are analogous to the causes of impotence, and treatment follows the same lines.

MENTAL SIGNS OF BODILY ILLNESS

It is of the greatest importance to recognize that mental symptoms may be caused principally or exclusively by physical disease. It is not possible to give here an exhaustive list of these, but a few typical examples may usefully illustrate the principle.

Influenza is an exhausting and depressive illness at the best of times. If a person who is struggling with an emotional conflict, and is just managing to carry on with life in spite of it, has an attack of influenza, it may so weaken him that he breaks down and exhibits a severe anxiety state. Similarly, such an illness may precipitate a phase of pathological depression. Again, a certain number of women develop insanity after childbirth. As will be shown (page 354), there is undoubtedly a predisposition to insanity in those who succumb to this form of illness, but were it not for the fatigue of labour and subsequent poisoning from infection—even though this is not severe or even very obvious—there is no reason to suppose that insanity would have occurred. It is important, then, that everything should be done to mitigate the trials of childbirth, and it is essential to do everything to avoid infection of womb or breast afterwards. It is probable that the wise use of anaesthetics and of sulpha drugs and penicillin will in the near future reduce the number of cases of puerperal insanity with which we have to deal.

Fear of Impending Disaster. In certain acute anxiety conditions due to an insoluble and intolerable emotional conflict, the patient may experience a most distressing fear that something terrible is likely to happen. This feeling of impending disaster is also experienced in certain diseases of the heart and large blood-vessels. It is often associated with the intensely painful condition known as angina pectoris, and may be thought to be determined by the dread of the excruciating pain of an attack of angina. Sometimes, however, the dread may occur without the pain and may possibly be the result of a sudden alteration of the normal circulation of the brain.

HIGH BLOOD PRESSURE

Irritability. In pages 313–14 attention is drawn to the probability that much high blood pressure in middle life is the result of continued emotional strain and of frustration of one sort and another. There is another form of high blood pressure, however, which occurs earlier in life and which is due, perhaps, to constitutional factors, and certainly to physical causes. In this condition the patient frequently exhibits intense irritability and explosive outbursts of temper resembling those described in pages 338–42. Inasmuch as the epileptic personality owes a great deal to constitutional abnormalities in the behaviour of brain-cells, as demonstrated by recording their electrical activity, it may be that there is some connexion between this type of personality and that which develops "malignant" high blood pressure early in life; at present, however, we do not know.

Mental symptoms associated with diseases of the lungs are much less common, but it is known that variation in the concentration of oxygen and carbon dioxide in the blood has a profound effect on the function of brain-cells. Thus, if a person breathes very deeply for several minutes more oxygen and less carbon dioxide will be present in the blood. This means that the blood will be relatively less acid, and that causes a diminution in control and a general confusion of mind. Those who are potential epileptics may suffer from fits in such circumstances.

Euphoria. It is a well-established fact that sufferers from consumption, even in the most advanced stages, are illogically hopeful and cheerful. And so, often, are those suffering from infantile paralysis, in spite of its seriously crippling effects. This so-called "euphoric" state is reminiscent of the illogical cheerfulness of the elated or over-cheerful type (page 343), though, of course, it is not so marked or erratic. The same condition is also found in the organic nervous disease called disseminated sclerosis.

Mental Effects of Digestive Disturbance. Indigestion is a potent cause of depression and irritability and, as is shown on page 313, indigestion may be caused by emotional conflict. There is no doubt that this indicates that a vicious circle can easily be established. Thus, many digestive disturbances, including ulcers of the stomach and of the duodenum, are partly due to emotional causes and partly to physical causes, which increase irritability and frustration, each intensifying the other.

That constipation can influence mood is a matter of common observation. We are all familiar with advertisements which recommend laxative preparations for irritable children. This emotional disturbance is probably not so much due to poisoning from waste products as is popularly believed, since poisons are not readily absorbed through the lower bowel. The cause is more likely to be alterations of pressure within the bowel. The almost instant relief of headache and depression which sometimes follows a dose of salts cannot be due to a washing of poisons out of the blood, but may be due to nerve impulses conveyed to the brain after a distended bowel has been emptied.

The familiar liverishness, with its headache, depression and irritability, is a very real experience of most of us when our livers become congested and inactive, and although none of these symptoms reaches the intensity which might lead to a serious diagnosis of mental illness, the subject's psychological reactions are certainly abnormal when he is suffering from these afflictions.

Mental Effects of Waste Products. More important mental reactions occur when the excretion of waste products by the kidneys is inefficient. The mental accompaniments of the accumulation of nitrogenous waste in the blood ("uræmia") are well known to all doctors and nurses. The patient is morose and depressed and loses his powers of concentration and clear memory; if the condition is not relieved he becomes confused, loses consciousness and finally dies. In the earlier stages of this process, discrimination between uræmia and the mental illnesses developing in the depressed and withdrawn types may, for the time being, be difficult.

One of the most painful maladies to which man is prone is stone in the kidneys and bladder; it is supposed that this constituted St. Paul's "thorn in the flesh". He, at any rate, probably correctly attributed to this disease his aberrations of mind and temper which occurred from time to time.

Mental Effects of Under-Nourishment. When the nourishment of the brain is inefficient, mental alterations become obvious, and in severe anæmia the patient finds he cannot concentrate or remember, and that any prolonged mental effort is impossible.

VITAMIN-STARVATION

Those deprived of certain vitamins show very definite mental symptoms. Nicotinic acid, one of the constituents of Vitamin B, is important in this respect, and many patients suffering from lack of this essential ingredient in the food, or unable to absorb it, exhibit clouding of consciousness, hallucinations and delirium. These symptoms may all be removed in a few hours by treatment with nicotinic acid, if this deficiency is the real cause of the trouble. Again, profoundly under-nourished people who have been below the minimal

306

level of intake for some time, may alternate between profound stupor and agitated delirium; while in pellagra, a disease due to deficiency of Vitamin B2 (nicotinic acid and probably other constituents), there may be a phase of paranoid reaction (unreasonable suspiciousness), in addition to profound depression or a marked withdrawal from reality. All these conditions can be relieved by intensive feeding with the necessary vitamins, but will reappear if the supply is not maintained.

THE PART THE GLANDS PLAY

Mental Effects of Endocrine Abnormalities. The most serious failure of proper nutrition of the brain resulting in deranged mental states occurs when the secretions of the endocrine glands are deficient, excessive or abnormal.

The balance of the thyroid gland is of the greatest importance. When the secretion is deficient (as in cretinism and myxœdema) the patient is dull, stupid and depressed, or even of such low mental grade as to fall to the levels of the imbecile or idiot. When the secretion is excessive or abnormal (as in Graves' disease, hyperthyroidism, or exophthalmic goitre) he becomes excitable, agitated, anxious, elated or confused, with delusions and hallucinations, and may simulate one or other of the varieties of serious mental illness from time to time. Feeding with dried animal gland (thyroid) in the deficient cases and surgical removal of most of the gland in the over-active type will generally remove all these mental changes.

The effects of other glandular abnormalities are not so clearly defined, but the influence of the internal secretions of the genital glands is marked. In the male the gentle but irritable, facile ineffectiveness of the eunuch is traditional.

In the female the rhythmic alterations of function of the ovary have definite, if rather subtle, mental effects. For the two days before the period and the first day or two of the flow, many women are irritable, "touchy", unreasonable and lacking in a just sense of proportion. It has been shown statistically that there is a diminution of efficiency, accuracy and rate of production in factory work during this time. Before, during, or just after the period, many women also experience a depression which in some cases becomes really profound.

Such symptoms become more marked and more prolonged at the change of life, and it is necessary for the patient and her friends to realize the temporary nature of these changes in personality and the strong likelihood of an eventual cure. Sometimes it is possible to bring relief by the administration of various endocrine extracts, but unfortunately their action and interaction are so complex that it is not possible to be sure of their results in any given case.

Other glands, by the irregularity of their secretions, produce a variety of mental effects, but the whole subject is so complex that it is hardly worth while elaborating the subject here, especially as it is often difficult to distinguish between the direct effects of over- or under-secretion of one gland and the direct consequences of a general upset in balance. For example, children suffering from excessive growth of the pineal gland, situated in the centre of the head, go through a stage in which they exhibit mental and sexual precocity, due not only to the abnormality in the pineal but also to deranged action of other glands. A child of under ten with the mental capacity and sexual virility of a man of over twenty will naturally exhibit mental characteristics and behaviour which are quite abnormal for a boy of his age, but which would not be remarkable in a grown man.

Mental Effects of Injury. Injury, new growth, or disease of the brain itself might naturally be expected to result in marked mental changes, and this certainly is the case. We must guard, however, especially in these cases, against attributing the whole of the mental changes to the direct effect of these physical factors, because there may be a predisposition to mental illness which is precipitated by the physical factor.

CONCUSSION

Injury may produce immediate or late effects, or both.

Immediately after concussion, when the patient is coming round from his initial loss of consciousness, there may be agitated delirium or gross confusion. He may even perform automatic actions, as the epileptic does after a fit. Later he may show marked irritability and a much greater susceptibility to the effects of alcohol, so that he easily becomes "fighting drunk". Again, he may be depressed and sometimes he may exhibit abnormal suspiciousness. There may be, of course, a lessening of mental capacity, owing to extensive destruction of brain tissue, and this is specially liable to occur if severe brain injury is inflicted in childhood, when the brain is still growing, though the power of "reserve" brain-cells to take on the function of those put out of action is to all appearances very remarkable.

Mental Effects of New Growths. Brain tumours produce mental symptoms of some sort or another in a large proportion of cases. Among such symptoms are the dullness and lack of mental capacity which might be expected to result from pressure within the skull, the pain of the resulting headache and the destruction of tissue.

Sometimes, however, hallucinations occur, and now and then attacks of excitement or violence. Some authorities hold that tumours of the front part of the brain are associated with a cheerfulness, a sense of well-being and a tendency to make rather feeble jokes which were previously foreign to the personality concerned, and that this is a sufficiently constant feature to serve as a valuable aid to diagnosis.

In the diagnosis of abnormal psychological manifestations it is clear that we have to treat the patient as a whole. We have to consider his body and mind, his heredity and his constitution, and all the complicated reactions of his own individuality with his environment. When we have done this, then and then only can we estimate the true cause of his abnormality and proceed intelligently, with whatever resources there are at our means, to restore him to normality.

The Failing Mind. Mental capacity starts to fail when large numbers of brain cells die. They may do this because they have reached the end of their capacity to live, and since the nerve-cells are such specialized and delicate structures, they are apt to die before the more robust cells of the rest of the body. Indeed, probably many such nerve-cells die early in everyone, but it is only when a disproportionate number die that we have to take notice of the mental failure.

Premature death of nerve-cells of the brain will also take place if they are subjected to certain poisons which specially affect them, the chief of which are alcohol and the germs of syphilis. The danger to the constant drinker who claims that in spite of all the alcohol he takes he is never drunk is that in the early sixties his memory, concentration and judgement may fail, ten or even twenty years before they should. Brain-cells will also die if they are not properly nourished, and in conditions in which the blood-vessels are diseased (e.g., arterio-sclerosis), which occur again in chronic alcoholism and syphilis and also as a result of strain, there may be a premature failure of mind.

Dementia. Apart from the generally decreased capacity of memory, concentration, judgement and reason which is characteristic of this failure (technically called senile dementia) and is due to the ageing and death of the brain-cells, the form of mental illness may be partially determined by the previous mental type of the patient. Some are depressed, some excitable, exploding into violent rages; others "withdrawn" or suspicious. Like those of the confusionals, whom they may closely resemble, their symptoms are never so clear-cut as in the primary insanities, since, for example, they are too muddled to formulate the logical systems of delusions of the paranoiac, or to conceive the guilty feelings of the "sin against the Holy Ghost" of the depressive, or to build up the marvellous schemes of the elated manic. (See Chapter XVII.)

LEGAL IMPLICATIONS

The illness of these patients is important in two special ways. From the medico-legal point of view, their making of wills or bequests or gifts may give rise to serious trouble. Lacking in discrimination, they may be very suggestible, so that unscrupulous attendants may influence them to leave their property to them or to give away large sums even before they die. Again, they may be suspicious or depressed, and may become quite unreasonably hostile to their nearest and dearest, or convinced that they have been robbed or have already lost all they are possessed of. In this case they may fail to provide for those people who ought to benefit and may die intestate, or else leave everything, or a substantial residue, to one who has no close interest or claim.

Care of the Demented. Since there is no hope of cure, for a dead nerve-cell

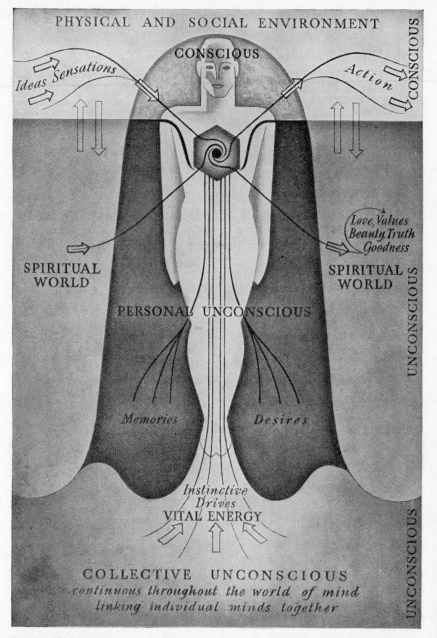

FIG. 87. *The Individual Mind. Vital energy, in the form of instinctive drives, wells up from the collective unconscious (Fig. 88) and is modified by personal memories and desires. By means of this modified energy the individual personality reacts by physical action or conscious thought to ideas, sensations or situations presented by the environment.*

cannot be replaced, and relatives are loth to send these patients to a mental hospital from which they know there can be no release, these old people may become an intolerable burden. The lives of conscientious younger relatives who devote their whole time to looking after them may be completely spoiled. Unfortunately, these patients may live a long time in a state of mental and physical degradation. Being confused, they have no idea of time and space. Although they have been for months or years in their own beds, they indignantly demand to be taken home, and bitterly accuse their all-too-devoted attendants of cruelty and neglect. In the last stages they are unable to control their excretions and can neither feed nor wash themselves. In every way they would be better dead, but since that cannot be, and they are really no less happy or unhappy wherever they are, special hospitals which cater for such cases are the place for them. Certainly, the younger members of the family, generally unmarried daughters, should not be sacrificed to look after them.

PHYSICAL ASPECTS OF MENTAL CONFLICT

Of recent years it has been recognized that certain illnesses previously regarded as being entirely due to physical causes, such as accident, infection, poisoning or new growth, are entirely or partially caused by conditions which we are accustomed to think of as mental. It is, of course, true that we cannot separate body and mind into distinct compartments and that

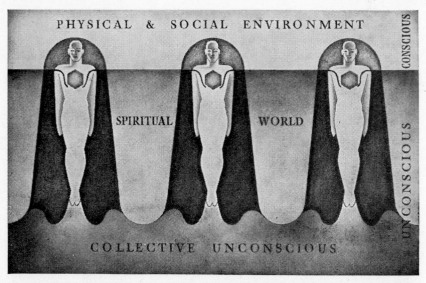

FIG. 88. *The personality of each individual forms but a minute fragment of one vast whole. Each human being's personal consciousness is isolated within his physical and social environment; his personal unconscious, too, exists for himself alone (Fig. 87). But below these, continuous throughout the world of mind, linking all individual minds together like a matrix out of which they grow, is the collective unconscious.*

311

whatever be the "state" in which we find ourselves, whether of health or illness, this state owes something to mind and something to body.

Hysteria. On page 320 attention is drawn to the readiness with which a subject of the complacent type manages to "convert" anxiety into physical symptoms. In other words, he succeeds in resolving, at least temporarily, an insoluble conflict by "acquiring" a disability which removes him from the difficult situation or gives him a "respectable" excuse for avoiding its implications. Such symptoms are, as a rule, paralysis or disorganization of movement of limbs or loss or exaggeration of sensations, such as blindness, deafness, excessive pain or troublesome derangements of the sensation of touch. Sometimes, however, they involve the internal organs, as in the case of train-sickness, which prevents the patient from travelling, or a persistent necessity to pass water, which prevents him from attending social functions.

With such symptoms we are not concerned at present, however, except in so far as they may persist as permanent structural changes. As will be seen, if treated early and efficiently, they can for the most part be removed by counter-suggestion, provided that some means be found of solving the underlying conflict at the same time or immediately afterwards. It is generally the neglect of the latter provision which prevents the cure of hysterical illness, with all its physical symptoms which may multiply as time goes on. Moreover, if such symptoms last for a long time, especially in older people, there may be such changes in the blood supply of the limb or of the tone of the muscles that full restoration of usefulness becomes impossible. Nevertheless, it is probably safe to say that hysterical symptoms—which notoriously can simulate almost any physical disease—do not as a rule result in permanent or even prolonged derangement of structure or function.

Anxiety. On the other hand, the prolonged anxiety consequent on conflicts which cannot be or are not resolved does produce alteration in the nervous control of the internal organs which, if it goes on long enough, may lead to permanent ill results.

EFFECTS OF PROLONGED EMOTION

In Chapter XVI are described (page 315) the physical effects of emotion, such as the rapid heart-beat, heavy breathing and sweating accompanying fear or anger, and the diarrhœa and poor control of the bladder associated with anxiety before an interview or an examination. It is there shown, moreover, that such effects may follow long-drawn-out emotion, even if the reaction is by no means excessive, just as readily as they accompany violent emotion; especially is this the case in people with an inherent tendency to instability.

These effects, if prolonged, may have serious effects on the organs concerned, especially if—as is undoubtedly the case with some organs in some people—they are of poor quality from the beginning.

Of the diseases which may be induced by conflict and mental illness in general no detailed discussion is possible here; however, a few of them may be mentioned:

Asthma is a troublesome complaint which may sometimes be traced to an abnormal sensitivity to the pollens of certain grasses and flowers, to the fur or hair of certain animals, such as the cat and the horse, or to certain foods. These causes, however, are not always admissible, and in many cases of asthma the attack follows fears, anger or disappointments, especially if such emotions are associated with, and intensify, unresolved conflicts.

The same is to some extent true of other so-called allergic diseases, such as gout, some varieties of eczema and certain forms of inflammation of the bowel (ulcerative and mucous colitis). The gouty person is notoriously bad-tempered, but it is sometimes difficult to be sure whether the loss of temper is due to the pain of an attack of gout, or whether the attack is due to a loss of temper. All of these conditions are associated with, and often seem to be the consequence of, prolonged anxiety.

RESISTING INFECTION

The ordinary view of infectious diseases is that they are the inevitable result of the invasion of the body by harmful germs, and no doubt this is true of many of the acute infections such as smallpox and measles; but, even so, not everyone who is exposed to the germs of measles catches the disease, so the factor of the patient's resistance to the infection has also to be taken into account. In conditions, then, in which there is less certainty about the invading germ, this resistance factor becomes very important indeed, and conditions which lower resistance contribute very considerably to the occurrence of the illness. Among such conditions, conflict, depression and anxiety are very potent, so that there is no doubt at all that if these mental manifestations are left unrelieved the patient is much more liable to be attacked by the germs of disease, and may be much less able to resist their onslaught.

Various kinds of indigestion are commonly associated with fear, anger, anxiety or depression, and some interesting experiments have shown that if these emotions are suggested to a patient under hypnosis, marked changes will occur in the secretions of the glands and in the movements of the muscles of the stomach and bowels, changes which are known to be associated not only with indigestion, but also with stomach and bowel ulceration. It is well known among medical men that when prices of stock go down in the City, the incidence of stomach ulcers increases. Cases of gastric and duodenal ulcers increase also in number and severity in times of trade depression and severe unemployment, and indeed in any time of anxiety and strain.

A most important condition of this sort is high blood pressure. No doubt the causes of this condition are multiple, but that it is associated with mental and emotional strain there is no doubt; it is a disease of so-called civilization, at least of high-pressure civilization. It can be proved that blood pressure is raised by rage or fear, and since many mental illnesses are expressions of prolonged and persistent rage and fear it is not surprising that there is a prolonged and persistent high blood pressure.

The basis of high blood pressure is laid down in middle life in the vast majority of cases, for it is at this stage of existence that many people begin to realize that their time for making a success of life is beginning to run short, especially in the more physically active pursuits. In many cases this engenders resentment, and sometimes fear that they will not be able to provide for themselves and their dependants in later life. This resentment and fear are not necessarily openly expressed, but may come out indirectly in a way which is not difficult to interpret for anyone but the subject himself. An example of this is seen in the vicarious valour at the expense of youth which is exhibited by elderly men and women in time of war. It is by no means improbable that if people were to modify their idea that the attributes of youth (sexual allure in the case of women, and physical prowess in men) are the be-all and end-all of existence, there might be less high blood pressure in later life. At any rate, it is very common for those who have resented the waning of youth and have not been able to do anything about it, because they have no interest in pursuits suitable to later years, to develop high blood pressure. This is assisted, no doubt, by increasing indulgence, especially in alcohol, which, incidentally, is only another manifestation of their spiritual discontent.

Test Yourself

1. What are some of the chief causes to which abnormality of mind may be ascribed?

2. McDougall describes the development of "sentiments" such as love, hate, business interests, etc. Can you give examples of how such sentiments may conflict (*a*) in the short run, (*b*) throughout longer periods of life?

3. Enumerate some of the more obvious mental effects of bodily illness.

Answers will be found at the end of the book.

CHAPTER XVI

ANXIETY, OBSESSIONS, FEARS

NXIETY is a common human emotion which is felt by all normal
people from time to time, and it is only when a person experiences
this anxiety persistently, and when the degree of anxiety felt is
out of proportion to any cause apparent to the subject or his
friends, that he can be described as abnormal. Anxiety is the result of conflicting emotions. Thus, when we are anxious about a sick child we are
alternately, or even simultaneously, swayed by fear and hope—fear for his
death or pain, and hope for his recovery or easement. So, too, is the pathologically anxious swayed by conflicting emotions, though both the subject
of the conflicts and the nature of the emotions involved may be hidden from
the patient's consciousness. Nevertheless, we may be sure that fear of something must be at the bottom of the trouble—yet not pure, uncomplicated
fear, for that is panic, not anxiety. There must be another side to the situation
—hope, aspiration, ambition, self-respect, or whatever it may be.

EMOTIONAL STRESS

The pathologically anxious person not only does not know, or at least
fully know, what he is anxious about, but he may not even know that he *is*
anxious. When we experience emotion we are commonly afflicted with certain
bodily discomforts or even disabilities. Who has not broken out into a sweat
of fear, felt his heart racing when angry, experienced the sensation of goose-
flesh when listening to eerie sounds in a dark house, or had a sudden overwhelming desire to pass water or even to relax his bowels when waiting to
go into an examination room or to interview the "boss"? All these, coupled
with an inward tension, are the results of emotional stress and nothing but
emotional stress; and the over-anxious type may just feel these things and be
quite unaware that they are due to mental and not physical causes. So he may
go to his doctor and demand to be treated for palpitations, diarrhœa, pains in
his back and the like, and the doctor may be deceived and accept the patient's
estimate of his trouble. When such symptoms have been going on for a long
time they may become fixed, and their true nature may be very difficult to
disentangle.

Whether the patient suffers from obvious mental anxiety or from tension
and physical symptoms, he certainly requires treatment, for he is a very
unhappy and a truly sick person. Treatment consists in finding the cause of
the anxiety, that is to say, the conflicting emotions which have not been

315

adjusted. If the tangle can be resolved, it is often found that the patient can adjust himself to life without great difficulty, and then of course he is sufficiently well to carry on. Often the original conflict has resulted from some particular incident, but as a rule the trouble is caused by a whole series of related incidents which make it more and more difficult for him to adjust to life.

There is no doubt that some people can adjust to life less easily than others, and so are more subject to conflict and consequent anxiety. It takes very little, therefore, to upset them, and they are the people who are apt to be called "neurotic". Theoretically, however, anyone may acquire a pathological anxiety if the stress to which he is subjected is sufficiently great.

CHILDHOOD CONFLICTS

The initial incident giving rise to a case of pathological anxiety may be encountered in adult life, but in the majority of cases amongst ordinary citizens the original situation occurred in childhood, and often in early childhood. The conflicts are as a rule based on difficulties in the relationships between the young child and his parents. This takes us back to very early mental processes and to conflicts between the instincts and the requirements of society. The young child is an egotist and desires to gratify his instinctive demands in the most direct way; but he also wants security, especially the security of being loved. To obtain this he depends on those around him, especially on his mother. If he is to get security, he must do what his mother wants him to do; but if he is to gratify his instincts directly, he often finds he is doing something of which his mother strongly disapproves. Here is a fruitful source of conflict, and it is perhaps more remarkable that so many children grow up without becoming pathologically anxious, than that some develop into anxious types later on.

Importance of Early Security. It is this sense of security and love during the first five years of life that is so essential to the mental well-being of the individual. After that he is more naturally adventurous and requires much less cossetting—indeed, he is better without it. But in his early days he can't have too much. That is why breast-feeding is such an advantage from the psychological, as well as from the physical, point of view. A mother cannot cuddle her baby to a bottle as she can to her breast. She cannot encircle him and hold him safe and secure in her arms so well, and if a bottle must be used, then it is all the more important that the child should receive this protective envelopment of mind and body in all possible ways. It is for this reason that the upbringing of under-fives in institutions is so difficult and often so unsatisfactory, for all the scientific rules and regulations for the upbringing of the infant are worth nothing in the balance compared to a "cuddly" mother. It is not too much to say that if you can give a child real emotional and intellectual security in his early years you can depend on him to secure for himself all the freedom he needs in later years.

316

Security depends not only on physical protection in the early months but also on parental consistency later on. There must be harmony in the home between father and mother and no "playing off " the child from one parent to the other by deputing to the father the infliction of punishment while the mother does all the loving.

Strict fairness in the treatment of all the children is equally essential. Rivalry between children for the affection of their parents must be avoided.

Here must be mentioned the problem of jealousy of the next child—a very important one. There is, indeed, a psychological reason, as well as a physical one, for a wise spacing of the family. If a child is at least two years old before the next baby arrives, he is old enough to be told that a new baby is coming and encouraged to help to take care of it. He is by this time not quite so dependent on his mother, and it is now that the father can be so useful by making a special effort to take an interest in, and to play with, the older child, and so for the time being allow the mother to devote her time and attention to the new arrival.

But too long an interval between the children is also inadvisable, because the sooner the children of the family can play together and depend upon each other, the sooner will they feel less dependent on their parents, thus allowing the latter to get on with their own lives, both individually and together—which is essential for the continued harmony of the family.

The Anxious Child. If a child in his early years enjoys physical security and emotional calm, he is likely to be able to meet the demands of his future with equanimity, so that it will require a major disaster to throw him off his balance. But if he has not this foundation of security, he soon develops an attitude of mind which expects the worst and looks for difficulty. This way lies anxiety—anxiety about going to school, divided loyalties between home and school, between home demands and work, between love for his parents and family and that for his friends and sweethearts. He lacks enterprise to strike out for himself in thought, in action, in learning and in his sexual relationships, and when he comes to have to adjust to the demands of sex, that most difficult of all the adjustments which he is called upon to make, he is filled with anxiety as to whether or not what he wants to do is right, or what he thinks is right is what he wants to do.

DEMANDS OF SOCIETY

This brings us back to the demands of instinct and demands of society, and it is in the realm of sex that these demands are most likely to conflict. That is why, in investigating the conflicts and causes of anxiety in the "neurotic", sexual problems are so often found to be the basis of the trouble. In the established neurotic the term "demands of society" must be modified. To begin with, the instinctive demands of the infant are countered by the wishes of the parents and the rules laid down by the latter, but before long

317

these wishes and rules are incorporated in the child's own mental make-up and form what has been technically called his super-ego, his ideal for himself. This ideal of what he would like to be and would like to do is, however, complex, and by the time he is grown up it is much modified from the stage when it was represented by the simple rules of his mother. Indeed, his own instincts help him to form it, and these instincts not infrequently come into conflict. For example, there is often conflict between fear and curiosity: he would like to go and see what this object is, but its threatening aspect deters him and he has to adopt some working compromise, and such working compromises help to make up his ideal of conduct.

IMPORTANCE OF SELF-RESPECT

The neurotic is, in fact, much more concerned with the conflict between what he feels he would like to do on the spur of the moment and what he would think of himself if he did it, than he is concerned with what other people are likely to think of him. That is why he is sometimes able to solve his conflict for the time being by reactions which—at least, to his own temporary satisfaction—save his face, though from every other point of view they are utterly unsatisfactory. This is why, also, if the neurotic is to be successfully treated, his self-respect must be restored and maintained, and he must be given a reason for his illness which is satisfying to his intelligence and not wounding to his pride.

The essence of the mental state of the person suffering from pathological anxiety is that he suffers from insecurity because of a conflict between what he immediately wants to do and what he thinks he should do. This conflict and the effort to reassure himself and re-establish his security may show themselves in different ways.

Shyness. He may throw up the sponge and think of himself, and appear to other people, as inferior. He is not so good as his neighbour, therefore he cannot be expected to do this or that which is really within his capacity. He is shy, diffident—he may even be cringing and afraid. In this way he goes through life singularly ineffectively. But now and again this sort of person feels that his self-respect is being completely outraged, and he suddenly bursts into aggressive, rude, and even violent behaviour. We have all seen the shy, retiring person who suddenly surprises everyone, not least himself, by becoming noisy and hearty, and then, perhaps equally unexpectedly, is covered with confusion and retires more deeply into himself than before.

Such a person is insecure. He is afraid of taking action lest his actions run away with him beyond the point at which he feels safe, and since the margin of safety becomes narrower and narrower, he becomes more and more restricted, until he can stand it no longer and for a brief moment he bursts the bonds. If he is to behave normally, he must see the situation clearly;

first he must understand that his inferiority is not, at any rate entirely, due to lack of capacity, but to lack of security. Let him see why he is insecure, let him look his conflict in the face, see how it has been built up and enlarged on the foundations of something which happened long ago, probably in early childhood. Let him get a true assessment of the real importance, or rather unimportance, of that long-past episode. Let him acknowledge his present capacities. Let him see how his overweening criticism of himself limits him. Let him appreciate the good opinion of at least quite a number of his fellows. Let him understand how, with the constructive help which can be given by someone who really understands the mechanisms of these conditions, his difficulties can melt away. Then, very often, he is able to take his proper place in the community, and achieve a happiness and a success which he never believed possible.

Snobbishness. Another victim of insecurity may buttress himself by trying to assume a position which he would like to take, but which he is not sufficiently secure to take naturally. He becomes a snob. As Thackeray pointed out, there are snobs of every sort and kind, social, intellectual, artistic, and all the rest, but all these snobs are insecure, insecure as they can be. The natural aristocrat is at ease with all classes—duke's son, cook's son, all come alike to him. Not so with the snob. He entrenches himself behind what he thinks are the manners and the customs of the group he has chosen, and he dare not admit to himself, much less to others, that he might be vulgar or stupid or unappreciative of beauty. As someone once said, "The worst of all snobs are the spiritual snobs, who would convert the very house of God into self-contained flats". But the snob will not be happy until he is natural, and he will not be natural until he has realized that his snobbishness is an artificial and really ineffectual barrier against the threat of his insecurity. Indeed, such a realization is a sign of grace, for it is the first step to real self-knowledge and, therefore, to ultimate cure.

INTELLECTUAL SNOBBERY

Intolerance. Another defence reaction against insecurity is intolerance and the adoption of a hypercritical attitude. Such a person feels that, far from being inferior, he is superior. Nothing comes up to his exacting standards, everything is poor or wrong or inartistic. In fact, he is an intellectual snob, but his superiority is only a defence; even he himself is not really convinced of his superiority, and the less secure he feels the more unreasonable he is and the more absurd he appears to others. The mechanism is the same as in other forms of insecurity, and the treatment is the same. None of these people can be happy, or indeed useful, in society until they realize the truth, and only then may they recover health.

Anxiety is a fundamental manifestation of abnormal psychology and is constantly being encountered in a variety of conditions, especially in those in which the patient is "depressed". So the depressed patient is frequently anxious as well; and, of course, the true anxious type is often, if not generally, depressed. (In psychiatry, however, the word "depression" is generally used in a special technical sense.) Similarly, the "withdrawn", the "suspicious" and the "confused" types (see Chapter XVII) may exhibit marked anxiety, as also may those whose minds are failing.

COMPLACENCY

Paradoxical as it may seem, pathological complacency is a derivative of anxiety. As has been demonstrated already, anxiety is the result of an emotional conflict which cannot be solved, at any rate for the time being. This failure of solution may become so intolerable that it must be got rid of somehow. If it can be dispelled by the development of what is technically called "hysteria", the most remarkable complacency may be developed.

War Hysteria. An example will show how the process takes place. Let us take the case of a sufferer from battle neurosis, whose conflict entails a struggle between self-preservation and his ideal of patriotism and courage. In wartime he cannot avoid service, and so if the conflict is to be solved something has got to happen to enable him to get away from danger without "losing face". The type who develops the hysterical symptom and so becomes complacent is suggestible and rather non-critical. If he receives a slight injury to a limb, or is suddenly frightened so that he becomes speechless or shakes and shudders, he very easily accepts the suggestion that his limb is useless, that it is paralysed or that he has become completely dumb or is seized with an uncontrollable shaking (tremor).

In such a condition he has become useless in face of the enemy, so he has to go to a hospital in the rear. This solves the conflict for him, for he has got away with an injury which in his eyes, and the eyes of most people, is obviously disabling and therefore respectable. It is the sudden resolution of the conflict which makes him so complacent and enables him to assume the role of *belle indifférence*, as it is so admirably termed by Janet. But his very complacency has an air of unreality about it, for he seems to be, and for the time being is, quite content to have this definitely disabling condition, and he gives up any attempt to make a real adjustment to life. The person who has really and satisfactorily solved his conflict is not complacent in this way, because he is back again in touch with life and is making a real effort to adjust. Adjustment to life is always difficult, and anyone who is making a conscientious effort to adjust can never be really complacent.

The Nature of Hysteria. These physical conditions which are developed under the influence of suggestion in order to solve a conflict are known as hysterical symptoms, and the illness so developed is called hysteria. They do not correspond to structural changes in the body. Thus the examining doctor does not find that hysterical paralyses are associated with the alterations in

320

reflexes which indicate damage to brain, nerve fibres or muscles, and so he may think that the paralysis has been consciously assumed—in other words, that the patient is malingering. The wise doctor does not think this, however, for he knows that it is very difficult to keep up malingering for long. True malingering is, in fact, rare, since whoever tries it is very soon found out. The essential characteristic of the hysterical symptom is that it is unconsciously determined, while the malingerer quite deliberately sets out to deceive his neighbour. The hysterical patient cannot remove the paralysis by an effort of will, or, more accurately, cannot make the effort of will necessary to remove it. The malingerer can stop the symptom whenever he wants to.

Characteristic of both hysteria and malingering is the fact that the symptom always achieves a purpose, although in the hysterical this purpose is not obvious either to the patient or the observer, since neither is generally aware of the true nature of the conflict. In the case of the war neurotic the purpose is to get the patient out of the battle without "losing face". A further characteristic of the hysterical symptom is that, unless the passage of time has altered the circumstances which determined the conflict, the removal of the symptom—which can usually be effected by counter-suggestion without much difficulty, except in cases of very long standing—leaves the patient in a state of anxiety and, of course, destroys his complacency. To cure the patient it is necessary, therefore, in the case of hysteria, not only to remove the symptom, but to see that the conflict is solved as well.

There are other types who may be very complacent and pleased with themselves, especially the over-excited type who is not in a very violent phase (pages 343–4) and the general paralytics if they entertain grandiose ideas of themselves (pages 354–5).

DOUBLE PERSONALITY

As a rule, there is included with the hysterics a group of cases of double personality and loss of memory. Such cases are so bizarre and remarkable that when they occur they usually attain a considerable notoriety. However, the reader should bear in mind that these cases are rare and relatively unimportant.

In his fictitious presentation of Dr. Jekyll and Mr. Hyde, Stevenson has depicted the double personality vividly and sufficiently accurately. The personality of everyone is made up of various and often conflicting characteristics, and if these are so divided that for a time one set of characteristics becomes dominant and the opposing set is overlaid, there will be produced from one individual two or more different, and even contrasting, personalities, one of which will appear at one time and another at another time. As a rule, the personalities have no conscious knowledge of each other; but sometimes A knows all about B, while B knows nothing about A, so that when he wakes up in the circumstances and surroundings of A, he is completely mystified. Thus, in the case of the Rev. Anselm Bourne, who was a city parson in one phase and a provincial grocer in another, he could not understand, when the phase changed from "grocer" to "parson", how he came to be in such strange surroundings and clothes and such a long way from home; the "grocer", however, did know about the "parson".

Cases of completely dual personality are very rare, but less uncommon are those people who suddenly lose all memory of their true identity and yet, during this period of lost memory, wander away and may appear to behave logically and "normally" so far as the observer can see, though the behaviour is not normal for the individual himself. Such wanderings are called "fugues", and these may last for considerable periods. There are all gradations, from the complete fugue, which almost amounts to dual personality, to short periods of loss of memory, during which the general consciousness of the person is retained. Such conditions can generally be treated by appropriate analytical treatment, often helped by hypnosis, during which treatment the memories of the patient may be restored.

OBSESSIONS

We have seen that in severe cases of anxiety the insoluble conflict may be dealt with by the suggestible, non-critical type of person by the formation of a hysterical symptom. This was common in war neurosis, especially in the First World War among non-commissioned ranks, because they were trained to implicit obedience, and criticism and personal initiative were discouraged. Hysteria was less common in the Second World War, because, being a war of movement, situations were less static and so could more easily be got out of, and also because all ranks were trained to exercise enterprise and initiative. In ordinary life the displacement of intolerable anxiety occurs less commonly, and so the straightforward anxiety (if such a word as "straightforward" can be used of such a complex condition as a psycho-neurotic illness) is more usually met with, in which conflicts cannot be solved by the patient himself.

The Obsessional Type. However, in the case of a certain type of person who is specially prone to severe conflict, the original anxiety is transformed into what is called an "obsession". There are two types of obsession, a "phobia" and a "compulsion". Each of these types will be discussed presently, but first we must consider the type of person who may develop an obsession. Some people claim to be able to recognize the hysteric before he develops a hysterical symptom, but, except that he is over-suggestible and not sufficiently critical of himself, his characteristics are too vague to make a distinction of the hysterical type useful. But the obsessive type, which in many ways is the opposite to the hysteric, is much more easily recognized. Such a person is essentially over-conscientious. There can be no doubt that in the make-up of this type there is a considerable inherent constitutional factor, which probably accounts for the fact that obsessions are much more difficult to treat than either plain anxiety or hysteria. It is much more easy to remove the effects of, or to modify, the environment than to alter the person's inherent constitution.

The over-conscientious person of obsessional type is always scrupulously neat in his behaviour. He is the person who makes a fetish of "a place for everything and everything in its place". In his bedroom his clothes are always neatly folded; every coat has its special peg on which it hangs, and every shoe an exact place in which it rests. Untidiness is a terrible anguish to him, and should anything be displaced he is very angry or even weeps. In his study or his office everything is carefully docketed and "lives" in its own pigeon-hole. He is "file-mad". He never throws anything away in case it may be wanted, and his indexing system and arrangements are so complete, and consequently so complicated, that in the end he cannot find his way about in it himself.

In his conduct, too, he is over-scrupulous. He is forever on the look-out lest he should do something wrong, or lest others should not do the right thing. Formulas and formalities, red tape and the right method tend to become more important than the actual achievement. We are apt to find these over-conscientious people in the Services, especially, perhaps, in the Civil Service. Their exaggerated sense of orderliness disposes them to be fitted into a hierarchy, with its grades and ranks; and they feel secure as part of a system that implies that, so long as they do not do anything wrong, they will be sure of steady promotion and an eventual pension. For work which requires a meticulous attention to detail they are invaluable, but as they will not take risks which may disturb their orderliness, anything which requires a degree of enterprise or initiative is not for them.

INHIBITIONS

How far such over-conscientiousness may be regarded as normal is a matter which is open to question, but it is obvious that such people will be specially prone to conflicts, more particularly about their own behaviour, and so they are almost always anxious. They have built up such a complex and inflexible order of ideals that it is practically impossible for any spontaneous, instinctive urge not to conflict with it. They accept the opinions of others, especially of the majority, in politics, ethics and religion, so that anything unconventional shocks them, and they are continually terrified that their conduct (which, like that of everyone else, owes much to instinctive drives) will come up against these conventions. Since sex and religion are more subject to conventional inhibitions than all other activities in life, we often find that their troubles centre around these subjects.

Since these unfortunate people are almost constantly subject to anxiety, their conflicts tend to grow and grow, both in complexity and intensity, so that it is not surprising that they frequently become quite intolerable. As has been said, when a conflict becomes really intolerable something has to happen, and we find these obsessionals, these over-conscientious people, figuring in certain types of Abnormal Psychology which are discussed in the following pages.

These types are the "fearful", the "compulsive", the "weak-willed" and the "suspicious". The first three of these are usually included among the sufferers from obsessions; they are inflicted with "psycho-neuroses", the less severe and dangerous forms of mental illness. But the last is a "paranoid" —a sufferer from one of the most serious and dangerous of the "psychoses", or insanities. (For details of this condition see pages 350–1.)

BELOW CONSCIOUSNESS

An obsession is defined as an irrational thought or action which the subject knows to be irrational, but which he is powerless to prevent or to control. He is powerless to prevent or control the obsession, just as it is impossible for the hysteric to prevent or control the hysterical symptom, because the whole mechanism is below the level of consciousness and therefore is not subject to the patient's will-power. As we have already stated, the obsession is a means by which an insoluble conflict is mitigated. People of the over-conscientious type—those in whom obsessions occur—are probably more aware, though still only dimly so, of the nature and content of their original conflict than is the hysteric, because they are more introspective and more sensitive to the incompatibility of their instinctive urges and their meticulous code of conduct. But when the obsession has developed they are quite unconscious of its connexion with the original conflict. Yet connexion there is, because when an obsession is analysed it is found that the obsessive object is symbolic of the original situation.

The various forms that obsessions assume can be divided into two classes, the first comprising fears or "phobias", in which the person feels that he must not on pain of disaster touch certain things, perform certain actions or place himself in certain situations; the second class consists of feelings of "compulsion", in which the patient feels compelled, in face of unavoidable disaster, to do certain things; or, again, certain ideas come into his head unbidden, with a compulsive force. While the savage implicitly believes in his taboos and rites, the obsessional—as a rule, a highly intelligent civilized person—is only too aware that his taboos and rites are absurd.

These fears and actions bear some sort of symbolic relation to the original conflict, though their actual form may owe something to suggestion; and perhaps because of this connexion the patient cannot rid himself of them, however much he tries.

Fear is, of course, a common experience of us all, but here we are dealing with pathological fear, and this may be discussed under the four headings:

(a) Obsessive fear
(b) Depressive fear
(c) Fears associated with suspicion
(d) Fears of the confused.

(a) *Obsessive Fear* (*Phobia*). The nature of the obsession has been discussed already; a few examples of obsessive fear may suffice to illustrate the mechanism involved. It should be recognized that it is definitely not true to assume that the mechanism is the same in every case, even though the obsessive symptom, such as a fear of small rooms or of sharp instruments, is apparently the same. Each case must be judged as a separate problem.

Claustrophobia. A very common example of an obsessive phobia is the fear of enclosed spaces or small rooms, commonly known as claustrophobia. It used to be thought that this phobia might be caused by the patient's experience of a severe fright in childhood, such as that resulting from being shut in a dark cupboard, and that the recollection of this event by the patient would be sufficient to effect a cure. In the great majority of cases, however, the simple restoration of such a memory is not curative. It is a working rule that to cure the patient *all* the relevant memories must be recalled. This means that the original situation and all subsequent series of situations and their relationship with the general difficulties in adjustment to life experienced by the patient must be unravelled and explained. It may then be expected that the patient will be relieved of his symptoms—in this case the obsessional fear—and cured of his psycho-neurotic illness.

HISTORY OF AN OBSESSION

So in claustrophobia, more elaborate investigation is needed than the restoration of the memory of the dark cupboard; and this shows that, although the cupboard may have had some influence in suggesting to the patient the form which his subsequent obsession may take, the fault for which the shutting in the cupboard was a punishment is much more likely to be of real significance.

The patient's mother, we shall suppose, locked him in a dark cupboard—a foolish and wicked thing to do, in any case—because he had been naughty and had displeased her. To the child this was a terrible punishment, involving as it did such fear and misery and loneliness. Although he may not have understood why the fault was so bad, he realized that it must have been a serious one, serious enough to have forfeited his mother's love and affection. Being very insecure, as such anxious obsessionals are (partly, perhaps, as a result of his inherent constitution, but also because of the difficulty of fending for himself in life), the loss of this love and affection was the most dreadful thing that could happen to him. Although later all may seem to be well again and the mother has probably forgotten all about it, the child, if he is of this over-conscientious type, is never quite sure, and he becomes more and more scrupulous in his behaviour lest he should commit the mysterious fault which brings upon him this awful punishment.

MORAL FORTRESS

With his over-conscientiousness and orderliness he builds around himself a protective shell of correct behaviour to ensure that whatever he does will be "right" and dire punishment will not overtake him. By this time he is neither clear in regard to the nature of the forbidden sin nor to the whys and wherefores of the dire punishment, but he lives his life in fear of it, and the enclosed space seems to be symbolical of all his terrors. Then he comes up against a situation in which he seems forced to behave in a way which is contrary to his rules and orders. He has to go outside his fortress, to lose protection, and he vaguely harks back to the memory of the time when he seemed to lose his mother's love, and this is associated with the terrible punishment of the dark cupboard.

Then the processes in his unconscious mind operate somehow like this: if he hadn't been in the dark cupboard it would have meant that he had not forfeited his mother's love and protection, and had not committed the mysterious fault. If that had never happened, he would not have had to build such a rigid fortress round himself and this necessity to get out of this fortress would not be so dreadful. But now, if he can keep out of the dark cupboard (the small room or the enclosed space), the symbol of all that is dreadful, the situation which is such a conflict and produces so much anxiety will no longer be so insistent. That, in fact, is what happens, for the obsessive consumes so much of his energy in thinking about and avoiding his phobia that he has no longer any interest or energy left to deal with the present conflict, and for the time being at least it is shelved, and the momentous decision as to what he should do is postponed.

FEAR OF THE OPEN

Agoraphobia. The phobia, or irrational fear, of open spaces may be much more simple, signifying a fear of being deprived of the support and protection which the patient has always felt to be so necessary. If he can be shown that the artificial fortress is really unnecessary and, in fact, harmful in the present situation in which he is involved, he may be relieved of his phobia and his conflict. Even here, however, the process of elucidation is not likely to be simple or swift, for the genesis of all obsessions is complex and involved, and the obsessional is always difficult to treat.

Fear of Sharp Instruments. The phobia of sharp instruments may have a specific meaning, but it must not be supposed that the mechanism is the same in every case or that the symbolism can always be translated by the same idiom. The same instrument may, however, be a symbol of the male sexual organ and it may be found on elucidation and analysis that the patient (who may be of either sex) has had an experience in early life of some sexual fault involving the penis over which he felt very guilty and in connexion with which he felt that he was in danger of losing the love and approbation of his parents. Sex and everything connected with sex has then become abhorrent, and he has surrounded himself—or in this case, perhaps, *she* has surrounded *herself*—with a fortress of puritanical prudishness. Then, to her horror, she vaguely recognizes that she herself, the pure, the virginal, soul, is being tempted by, or has even become interested in, sex; she may get ideas or even visions of the penis, a sharp instrument which, she believes, is threatening her morally, even if not in a physical sense.

SEX AND SYMBOLISM

Such a situation is quite intolerable, yet will not be denied. She cannot bear to think of sex, even in order to avoid it, but if she symbolizes it by thinking of it as a sharp instrument she need no longer think of sex at all; and she can and does take all sorts of elaborate precautions to avoid sharp instruments, until her life becomes a misery, since she can hardly avoid contact with knives, forks, nails or pegs. Again, she must be got to face the old situation, and from that the present situation, and if possible made to realize that sex is a natural function of everyone, and is, in fact, not so very difficult to control if it is squarely faced and clearly understood. It should be stressed, however, that all phobias of knives and daggers are not symbolic of sexual difficulties. They may represent guilty feelings in relation to ideas of suicide or even homicide, and every case must be investigated on its own merits.

(b) *Depressive Fear*. Depression will be dealt with more fully in Chapter XVII (pages 344–7); it will be seen that in the truly depressed patient there is a basic feeling of guilt and often definite impulses to suicide. Here we are dealing with fears which may be irrational to the observer, but, unlike obsessive fears, to the patient himself they are most definite and real. He is quite sure that everything is wrong, that he has committed the unforgivable sin, that he has no hope in this world or the next, and so it is no wonder that he is afraid. We may use all the arguments and all the persuasiveness in our power to try to show him that his fears are groundless, but he remains convinced that they are all too well founded. We may think that we can connect his fears with deeply buried conflicts and try to bring him to see the connexion, as we do with the obsessive in relation to his phobias, but this has seldom any real effect. Sometimes, however, depression, and fears depending on depression, pass away for no obvious reason and without the intervention of any particular treatment.

(c) *Fears Associated with Suspicion*. Abnormal suspicion will be dealt with in Chapter XVII. In this case the patient is afraid because he thinks that all

327

the world is against him and that certain people are plotting to do him grievous harm. Since these ideas are false—they are, in fact, what are technically called "delusions"—the observer readily realizes their falsity and tries to assure the patient that they have no foundation. But they are very real to the patient, and no argument can convince him of the contrary. They may not be quite so terrible as the fears of the depressive, for the depressed person is as a rule passive, while the suspicious person is much more active and may, and frequently does, attack his supposed enemies. In this way he gets some relief, since he goes out to meet his fears and does not give way to the black despair of the depressed. As he is not withheld by doubts or scruples, it may, of course, go hardly with his "enemies", who may, very justifiably, be afraid of him.

(d) *Fears of the Confused.* In the confusional conditions which are discussed in Chapter XVII, it will be noted that hallucinations are common. These are "false images", that is to say, sensory impressions of sight, sound, smell, touch and so on, which, though not founded on objective fact as observed by the patient's neighbours, are absolutely real to him. Some of these hallucinations are very alarming and the patient may be absolutely terrified by them. The traditional pink mice and green snakes of delirium tremens, a condition which may be the result of acute alcoholic poisoning, are examples of such terrifying hallucinations. It is no use telling the patient that these objects are not real; he is quite convinced that they are, and that they are coming at him rapidly and inevitably. He will lose neither the fear nor the hallucination until his insanity is cured.

LOSS OF SECURITY

Compulsions. People sometimes say of their actions, "I felt compelled to do it. I was obeying an irresistible urge." In many cases all that this means is that they very much wanted to do something and weren't going to be put off by anything. For an urge to be pathological, it must be genuinely irresistible. A truly irresistible urge is met with in several sorts of mental illness.

The obsessive compulsion has already been referred to and may be considered first. In this case the patient is quite aware that his action is unnecessary, unproductive and probably ridiculous, but even though he tries hard to stop himself he cannot do so for long. Like the phobias, compulsions represent a symbolic displacement of anxiety from an insoluble and very distressing conflict, involving a loss of security, generally moral security. The conflict in such cases is between some instinctive urge to action which is in opposition to the patient's own ethical code. An example of a common compulsion is the case of a person who experiences an imperative feeling that he must go and see if a door is locked or a gas-jet turned out, and he has to do so again and again, even though intellectually he knows that the door is already securely shut or the gas-jet turned off. It is easy to see that such an action symbolizes security and that he is unable to convince himself that he really is secure. This symptom can only be removed when the patient is persuaded that his (moral) security is not threatened, and this will only be achieved where he has understood the mechanism of his compulsion.

Another phenomenon, usually included amongst the obsessive compulsions, is the unbidden appearance in the patient's mind of words or phrases usually obscene or sacrilegious. Such obsessive thoughts are apt to occur, moreover, in people who are particularly prudish, puritanical, or tied to the forms or ceremonies of some particular cult. These thoughts generally come at the most unsuitable times and places—in church, when taking communion, or on some other solemn occasion—and cause the subject a great deal of distress.

MORAL BARRIERS

The story generally is that such people have been very strictly brought up, and have built up in their minds a tremendous barrier against any behaviour which might run counter to their ethical code relating to sex or religion. This is intensified if they have in childhood experienced something of a sexual or profane nature which has frightened and shocked them. Even such people cannot pass their whole lives without thought, inclination, or action which is, or seems to be, in some way sexual or against their religious code. So any chance thought of this nature, still more any conscious desire, shocks them, and every recurrence upsets them more and more, with the result that the offending subjects are pushed farther away and the walls of the fortress are further strengthened. What they are really afraid of is that they will be assailed by a temptation to perform some sexual or sacrilegious act which they will not be able to resist, and they try to persuade themselves that such a temptation does not and cannot exist.

DANGERS OF REPRESSION

But neither the world nor the flesh can be pushed right out of the personality, and at some time or other these enemies must make themselves felt, even though they may be reduced to isolated words or phrases by the barriers which have been unconsciously erected in the effort to keep them out of the mind. It should be noted that the control, instead of being conscious, voluntary and rational, as it should be, is unconscious, involuntary and irrational and not subject to the patient's will. Then it seems to these unfortunates that the devil has entered into their souls and is sending these words, so foreign to their conscious selves, to torment and terrify them. Attempts at complete repression of material which is an essential part of us is never successful and never desirable, and the occasional consciously permitted bawdy story is better than the obsessive compulsive oath, coming unbidden into the patient's mind.

A word may be said here about "kleptomania", a term which is apt to occur quite often in press reports of police-court cases. A respectable woman steals some silk stockings from a drapery store and a defence of kleptomania is put up. The implication is that she had been driven by an irresistible impulse and could not help herself. The word "kleptomania" is unfortunate, because in psychiatry "mania" means something quite different. It would be much better to call it "compulsive stealing". Obviously, such a defence must be closely criticized and should only be accepted if there is positive evidence of a compulsive act. There is a pathological condition of this sort ("compulsive delinquency"), but it is by no means common, and it should be shown that the stealing has a symbolic relationship to an insoluble conflict within the patient's personality. Many cases of "kleptomania" are just plain stealing, the word needing no qualification.

COMPULSIVE STEALING

Pathological stealing—that is, stealing due to mental illness, which should not be punishable by law—is not always compulsive, but if it is compulsive the stealing will in some way represent to the patient a lesser evil than that involved in the original conflict. The formula may be: "I have recognized in myself an impulse to outrage or to kill so-and-so, but such a thought is quite intolerable. Yet the impulse is strong, and so must be displaced—better to steal money or goods than to deprive the person of virtue or life." If this is so, compulsive stealing is more likely to be from an individual or small group of individuals, often close relations of the patient, than from a public store. It sometimes happens, however, that thefts are committed by a person who is eager to be punished. Then the theft will be as public as possible, with no attempt at concealment. These crimes, though sometimes included in the category of compulsive stealing, should not be so placed, for the desire to be punished is associated with an overwhelming sense of guilt, which is more characteristic of depression than of obsession.

ANTI-SOCIAL URGES

Other compulsive acts may be performed by the insane ("psychotic"); the last-mentioned stealing in order to be punished is an example, as is the suicide of the depressed. Similarly, serious crimes may be committed by the over-excited, the suspicious and the confused types (see Chapter XVII). To the insane patient, however, these actions are not unnecessary or ridiculous—they are absolutely imperative, and no argument, pleading, or ethical consideration can deter them from committing their crimes. The whole personality is behind them, and so far as these actions are concerned there is no conflict involved. There may have been a conflict, but at the time of committing the crime any opposition to action has been completely submerged.

Although these actions, whether obsessional or psychotic, may be anti-social, it may be right that they should not be punished by the law, but if the "culprit" is not to be punished, he should be treated by a specialist in psychological disorders, who, possibly, may be able to cure him of his disability.

Psychasthenics. A class of people who are quite incapable of making up their minds or of undertaking any task at all is usually included among the obsessives; but, although certain obsessives are weak-willed and are so strangled within their moral fortress that they have difficulty in starting anything lest they be led into some action which would not be acceptable to their ethical code, they are not quite the same as the "psychasthenics", as they were called by the French physician Janet, who first gave a clear description of these subjects.

Although he classed them among the obsessional types, Janet postulated that the psychasthenics lacked something in their make-up, though he did not make it clear what that something was. Though many people now agree that these people are in some way inherently abnormal and so class them with the psychopathic personalities, we are no nearer knowing what it is that is lacking. It may be that they lack some component in the structure of the brain, as is the case with the mental defectives, though this seems unlikely. It is more probable that there is something wrong with the way in which the brain works, as with the epileptic (pages 295 and 338), or, as with the cretin, with the glandular secretions which regulate brain action and enable it to be co-ordinated (pages 307, 335), though in the latter case it is development to the state of adulthood, rather than the smooth working of the grown-up mind, which is prevented by this condition.

EXTREME INDECISION

Whatever the cause may be, such people are quite ineffective in life. In the most severe cases they cannot even make up their minds how to tie their shoe-laces. They can apply themselves to nothing, and so do poorly at school (though they are not actually lacking in intelligence), and they can never take up any useful employment. They are often artistic, but only on the receptive side. They like to listen to good music or poetry, or to look at good pictures, but they cannot play an instrument or compose or paint, so their marketable value is nil. Efforts to find conflicts and hidden emotional situations are generally futile, and even if they are found they do not seem to be particularly significant, and the discovery has no obvious curative value. Possibly in the future it may be found that some glandular treatment may be of use, but so far no such remedy has been discovered, and all that can be done is to provide what Janet called a "director", a keeper who will guide them and shepherd them through life, telling them what to do and making sure that they do it.

Other Forms of Weakness of Will. Almost all patients afflicted with mental

331

illness may suffer from apparent weakness of will, except perhaps the over-excited and suspicious types. The anxious type is so taken up with his anxieties that he has neither the energy nor the time to be as enterprising and decided as he should be. The complacent type is too satisfied by his temporary relief from his conflict to bother with problems and, in any case, the symptom which he has acquired may make it impossible to perform any task. The obsessional type has already been mentioned in this connexion as being so bound up in his fortress of rules and regulations that he is handicapped in everything, and the depressed type is so miserable that he has not the heart to apply himself to any new occupation.

The withdrawn person, as will be seen, is frankly not interested, but he has plenty of will-power in certain activities in his own peculiar world of make-believe; while the confused person is in such a muddle that he cannot follow any line of thought or action for very long. In all these cases, however, the will is more deflected than essentially weak, and these people only appear to be weak-willed, not because they cannot, but because they do not apply themselves to the work which the normal person thinks ought to be the object and endeavour of his fellows.

Test Yourself

1. What may be done to relieve an anxiety state?

2. What is an obsession? Distinguish between its two most common types.

3. Why is it so important to give young children a sense of security?

Answers will be found at the end of the book.

CHAPTER XVII

PSYCHOLOGY OF THE ABNORMAL

Ow TO present any comprehensible classification of psychological abnormalities to the general reader is a difficult problem. He is not concerned with scientific groupings so much as he is interested in the various queer, difficult, or even dangerous people he sees in the course of his contacts with, and studies of, society. He remarks that someone is unduly depressed without apparent cause, and he goes perhaps to his doctor friend and wants to know what sort of an abnormality this depression is. He may be told, and correctly told, that depression is only a symptom and his depressed acquaintance may be suffering from "a manic-depressive psychosis—an involution melancholia—schizophrenia—an anxiety type of psychoneurosis—or even G.P.I." Our inquiring citizen may be impressed by his friend's use of long words, but he is certainly not much wiser. We shall, therefore, give some description and explanation of the various types of mental abnormality which we encounter in our daily lives. The reader should realize, however, that when we put an individual into a group and describe him as being of a special type, all that is meant is that his dominant characteristics correspond to those of that type; he will probably show plenty of the characteristics of other types, although these will not be so marked.

MENTAL DEFECTIVES

Some low-grade mental defectives owe their condition to heredity factors. These are inherent in the germ-plasm and so are handed down from parent to child, but since these low-grade people are as a rule sexually most unattractive, they do not transmit their characteristics easily. Many such cases are the result of birth injuries and constitutional factors, while infection with the germ of syphilis before birth is responsible for a small (but only a small) number of them. Legally, such persons are defined as "idiots", that is to say, "persons so deeply defective in mind from birth, or from an early age, as to be unable to guard themselves against common physical dangers", and as "imbeciles"—"persons in whose case there exists from birth or from an early age mental defectiveness not amounting to idiocy, yet so pronounced that they are incapable of managing themselves, or their affairs, or, in the case of children, being taught to do so".

As adults they are quite unable to fend for themselves in society. In rural districts a few may still be found, protected by their families and the community as village idiots. This once-familiar object of derision and pity is, however, becoming rare, since the vast majority of idiots and imbeciles are now ascertained during their school age and, having been certified under the Mental Deficiency Acts, are segregated in colonies where they are cared for and given such simple tasks as come within their mental scope. Their demands on life are very few, and they may be happy enough in repeating over and over again the most simple actions. If such actions can be made useful, they may perform a worth-while task; but these low-grade defectives are essentially unreliable, and their attention quickly wanders, so that they have to be constantly supervised.

As a rule, they are easy-going and give no trouble, but if thwarted or teased they may lose their tempers, and, being quite uncontrolled, they may then be destructive and even dangerous.

As young children, they may give an appearance of an intelligence which they do not possess, but as they grow older this early promise soon disappears and they fall further and further behind. They are difficult to rear as infants, often being unable to suck, so that they have to be laboriously fed with a spoon. Everything in their development is late—their teeth appear late, they are unable to hold up their heads, still less sit up, until the age of twelve or eighteen months; they do not walk or talk until they are three or four years old. When he at last succeeds in walking or achieving balance, the imbecile is apt to roam round continuously until he is quite exhausted. This may give a false appearance of noticing things and therefore of intelligence, but if the child is closely watched it is easily seen that he fixes his attention on nothing and is inclined to knock things off tables and shelves or pick things up at random and, having no interest in whatever he has found, to drop them.

"MONGOLS" AND "CRETINS"

Physical deformities of one sort or another are more common in mental defectives than in normal children, but many imbeciles (and even idiots) may be to outward appearance normal enough. There are two types of particularly characteristic appearance which are worth noting. These are the "mongols" and the "cretins".

The mongol is a distinctive type of mental defective which can be easily recognized. These children, for they seldom survive for long into adult life, are usually small and rather puny, with round heads and faces and with a pronounced red flush on their cheeks. Their most characteristic feature, however, is their eyes, which slant outwards and upwards, giving them a Mongolian look. They often have scanty, thin hair and fissured tongues; and their little fingers are crooked, so that the point turns inwards and the middle joint curves away from the rest of the hand.

The cause of mongolism is unknown, though it has been the subject of much speculation, including Crookshank's theory that it is a reversion to a more primitive type of humanity. Mongolism is quite untreatable, and since these defectives are peculiarly susceptible to, and have little resistance against, catarrhal infection, they generally succumb to affections of the lungs at a comparatively early age.

Better understood are the cretins, since they owe their special features to a lack of secretion of the thyroid gland, one of the so-called endocrine glands which is situated in the front of the neck, at the base of the throat. If this condition is uncomplicated and is not just one feature in a general mental and physical defect, and if it is recognized early in the first few months of life, this group can be successfully treated by the administration of dried thyroid gland; and, provided the supply is continuously kept up, the cretin may grow up a normal citizen. This is the only form of mental deficiency susceptible to direct medical treatment, but this must be continued throughout the life of the cretin.

The cretin is a small, stunted child with coarse, thick skin, scanty hair, a large, protruding tongue, large belly, thickened joints and flat feet.

INCURABLE CONDITION

As has been indicated above, the low-grade mental defective is of very little use to himself or to anyone else, but just because he has been so difficult to rear and his mother has had to expend so much care and trouble to bring him up at all, she is apt to devote a disproportionate amount of attention to him afterwards, perhaps to the detriment of other normal children. She is unwilling to abandon the hope that he will "grow out of it", but unfortunately the low-grade defective does not do so. It is really kinder, in fact, to tell the parents the unpalatable fact and better for everyone concerned to send the child to a colony or home where he can be looked after, together with others of his kind, by those who have special skill and training for this task.

There is no hard and fast demarcation between the low-grade mental defective and the high-grade, on the one hand, or between the high-grade defective and the less intellectual "normal" on the other. On page 142 the method of determining the Intelligence Quotient is described. The upper limit of imbecility is usually held to be an I.Q. of about 50, while the upper limit of feeble-mindedness is about 70.

The Feeble-Minded. Feeble-minded persons are legally described as: "persons in whose case there exists from birth, or from an early age, mental defectiveness not amounting to imbecility, yet so pronounced that they require care, supervision and control for their own protection or for the protection of others: or, in the case of children, that they, by reason of such defectiveness, appear to be permanently incapable of deriving benefit from the instruction provided in ordinary schools".

This does not mean that, when grown up, the feeble-minded person is incapable of undertaking simple work and to some extent of maintaining

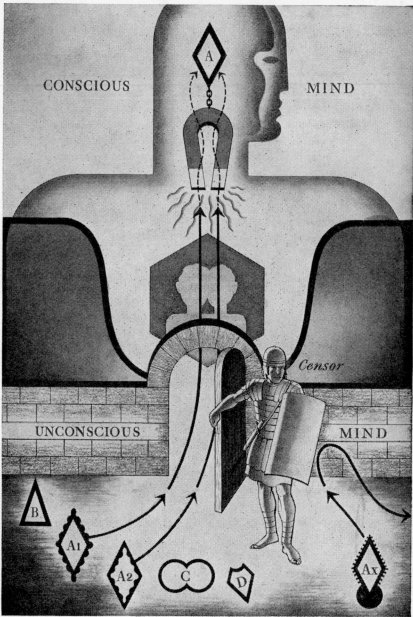

FIG. 89. *The Censor. An idea (A) in the conscious mind calls up ideas and memories from the unconscious which are associated with it (A1, A2). But if an associated idea (Ax) is strongly linked in the unconscious mind with a powerful emotion of fear or shame, recall to consciousness is impeded by an unconscious process, to which the name of "Censor" was given by Freud. (B), (C) and (D) are ideas unassociated with (A), and so not attracted by it.*

himself economically. Such people are, however, essentially the hewers of wood and drawers of water and in ordinary times are the last to get a job and the first to lose it. Feeble-minded girls are supposed to be specially suited to domestic work, but they are the crockery-breakers, the conveyors of wrong messages and the tearers of garments in the laundry.

Often physically strong and hardy, at any rate in the earlier decades of his life, the feeble-minded man is probably best employed on the land, though even here he requires fairly constant supervision by his more intelligent brethren.

Some people seem to have the idea that mental defectives are "dangerous" and that they are all criminally minded. This is emphatically untrue, for, if properly treated, the feeble-minded person is as a rule an amiable and easy-going individual. He is not easily roused, but if he is, his control being by no means good, he may lose his temper and become violent. At the same time, he becomes frightened immediately efforts are made to restrain him, so that he may appear vicious, and as he cannot be reasoned with once he is roused, it may be difficult to quell the storm.

CATSPAWS

So far as crime is concerned, however, it should be remembered that mental defectives are very suggestible and so they very easily become the catspaws of those who are less moral and more astute than themselves. But they are as a rule easily caught, and so their criminal careers tend to be short-lived. Similarly, mentally defective girls are easily seduced and persuaded into various sexual misdemeanours, but certifiable mental defectives do not form a large proportion of prostitutes because they are neither sufficiently attractive nor enterprising to succeed in that somewhat overcrowded profession. There is a large number of prostitutes, however, in the dull and backward groups.

The Dull and Backward. As we have seen, an I.Q. of 70 marks the upper limit of feeble-mindedness, and those with a quotient of between 70 and 85 comprise the dull and backward. At school such children do not do well; they fall behind their fellows and are nowadays usually dealt with in special classes. In industry they do poorly also, so far as continuous employment is concerned, but they are the people who may be content to follow the more mechanical and monotonous tasks. Mere lack of scholastic or social progress of this order is not always due, however, to inherent incapacity. It is very necessary to consider carefully why a pupil is falling behind in school, for it sometimes happens that a child of normal or even of superior intelligence does badly because his attention is deflected by anxiety and emotional conflict (Chapter VII). This state of affairs is disclosed by careful intelligence testing, which should, and in skilled hands does, discriminate between those whose inherent incapacity causes them to fail in such tests and those whose failure to acquire knowledge does not prevent them from performing the tests adequately, since the capacity is present.

Temporary failures may be due also to physical factors or illness, or more often to delayed convalescence after measles, whooping cough or the like, or to glandular changes which occur in relation to puberty.

Intellectual failure, therefore, does not necessarily mean intellectual defect, and the traditional school report "could do better if he tried" needs critical consideration. If the child is inherently lacking in mental capacity he could not do better, however much he tried. If he is the subject of anxiety or of physical defects leading to insufficient nourishment (or even poisoning) of his brain, he could do better, but it is of no use his trying until the disability has been remedied by either psychological or physical treatment.

That is not to say, however, that the report is not justified in many cases and that, in the case of some of those who receive such reports, punishment, judiciously applied, may not be the best remedy; but if exhortation or punishment persistently fail it is necessary once more to look for the real cause. The pupil's lack of progress may be due to failure by the teacher to capture the interest of the child, or even to make the subjects which he is trying to impart intelligible, or it may be due to the fact that his pupil is psychologically or physically abnormal. It is no use trying to treat or to beat the child until the true cause of his trouble has been discovered.

PSYCHOSES

In Chapter XVI we have mainly dealt with the conditions which we call "psycho-neurotic", conditions which may owe something to inherent abnormality, but which are chiefly caused by difficulties of adjustment to environment and for which a great deal can be done almost exclusively by psychological forms of treatment (psychotherapy). Now we have to discuss types which are for the most part "psychotic", a term which corresponds fairly well, but by no means exactly, with the popular term "insane". These conditions are probably due much more to inherent abnormalities and are very much more difficult to treat, especially by psychological means.

People with bad tempers are common enough; they generally want their own way and are deficient in control. The same characteristics of concern for themselves and loss of control are found in those whose explosiveness must be regarded as abnormal.

The Epileptic. Belonging to the principal group of this type are the epileptics. These are classified as "psychopathic personalities"; that is to say, they owe their disability chiefly to some inherent abnormality, and only to a minor extent to conditions determined by environment. We are beginning to know something about the nature of this inherent disability, namely, that, as is mentioned on page 295, there is something wrong in the way in which the brain works. This is shown by abnormal records of the very minute electrical discharges which emanate from all living tissue, including the nerve-cells in the brain. After being amplified by thermionic valves, these discharges are recorded by a special apparatus called the electro-encephalograph. Certain specific abnormal tracings are found not only in people who suffer from epileptic fits, but in many others, some of whom exhibit this explosive type of behaviour.

These people may have convulsive attacks (fits), but we cannot here discuss fits in detail, since their province is too much a purely medical one. It must suffice to say that the fit seems to be determined by some sort of stimulus to which the subject is over-sensitive. At the same time the convulsive activity is let loose, so to speak, because there is too little control of lower centres of activity by the higher levels of the brain.

"EXPLOSIVENESS"

The Epileptic Personality. Many epileptics and certain other people who do not actually have fits are very egocentric. They always want their own way, and they have to be the centre of the picture so that everyone and everything in the neighbourhood has to revolve round them. Such people are, of course, deficient in affection and regard for other people. The type of person we are considering is often singularly inconsiderate of others, even of his nearest relations. This being the case, he is peculiarly sensitive to anything which threatens or interferes with himself and especially with his pride. When this happens he is apt to explode into ungovernable tantrums and outbursts of rage. Often it is difficult for the onlooker to determine what it is all about, since it is only with difficulty that he can realize the extreme sensitivity and remarkable egocentricity of these subjects. Nor is it easy to deal with them, since they think that regard for themselves overrides all other considerations; and since they have little or no affection for others, there is nothing to appeal to in the way of altruistic feeling or rules of ethical behaviour.

Convulsions and Automatisms. In the epileptic fit, after the outburst of the convulsive movements which correspond to the outburst of rage, there is generally a period of unconsciousness or semi-consciousness in which the patient is only dimly aware of his surroundings. After he returns to full consciousness, he can remember nothing of what he has done or what has been happening. After a fit or an outburst, or even without these manifestations, epileptic personalities may do things which to the onlooker appear rational and deliberate, but for which they are not responsible, since they remember nothing about them.

Such actions are called automatisms. A claim that anti-social behaviour has been automatic is often put forward as a defence in criminal cases. If the crime (which, if a true automatism, is generally one of violent assault or even murder) has been committed soon after an epileptic fit, and the subject can be proved to be prone to fits and to take some time to return to full consciousness after them, the defence is probably good. Indeed, it may be good even though the subject does not have epileptic fits, but in this case it is much more difficult to be sure. Further positive evidence is significant if the defendant is subject to explosive outbursts, or if the tracings of his encephalograph are abnormal. In that case, the crime may be a true automatism and the prisoner should not be held responsible in law. Such people, whether criminal or not, may respond to treatment. Although the inherent abnormality cannot be altered, the actual attacks—whether these are fits, or outbursts, or automatisms—may be controlled by suitable drugs, though their action is less certain than we might wish. In any case, no one can guarantee a "cure" until the patient has been free from abnormality for from two to five years. If it is a question of criminality, it is difficult to know how long a person should be kept under treatment and control. If he is liable to commit dangerous actions unconsciously, to let him loose in the community (unless it is perfectly certain that he is cured) is like allowing a blind man to drive a high-powered motor-car along a crowded thoroughfare.

Uncontrolled Action. Explosive actions may take place in several other psychotic conditions (insanities), for it is a general rule that when he becomes really insane the patient loses touch with reality to a greater or less extent and becomes a law unto himself. So the normal control exerted by the dictates of society and consideration for others is not operative. Thus, if the patient is subject to a sudden impulse, it is likely to be gratified without delay and without consideration. Furthermore, the patient's own personality becomes disintegrated; therefore, certain instincts and impulses which normally oppose and restrain others no longer do so. For example, in the normal individual the instinct of self-preservation is very strong indeed, and it is very difficult for him deliberately to run into serious danger of actual injury to himself, or to run the risk of severe punishment for a crime which he has committed. Still more is it difficult for the normal person to take his own life. To do this, either the stimulus from the environment must be overwhelming, or his own conscious resolution must be tremendous. Indeed, some people would say that it is not possible for the normal person to commit suicide and, if he does so, this very action may be the first sign of insanity. This may be going too far, but it is too difficult a question to discuss here at length. When a person is insane, however, restraints apparently have little effect, and assaults on the self or on other people seem to happen with surprising readiness.

If these external and internal restraints are thus absent, it is only logical to expect that action will follow impulse immediately, and the behaviour will be explosive in character. Thus persons of the depressed and guilty type (page 344), who are particularly prone to self-injury, may commit suicide quite unexpectedly, and that is why the depressed person should be watched

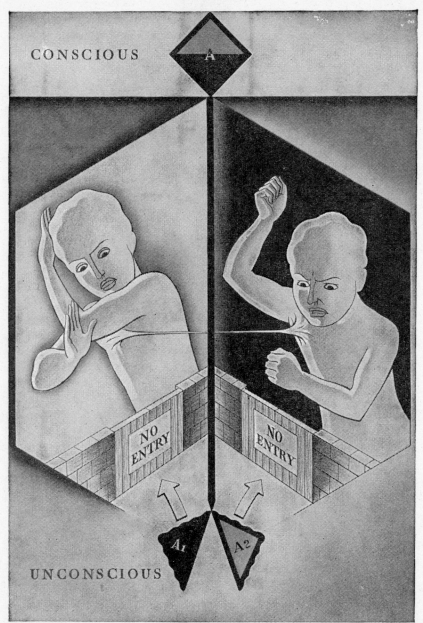

FIG. 90. *Conflict. A complex idea* (A) *which presents a problem to the personality requires energy-charged ideas* (A1, A2) *from the unconscious for its solution (see Fig. 87). If any of these is unacceptable to either of the "Twins", conflict results. If the Twins do not find a compromise, the bonds between them may be stretched to breaking-point, setting up mental tension of various degrees of severity or even entailing serious mental disease.*

veıy closely and continuously if attempts at self-destruction are to be avoided. Similarly, the over-excited type is liable to sudden, unexpected actions, generally of a destructive or aggressive nature, though sometimes the behaviour is childish or ridiculous. Again, with one group of the withdrawn type, members of which seem to be particularly out of touch with reality and mentally divorced from their surroundings, the patient may suddenly and most unexpectedly burst out into violent and aggressive behaviour, which may be very unpleasant for all concerned. Again, in the confused type, consisting of those whose minds are in a complete turmoil and muddle, a sudden impulse may come uppermost and result in immediate action. As will be seen (page 354), these confused people are specially liable to hallucinations, though other sufferers from insanity may likewise be affected. These hallucinations may take the form of voices which tell them to do various things, and again the action may be sudden and violent.

It will be seen, therefore, that though the typical explosive action, the outburst of temper or anti-social conduct occurs in the epileptic type (and confirmatory investigation by encephalographic and other studies to confirm the diagnosis of epilepsy is always justified and, indeed, desirable) unexpected violence against the patient's own self or other people or property may occur in any form of insanity. If such explosive behaviour does occur, the patient is much more likely to be psychotic than psycho-neurotic. This means that his mental illness is of a serious nature and that its treatment may present great difficulties. Since he is not properly restrained by external or internal prohibitions in these illnesses, care and restraint in a mental hospital may be very desirable or even necessary for his own sake and for that of others, even though at the moment his behaviour does not seem very abnormal in the eyes of the casual observer. In such cases it is better to be safe than sorry, and it by no means follows that because in the protected atmosphere of a mental hospital the patient is quiet and gives no trouble, his behaviour would have been so satisfactory in the rough and tumble of the world outside. This implies that expert judgement is required before it is safe to release a patient from certificate, however much the man in the street, visiting the hospital, may think that he is perfectly sane.

FUNCTIONAL PSYCHOSES

The mental conditions which we shall now discuss, known as "functional psychoses", undoubtedly owe something, probably a great deal, to inherent abnormality, but what the nature of such abnormality may be nobody knows. Often conflicts and anxiety can be discovered in the functional psychoses, and their resolution relieves the symptoms, but seldom cures the condition. Even when such treatment seems to effect a cure, we must be careful of drawing conclusions, for these conditions are prone to remissions of greater or less duration, whose cause is as obscure as that of the disease itself. Therefore, any successful treatment may only be coincidental to the remission. At all events, treatment which at one time seems to have caused a remission may have no effect whatever when the same patient has a relapse. It may be that physical factors such as infections, chemical changes in the body or abnormal secretions of glands play a considerable part, especially in determining the remissions and relapses which frequently occur, but it must be confessed that our knowledge of the causes of these conditions is woefully scanty.

The Hypomanic. Many people are very energetic, very enthusiastic, full of ideas and capable of very hard work. They may be like this all the time, or only at certain times, sinking down in the intervals to normal levels or even to a condition of depression and lethargy. Such energetic people ("hypomanic", as they are technically called) are useful members of the community and may get a very great deal of work done. The trouble is that their energy is apt to be uncontrolled and even misdirected, and they may undertake so many tasks that they cannot complete one of them efficiently.

The Manic. When this condition becomes really abnormal we have the condition that is technically called "mania". In mania, all activity is exaggerated, but the lack of control and the diffuseness of activity are especially marked, so that the energy is dissipated and entirely wasted. In extreme cases this energy may be seriously misdirected and the patient may be led into wasteful monetary expenditure or into seriously asocial conduct.

ALTERNATE ELATION AND DEPRESSION

As has been indicated, the excitement may be either continuous or intermittent, the patient returning to normal or sinking into depression, as is described on page 344. In the latter case, the condition is described as "cyclic", there being alternating cycles of elation and depression lasting, perhaps, all through life. As a rule, the cycles last a few months, but their duration varies from single days to many years. It varies not only from patient to patient, but in the same patient at different periods of his life.

The patient in an elated cycle (the manic) is continuously over-excited, sleeps little, and yet seems always to have unbounded energy. All his functions go at top speed and yet he suffers curiously little, if at all, from fatigue. His ideas race, and he is apt to talk rapidly and incessantly, dashing from subject to subject faster than he can get his words out, so that he may appear quite incoherent. He is, however, unlike the confused person, who is really incoherent, for if there were a means of recording sufficiently rapid it would be found that there was some order, if not a very logical sequence, in the thought processes of the manic. Similarly, he may cover reams of paper with almost illegible script, so fast does he have to write. In these records he describes all sorts of wildcat schemes, such as a machine to supply a whole continent with light and heat, fixed to a raft out at sea and driven by the waves.

But this is not the worst, for the manic subject has a most inflated idea of his own grandness and importance, and anything or anyone standing in his way may have to be swept aside. The severely excited person may be very destructive and a serious danger to life and limb. Though less commonly, he may also do damage to himself—not from despair, as do the depressed, but because in his God-like condition he is no longer bound by natural laws. So he may believe that he can step out of an upper window and will not be hurt; or he may jump overboard at sea, for he can walk over water as easily as over land; and he can run so fast that he can easily cross the road before the swiftly oncoming motor-car can reach him. He is apt to suffer from hallucinations, and "voices" may seem to tell him to do these things.

Obviously he is so excited, so sure of himself and so certain that he is right, that no argument or persuasion advanced in an attempt at treatment can have the least effect. Psychological methods have therefore no place in the manic phase, though in the quieter periods of the patient's life something may be done to reduce the disproportion of the ideas. Nevertheless, it must be repeated, there is much more than this behind the condition, and psychological treatment can at best be palliative.

MELANCHOLIA

In contrast to the excited type, many people are naturally gloomy, pessimistic and morose, either all the time or at intervals. From what has been said on page 343, it will be seen that pathological depression may be met with in patients in the opposite phase of an alternating cycle, but sometimes the depression may last a very long time, especially if it comes on in middle life in either sex. This type of depression is called "involution melancholia". While some authorities believe it to be a separate disease, others regard it as an unusually prolonged phase of the cyclic type, determined perhaps by the chemical and glandular alterations which are characteristic of the change of life.

The Depressed Type. Whatever the cause of the depression, the result is very much the same. Mentally the patient is gloomy, introspective and uninterested in the things that go on round about him. His thought processes are slowed down and his outgoing emotions are dulled, so that, as he often complains, he loses all capacity to be fond of those nearest and dearest to him. With regard to himself, however, he has plenty of emotion of a negative kind. Being concerned with his own unworthiness, he loses touch with the environment, though not in the same way as does the withdrawn type, who replaces reality with a very definite and lively world of imagination in which he may be happy or very miserable. The depressed type, moreover, may have decided impulses towards self-destruction.

The Guilty Type. When his symptoms are severe, the depressed type feels very guilty. He is convinced that he has committed some quite unforgivable sin, but cannot describe what the sin is or when he committed it. He is very vague about it and often refers to it as the "sin against the Holy Ghost" or by a similar expression. Having, in his own incontrovertible opinion, committed such a sin, he feels that he merits the worst sort of punishment. In his own view, he is quite unworthy and he would much prefer that people did not try to help him, because it is not worth while, and they ought to have much better things to do. In a sense it is not worth while, because, like the over-excited manic, he is quite incapable of accepting any argument.

FALSE CONFESSIONS

Yet steady encouragement does help these people, as they will confess when they return to normal, although they seem to pay so little attention to it at the time. Patients who feel this degree of guilt may commit delinquencies and even major crimes with the explicit expectation of being discovered and punished. Not only do they take no pains to cover up their actions, but they may actually draw attention to what they have done. These, too, are the people who confess to crimes, even murders, which they have not committed, in the hope of being punished and so expiating their intense feeling of guilt. This may cause considerable annoyance to the police, who may be led to follow up false clues, so delaying pursuit of the true criminal and, perhaps, preventing his apprehension.

The treatment of depressions, like that of over-excitement, is on the whole unsatisfactory, at least by psychological methods. Conflicts and anxiety can be found, and these may colour the guilty feelings and modify the nature of the imagined sin. For example, sexual conflicts may be discovered, in which the patient's natural sexual urge has come into conflict with his over-puritanical ideals. In such cases, he may imagine he is guilty of grave sexual depravity and hint vaguely that his sin consists of such things as incest or gross perversions. The details are, however, still wanting, and it is seldom that the patient will describe exactly how or when the sin has been committed. As has been said of the manic, we must suspect that apparent cures by analysis may only have coincided with the remissions which, at least in the cyclic type, are so apt to occur. Actually, it seems that while elaborate psychological analysis does little if any good, medical care does help the patient to feel that someone, in spite of everything, is taking an interest in him and encouraging him throughout.

New Methods of Treatment. In recent years, two physical methods of treatment have been evolved which certainly seem hopeful. The best established and most successful method is called shock therapy. In this the patient is given drugs, or nowadays more often controlled electric shocks, which cause convulsions. For some reason not at present by any means fully understood, these seem to "shake" the person out of his depression. Sometimes the effects are spectacularly good, in which case the patient was probably "coming out"

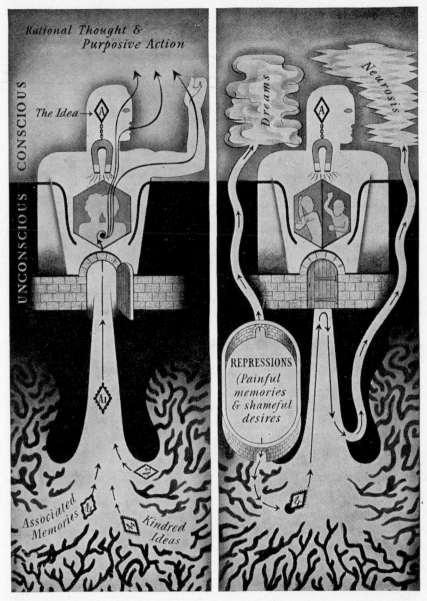

FIG. 91. *Repression.* Left: *the idea* (A) *attracts kindred ideas, memories and desires* (A1, A2, *etc.*) *which the whole personality is prepared to accept and use, so that they pass unimpeded into consciousness.* Right: *memories, etc.* (Ax), *that were closely associated with painful or shameful emotions may have been purposefully forgotten, that is, repressed, and can no longer return to consciousness. This illustration shows, as a whole, the factors in the causes and the results of repression that are treated in detail in Figs.* 89, 90 *and* 92.

anyway. In others, relapses are apt to occur, but repetition of the treatment may act favourably.

Still more may this be said of the second method of treatment, which has had some success, especially in agitated cases. This consists of a surgical operation by which certain areas of the brain are separated from each other so that the intensity of emotion is reduced. This would appear to be a very serious interference with the integrity of the most important organ of the body, but it must be confessed that, so far as can be ascertained at present, the results are less damaging than might have been expected, and there is an undoubted calming of the whole personality.

RISK OF SUICIDE

Apart from this true psychotic depression, general depression may be met with in all mental illnesses. Anxiety cases and obsessionals may be very depressed, though hysterics are probably not so, at least while they enjoy the satisfaction of the temporary solution of their conflicts and the relief from anxiety. The unhappiness and depression of some withdrawn people is often very great, and the same applies to the suspicious group. Excitement and depression may colour other psychotic conditions, especially the confused group. As will be seen, the insanity following childbirth comes within this group, and these patients may be elated, noisy and obstreperous, or depressed and suicidal. Similarly, in general paralysis of the insane, a form of confusion associated with syphilis and characterized by a marked exaggeration of the personality, the patient may be very happy and think himself the most marvellous scientist or a super-Napoleon who has conquered the world; or, on the other hand, he may be terribly depressed and regard himself as the most unfortunate or the most guilty of the human race. The same colouring applies to alcoholic insanities and to those associated with failing mental powers in old age. Whatever the underlying condition, wherever there is severe depression there is risk of suicide, and when there is risk of suicide the responsibility of friends and relations is correspondingly great. In these cases certification and the transfer of responsibility to skilled experts should be seriously considered, for the benefit of all.

MORBID SECLUSION

The Withdrawn Type. There are many people who do not make friends and who tend to live rather solitary lives occupied with their own imaginations. Intellectually they are usually quite up to standard, and do well enough at school while absorbing theoretical knowledge, but when it comes to practical work and the application of this knowledge they tend to fall down rather badly. They are generally artistic, as might be expected from their strong interest in imaginative activities, and some rise to high levels of achievement. Perhaps the best example was the artist van Gogh, whose

347

pictures are so widely reproduced, but who at the end of his life passed beyond the bounds of normality.

Schizophrenics. If and when these bounds have been passed, such people are known technically as "schizophrenics", which, literally translated, means "persons whose minds are split". Normally, reality and imagination are integrated and one plays upon and controls the other. In the schizophrenic these two aspects become more and more divorced, so that the patient becomes interested only in his fantasy or imaginary life and pays less and less attention to the world around him, although for a time he may alternate between his interest in reality and his preoccupation with fantasy.

There are three types of patients met with who suffer from schizophrenia—the simple, so-called "hebephrenic" type, the "catatonic", who have the most peculiar bodily manifestations, and the "suspicious" or "paranoid" type, who will be described together with those who suffer from those forms of mental illness in which abnormal suspicions are a prominent feature.

Simple Schizophrenia. The first type, the hebephrenic, is the exaggerated form of the ordinary withdrawn and solitary person, who is sometimes technically called "schizoid". These hebephrenic patients become more and more involved in their world of fantasy, but before they become too detached it is possible to explore their mental processes. They have the most wonderfully elaborate dreams—both ordinary dreams and daydreams—which contain a great wealth of imagery and symbolism. It has been found that this imagery and symbolism can be elucidated and analysed; and it has been largely from the material supplied by these moderate schizophrenics that it has been possible to understand the workings of man's unconscious mind, for this material provides the unbroken series, from the dreams, unconscious mannerisms, slips of the tongue and tricks of behaviour of the perfectly normal person to the ravings of the most abnormal lunatic.

PRIMITIVE MAGIC

What is even more interesting is that there is a close correspondence between much of this unconscious material and the religious ceremonials and beliefs in magic of primitive man. A great deal of work has been done and many books have been written about the borderline between the normal, the abnormal and the primitive, and there can be no doubt that a great deal of light has thus been thrown upon human behaviour. The fact that much of the original material came from abnormal and even insane people does not detract from its worth, for, as has been indicated here, the behaviour of insane people is not fundamentally different from that of normal people—it is only exaggerated and differently directed.

When the schizophrenic becomes really detached from reality, he may become very troublesome. At this stage he is quite unapproachable and very difficult to treat. He may sit by himself in a corner, paying no attention to anything, but making faces, gesturing and from time to time breaking out into short cackles of laughter, presumably in accordance with the contents of his daydreams. He resents interference, because his world of make-believe is so much more important to him than the world outside. Consequently, he neglects his personal appearance, forgets to feed himself or wash, and, when those responsible for him insist on these interruptions to his fantasies, he may become violent and attack his attendant. As a rule, however, he is docile and harmless, but it is impossible to be quite sure that this docility will continue. As has been indicated, his fantasies may lead him into all sorts of curious and often primitive methods of thinking; strange voices seem to talk to him and all sorts of magic rites and ceremonies are performed. As with the primitive himself, some of these are violent and cruel, and, whether in obedience to hallucinatory voices or in accordance with a magic formula, the patient may suddenly spring into activity and commit suicide or murder.

FANTASY REPLACES REALITY

Often the fantasy involves identification with prominent people, and the patient may believe that he, or she, is Queen Elizabeth or General Booth, or even be convinced that he is God. Since he believes implicitly in his fantasy, and reality is of no importance, he may be persuaded to carry round the mail or scrub the floor, but the incongruity of Queen Elizabeth's washing floors does not disturb the patient, for the floor and the scrubbing-brush are of no significance to him, while the imagined royalty is real. This concentration on fantasy causes these patients to break off in the middle of something they are doing and assume weird attitudes or exhibit apparently inexplicable gestures. If the "queen" who is washing dishes suddenly drops all the plates and stretches out her hand in an attitude of command or blessing, it may well be that in her mind's eye her adoring subjects are kneeling at her feet.

The Catatonic Type. The catatonic type is less common, but very interesting, because in these patients the detachment from reality seems to have spread not only to the mind but to the nerves and muscles of the body as well. If a limb of such a person is put in any distorted position by the observer, the patient will pay no attention and the limb will be held in this position for periods far longer than would be possible with the greatest voluntary concentration. Normally, muscles tire relatively quickly and cannot maintain a limb against gravity, however much the patient tries, if the position is not a habitual one. Try holding the leg at a right angle to the body while standing up. It cannot be so held for long, yet the head is maintained in the erect posture all day long— a position which probably expends as much muscular energy as would the maintenance of the leg at a right angle. With the catatonic, this capacity for maintenance of posture seems to be independent of habitual use, and so he can maintain the most grotesque positions without difficulty or fatigue, just as the normal person can hold up his head almost indefinitely. Possibly because he is so much withdrawn, the catatonic is liable to the most violent outbreaks of aggression. These have already been referred to in dealing with the explosive type.

In the last few years shock therapy (page 345) has been given to the withdrawn type—indeed it was first used for this type—and still more recently insulin has been injected until the patient lapses into coma. Although the immediate results of these treatments may be quite good, it is found that most patients relapse relatively soon. Indeed, the outlook for the schizophrenic who is advanced in his illness is a gloomy one.

ABNORMAL SUSPICION

Many people are abnormally suspicious and are always afraid that others have a "down" on them or are doing them harm. They are constantly on the look-out for slights and are always expecting insults. This is really because they are so unsure of themselves that they think they must be in a position to be insulted or over-reached, or they may feel guilty because they feel hostile and vindictive towards other people. This may be reflected at times by a fear that they are liable to injure other people, but this does not as a rule last for long and soon this feeling is "projected", as it is called. This means that, instead of feeling that they may injure people, they feel that other people will injure them. This is, on the whole, a more tolerable feeling than the former, because at least they feel that they are not in the wrong and that they have the consolation of martyrdom. They persuade themselves, and try to persuade others, that wicked people are persecuting the innocent (themselves). There does seem to be something inherent in this attitude to life, for although, as in the case of the withdrawn type, very numerous conflicts may be discovered by analytic treatment and much unconscious material of a complicated nature may be elucidated, this analytic procedure does relatively little good; and, like other people of analogous types, reasoning or persuasion has no effect upon patients of the suspicious type.

Actually, the tendency to withdraw from life and the tendency to develop suspicion and ideas of persecution seem to be closely associated, for one form in which schizophrenia may manifest itself involves abnormal suspicion. This is usually referred to as the "paranoid" type of schizophrenia. Some psychiatrists would classify all forms of abnormal suspiciousness, technically called "paranoia", under the general heading of schizophrenia, but others consider this reaction of suspicion so specific that they prefer to place those suffering from it in a separate group.

The Paranoid Schizophrenic. Abnormal suspicion may occur throughout adult life, but certain differences are observed according to the age at which it occurs. As has been said, schizophrenia, the abnormal manifestation of the withdrawn type, is a disease of youth. Some of these young people, perhaps those who are particularly introspective, or who have a special love for themselves, develop suspicions and ideas that other people are persecuting them. Perhaps this group is not withdrawn so completely from the world around them as are other schizophrenics. They are not indifferent, but they are bitterly hostile and feel at war with everything and everyone. For this reason they may be dangerous, but seldom to themselves, unless they feel that the persecution of the world is so overwhelming that it can no longer be borne. But more often they act on the theory that the best form of defence is attack, and so they may assault those whom they suspect to be their enemies. Such enemies may be people whom they see every day, even people who are doing their best for them, or they may be total strangers.

Young schizophrenics are always a potential menace to others, but warning of the danger may be obtained, because they do show other signs of abnormality. They exhibit eccentricities and mannerisms, such as are described on pages 348–50, and the suspicious behaviour may only be a phase in their illness, during the whole course of which they may have shown other manifestations of the simple or catatonic type. As a rule, therefore, their friends and relations know that they are abnormal and, as a result of this knowledge, should be on their guard against asocial or dangerous behaviour.

DANGEROUS TRAITS

This is not by any means always true of the other two groups, the "paraphrenics" and the true paranoiacs, whose dangerous traits may develop with very little warning. It is convenient to describe the latter group first.

The Paranoiac. True paranoia occurs in men in the fifties and sixties. They are of the suspicious type, having all their lives thought that they were right and other people were wrong. Easily thinking themselves slighted, they have adopted rather a cold and defensive attitude, not mixing easily with their fellows. Otherwise they are intelligent, and are often capable of making a great success of their business or profession. For this reason their friends and relations think a great deal of them, and those dependent on them admire their business acumen, on which their own wellbeing depends.

One day, however, everybody is horrified and shocked, because this clever, successful man has committed an assault on someone, perhaps a stranger who certainly has never done him any real harm. There is a scandal, with police proceedings, and perhaps even a charge of murder. The relatives, realizing that his behaviour has really been abnormal for some time, ask plaintively why they were not told he was mad. Both medically and legally, these cases are very difficult. Unless the abnormal suspiciousness of these people is recognized early and something is done about it, tragedy is almost bound to result, and yet the patients are so logical, so normal in every other respect, that it is very difficult to take any restraining action before a crisis occurs.

The Paraphrenic. Paraphrenia is a less distinctive type of mental abnormality, which some people think should not be differentiated from paranoia. But

351

there are differences. The patients are generally women about the change of life, that is, in the forties or fifties. They have "ideas of reference", impressions that people are persecuting them and doing them harm; but sometimes these ideas are preceded by the notion that they themselves are likely to harm others by writing libels about them on odd pieces of paper, and that they might leave these about. Or they are afraid they may draw obscene pictures which may get into the hands of children and corrupt them, so that they develop pathological fears of pencils or paper. Often these people are at first diagnosed as "obsessives" (Chapter XVI), but sooner or later these ideas are "projected" and it is imagined that others are likely to harm them. In the paraphrenic, however, these delusions are never so clear-cut, and the arguments by which the ideas are supported are not so logical and convincing, as are those of the true paranoiac. Moreover, the paraphrenic is likely to exhibit a few other symptoms of abnormality, which take a middle place between those of the paranoid schizophrenic and the true paranoiac.

Ideas of Persecution. In all forms of paranoid delusion the supposed ways in which the "enemies" attack the patients are often peculiar. They may work from a distance by means of machines producing a new ray. Often they are supposed to carry out their nefarious schemes through hired "natives" or "assassins", or by means of the telephone or the wireless—usually, as a matter of fact, by the latest scientific invention. In future, no doubt, it will be by means of some sort of atomic energy that they will operate.

CONFUSIONAL INSANITY

When we are very tired or have a bad cold, or, in the case of women, at the time of the monthly period, we find our memory is confused, our powers of concentration are diminished, and we are irritable and apt to get things out of proportion. If the illness or fatigue is much more severe, and/or if we are people of a certain type, our psychological reactions become really abnormal and we suffer from confusional insanity. It is necessary to understand clearly what is really meant by this "and/or".

If we suffer from an illness which results in a state of severe exhaustion or poisoning of our brain, then our mental reactions will suffer, and the worse the exhaustion or poisoning the worse will be the effects. The results will be a lessening of capacity for the highest functions of our brain and mind, namely: integration—the welding together of sensations, memories and ideas into coherent, rational concepts; discrimination—the power of analysing meanings, estimating values and so of getting things into proper proportion; and control—the power of regulating our thoughts, feelings and actions to suit the situation. We may say, then, that, given a sufficiently severe illness, everyone may suffer from this pathological confusion. However, many people suffer from confusion without being as ill as those who show no confusion.

It seems likely, then, that people who are less stable than their fellows,

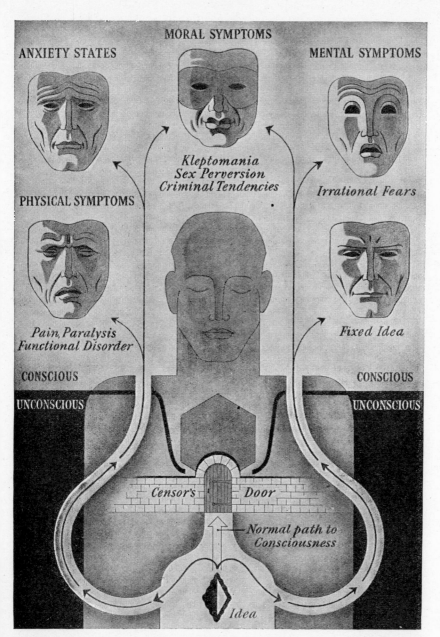

Fig. 92. *If an idea strongly charged with emotion is repressed (see Fig. 91) in the unconscious, it may be transformed into a neurosis, which may take the form of an anxiety state or a physical symptom or pain; or it may generate irrational fears, fixed ideas and other mental symptoms; or it may blind the moral sense and cause kleptomania, sex perversion, and so on.*

because of heredity, constitutional abnormality or previous conflicting environmental experiences, are apt to be more affected mentally by these illnesses. It is because of this that the confusional cases are so very varied in their manifestations. They seem to take colour from their backgrounds— some are depressed, others explosive or excited, others again withdrawn or suspicious. There are many different conditions included among the confusional insanities, and it is only possible here to notice a few of them briefly.

RAMBLING AND DELUSIONS

Deliria. First, there are the deliria. In acute fevers, such as pneumonia or typhoid, the brain is severely poisoned and the patient "rambles". If close attention is paid to what he says, it is possible to make out that his half-finished sentences refer to all sorts of incidents, feelings and experiences, unconnected in time, space or mood. Some relate to childhood, others to last week, some to things which occurred at home or far afield. Sometimes the patient is gay, sometimes sad, at others angry or afraid. Sometimes he refers to imaginary things—hallucinations based on delusions—sometimes to visions of horror or to pleasant little fairy people the size of small dolls. Again, in acute alcoholic poisoning, the patient experiences the horror of "delirium tremens" (D.T.s), with its green snakes and pink elephants.

Confusional States. Other confusional states are "slowed-down deliria", with the phantasmagoria perhaps less jumbled, but in any case working at a slower rate. Examples of these are the puerperal insanities which occur now and then after childbirth. Probably fatigue, mild infection and poisoning are the determining factors, but since there are vast numbers of women who give birth to children and only very few who suffer from subsequent attacks of insanity, the background of instability must be taken into account. This is borne out by the great variation in the manifestations of these attacks, for some patients are excited and may injure others, especially their child; others are depressed and may harm themselves and even commit suicide; others are withdrawn, taking no interest in their bodies or their surroundings; while others again are suspicious or resentful.

General Paralysis. When the patient has suffered from syphilis, but not unless he has done so, he may contract a special form of this confusional insanity called "general paralysis of the insane" (G.P.I.). Here again the background is important, for only about 2 per cent of those infected with syphilis contract G.P.I., and the form of the illness varies as do other confusional states. These cases, however, are characterized by the intensity of their symptoms. If they are exalted and excited they imagine themselves to be very great indeed—God, Emperor of the Earth, Queen of the Solar System, and so on. They are, moreover, dangerous, for they may be very violent. If they are depressed, no one has ever been so unfortunate or guilty of such terrible sins. If they are suspicious, not one or two persons or groups of people, but the whole world is against them. They are often very confused and incoherent and their mental processes may be quite impossible to follow. In the final stages the body is affected as well as the mind, and they become totally paralysed.

Prospects of Cure. On the whole, the outlook for these confused patients is favourable, and there is a fairly high rate of recovery nowadays, even from general paralysis. If the patient can rest and recover from his fatigue, if the infection can be dispelled and the poison be eliminated, then the patient will recover from his illness.

Two factors operate against this. If the background of mental instability is too strong, then, although the precipitating illness or fatigue may be cleared up, the patient may continue to suffer from the particular form of mental illness to which his background makes him liable, that is, manic depressive (cyclic) psychosis, schizophrenia, or paranoia. The fatigue or poisoning has only acted as a trigger which has set off the other illness, and so the latter remains behind when the effects of the former have been as far as possible removed. Secondly, the poisoning may continue so long or be so intense that the cells of the brain are destroyed. As is explained on page 309, if enough of these cells are destroyed there will inevitably be mental or physical deterioration, or both.

Since the germ of syphilis is very difficult to kill once it has found firm lodgement in the body and especially in the nervous system, and since the nerve-cells are very easily destroyed by its poison, general paralysis of the insane is markedly resistant to treatment. Until recently nearly all cases gradually got worse until the patients died as mindless, paralytic wrecks. It was found, however, that if the temperature of the body could be raised sufficently in the early stages of the disease, these germs (spirochaetes) could be killed, so various methods have been used to give the patient a high fever. The most effective of these methods is to infect him with malaria, which gives him bouts of fever. It is possible to cure him of this imposed infection with quinine, when he has had sufficient attacks. For other forms of confusion, rest and the treatment of whatever infection has attacked the patient are used, with encouragement of elimination by kidney, bowels and skin. It is obvious that in his confused state the patient cannot appreciate psychological treatment, and, indeed, in this group of cases psycho-therapy has no place, at least until the condition of confusion has been relieved.

HYPOCHONDRIASIS

There are a number of people whose minds are abnormal, but whom it is difficult to classify among the types we have already described because the behaviour which they exhibit may be met with in persons belonging to widely different types.

Among these people of doubtful classification are those who are abnormally and morbidly interested in their health. Such people are known as "hypo-

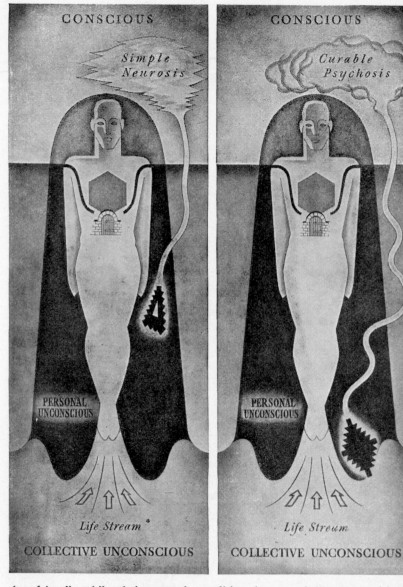

CONSCIOUS

Simple Neurosis

CONSCIOUS

Curable Psychosis

PERSONAL UNCONSCIOUS

PERSONAL UNCONSCIOUS

Life Stream

Life Stream

COLLECTIVE UNCONSCIOUS

COLLECTIVE UNCONSCIOUS

chondriacs", while their mental condition is termed "hypochondriasis". Hypochondriasis can only be said to be pathological, however, when nearly the whole of the person's attention is directed to the supposedly abnormal working of his body. Abdominal symptoms—especially those of stomach and intestines—are most commonly the subject of the hypochondriac's attention, and sometimes the sensations which are present, or are elaborated by the

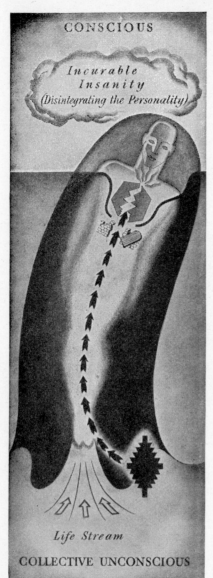

CONSCIOUS

*Incurable
Insanity
(Disintegrating the Personality)*

Life Stream

COLLECTIVE UNCONSCIOUS

FIG. 93. *Neurosis and Psychosis. A psychosis is caused, like a neurosis (Figs. 91 and 92), by a conflict-producing idea, charged with emotion (usually fear), that is buried in the unconscious. In the case of a psychosis, however, the cause lies deeper and poisons the life stream. Both are escape mechanisms, but, whereas a neurosis involves escape from a particular situation, a psychosis entails escape from reality. Severe forms of psychosis constitute insanity.*

patient's introspection, are the basis of far-fetched delusions, such as that crabs or scorpions inside his body are slowly eating him away.

Sometimes hypochondriacal ideas are based upon symptoms of genuine structural disease. At other times the symptoms are due to changes in the working of the circulation, muscles or glands induced by anxiety, as is discussed in pages 312–13. In both cases the attention given to the symptom, be it real pain or merely discomfort, increases the sensitivity of the patient to the sensation, so that his hypochondriasis proceeds in a vicious spiral.

The Hysterical Hypochondriac. The hysterical subject, as we have seen (page 320), substitutes a bodily symptom for an insoluble conflict and becomes for the time being complacent, because the conflict has been solved. But his interest in his hysterical symptom must be constantly maintained, if his new-found peace of mind is to persist. Such symptoms are now made to serve a purpose in forming a most plausible excuse for avoiding the action involved in the unsolved conflict, so that more and more attention is paid to the symptom, until the complacency is replaced by a true hypochondriasis. If the symptom is a painful or unpleasant one it becomes a conflict in itself. It cannot be relinquished or the original conflict will be unmasked, but the more it intrudes upon the patient's consciousness the more does he complain of it, and the more hypochondriacal does he therefore become.

357

The Psychotic Hypochondriac. The depressed and guilty type of person (pages 344–5) is anxious to punish himself. Only in this way can his conscience be assuaged, and only thus can be pay for his sin and wash away his guilt. A pain or an unpleasant feeling in his body may be the means of punishment. He loves his pain, he takes a perverted pleasure in it; it serves its purpose, but he must never let himself (or others) forget it. Again hypochondriasis is established.

The suspicious person is sure that his enemies are doing him harm. Pain or discomfort is the result of his enemies' malice and a proof of their malignity. His attention is fixed on this, for he regards it as the incontrovertible proof of the truth of his statements, which his friends and relatives are so unwilling to believe. Again hypochondriasis is established.

The treatment of hypochondriasis consists in alleviating the underlying mental illness. Since the hypochondriasis serves a very useful purpose to the patient, it will not be removed by direct attack and all such attempts to persuade him to abandon his symptom are useless. The only practical line of treatment is to bring about such a change in his outlook on life that the symptom no longer serves any useful purpose and, as a result of this, ceases to occupy the patient's attention.

TREATING MENTAL ILLNESS

It is not very long since those who were mentally ill were left to suffer without any attempt at treatment at all, either as ailing and unhappy members of the community, or, if dangerous or troublesome, in asylums, where little more was done than to protect them against themselves, while society was relieved of their presence. Only 150 years ago they were not even given refuge, but were imprisoned, chained up, and left to rot and die in insanitary hovels worse than those provided for dogs and cattle.

Modern Methods. In the last half-century, however, real progress has been made in classifying the various categories of mental illness, in understanding the causes, nature and course of these different disabilities, and devising means whereby they may be relieved. Perhaps the most important single contribution has been that of Freud and his followers, who since the early years of this century have elaborated the concept of unconscious mental processes and the formation of emotional conflicts, and have devised the means of resolving these conflicts. Although the technique of treatment devised by Freud has not proved quite such a panacea for the relief of individual and social maladjustment as was at one time hoped, the much greater understanding of how the mind works in both health and disease which has resulted from his pioneer work has been of great service to humanity, and if properly applied may still promote great benefits to mankind.

Treating Mental Deficiency. Unfortunately, if we begin with the mental defective, we must begin on a note of pessimism, for, with the exception of cretinism, mental deficiency is not susceptible to treatment by medical means. If there are not sufficient healthy nerve-cells present in the brain for full mental capacity, nothing can put them there, although it is possible to make the best use of those which are present. To do this, education and training, not medicine, are necessary. Theoretically at least, every individual has a right to the education by which he can most benefit. It is certain that all mental defectives in Britain do not enjoy this right; however, a great many do, and no doubt that is as it should be.

Treating Psycho-Neuroses. The cure of the anxiety state depends on the discovery and resolution of the underlying emotional conflict. Many cases of anxiety are, or seem to be, "reactive"; that is to say, there is an obvious conscious cause for anxiety. Illness of relatives, lack of news of someone dear to the patient, financial loss or insecurity of employment are examples of such causes. However, the fact that the anxiety persists and is often out of proportion to the cause indicates that behind this reactive anxiety there is in many cases an abnormal attitude of mind, based on analogous experiences in the past. Such experiences will be especially potent in producing abnormal mental attitudes if they have involved self-criticism. Removal of the obvious source of anxiety may or may not remove the anxiety. Even when a conflict or an apparent cause of anxiety has been discovered, it may be that this is only the last link in a chain, and before the patient's attitude of mind can be changed many more conflicts will have to be explored and dealt with.

Indirect approach is necessary, for the patient is not aware of the true nature of his illness, and various clues to the material required may be used. First, the patient's story of his life and his opinions and reactions throw a good deal of light on his attitude of mind. To the skilled observer his mannerisms and tricks of speech or gesture may be very enlightening, as may his emotional reactions to various people and situations. Dreams, if carefully studied and compared, throw much light on unconscious conflicts and are often useful in estimating the progress of the case, for the patient may often become successful in his dreams before he achieves success in his waking life. For example, the dream of always running after and missing a train is indicative of an attitude of failure and frustration, but if the patient begins to catch the trains in his dreams it is a definite sign of improvement.

FINDING THE ROAD BACK

While the unravelling of the tangled skein of the patient's emotional reaction and the solution of his conflicts give him the capacity to make a new and more successful adjustment to life, he generally requires sympathy and kindly help in making his new adjustment, and between elucidating the basis of the trouble and helping him to make his readjustment, treatment can take a long time. We are now learning many short cuts, compared with the laborious analysis of twenty years ago, such as the extraction of buried memories when the patient is recovering from a sleep induced either by strong hypnotic drugs or by hypnosis. If results are to be achieved, there must be much patience on the part of everyone concerned.

In the treatment of hysteria (pages 320–21) it is generally advisable to remove the symptom first, before tackling the underlying conflict by such methods as are described above. After explaining clearly to the patient the nature of his symptom and showing him that it is not due to structural or irreversible processes, persuasion or suggestion is generally quickly successful, provided that the symptom has not been established too long, so that it has sunk to the level of a muscular or sensory habit over which the patient's conscious will, even under the most favourable circumstances of understanding and properly directed effort, has very little influence. Care must be taken in all cases to retain the patient's self-respect throughout treatment. He must be made to realize quite clearly that the disability was not his fault, that he need not be ashamed of acquiring it, and that by making a real effort to get rid of it he is not confessing to conscious fraud.

DEEPLY-BURIED CONFLICTS

Ultimately both the hysteric and the obsessional (the fearful and the compulsive types) require analytical methods for their cure, but the obsessional is notoriously difficult to treat successfully. Usually the relevant conflicts are more deeply buried in the unconscious mind, and the abnormal attitude of mind is determined by more complex and numerous adverse situations than is the case in the hysteric or the simple anxiety case. Sometimes the relevant material can be brought into consciousness more easily by setting the patient "tasks", usually with the object of forcing himself to face his fear or neglect his compulsion, and while these tasks will not directly benefit his condition, they may indirectly pave the way for his release from the tyranny of his symptoms.

Treating Psychopathic Personalities. The treatment of the severely weak-willed (psychasthenic) type is very difficult, and while analytic methods are occasionally successful, it is generally necessary for someone to guide and control the patient throughout his life.

The explosive type can be controlled to some extent with certain drugs which prevent the occurrence of convulsions and may also prevent the outbursts of temper. For the rest we must try to ensure that these people lead as normal lives as possible, though the occurrence of convulsions is bound to restrict them considerably, giving them a sense of frustration all the time.

Treating Psychoses. The over-excited people will, as a rule, return to normal or even pass into a depressed phase within a certain time, though it is always difficult to foretell how long this time is going to be. Meanwhile it is necessary to restrain them from harming the persons or property of themselves or others. Although these people seem to be able to manage with very little sleep with relative impunity, rest is essential for their recovery; therefore sedatives and sleep-inducing (hypnotic) drugs are always valuable. If they get too excited they must be treated in a mental hospital, where they can be looked after and where special treatments can be given. They may be put to sleep by hypnotic drugs for several days together, being allowed to wake only for necessary meals, or they may be immersed in baths at blood heat for several hours. This has a remarkably soothing effect, and even very excited people may go to sleep while in the water.

The depressed and guilty subjects will likewise return to normal or pass into an excited phase in due time, though the phase of depression accompanied by the almost intolerable guilt feeling is only too liable to recur. It is necessary to try to encourage these people and attempt to keep them reasonably active until the end of the depressed phase. It must be remembered that these patients are very liable to suicide and this danger persists until the depression has entirely passed. The modern form of treatment is to induce convulsions in these people, and in a certain number of cases this does seem to be remarkably successful. It is as if they were shaken out of their depression by this throwing into activity of large areas of the brain. Drugs used to be used for this purpose, but nowadays it is done by a special electrical apparatus.

PROLONGED ANALYSIS

The treatment of the withdrawn type is very difficult indeed. If analytical methods are used a surprising wealth of material is obtained; whole series of conflicts may appear to be resolved, but, unlike the anxiety case, the schizophrenic is not cured or even much relieved by all this. Claims have been made that cases of schizophrenia have been cured by very prolonged analysis, but it must be remembered that these cases tend to have remissions in which for a time they may become quite normal again, and therefore the validity of these claims is open to question.

There is very little to be done for the suspicious type. Encouragement and persuasion do some good, and if anyone can really gain the confidence of the paranoiac, he may guide and restrain the conduct of the patient to a remarkable extent. However, the retention of this confidence is precarious and may be lost very suddenly.

Patients of the confused type are too muddled to benefit by any direct psychological treatment, at least until their fatigue is relieved by rest and the infections and poisons by which they are afflicted are removed by the defences of the body itself, aided by appropriate medical means.

The failing mind cannot be cured. This condition is due to the death of a large number of nerve-cells in the brain and since a nerve-cell cannot come to life again once it is dead, or be replaced by the growth of new cells, it is obvious that treatment is impossible. All that can be done is to care for these people and ensure that they are as comfortable and as happy as possible, while their dependants do not suffer more than is necessary from their vagaries.

Although it would appear from all this that little can be done to relieve sufferers from some mental illnesses, yet really there is a great deal that can be done. The popular belief, too often held, that to pronounce a person mentally ill is to imply his condemnation to permanent invalidism or worse, is emphatically not true. All sorts of methods of treatment are available—purely psychological treatment by analytical methods, suggestion and persuasion, physical treatment by electricity and heat, treatment by baths and by various sorts of drugs, all of which can be used to great effect if skilfully combined in a programme suitable to the individual patient. But in addition to all these there is a most important form of treatment which has so far not been mentioned because it is applicable to all forms of mental illness. This form of treatment is occupation.

Occupational Therapy. It is a good rule that all sufferers from mental illness should remain at work or engage in some sort of occupation, if at all possible. If the mental defective is removed to a colony he must be put to work. It is much easier to treat the psycho-neurotic if he is at work, and the great difficulty of treating the industrial neuroses is that in the majority of cases they are off work pending the settlement of their compensation.

It should be remembered how short a time it is since pessimism regarding treatment of mental disease was all too justified, and so we may look forward to the future with hope and confidence, in spite of the increase in the strain and complexity of life which makes adjustment all the more difficult.

Test Yourself

1. What is shock therapy and when is it used?

2. What measures might be recommended for bringing up children who show signs of emotional or mental want of balance?

3. Why is occupational therapy important in the treatment of incipient mental trouble?

Answers will be found at the end of the book.

GUIDE TO FURTHER STUDY

THIS volume has touched upon many aspects of the science of psychology. Being the work of several authors, it will already have taught the student that there are various approaches to the study of man's nature, and that at the present day many hypotheses are being tested. Some of these hypotheses insist more upon what human beings have in common with the animals, others fix our attention upon those features which, as they belong uniquely to man, are characterized by the epithet *human*.

Why does psychology touch upon so many and such varied subjects? The answer to that question lies in the many-sided activities of man as well as in his great adaptability. For the human being can not only see, hear, handle and enjoy the material objects which surround him, but he can trace in all the intricate structure and interrelations of these objects a law and order which in some wholly satisfying manner, corresponds to the law and order which he finds in his own mind. And the first step towards this inward harmony between himself and the material world is taken by means of that mental power which enables man, when he perceives material objects, first to mirror them in his own mind, and then to hold and possess them in his memory and in his imagination. Moreover—and this is man's highest glory—he can so compare and consider the various objects around him as to penetrate and define their essences, and thus he can form those abstract concepts or general ideas which are the very stuff of his reasoning and of his creative activity.

The student who would study the nature of man's intelligence will find help in F. Aveling's *An Introduction to Psychology* and A. W. P. Wolters's, *The Evidence of our Senses;* or, if he would penetrate more deeply, in C. Spearman's *The Nature of Intelligence and The Abilities of Man.*

THE STUDY OF PSYCHOLOGY TO-DAY

The study of psychology is given pride of place in our day partly because recent discoveries in biology, in physiology or in medicine have helped to throw light upon the working of man's nature, but also and chiefly because the unprecedented upheavals of the past forty years have inevitably caused much psychical disturbance. Numbers of men and women have had to face situations of terror or bereavement which have thrown them off their balance. These people have needed the help of the psychiatrist in order to recapture the poise and the easy rhythm lost in years of unrest and warfare.

But we need not look only to pathological cases for an incentive to study psychology; years of warfare are years of effort and years of invention. The very unrest of the world has turned the minds of men to the creation of new and more efficient organization, new and more efficient training, new and more efficient machines. The psychologist has had to study the adaptation of these inventions to the business of life. He has had to work out the problem of making greater efficiency in production go hand in hand with the happiness and the spiritual and material welfare of the worker. Much has been achieved. Very much has still to be done. A vast field lies open to those interested in the subject of psychology. R. S. Woodworth's *Contemporary Psychology* might be read with profit. Other recommended books are: Knight, R. and M., *A Modern Introduction to Psychology;* Munn, N.L., *Psychology;* Boring, Langfeld and Weld, *Foundations of Psychology.*

The reader would do well, at this stage, however, to ask himself what he has learned from this volume. The answer will probably be in terms of his own particular interests, for we generally obtain from our reading much of what we originally went to seek. Perhaps, however, new interests have been awakened. The reader's appetite may have been whetted. He would like to know more, to see wider. In such a large field, he feels the need of a guide to map out the country. It may, therefore, help towards that end if we group a few subjects under two main headings: Psychology and our own lives; Psychology and the lives of others.

PSYCHOLOGY AND OUR OWN LIVES

Self-Development. We all know the saying that "the proper study of mankind is man", and we all have an innate interest in the working of the human mind, particularly our own. It is not a good thing to be for ever turned inwards upon ourselves, nevertheless we can sometimes with profit turn our minds to moments of inward experience, and so realize, perhaps for the first time, something of the essential creativeness of the human mind and of the essential independence of the human spirit.

Tennyson speaks of the wonderful moment when the young child first realizes "I am I". To every one of us there have come moments of intuition when we have become aware of how, in spite of all the adverse forces which may seem to be against us, we are in truth the "captains of our souls". We have known that by controlling our attention we could decide which of two conflicting motives should prevail. And thus we have seen that happiness is more a matter of the mind and spirit than of outward circumstance, and that contentment is the fruit of self-discipline. The "sane mind in the sound body" prized by the Roman philosopher has then appeared as the product of the rational organization of all our powers, working in harmony under the influence of a worthwhile ideal.

Seeing, therefore, that a harmonious development of human powers is a matter of such fundamental importance, the reader may wish to study in some such book as Betts' *The Mind and its Education* the differences and the relationships between our knowing and our striving powers. He will want to understand more deeply the role of sensation, perception, imagination, memory, intellection, reasoning in our conscious life; and he will want to trace to their sources the manifestations of man's desires, be they instinctive, passionate or of the rational will.

CHARACTER AND THE EMOTIONS

In such a book, the reader will be able to study the influence of the external world on man's nervous system and on his external and internal senses. He will learn to distinguish the part played by instinct, emotion, sentiment and some of the great unconscious forces which influence our thought and action. But, above all, the student will do well to trace the working of that subtle, less-easily analysed power of forming concepts, judgements and logical reasoning. From this step he will pass on to the consideration of the control of attention, desire, conduct. A book like Shand's *The Foundations of Character* will teach him much about the part played by emotion, or by what psychologists sometimes call the affective side of life. It will show him how our emotions tend to group themselves into complex systems which Shand calls *sentiments*. This tendency is vividly illustrated in Jane Austen's *Pride and Prejudice*, where hero and heroine group all their feelings for one another, he around his pride and she around her prejudice. On the subject of character-building or character-analysis the reader may also find much that is helpful in the chapter on *Habit* in William James's *Psychology* or in Rudolf Allers's *The Psychology of Character*, which is largely based on the well-known work of Adler.

At this stage one would suggest depth of reading rather than breadth, that is, reading accompanied by some healthy self-questioning which must not degenerate into morbid introspection. Let the student deliberately ask himself in the light of his experience and of his studies: What is my goal? What are my powers? What do I seek from life? Where am I going? This is a necessary foundation to all self-discipline and self-development.

DEVELOPMENT WITH AN OBJECTIVE

In connexion with the idea of harmonious self-development a caution is necessary, however; for the harmony of which we speak must be considered rather in terms of the quality of the whole man than of the quantity in the measure of development. In other words, a man's powers should not all be developed to an equal degree merely for the sake of being developed. Rather should we, in our self-education, consider our special objective, our individual needs and difficulties, our gifts, handicaps, circumstances. We have learned that unhealthy repression may be very harmful, and we should avoid atrophy or neglect of any side of our nature. But, just as an athlete will make sacrifices of time, pleasure and inclination in order to achieve a degree of physical fitness not necessary to every man, so in every achievement in life sacrifices are legitimate. It is for the good psychologist to see that these sacrifices should not be excessive. Such books as W. F. Book, *The Psychology of Skill; or* T. H. Pear, *Skill in Work and Play*, and S. Colvin, *The Reasoning Process,* and C. A. Mace, *The Psychology of Study* will be of use to those who wish to apply the principles of psychology to their own self-education.

OUR VOCATION

All men have to face a choice when they come to consider their career or vocation. There is a great deal of difference in the attitude towards one's life's work if it is approached merely as a way of making money, or if it is considered as the individual's response to his special call, his own personal contribution to the world in which he lives. Dorothy Sayers's *The Mind of the Maker* lifts the whole question of work on to a plane of personal responsibility very much above mere considerations of gain.

In general, one may say, life offers a choice of two different types of work, the one which is of real interest to the worker and which will claim the utmost of his time and energy; the other, of less interest, making fewer demands upon him but leaving him time and leisure to develop his own activities. Both types of work have their attractions. The doctor, the architect or the research worker may use up every fibre of his being in pursuit of an ideal. The man who performs less creative work must be sure he knows how to use his leisure and must develop his own interests.

The student who is faced with a choice of career can obtain help from his study of psychology. He will have learned that instincts and abilities do not all develop at the same rate. Some abilities develop late in certain people owing perhaps to their upbringing, perhaps to some reason of health or temperament. The young man or woman seeking his or her vocation will do well to experiment with different types of work. Vocation courses, agricultural holiday-camps, summer schools and suchlike activities provide varied experiences that will often help young people to get to know themselves and their capabilities.

PERSONAL EFFORT

It is because of its many-sided activity that the Scout movement with its holiday-camps has had such a deep and beneficial effect, not only on the lives of its adherents but also on all subsequent youth movements. Many boys have found their place in life through their experiences as Cubs or Scouts. Young people can also receive advice and guidance through Youth Clubs, through After-Care Committees attached to their schools, through the Junior Employment officer and the welfare officers of firms or factories. These trained workers can be of very real help provided young people will co-operate and will "play the game" by personal effort and perseverance. "One man can take a horse to the water," says the old proverb, "but ten cannot make him drink". An elementary lesson to be learned from the psychology book is that personal choice must be accompanied and followed by personal effort. If we want an end we must also embrace the means.

CULTURE

If many people in a country are choosing with reasonable seriousness and freedom a way of life which points towards a definite ideal, sooner or later these individual ideals fuse into a social outlook which we call culture. Now a national culture can be created in two ways. It can be imposed upon a people by an all-powerful state which organizes every detail of the education, the choice of work, the finances and the recreation of its people; or it can be evolved by the free response of a people to leadership in school, in University, in the pulpit, in social life. T. S. Eliot, in his recently-published *Notes Towards The Definition of Culture*, sees culture as a people's lived religion. Sir Richard Livingstone, in *The Future of Education*, takes us back to the Greek idea of culture, of the education fit for a free man. The Greeks, he says: "held that the free man, the real man, the complete man, must be something more than a mere breadwinner, and must have something besides the knowledge necessary to earn his living. He must have also the education which will give him the chance of developing the gifts and faculties of human nature and becoming a full human being".

LITERATURE AND PHILOSOPHY

Poetry is vision and so is all great literature. The study of psychology may begin with self-questioning, but it will inevitably lead us outwards from ourselves, especially to the books which enshrine the thoughts, experiences, vision of the great men of the past. As one French writer has put it, the classics teach us "that the great men whom we are tempted to look upon as spirits in the realms of literature have lived through times as stormy as our own. They have taken part in the battle of life and have suffered like us. These men that seem at first glance to be so serene have been buffeted by storms, and bear each one in his own heart the wounds of life's sorrows". One of the best fruits of the study of psychology is a deeper and more serious approach to books. The man or woman who has looked upon reading as a mere relaxation, an escape from the realities of life, will learn to find in books a higher reality, a wider vision. Encouraged by this discovery, he will learn that inner adaptability which will enable him to project himself into the lives and thoughts of others.

The study of psychology and literature is sure to lead to philosophical ideas. Indeed, in some countries, notably in France, a course of philosophy is planned in connexion with the literature classes in the upper forms of secondary schools. Such a course would generally comprise a year's Logic (which is made to follow a year of formal grammar and syntax), a year's Ethics, a year's Psychology, and a year's Metaphysics and Natural Religion.

Lately the B.B.C. broadcast a series of talks for Sixth Forms under the title "Religion and Philosophy" and in doing so has supplied a need felt by many young people. The student of human nature turns by instinct to the philosopher for the answers to his mental and moral problems. The age-long questionings of man, his aspirations after immortality, his heart-searchings and inner conflicts find echo, at least now and then, in the heart of every thinking person.

The student of psychology must push his mental excursion into the larger field of philosophy, which will teach him the why and the wherefore of much that he has taken for granted. In this field he will need a guide, but he can also do some reading for himself of books, for example, like Plato's *Republic* or Jacques Maritain's *Introduction to Philosophy*. The first will teach him to think, the second will show him something of the great philosophies of the past. Both ought to show him what Sir Richard Livingstone calls "the most serious danger to our civilization", namely, the widespread lack of a widely held philosophy of life. What more practical advice could be given to the reader or student than that he make an attempt to discover the principles which govern his life, and to see where he fits in to the scheme of things. What are his responsibilities, his hopes, his standards?

PSYCHOLOGY AND THE LIVES OF OTHERS

The study of psychology can give us much of that sympathetic understanding of others so necessary for the peace and fruitfulness of social life.

If we understand the inner motives, the underlying forces, which govern human behaviour, we are much more likely to avoid the misunderstandings, the hatreds and the quarrels which set man against man, class against class, and country against country.

From the first, more introspective, study of psychology, the student is invited to turn to its applications in education, industry, politics, medicine and other fields. The reader would do well to begin by reading M. Collins and J. Drever, *Psychology and Practical Life.*

THE DEVELOPMENT AND EDUCATION OF CHILDREN

Few are the people who have not at least some interest in the upbringing of children, whether from the standpoint of parents, teachers, welfare workers or merely kindly friends. More and more importance is being laid upon the pre-school years, about which the student will have read in Chapter VII. On this question the following books will be of interest: A. H. Bowley, *The Natural Development of the Child;* Freud and Burlingham, *Infants without*

Families; S. Isaacs, *The Nursery Years;* B. Tudor Hart, *Plays and Toys in Nursery Years;* C. Butler, *The Child and the Family;* S. Isaacs, *Intellectual Growth in Young Children, Social Development in Young Children;* K. Bridges, *Social and Emotional Development of the Pre-School Child.*

WELFARE WORK

There are many types of social welfare. In the Citizens' Advice Bureau, the After-Care Committees, the Marriage Guidance Council, young and old can find help to meet their problems of adjustment to life. The Almoner and the Probation Officer both play an important part in dealing, the one with those who are physically weak, the other with those who are morally weak and yet who can be helped to lead sane and healthy normal lives in their own homes.

The standard work on the maladjusted or "problem child" is Cyril Burt's *The Young Delinquent.* Other books which approach the subject of adolescence, not only in its difficulties but also in its possibilities for good are: P. Jephcott, *Girls Growing Up;* Home and School Council, *Understanding the Adolescent;* Burbury, Balint, Yapp, *Child Guidance;* O. Wheeler, *Youth.*

From the study of the adolescent, one is led to that of the choice of career, with all the possibilities of wise, psychological guidance; and on this subject the student should read: F. M. Earle, *Methods of Choosing a Career;* A. Macrae, *Talents and Temperament;* Hunt and Smith, *A Guide to Intelligence and Other Psychological Testing;* and Aveling, *Directing Mental Energy.*

INDUSTRIAL PSYCHOLOGY

The organ of the National Institute of Industrial Psychology, *Occupational Psychology,* lays special emphasis on the human side of the relation between individual welfare and industrial efficiency.

We are learning more and more the importance of understanding our work and all the demands which it makes upon us, but still more vital is the necessity of understanding our fellow workers. As a study of work and its conditions, the student might read: F. Galbreth, *Fatigue Study* and *Motion Study,* and A. G. Shaw, *An Introduction and Application of Motion Study* (H.M. Stationery Office, 1944). As a study of the personality of the worker, "Psychological Methods of Personnel Selection in a Woman's Service" (*Occupational Psychology,* Vol. XIC, No. 1, 1945) is recommended, while for a wider view of the problems involved in industry, F. Watts, *Introduction to the Psychological Problems of Industry,* may be found useful.

SOCIAL PSYCHOLOGY

The consideration of Industrial Psychology, or the psychology of a group of workers, leads us on naturally to that of the larger unit, of society in general. In what sense can we talk about Social Psychology? The psychologist will find that human beings in the mass will exhibit traits not to be accounted for by the mere aggregation of individual characteristics. He will learn to expect from a large group of people reactions which are often the effect of suggestion, emotion or other sub-rational factors, and will not look only to motives of reason but to the part played by leadership, prejudice, instinct, racial memory. Social study may sometimes be merely an investigation into the welfare of a particular class or of a group of people, or it may be extended to the study of racial characteristics and thus overlap the domain of the anthropologist. Or, again, it may be concerned with a national system such as Fascism or Communism, in which case we would class our study as belonging to Politics.

There is a real connexion between psychology and politics, for ultimately our judgement of any system of government, of any law or ordinance must be conditioned by what we think of man. The adherents of Communism, if they are sincere, must accept the philosophy of Karl Marx; those who read in *Mein Kampf* Hitler's ideas of the hopelessness of arriving at a true and healthy democracy could understand the principles upon which Nazism was built. If we are to-day to keep alive the civilization of Europe, we must hold fast to the fundamental values upon which that civilization is built. The foundations of European civilization are Greek Philosophy and Greek Literature, Roman Law, Christian ethics and Christian worship, these last having their roots in the Jewish religion. U┌on these foundations was built that Christendom which still forms the background of Western thought, of Western law, and Western manners.

The following books may be recommended to the reader: Alexander and Stank, *The Criminal, The Judge and The Public;* C. Murchison (edited by), *Social Psychology;* J. Drever, *Psychology of Everyday Life;* R. S. Woodworth, *Contemporary Psychology.*

EXPERIMENTAL PSYCHOLOGY

Although readers of this book will hardly need experience in a psychological laboratory, nevertheless they may be interested in reading about methods of testing our psychological processes. Already in Chapter VIII they will have seen examples of intelligence tests and tests of attainments. Probably in their own experience they have become familiar with such tests as those for intending motorists, in order to ascertain the rapidity of their reaction to a danger signal. The framing of a psychological test is a matter requiring not only skill but wide experience, and no single one is considered valuable unless it has been tried out on hundreds of subjects and unless careful records have been kept of its effectiveness. The amateur should not be encouraged to experiment with psychological testing, but he may take an interest in reading about the advance of this branch of psychology, whether it be used in connexion with psychiatry, with education, with industry or with any other form of human effort. A book like C. Murchison, *Text Book of*

Experimental Psychology; or Collins and Drever, *An Introduction to Experimental Psychology,* will give to the reader who is interested in this aspect of the subject a sufficient insight into methods and techniques.

PSYCHOLOGY OF THE ABNORMAL

Psychological tests are often used in that branch of psychology which deals with those less fortunate people whose happiness is threatened by mental or nervous abnormality. We have come a long way in our attitude to such misfortunes. In contrast to earlier tendencies to regard these victims with fear, with unfeeling hostility, perhaps even revulsion, the great strides recently made in the investigation and treatment of mental disorders have done much to banish prejudice and ignorance and to substitute for them sympathy, understanding and helpfulness.

The neurologist, the psychiatrist, seek to penetrate to the root of mental trouble and to counterbalance undesirable tendencies by sane and steady developments in normal living. Very great discretion and delicacy of touch is needed in all fields of psycho-analysis. All probing of the personality of another must lead to constructive help in re-education and in establishing inner harmony.

The general reader may find the following books interesting and not too difficult: C. M. Fleming, *Adolescence;* R. G. Gordon, *Abnormal Behaviour;* W. Moodie, *The Doctor and the Difficult Child;* Gordon Harris and Rees, *Introduction to Medical Psychology.*

Psychology is a challenge to thought rather than to action. Nevertheless, a little reflection will show how wide is its application. Psychology digs deep roots, but these roots send their tentacles out very far. There is hardly any branch of study which will not benefit from the student's initiation into psychological principles. The biologist, the novelist, the soldier, the industrialist, the teacher, the poet must sooner or later find out for himself the fundamentals of man's nature. Do you remember the Elizabethan poet who was sighing at his inability to sing the glories of his lady-love, and how, in a flash, intuition came to him as the very teaching of the Muse herself:

"Fool," said my Muse to me,
"Look in thy heart and write . . ."

The student of psychology will learn to look into his heart and *act.*

ANSWERS TO "TEST YOURSELF"

CHAPTER I

1. The basic division which can be made of the activities of an organism is that which differentiates those activities directly concerned in maintaining the life of an organism from those which are concerned primarily with environmental stimuli and therefore with the adaptive side of the organism's life. Examples of the first group in man are the blood system and the digestive system. The second group is represented by the nervous system, although it must be realized that the interaction between the two groups is both constant and vital.

2. The two chief methods used in the science of psychology are introspection, or looking within at the workings of one's own nature, and observation of others by looking out from ourselves to others and trying to penetrate the motives, feelings, acts and reactions of others. This second method has many degrees and can vary from the simple study of human nature by any thoughtful person, to accurate, scientific tests, sometimes made in a laboratory, or to the sensitive scrutiny and sympathetic analysis which a trained psychologist can make of the mind of another person. The two methods, that of looking within and that of looking without, complement one another.

3. The social heritage of a child is what his personality received from his environment, at first immediately in the home, then, in an ever-widening circle, through education, through the influence of friends or playmates and even from more casual everyday contacts. From all these he receives influences which bear upon his way of thought, his standard of right and wrong, his manners, bearing, and outlook. He in his turn reacts, through his individual mental and emotional make-up, upon his social heritage, and in the interplay of forces his personal character is formed.

CHAPTER II

1. A percept is our awareness of some object or event outside ourselves. This awareness comes to us first through some sensation, e.g. of sight, of touch, of hearing. When we receive the sensation and turn our consciousness upon it we read into it some meaning, however vague. This meaning is to us the percept. Thus a man may sit reading in a room in which people are talking. The sound strikes his ear, but if he is deep in his book he may not receive it as a percept. When he becomes aware of the sound it is a percept.

2. This is the name given to the generally accepted fact that an object, although viewed from different angles or in different lights, always produces in us substantially the same effect. In other words, an object looks pretty much the same on dark days as on bright, or when seen in varying circumstances. This fact makes the psychologist distinguish between the phenomenon (what a thing looks like to the person) and the actual sensation produced by a certain amount of light.

3. By a concept we mean a universal abstract notion by which a man may know, however simply, the nature of things around him. When we say "this book is well bound" we have in our minds a notion of "book" (which, incidentally, we expect others to understand), and we have also a clear understanding of what we mean by "good binding". Both these abstract notions are dependent on the work of the senses and the formation of percepts which have been made on previous occasions.

CHAPTER III

1. Most people will find that they use both auditory and visual images, but,

probably, one or other type will pre-dominate. If you have an auditory imagina-tion you will tend to recall your friends more by their voices than by their appearance. If your imagination is visual you will tend to think of your friends as they appeared when you last met them as well as the place of meeting. Certain features, certain gestures will stand out and if you could draw them you would have your model in your mind.

2. The study of a person's daydreams gives us an insight into his mind, chiefly by showing to what his mind swings back at moments when he is off his guard. We can get to know, in this manner, his chief preoccupations, and his secret interests and longings. Daydreams are nature's method of compensating for all the frustrations from which we suffer. What we cannot have in reality we seek in our dreams. By showing us the extent and the particular direction of our desires they are self-revealing.

3. The poet here uses a metaphor, that is, he appeals to our imagination in order to bring out more vividly an intellectual abstract meaning. He wants us to know that he has had a full life of happy ex-periences and that he does not fear death. He shows us the picture of a man with hands outstretched before a cheerful fire. We see the fire gradually sink. We know he will leave it as it goes out. The little para-bole illustrates for us the poet's feeling towards life.

CHAPTER IV

1. Various factors may halt the progress of learning. Let us take, for example, a student of mathematics who has been getting on well and then, quite suddenly, can make no further progress. He may be physically tired and off-colour. Sleep, fresh air and exercise will stimulate the flow of blood to the brain and make his work easy and pleasant when he returns to it. On the other hand, he may have outrun his habits of work; that is to say, he may have learned the meaning of certain pro-cesses or theorems but not yet have gained skill in their use. He needs practice before he can break new ground. Again, other factors may be hindering him: a violent dislike of a teacher or method; or, perhaps, a great distraction. He may be so saturated with other lessons and exercises that his mind has no leisure for that subconscious assimilation which is part of the process of learning.

2. Habit, we are told, is second nature. It is nature's way of enabling us to carry out the multifarious routine jobs necessary in ordinary living. Once a choice and decision have been made, we can relegate to the unconscious such habitual and nec-essary actions as dressing, journeying from home to work, performing mechanical processes. Habit thus sets the mind free to dwell on higher matters.

3. By deliberately recalling what he is trying to learn the scholar fixes the matter in a system of associations, grouping all the facts around certain key points. In this way he helps himself by splitting up the matter into manageable parts. By the law of association, one fact remembered will be likely to recall the next and all those connected closely with it. The repetitive recall fixes this association in the mind and in the nervous system, creating all kinds of associated images and forming a distinct part of nervous activity. The alternative to this method of recall is merely to read the matter over again and trust that chance associations will make it live in the memory.

CHAPTER V

1. This is simply a discussion of what counts most in a child's upbringing—in the formation of his character, his par-ticular temperament, his mental, moral and physical make-up. Can we by educa-tion eradicate, transform and sublimate traits which are natural to a child's charac-ter? Some people lay great stress on very early training because they believe that *Nurture* or education (in its widest sense) is most effective in early days. Others are of the opinion that "the leopard cannot change its spots".

2. For the psychologist, the answer is *No*. Children from the same home may appear to have much the same lives out-wardly but may be poles apart in their

thoughts and habits. The eldest child in a family has a different environment from that of his younger brothers or sisters. A boy has a different environment from that of a girl; a pretty girl from that of a plain one; a clever boy or one good at games from that of a lad less gifted. It is the differences in home environment particularly which affect a child most deeply and permanently and they should be carefully studied.

3. It would be well to re-read the answer to question 1 above. Nature gives us our temperament and a tendency to form certain habits. *Nurture* makes us deliberately choose what habits we wish to form, and to exercise ourselves in them. Obviously, then, a person who is by nature fiery, pugnacious, irritable, must deliberately cultivate control of speech, a disciplined reaction to the rubs of life. A person who is naturally lazy will benefit enormously by cultivating a standard of brisk and thorough work. In so far as this attempt is made will there be balance in the character.

CHAPTER VI

1. The baby first makes some random reflex movements such as grasping with his fingers if an object is placed in the palm of his hand, or fanning out his toes when the sole of his foot is touched. Then there will be spontaneous and random movements of the whole body, wriggling, or stretching in a recumbent position. After two or three months the baby will stretch out his arms and touch the limits of his cot, his toes, his mother. About the fourth month he can lift his head, about the fifth or sixth he can sit up, and after this he begins to roll and crawl. At twelve months he will pull himself on to his feet—at about fourteen months he will walk and begin to co-ordinate his muscles.

2. Bricks, pull-along toys, a barrow or a wooden horse to push, will still be popular at this age and for some time to come— along with such old favourites as the teddy bear and other soft toys. Peg-boards and nests of boxes to be fitted one into another will usually amuse (and at the same time develop) the infant mind. Out-of-doors the

child may be left in a safe garden, although, almost certainly, he will require an occasional visit from his mother. A lively romp will be much appreciated and will do no harm if care is taken to avoid over-excitement. If water (a shallow pool or perhaps an old tin bath with no sharp edges) is available, so much the better, and a sand-pit will amuse most children for hours. Always, in the evening, there should be a period of quiet in preparation for bed, and the traditional bed-time story (with no horrors), told or read by parent or friend, is probably the best method of securing the desired atmosphere.

3. A young child has a fundamental need of affection, of the presence, the approval, the notice and the love of its parents. This affection is sunshine to its growing powers and fosters their development as nothing else can do. It is also a buttress against that fear which is engendered by the sense of helplessness felt in the face of a grown-up and complex world. Affection means security, mental stability and the sense of home. A child deprived of affection may develop neurotic tendencies which last into later life.

CHAPTER VII

1. The Nursery school can give the pre-school child many advantages which he can seldom find in his home. It gives space, order, a "world of his own size" with chairs, tables and other material things with which he can cope. Above all it gives him companionship, the training which results from having to consider others, opportunities for play, imitation and speech. He can have rhythmic exercises, so important at this stage, as well as settled times for sleep and meals. When these advantages come as *an addition* to the love and security of a good home they are precious, but they can never compensate for home training and the loss of parental love and care.

2. The social adjustment of the pre-school child has to be made in the teeth of emotional difficulties. Love, fear, an innate self-centredness hold back the pre-school child from open, friendly intercourse with his fellows. The wise

teacher leaves young children to work out this adjustment very slowly. They need periods of silent solitary games. Above all, they need affection and security. The child over five years of age has, normally, achieved a greater measure of security. He is more objective because more at home in the world. He can quarrel without emotional disturbance, is imitative, more gregarious, more ready to learn from others.

3. In adolescence new tendencies begin to develop, sometimes with disconcerting rapidity. Sexual development comes at this time, and with it the power of intellectual, abstract thought. The adolescent senses the reality and importance of his own personality and begins to look out upon the world and to ask himself what it is that he desires from life. The youth and the girl meet obstacles with dreams, and disappointment is held at bay by plans for a golden future. For these young people to adjust themselves to society, an outlet for the expanding intellect is required, and this need can be met by satisfying work; adequate recreation (physical and mental); the companionship of both sexes; and, when it is sought, the advice and guidance of older people.

CHAPTER VIII

1. Backwardness in reading does not necessarily imply lack of intelligence. On the contrary, it is often found among more favoured children of large families who have a rich and varied experience at home and do not feel the need of books. Sometimes such children have had adults to read to them and, therefore, have had little incentive to master the difficult art for themselves. There comes a time, however, when learning to read is seen to be desirable, necessary even, if only to escape from a teacher's disapproval. If the child makes the effort and still does not succeed, the teacher must suspect some impediment, but it may be a purely physical one such as poor eyesight and need not be lack of intelligence.

2. According to Burt's Reading Test on pages 140–41, the first ninety words are generally read by children of twelve years. Therefore, as this is a standardized test,

we can conclude that the child of ten has the Reading Age of a child of twelve and that his Reading Quotient is 12/10 x 100 =120.

CHAPTER IX

1. Children in the gang stage use their imagination socially, that is, they will play at being "Red Indians", "Robin Hood and his Merry Men", "Parachutists", or other groups of romantic characters. Girls will sometimes set up "families" or "schools", but they often enjoy more adventurous gang-play. Virtues of loyalty, co-operation and good-fellowship are prized. There is often an element of secrecy, a secret society, a special language, a guarded treasure. Sometimes a feeling of hostility to the adult world is present. Ideally, as in the Scout movement, the gang spirit can be guided into channels of service to society.

2. A mental test may be a test of general intelligence and/or of specific abilities, as described in the answer to question 4, below. An attainment test, however, is concerned with what the pupil has learned in any special branch of knowledge and this more nearly approaches to the ordinary school examination, though it is framed in such a way as to allow a standardized method of marking. A diagnostic test combines tests in general and specific abilities in order to see where there is any special weakness or special talent.

3. The term "maturation" denotes the ripening or normal development of the brain and the nervous system. This development, on which all human ability depends, takes place progressively and at an accelerated rate in normal children up to the seventeenth year. By learning-readiness we mean the common order of intellectual, emotional and social development which is largely dependent on maturation. The study of children reveals that there are certain types of interest and activity which can be associated with the stages in maturation.

4. General intelligence is an intuitive power difficult to define. It has been called "the power of seeing through a brick wall". The intelligent person sees to the heart of

things, reads meanings, sees analogies, reasons quickly, gets things in proportion. This power must not be confused with wisdom, experience of life, or with scholastic attainment. It is measured by a simple reasoning test such as that of Sir Cyril Burt, given in Fig. 45. Special abilities are those connected with some eight groups of special techniques—such as linguistic, mathematical, or artistic skills. They are tested by questions which are designed to eliminate any previous knowledge. For example, linguistic ability is tested by an exercise in reading a "nonsense" language after being given a few of the basic words or rules.

CHAPTER X

1. A first requisite would be, of course, kind reliable foster-parents, who accepted the recognized moral code of our society and the qualities of cleanliness, order and decency. Then the potential educative value of the home should be considered. Would the child find affection, interest, companionship and an intelligent environment in which to develop his growing powers, and would the general effect of the home be one of stability, happiness and encouragement?

2. The classroom illustrated in Fig. 56 seems to be pervaded by a general air of gloom and strict uniformity. The walls bear evidence of the practice of teaching by text and there is no display of the children's individual work, nor any attempt to brighten the room with decorations. Such surroundings (and the type of life that may be inferred by the signs that are visible) may well have cramped and fettered the development of thought and personality. The attainment of self-confidence is made difficult for those who are deprived of free expression in dress and movement.

3. As a contrast to the picture in Fig. 56, that in Fig. 57 shows a spirit of freedom which engenders contentment and a power of original development. The boys are not dressed alike. Their attitudes are relaxed, yet their attention is concentrated. They are not in a crowd, but stand alone, working with interesting material which can be used for creative activity. They have a common problem and are free to discuss it and to tackle it in their own way. An enormous achievement in teaching and in methods of discipline is suggested by the attitude of these boys.

CHAPTER XI

1. Methods of assessing personality and temperament cannot, by their nature, be so accurate as those which aim at testing specific abilities. The reactions and conduct of the examinee when performing tests of any kind are a revelation of his temperament. The questionnaire is used, and a subsequent discussion of the answers given, between the psychologist and the examinee, proves of great value. The interview has always been of first importance to the psychologist. If this can be supplemented by a scrutiny of the examinee at work (the teacher in his classroom, the mechanic with his machines) and by reports from school or employer, the general consensus of informed opinion is likely to result in a correct estimate.

2. The information needed would concern (i) his physical standing, i.e. height, weight, record of illness, present health; (ii) home conditions, education; (iii) financial position; (iv) his desires and ambitions; (v) his general intelligence quotient; (vi) special abilities; (vii) attainment in basic elements of education—Reading, Writing, Arithmetic, Handicrafts; (viii) his special fitness for the trade of his choice, and/or other capabilities which would suggest reorientation; (ix) personality—that is, qualities of self-confidence, reliability, perseverance, leadership—or the absence of these qualities; (x) willingness or ability to conform to conditions of entry or training.

3. Vocational Guidance and Vocational Selection are obviously closely interrelated. In the former, emphasis is laid on the character and aptitudes of the person in order to find out what type of work would enable him to give his best to the community. In the latter, emphasis is laid on the nature of the work, in order not to place it in the hands of people not capable of doing it efficiently. Ultimately,

both *subject* and *work* must be studied, but the difference lies in the emphasis placed on either.

CHAPTER XII

1. Three main points of interest might be:

(i) Physical conditions: warmth, ventilation, space, and sensible arrangement of the working rooms in order to eliminate unnecessary walking or other movement.

(ii) Contentment: the maximum of interest, intrinsic or extrinsic, should be given to the work. Where work has to be piecemeal and mechanical, music and recreative pauses have been found to have their uses. The personalities of heads of departments and managers are also important factors.

(iii) A right rhythm of life: length of hours, spacing of rest pauses, holidays, communal recreational activities.

2. The first duty of the welfare officer is to consult the medical officer so that an opinion may be formed of the genuineness of the illness. If some degree of malingering is suspected, then the following points may well be considered:

(i) What help is given, inside the factory, to those who do not feel well? Is there a warm room in which they may rest for a while, or change wet clothing?

(ii) What incentives are there for the employee to return to work? The feeling of being trusted and the existence of a good "factory atmosphere" is important here.

3. Each one must answer the question for himself. Consider your normal day. The following pointers may help:

(i) Beginning work—importance of a prompt and early start—having all tools ready—order and method.

(ii) When do you begin to feel the need of a rest pause? How long should it be? What do you do in the time? How do you relax? Note that a pause may scatter your energies or may send you back to work refreshed. To what causes do you attribute the different effects?

(iii) On returning to work, do you get right into your activity at once?

Can you draw a curve showing the peak of your activity?

(iv) How are rest pauses distributed in a day—a week—a year?

(v) What do you find your best recreation? What *rests* you: a book, a walk, strenuous exercise, conversation with a friend?

(vi) Look back on days of emergencies when you worked *all out* with no special rhythm. Contrast these with an ordered day and note the difference.

CHAPTER XIII

1. First the lay-out of the room and of the plant should be investigated, so as to eliminate unnecessary movement from place to place. Then the job itself should be studied, in order to eliminate any further superfluous movement. Next, consider the team—does any branch of the work overlap that of another branch? Finally, are there good incentives to work and rational safeguards against fatigue? Sometimes a reduction of hours worked will produce better results; or, again, a redistribution of rest pauses, more fresh air, more warmth, some music or community singing will make for increased efficiency.

2. In a modern factory the worker is taught to handle his material with precision and concerted movement. Where appropriate, movements should be simultaneous, sometimes performed to music, always planned so as to give the minimum of fatigue. In general, rhythmic movement necessitates the correct placing and handling of work and tools. Movements should be symmetrical round an imaginary line passing through the centre of the body, both hands being used together, if possible. Movements should be habitual, natural and rhythmical. When employees work in a concerted rhythm there is generally a gain in team-spirit and efficiency.

3. The industrial psychologist can think out excellent methods of handling tools or loading weights, etc., but he must never forget that it is Tom and Dick who have to do the job. In dealing with human beings, human differences, weaknesses and prejudices must be allowed for. The investigations and suggestions of the

psychologist may appear to the worker an invasion of the little private initiative left to him.

Suggestions will be received more readily if fully explained. If possible, they should be illustrated by a slow-motion film, or even by means of demonstrations by trained workers. Some reward or incentive should be associated with the adoption of new methods. Such methods should never be forced on the individual; and, above all, if good work is already being done by a different method, it is often better to leave well alone.

CHAPTER XIV

1. The employer who selects an unsuitable employee will lose money because his work will not be efficiently done. He will lose some of the confidence of his personnel, for the deficiences of the new worker will be felt throughout the whole department. An unsuitable person is often discontented and blames the authorities, the system, the conditions of work. Even when the employer decides to discharge him, there is a likelihood of more criticism and reproach.

Moreover, the employee who enters unsuitable employment is excluded from work which he might be able to do successfully. He wastes time and energy in training for a job that is not his vocation. He may sense that he is a failure and become embittered and discouraged in consequence. When he applies for a new job his sense of failure in the previous one may obtrude itself and count against him. The worst danger is that he will cling to his unsuitable post through fear of unemployment. A brave man with the spirit of adventure can, however, cut through these difficulties and learn from his experience.

2. The human relationship is always the most important factor. According to the size of the organization, efforts must be made to put employer and employed into contact with one another. In a large organization, therefore, authority must be given to heads of departments to treat openly, freely and courteously with the personnel. Employees value most highly some freedom of action—absence of minute supervision and regimentation. They appreciate some form of self-government, and like to be consulted on matters appertaining to the work they are doing, as well as in matters of welfare. If some kind of co-operative financial arrangement can be made whereby the staff can benefit directly from extra effort at times of greater pressure, such periods of strain may be accepted cheerfully.

3. Apart from obvious precautions against industrial accidents, such as due observation of the official regulations regarding the fencing of machinery, care of noxious chemicals, explosives and so on, attention should be given to a suitable arrangement of the work, of tools and materials, in order to obviate constrained, awkward and possibly dangerous bodily movements. Other fertile causes of accidents are boredom and fatigue (and hence inattention) on the part of the worker, unsuitable temperatures of workrooms and inadequate lighting. All these details are capable of improvement. Apart from material causes, however, investigation has clearly shown that some people are more susceptible to accidents than others. This accident-proneness can be traced to peculiarities or defects in physical or psychological make-up, and tests have been devised for revealing such shortcomings in intelligence, temperament, nerve and muscle co-ordination, and so on. Thus the accident-prone person can be eliminated from work that is unsafe for him, and diverted to more suitable employment.

Key to potential accidents in Fig. 83:— Man hammering on roof—no crawling boards; hammer and asbestos sheet on roof insecure; scaffold badly designed and insecure; ladders in bad repair, not secured and badly placed; brazier close to ladder and insecure; men smoking in inflammable surroundings; coke litter on ground; manhole cover off; fire extinguisher missing and bracket out of reach; oil leaking; drums stacked without chocks; badly stacked goods in truck; no clear view for man with truck; planks, with nails, on floor; man oiling shafting in motion and ladder insecure; machine-belt guard removed; no guard on machine tools; no operator at machine tool; unshaded light; loose belt; buckets in fairway; no guards on belts and pulleys; man with plank unable to see round corner; inadequate gangways in machine shop; load on crane badly slung; crane-driver cannot see signals; anchorage for pulley-block insecure; planks on hoist badly slung; plank leaning against back of lorry; planks on lorry badly placed; wheelbarrow badly trimmed; hose badly placed and leaking near lamp; guard removed from lamp; flex led through window and knotted; flex liable to trip workmen; pipes (in background) badly stacked; handrail on crane gantry broken; man on roof cannot handle goods with safety—also danger from travelling crane; danger sign knocked over; general litter in yard.

CHAPTER XV

1. Abnormality of mind is chiefly due to heredity or to physical defects, such as insufficiency of brain development, defects in the nervous system, in glandular secretion, in the condition of the blood. It may also be due to early upbringing in home surroundings where there is emotional tension or lack of control, or where the child has grown up unchecked and un-disciplined, or where, on the other hand, he has been depressed and cowed by lack of understanding and affection, or even by cruelty. Mental abnormality may also be caused by degenerative changes in the tissues of the body and especially of the brain, the result of injury, shock or disease.

2. (*a*) At any moment of danger, such as in battle, the sentiments of self-respect, of pride in one's own courage, of pat-riotism, hatred of the enemy, and so on, may conflict sharply with the urge to self-preservation, which is an instinctive reaction in time of danger; and the result of this conflict may be a momentary act of cowardice.

(*b*) An example of "long-term" conflict between sentiments is that which might occur in the case of a successful business man who finds it impossible to reconcile unethical practices, to which he finds it expedient to resort in his business, with the sentiments of rectitude permanently implanted in him by a highly respectable or, possibly, even pious, upbringing. It is impossible for him to resist the urge to make money, and he recognizes no ethical barriers in the process; but his innate sense of morality (which, in the form of "conscience", he may placate from time to time by making charitable donations) gnaws away at him incessantly. The con-flict poisons his whole life and may cause deterioration of his personality and of his mental and physical health. If the conflict is repressed in the unconscious, its ravages may become more dangerous and insidious still.

3. Outstanding examples of abnormal mental symptoms consequent upon bodily illness include the following: the insanity following childbirth, when poisoning of the blood has occurred; the groundless optimism which sometimes accompanies tuberculosis and infantile paralysis; the mental confusion sometimes resulting from kidney disease; the special mental symp-toms associated with vitamin deficiency, ranging from stupor to hallucinations and insanity. Abnormal functioning of the endocrine glands also produces charac-teristic mental disorders. Thus, deficiency of thyroid secretion produces cretinism and idiocy, while excess of this secretion results in agitation and delusions. Again, the poisoning of chronic alcoholism may result in the terrifying halllucinations of delirium tremens, while the germs of syphilis may induce general paralysis, with its mental confusion and grandiose delusions.

CHAPTER XVI

1. The treatment of an anxiety state consists primarily in finding out the cause of the trouble. Psycho-analysis, shock-treatment, hypnosis and drugs may be used in order to get the patient to reveal the deep-seated cause of the anxiety state, which may be entirely hidden from himself. Sometimes the mere recognition of the cause may effect a partial cure. The psy-chologist has to eliminate strain, first by physical means, such as rest, fresh air, sleep, warmth, good food. Then he builds up self-confidence by re-education along

the lines affected by the anxiety. It is good to develop other strong points, to try to get the patient to forget his trouble through a new interest in life. Love, attention, guidance and patient understanding are the chief requisites in this re-education.

2. An obsession is an irrational thought or action which the subject knows to be irrational, but which recurs again and again and tends to get out of his control. The two main types of obsession are the "phobia" or haunting fear of certain objects, places or situations, and the "compulsion" or irrational urge to perform certain unnecessary or almost ritualistic actions.

Examples of phobia are the fear of enclosed spaces, of falling, of hearing one's own voice, of being in the dark. Examples of compulsion are exaggerated attention to details of tidyness, or the sudden urge towards the use of undesirable words or the doing of actions which would normally be considered reprehensible. Possibly about nine-tenths of such an urge is made up of fear of being guilty of such conduct.

3. A sense of security is the great safeguard against the development of anxiety complexes in children. A very young child is like a tender, delicate plant. He must be given time, space and leisure to grow. It does not matter very much if he develops slowly; it does matter enormously if his development is unhealthy. He needs a firm support on which to lean, he needs the sunshine of affection and approval, in which his latent powers may unfold and develop. Under these conditions he will avoid those deep-laid fears in which may develop the seeds of future neurosis.

CHAPTER XVII

1. Shock therapy is a form of treatment in which mental patients are subjected to drugs, or more often to controlled electric shocks, in order to produce convulsions. Such shocks have sometimes the effect of shaking the patient out of excessive depression, sometimes of bringing to his mind deeply-hidden memories, fears and obsessions. He will then readily reveal his personality and thus help the psychiatrist to treat his trouble. Shock treatment is only given in serious cases of mental trouble and by skilled practitioners.

2. A child who shows signs of want of balance, mental or emotional, needs a very calm, secure environment. He needs more love, more attention more physical care than other children, and, above all, he needs all the patience of the educator.

Lessons should be simple, always well within the child's capacity, and so skilfully taught as to engender in him a generous measure of self-confidence and self-reliance. Praise should be more in evidence than fault-finding, for the unbalanced find it difficult to accept criticism and will argue endlessly about trifles. When enough self-confidence has been induced, the child should be encouraged to bear some responsibility, but anything in the shape of emotional strain should be avoided at all costs. If punishment is necessary it should be short and sharp and of a material kind rather than of the kind which seems to imply disgrace, fear, or humiliation. Good points of the child's personality should be brought out and strengthened.

3. In the first place, while the patient is working, he has at least the illusion of normal living. Habits of industry, of attention, of skill may be exercised and may militate against the mental trouble.

Secondly, while he is at work, the patient's attention may be deflected from himself. He may even be forced to mix with his fellows. Adjustments of eye, of hand, of bodily movement, may help to keep the nervous system functioning normally.

Thirdly, work achieved gives confidence and joy. It may be the last link between the patient and the real life which he has known. As long as he can be interested in producing something he still has a hold on life. By occupational therapy the patient may be saved from complete breakdown and led back to a well-balanced life.

INDEX

(Page references printed in italics indicate illustrations

INDEX

ACKNOWLEDGEMENTS

The publishers wish to make grateful acknowledgement to the following for permission to reproduce photographs in this volume:

London County Council, Education Department, Fig. 60; The Controller, H.M. Stationery Office, Fig. 56; City of Manchester Education Committee, Fig. 57; National Children's Home & Orphanage, Fig. 55.

The example of a graded reading test in Fig. 45, the reading test in Fig. 46, and the facsimile reproductions of handwriting in Figs. 47 and 48 are from *Mental and Scholastic Tests*, by Sir Cyril Burt, M.A., D.Sc. (Oxon.).